The Program Evaluation Standards

3rd Edition

This edition of the Program Evaluation Standards is dedicated to the previous Joint Committees and the chairs who so effectively guided their efforts:
Daniel L. Stufflebeam (1975 to 1988)
James R. Sanders (1988 to 1998)
Arlen R. Gullickson (1998 to 2008)

Joint Committee on Standards for Educational Evaluation

The Program Evaluation Standards

A Guide for Evaluators and Evaluation Users

3rd Edition

Donald B. Yarbrough • Lyn M. Shulha

University of Iowa *Queen's University at Kingston, Canada*

Rodney K. Hopson • Flora A. Caruthers

Duquesne University *Office of Program Policy Analysis and Government Accountability, Florida Legislature*

Los Angeles | London | New Delhi
Singapore | Washington DC

JCSEE PGES3-2010
(Part I–Part V, pages 3–252)
Approved by the American National Standards Institute as an American National Standard.
Approval date: June 21, 2010

For information:

SAGE Publications, Inc.
2455 Teller Road
Thousand Oaks,
California 91320
E-mail: order@sagepub.com

SAGE Publications Ltd.
1 Oliver's Yard
55 City Road
London EC1Y 1SP
United Kingdom

SAGE Publications India Pvt. Ltd.
B 1/I 1 Mohan Cooperative
Industrial Area
Mathura Road, New Delhi 110 044
India

SAGE Publications Asia-Pacific Pte. Ltd.
33 Pekin Street #02-01
Far East Square
Singapore 048763

Printed in the United States of America

Library of Congress Cataloging-in-Publication Data

The program evaluation standards : A guide for evaluators and evaluation users/editors, Donald B. Yarbrough . . . [et al]. — 3rd ed.
p. cm.
Includes bibliographical references and index.
ISBN 978-1-4129-8656-4 (cloth)
ISBN 978-1-4129-8908-4 (pbk.)
1. Educational tests and measurements—United States. 2. Educational evaluation—United States. I. Yarbrough, Donald B.

LB3051.P648 2011
379.1′54—dc22 2010010922

This book is printed on acid-free paper.

10 11 12 13 14 10 9 8 7 6 5 4 3 2 1

Acquisitions Editor:	Vicki Knight	*Typesetter:*	C&M Digitals (P) Ltd.
Associate Editor:	Lauren Habib	*Proofreader:*	Susan Schon
Editorial Assistant:	Ashley Dodd	*Indexer:*	Jean Casalegno
Production Editor:	Eric Garner	*Cover Designer:*	Candice Harman
Copy Editor:	Alan Cook	*Marketing Manager:*	Stephanie Adams

❖ Contents ❖

❖ The Joint Committee on Standards for Educational Evaluation, 2005 to 2010 ❖

Donald B. Yarbrough, chair, 2008-present

Arlen Gullickson, chair, 1998-2008

❖ COMMITTEE MEMBERS

Ronald Fuller and **Terry Duggan Schwartzbeck,** representing the American Association of School Administrators (AASA)

Patricia McDivitt, representing the American Counseling Association (ACA)

Stephan Henry and **Raymond Pecheone**, representing the American Educational Research Association (AERA)

Hazel Symonette and **Elmima Johnson**, representing the American Evaluation Association (AEA)

Carrie Billy, representing the American Indian Higher Education Consortium (AIHEC)

Frank Worrell and **Jeff Braden**, representing the American Psychological Association (APA)

Edith Beatty, representing the American Society for Curriculum Development (ASCD, through 2006 only)

Rolf Blank, representing the Council of Chief State School Officers (CCSSO)

Brigitte Maicher and **James Cullen**, representing the Canadian Evaluation Society (CES)

Paula Egelson, representing the Consortium for Research and Educational Accountability and Teacher Evaluation (CREATE)

Lyn Shulha, representing the Canadian Society for the Study of Education (CSSE)

Fred Brown and **Richard Barbacane,** representing the National Association of Elementary School Principals (NAESP)

Dede Bailer, Mary Beth Klotz, and **William Strein,** representing the National Association of School Psychologists (NASP)

Leslie Lukin and **Donald Yarbrough**, representing the National Council on Measurement in Education (NCME)

Adriane Dorrington and **Segun Eubanks**, representing the National Education Association (NEA)

Flora Caruthers, representing the National Legislative Program Evaluation Society (NLPES)

John Sanders, representing the National Rural Education Association (NREA)

Vice Chairs: **Patricia McDivitt, Donald Yarbrough**

Administrative Staff: **Jennifer A. Jones, Sally Veeder**

❖ Acknowledgments ❖

Many people have made important contributions to *The Program Evaluation Standards.* We are indebted to the staff of the Evaluation Center at Western Michigan University, especially Sally Veeder, whose assistance from the beginning of the revision process was invaluable. The Cultural Reading Task Force of the American Evaluation Association's Diversity Committee reviewed the second edition line by line and produced a thorough and exceptionally useful set of documents and recommendations. Their *Cultural Reading of the Program Evaluation Standards* (AEA, 2005, available at http://www.eval.org/CRExecSum.htm) guided our efforts to attend to context and culture throughout the development of this third edition.

The Center for Evaluation and Assessment (CEA) at the University of Iowa provided funding and ongoing project support during the revision process. Jennifer A. Jones, CEA administrator, assisted with mailings and correspondence and helped organize and maintain the many data sets, comments, and revision drafts. She also helped administer the funds that allowed the task force to meet regularly to review comments and revise drafts for the next cycles. From start to finish of the revision, Jennifer has helped keep the process moving forward.

Numerous other CEA staff members helped support the work of the Program Evaluation Standards Development Task Force, including Jeanne Alnot, Dina Blanc, Doug Grane, Melissa Chapman Haynes, Julie Kearney, Emily Lai, Vernita Morgan, Margaret Mwenda, and Xuan Wang. CEA staff members Jeanne Alnot, Dina Blanc, Melissa Chapman Haynes, Julie Kearney, and Emily Lai also provided detailed comments and suggestions on various drafts. We are also thankful to the many students in our classes who read and tried out current and earlier versions.

Living in different regions of North America, standards development task force members were often looking for places to work face-to-face and to conduct field trials. Notable contributors to these needs were the National Science Foundation, whose travel grant for field trials (NSF Award Number 0742033) was ably administered by Rosemary Rynn in the Department of

Foundations and Leadership at Duquesne University; the National Education Association, who provided communication, refreshments, and the needed infrastructure for a joint field trial in Washington, D.C.; the Faculty of Education, Queen's University at Kingston, Canada, who contributed travel funds for task force meetings and hosted field trials; Duquesne University and the University of Iowa College of Education for hosting field trials and task force meetings; Hazel Symonette at the University of Wisconsin, who hosted and helped with not one but two sets of field trials; and Coe College in Cedar Rapids, Iowa, who hosted the task force for four days in its beautiful Alumni Center and provided entertainment in the guise of a real-life tornado warning, complete with a short-term trip to the basement but no long-term impact.

Many contributors to the development processes, including members of the Joint Committee on Standards for Educational Evaluation (JCSEE), participated in formal reviews, hearings, and the aforementioned field trials. The members of the JCSEE named in the front of the book provided help with definitions, debated exact wordings, provided oversight for all content and specific steps in the process, and ultimately voted to approve this edition. The more than 400 outside contributors are thanked individually in Appendix C and at http://www.jcsee.org under the heading Program Evaluation Standards Revision Process and Contributors. We have tried to maintain completely accurate records of all who contributed, but that was surely impossible because of the way that sign-up slips were distributed at hearings and the way that some review comments were sent via e-mail. If we have missed thanking anyone who contributed to any of these formal or informal data gathering processes, please contact the JCSEE and we will update the Web pages.

We also want to thank the independent validation panel: Marvin C. Alkin, chair; Jeffrey Braden; Joy Frechtling; Floraline I. Stevens; Sandy Taut; and Kevin Welner and express deep appreciation as well to Anne T. Vo, who served as the research assistant to the Validation Panel. Reviewing and providing perspectives on the extensive process documentation and multiple drafts required considerable effort and care. The panel's thorough and deeply appreciated Validation Report, available at http://www.jcsee.com, provided perspectives on the work of the JCSEE and guidance for the final revisions of the manuscript.

A few other professionals' in-depth comments outside of the regular review processes have made significant contributions to the final product. Among these are former members and leaders of the JCSEE: Arlen Gullickson, Todd Rogers, Jim Sanders, and Dan Stufflebeam. In addition, Stephanie E. Barry and Karen E. Kirkhart's line-by-line reading and critical commentary provided insights and suggestions that have enriched this final document.

With so many contributors and so much input, a major challenge for the task force has been to choose among the many and sometimes competing suggestions about features, content, and organization. We are indebted to all contributors in ways that defy adequate acknowledgment and appreciation. We hold ourselves entirely responsible for any remaining flaws and look forward to the continued improvement of *The Program Evaluation Standards* through subsequent revision processes leading to future editions.

We also want to thank Vicki Knight, Eric Garner, Alan J. Cook, and the rest of the able editorial and production staff at SAGE for their expert assistance in all phases of the production of this book. In addition, Susan Kistler of the American Evaluation Association also deserves special recognition for her assistance with stakeholder communication during all phases of this standards development process.

Last but certainly not least, we thank our families for their patience and support throughout this process: Kent Caruthers; Wabei, Hannibal, and Habiba Hopson; Dennis Shulha; and Nukhet Yarbrough. We especially thank our spouses, who provided professional and independent readings of these drafts well beyond any measure their professional or personal duties would have required.

—The Program Evaluation Standards
Third Edition Development Task Force: Flora Caruthers, Rodney Hopson, Lyn Shulha, and Don Yarbrough, chair

March 3, 2010

Royalties from the sales of this book will be used to promote effective use of *The Program Evaluation Standards* and to support ongoing review and revision activities.

❖ Preface ❖

The Program Evaluation Standards, Third Edition, provides an integrated guide for evaluating programs that foster human learning and performance across the life span. These standards apply to a wide variety of settings in which learning takes place: schools, universities, communities, governmental organizations, medical and health-care organizations, the military, private sector enterprises, and nonprofit and nongovernmental organizations.

These 30 standards are organized into five groups corresponding to five key attributes of evaluation quality: *utility, feasibility, propriety, accuracy, and accountability.* Parts I through V of the text are each devoted to one attribute. Each begins with a section introducing the key concepts related to that attribute, and subsequent chapters provide individual standard names, short standard statements, clarifications, rationales, implementation suggestions, and lists of hazards to avoid. Embedded case narratives illustrate the standards, individually and in concert. References provide documentation and opportunities for further reading.

This book addresses a wide variety of needs experienced by those who commission, conduct, or use program and project evaluations. It provides guidance and encourages reflective practice related to

- whether and when to evaluate,
- how to select evaluators and other experts,
- the impact of cultures, contexts, and politics,
- communication and stakeholder engagement,
- technical issues in planning, designing, and managing evaluations,
- uses and misuses of evaluations,
- other issues related to evaluation quality, improvement, and accountability.

In general, this third edition followed a development process very similar to that of other editions, characterized by transparency and a strong commitment to stakeholders' input. The process began in 2004 with a national survey of the membership of the Joint Committee on Standards for Educational Evaluation sponsoring organizations (JCSEE member list on page vii) to help identify features and content that needed attention. More than 300 stakeholders provided comments and suggestions. A subsequent survey sent to selected stakeholders investigated possible formats for the standard statements. Reviews of the scholarship and practice literature from the last four decades provided perspectives on substantive issues. Numerous formal and informal presentations and discussions at national meetings and other venues helped to provide broad and specific perspectives on what the third edition should accomplish. The four-member task force, appointed and supervised by the full Joint Committee on Standards for Educational Evaluation (JCSEE), reviewed this input and prepared successive drafts. At each annual meeting of the JCSEE, members reviewed task force work and provided guidance. As drafts were ready, more than 75 national and international reviewers provided comments and suggestions in an open review process. Participants at six national hearings discussed the contents and overall quality. More than 50 practitioners and other users tried out these standards and provided comments prior to final editing and approval. Then, after favorable review by an independent validation panel in 2008, the JCSEE approved the standards for finalization. Following a 45-day comment period in 2009 and thorough review by the JCSEE, these standards were readied for final certification as the American National Standards Institute (ANSI) program evaluation standards.

For readers who are new to *The Program Evaluation Standards,* we have tried to make your introduction to and subsequent use of the standards as valuable and enjoyable as possible. For those of you who have worked extensively with earlier editions, you will find much that is familiar and some important changes. The utility, feasibility, propriety, and accuracy standards retain their core importance. Case applications continue to be important for demonstrating how to apply the standards. However, in our surveys and reviews, we found that many stakeholders reported concerns about the individual cases at the end of each standard. These stakeholders asked for more integration of the standards into recommendations for reflective practice, taking into account the necessary trade-offs and compromises made necessary by limited resources and other features of evaluation settings. In order to create greater integration, this third edition provides a scenario for each attribute with applications spread across all the standards related to that scenario.

In addition, significant integrating themes, such as the roles of culture and context in evaluation, connect the attributes and standards with one another. For example, cultures and contexts have profound influences on how evaluators attend to and increase utility, feasibility, propriety, accuracy, and accountability. These influences are enumerated and illustrated in ways that bridge the various attributes and individual standards. Similarly, a recurring theme in high-quality evaluations is stakeholder involvement, not just because it is the proper thing to do and leads to more useful evaluations, but also because of its impact on feasibility and accuracy and its essential role in evaluation accountability. A third theme, high-quality communication and the need for communication planning, is addressed repeatedly throughout the attributes and standards. The concern is not just that formal and informal reports need to be accurate, or that communication needs to be timely in order for evaluations to be useful. High-quality communication is required to deal with conflicts of interests, with human rights, with many feasibility issues, with data selection and collection, and with quality planning and implementation. This third edition pays consistent attention to building these thematic bridges across the attributes and standards, even as it maintains the unique focus required by the individual standards.

A third significant change in this third edition is increased emphasis on the need to improve and hold evaluations accountable through systematic metaevaluation. In this revision, a new attribute, *evaluation accountability*, has been added to the previous core attributes. It is presented in Part V of this volume. Evaluation accountability is supported by three standards calling for rigorous documentation of evaluations, and their internal and external metaevaluation for formative and summative purposes. The standards call explicitly for all evaluations to be systematically metaevaluated for improvement and accountability purposes.

A number of smaller changes responding to stakeholders' concerns and suggestions have been incorporated into this book. For example, the discussion of each attribute begins with an overview that clarifies and describes its importance in evaluation. The standard names and statements have been revised to make the language clearer and more concise. The rationales for the individual standards have been removed from the standard statements and explicated more thoroughly in the following text. Suggestions for implementation and lists of hazards guide the reader in applying the standards.

The processes leading to this third edition have taken place in a period of rapid change in knowledge development and dissemination. Currently, the printed book as we have known it is being transformed by delivery systems that can augment and even replace physical pages bound together in a single volume. Electronic reading and other computing devices and worldwide networks are making it easier to transport, store, and access highly dynamic and interactive libraries. These electronic files also encourage and facilitate new search procedures and interaction with the contents of documents. The JCSEE continues to work on techniques for making *The Program Evaluation*

Standards and its supporting materials more user-friendly and accessible. Please visit our website at http://www.jcsee.com to read ongoing updates about new developments.

Our Web site will also inform interested stakeholders about the JCSEE and how to become involved in standards use and development. The members of the JCSEE are devoted to and passionate about evaluation quality and the contributions that evaluation standards can make to evaluation practice. We are committed to the development, revision, dissemination, and use of high-quality, useful evaluation standards. However, these evaluation standards can remain vital only with stakeholder input. Please use these standards and report your experiences to us. Once a volume of standards is completed, JCSEE procedures require review and possible updating no less frequently than every five years, and thorough review and revision no less frequently than every 10 years.

Consider being part of this development process, which begins immediately and will lead to a fourth edition in due course. Most of all, please view these standards as your standards, and visit our website for additional information and to volunteer. We need your ideas and contributions.

All of us thank you for your interest in and continued use of *The Program Evaluation Standards.*

❖ About the Authors ❖

Donald B. Yarbrough, PhD, is the director of the Center for Evaluation and Assessment and professor of Psychological and Quantitative Foundations at the University of Iowa. He is the current chair of the Joint Committee on Standards for Educational Evaluation (JCSEE) and has been a member since 1996, sponsored until 2008 by the National Council on Measurement in Education. He served as a writer for *The Personnel Evaluation Standards* and *The Student Evaluation Standards* and has helped organize and conduct numerous evaluation standards development activities, including national hearings and field trials. In addition to authoring and coauthoring more than 100 evaluation reports, he has published widely on assessment and evaluation. He has received funding from the National Institutes of Health (NIH), the National Science Foundation, the Fund for the Improvement of Postsecondary Education, the Department of Education, the Department of Health and Human Services, the National Education Association, and numerous private foundations. In addition, he currently serves as chair of the NIH Clinical and Translational Science Evaluators Definitions Interest Group. He maintains active memberships in the American Psychological Society, the American Evaluation Association, the American Educational Research Association, and the National Council on Measurement in Education.

Lyn M. Shulha, PhD, is professor and director of the Assessment and Evaluation Group, Queen's University at Kingston, Canada, and a charter member of the Consortium of Universities for Evaluation Education (CUEE). She has been a member of the Canadian Society for the Study of Education (CSSE) for over 20 years and has represented this organization on the Joint Committee on Standards for Educational Evaluation (JCSEE) since 2003. She is also a long-time member of the American Evaluation Association (AEA) serving as a chair of AEA's professional development committee and a member-at-large for the Evaluation Use topical interest group. She currently contributes to the editorial boards of the *American Journal of Evaluation*, *The Canadian Journal of Program Evaluation*, and *Evaluation and Program Planning*, and is an associate editor of the new international journal *Assessment Matters*. She continues to lead projects and publish in the areas of evaluative inquiry in school-university professional learning partnerships; collaborative, participatory, and mixed methods approaches to evaluation; teachers' classroom assessment practices; and, assessment as pedagogy. She currently chairs the JCSEE's Research Forum.

Rodney K. Hopson, PhD, is Hillman Distinguished Professor in the Department of Foundations and Leadership in the School of Education and a faculty member in the Center for Interpretive and Qualitative Research at Duquesne University. With funding support from the W. K. Kellogg Foundation, the National Science Foundation, the Robert Wood Johnson Foundation, the Annie E. Casey Foundation, and other sponsors, he has secured support for students of color in natural and social sciences to contribute to the development of interests that focus on democratically oriented evaluation and research approaches and practices in traditionally underserved communities in the United States. His recent book, *The Role of Culture and Cultural Context in Evaluation: A Mandate for Inclusion, the Discovery of Truth and Understanding* (with Stafford Hood and Henry Frierson, 2005), describes how the evaluation community attends to matters of culture and cultural context, especially in reconstituting knowledge production in the field. In addition, he has served on the editorial boards of several publications related to evaluation, including the *American Journal of Evaluation,* the *Encyclopedia of Evaluation,* the *Evaluation and Society* book series, and the *Journal of MultiDisciplinary Evaluation.* Recent professional service includes membership on the Board of Directors of the American Evaluation Association and time as the founding project director of the American Evaluation Association/Duquesne University Graduate Education Diversity Internship Program.

Flora A. Caruthers, EdD, is the staff director for technical services and staff development for the Florida Legislature's Office of Program Policy Analysis and Government Accountability, where she has served in a variety of positions, including conducting and leading a number of education-related program evaluations. Her previous professional experiences include service as an elementary school teacher, university administrator, faculty member, and postsecondary education evaluator and consultant. She also served as program chair, treasurer, and president of the Southeast Evaluation Association. For the last decade, she has served as the National Legislative Program Evaluation Society's liaison to the Joint Committee on Standards for Educational Evaluation and is in her second three-year term on the Executive Board. She is a member of the American Educational Research Association and the American Evaluation Association.

❖ Introduction ❖

Each year, people spend trillions of dollars on programs designed to improve knowledge, skills, performance, and attitudes. We invest in these formal and informal programs in the hope that we and our communities will change for the better. With so much time, money, and other resources directed to educational and social programs, how can we be sure that our programs are efficient and effective? How can we improve them and hold them accountable for results?

This need to address program quality systematically has helped program evaluation develop into a formal specialty. By the late 1960s, program developers, sponsors, and evaluators recognized the need for rigorous standards to guide program evaluation. In 1974, representatives from three national professional organizations came together to form the Joint Committee on Standards for Educational Evaluation (JCSEE). By 1981, the JCSEE was a 501(c)(3) corporation supported by 12 North American professional organizations and had published its first set of evaluation standards, the *Standards for Evaluations of Educational Programs, Projects and Materials*. A full, detailed history of the JCSEE is beyond the scope of this introduction, but additional references are available on our website. To learn more about the history and organizational support of the JCSEE, visit http://www.jcsee.org.

Today, the JCSEE is supported by 17 sponsoring organizations and has been a member of the American National Standards Institute (ANSI) since 1989. During its 35-year history, the mission of the JCSEE has remained constant: to develop and implement inclusive processes producing widely used evaluation standards that serve educational and social improvement. In keeping with this mission, it has developed and disseminated three sets of evaluation standards: *The Program Evaluation Standards* (1981, 1994, 2011), *The Personnel Evaluation Standards* (1987, 2009) and *The Student Evaluation Standards* (2004, in development).

❖ EVALUATION STANDARDS DEVELOPMENT

The cornerstone of JCSEE standards development is the ongoing involvement of diverse stakeholders representing different perspectives. JCSEE procedures encourage stakeholders from inside and outside North America, including stakeholders who have not previously contributed, to participate in each new standards development. Moreover, regular renewal efforts also keep the standards informed by current scholarship and practice. Following JCSEE procedures, formal reviews must take place on a 5-year cycle. Every 10 years, the standards must go through a complete review process. These reviews must take place in order to maintain ANSI approval.

The development process for this third edition of *The Program Evaluation Standards* began in 2004 and followed the same procedures as previous editions. It included the following key components:

1. Formal initiation of standards review
2. Needs assessment
3. Development of draft standards
4. External validation panel monitoring and oversight
5. Regular reports, process monitoring, and approval by the JCSEE
6. National and international reviews
7. National hearings
8. Revision of multiple draft manuscripts responding to stakeholder and JCSEE suggestions and comments
9. Stakeholder field trials of revised drafts
10. ANSI process monitoring and comment periods
11. JCSEE vote to approve the final version of the standards
12. Dissemination and research on standards use and quality

In 2002, the JCSEE approved an addition to these procedures: a task force to lead each specific standards renewal process. The change was in response to the increased responsibilities for three different sets of standards and was first used with *The Personnel Evaluation Standards* (completed in 2009). Continuing this model, a JCSEE-approved Program Evaluation Standards task force led the revision process and produced the revised manuscripts. The JCSEE retained its responsibility for regular review and final approval of the developing manuscript, but the manuscript was written, reviewed, and revised by the task force. Other procedures and components in the standards development process have remained the same as they were for previous editions.

In the development of the current edition, key considerations included the content and format of the standards statements and the clarifications and rationales for them. In the five years from initiation to final manuscript, the task force and JCSEE members conducted a North American needs assessment, a format survey about changes to the standard statements, numerous formal and informal presentations, discussions at national and international conferences, and extensive reviews of scholarship and practice literature on program evaluation, as well as all the steps in the process described above.

❖ TECHNICAL LANGUAGE IN *THE PROGRAM EVALUATION STANDARDS*

One important goal for standards in general is to clarify technical terms and make otherwise vague definitions fully operational and useful. Careful attention to terminology is not only typical for standards work but is also found in any craft or profession that has developed specialized tools and high-quality professional practices. For example, customers would worry about a plumber who could not read the local plumbing codes and skillfully implement standard practices effectively and efficiently.

Similarly, clarifying *The Program Evaluation Standards* requires concept and language specificity. *The Program Evaluation Standards* will use some technical terms that may not be familiar to all stakeholders; for example, *randomized field trial, quasiexperiment, ethnography, process use, instrumental use, program theory, service delivery,* and *institutional review boards.* In addition, they will rely on important concepts that have more nuanced meanings than in common parlance, for example, *programs* and *projects, standards, utility, feasibility, propriety, accuracy* and *accountability.* Key terms will be described fully in the text or in the appended glossary.

Clarifying these terms serves one primary purpose—to improve communication about value and quality. For example, not all stakeholders will be adept at implementing randomized field trials, ethnographies, or other evaluation methodologies and procedures. However, familiarity with such terms and concepts helps with communication about the nature and value of information to assist decision making. When program and evaluation stakeholders have knowledge of the concepts and terms used to ground the standards, they can engage effectively in conversations that guide programs and their evaluations.

❖ IMPORTANT ROLES FOR PROGRAM AND EVALUATION STAKEHOLDERS

Anyone whose life is affected by a program or its evaluation is a *stakeholder* in that program and its evaluation. The standards have been developed with consideration of the many different roles that stakeholders and groups of stakeholders play in program development, implementation, and evaluation.

With regard to program development and implementation, some roles are more administrative, such as reviewing programs for funding, guiding program designs and implementation, and deciding whether and how to implement programs. Other roles, especially those of the program staff and participants, support the detailed work of daily program implementation. Some roles, such as those of staff members or participants, usually engage numerous individuals. In nearly all programs, specific individuals may engage in multiple roles.

Similarly, many different stakeholders and groups of stakeholders play important evaluation roles. Some of the most important are

- proposal reviewers—those who scrutinize, evaluate, and decide which proposed programs receive funding based on considerations of needs and program quality, including the quality of the proposed program evaluation;
- sponsors—those who fund the program evaluation;
- clients—those who commission the evaluation;
- evaluators—anyone with professional experience and training in systematic program evaluation serving in a professional capacity;
- designers—evaluators and other stakeholders who work together to plan the evaluation and its purposes, goals, and objectives, including technical and domain specialists, selected program staff, participant group representatives, community or organizational representatives, government representatives, and consultants;
- implementers—evaluators and other stakeholders who work together to manage, administer, orchestrate, oversee, implement, and assure the quality of the evaluation, including evaluation staff, other technical specialists, selected program staff, volunteers, and consultants;
- evaluation participants—those who take part in the programs and provide information and perspectives for evaluation purposes;
- other respondents—anyone else who provides important information about the program;
- intended users—those whose needs are identified and addressed by evaluation processes and products, resulting in improved knowledge, skills, decisions, or other actions;

- other users—those whose needs are not specifically identified during evaluation planning but who have access to the evaluation processes and products, resulting in changes in knowledge and understanding of the program, decisions, and other actions;
- evaluation educators—those who help other learners, including program and evaluation stakeholders and beginning evaluators, develop more knowledge and skill in evaluation; and
- metaevaluators—those who evaluate program evaluations using these and other standards.

Just as with programs, individual evaluation stakeholders can play single or multiple roles in the evaluation.

❖ WHAT ARE *STANDARDS?*

The word *standard* as used in *The Program Evaluation Standards* has two key features. First, the standards identify and define evaluation quality and guide evaluators and evaluation users in the pursuit of evaluation quality. Second, these standards are not "laws" but are voluntary, consensus statements developed with extensive stakeholder input and then discussed, revised, and approved by the members of the JCSEE following ANSI procedures.

These standards are both similar to and unlike other types of standards in important ways. Like technical standards that specify exact dimensions and tolerances for manufactured items or content standards that outline learning processes and outcomes, evaluation standards identify ways to improve quality. However, unlike many technical and content standards, these evaluation standards do not specify exact procedures to be followed in any specific setting. They require responsiveness and judgment in each evaluation setting. In problem-solving terminology, these standards provide *heuristics* to be used in defining and addressing the novel problems that evaluation settings present.

An important characteristic of the individual program evaluation standards is that they exist in dynamic tension with each other. Few if any evaluations provide the opportunity to maximize quality in the application of each standard. Because of these limitations, a balanced application of individual standards depends on human values and choices in specific situations. In implementing the program evaluation standards, stakeholders must decide how to create the best quality evaluations based on prioritized needs. The standards can be applied to all evaluations, but the exact ways they are applied will differ.

Taken as a whole, the program evaluation standards address the possible dimensions of quality in program evaluations. To help clarify the standards and make them manageable, they are organized according to the five general attributes of quality: evaluation utility, feasibility, propriety, accuracy, and accountability. Each of these attributes of evaluation quality and their supporting standards are discussed thoroughly in separate parts of the book. Each part presents case scenarios and applications to address how the standards can help evaluators and evaluation users respond to complex evaluation challenges.

Another distinguishing characteristic of these standards is their lack of regulatory status. In contrast to standards defined by law or regulatory code, the program evaluation standards are *open standards. Open* in this sense means that they are voluntary and consensual even though they are developed with due process.

Evaluators and evaluation users can, however, agree contractually to be guided by *The Program Evaluation Standards* in specific evaluation work. They can agree to investigate whether the standards are well-implemented and how well they supported evaluation quality. The JCSEE strongly recommends that evaluators and evaluation users commit themselves to evaluation practices based on these standards.

❖ WHAT ARE *PROGRAMS* AND *PROJECTS?*

No discussion of *The Program Evaluation Standards* would be complete without describing and defining *programs* and *projects*. Earlier editions of *The Program Evaluation Standards* defined educational programs as "activities that are provided on a continuing basis" and defined educational projects as "activities that are provided for defined periods of time" (JCSEE, 1994, p. 3).

In this third edition, the definitions have expanded. Today, the general consensus among program and project managers and administrators is that programs and projects are not distinguished primarily by duration, since some projects last longer than some programs; nor do projects and programs consist of qualitatively different types of structures and functions. What distinguishes the two is their relationship to one another in specific situations. For example, it is quite common for federal programs to provide the framework for specific state-level and local projects, but rarely do projects provide the framework for programs. With regard to applications of these standards, it is not necessary to distinguish between programs and projects except to identify how they are related in specific evaluations.

This third edition also emphasizes that programs are much more than just activities. They consist of multiple components. In addition, all important components of programs can be the objects of evaluation in their own right or can be part of a componential evaluation of the whole program. Specific components that can be evaluated include

- contexts and how they interact with programs and program components;
- participants and other beneficiaries as well as those who encounter costs or loss of benefits;
- needs, problems, and policy spaces in programs and their contexts;
- goals and objectives;
- resources and costs of all kinds, including staff, facilities, materials, and opportunity costs;
- activities, procedures, plans, policies, and products;
- logic models, beliefs, assumptions, and implicit and explicit program theories explaining why and how programs should work; and
- outputs, results, benefits, outcomes, and impacts.

Our full description of programs includes the key elements discussed above. We describe programs as the systematic application of resources guided by logic, beliefs, and assumptions identifying human needs and factors related to them. Defined completely, a program is

- a set of planned systematic activities
- using managed resources
- to achieve specified goals
- related to specific needs
- of specific, identified, participating human individuals or groups
- in specific contexts
- resulting in documentable outputs, outcomes, and impacts
- following assumed (explicit or implicit) systems of beliefs (diagnostic, causal, intervention, and implementation theories about how the program works)
- with specific, investigable costs and benefits.

These standards are not designed to be equally applicable to all programs. Rather, they are tailored for educational, human services, human resource development, health, wellness, and other types of programs in which the goals include changes in human motivation, attitudes, knowledge, skills, and performance.

❖ WHAT IS *EVALUATION*?

Earlier editions of *The Program Evaluation Standards* defined *evaluation* as the "systematic investigation of the worth or merit of an object"

(JCSEE, 1994, p. 3). The "object" in this case is the program under review. While maintaining the core focus on systematic investigation and quality, more recent definitions of *evaluation* have expanded the number of terms that denote value to include *merit, worth, importance,* and *significance.* Other recent definitions focus more on active purposes, such as judgment, decision making, improvement, and accountability assessment. Sometimes evaluation is described by its position in the program development chronology; for example, as the judgment of quality made when a program is completed (a *summative* purpose) or while the program is still developing (a *formative* purpose).

In the third edition, we expand the descriptive definition of program *evaluation* to include

- the systematic investigation of the quality of programs, projects, subprograms, subprojects, and/or any of their components or elements, together or singly
- for purposes of decision making, judgments, conclusions, findings, new knowledge, organizational development, and capacity building in response to the needs of identified stakeholders
- leading to improvement and/or accountability in the users' programs and systems
- ultimately contributing to organizational or social value.

The first component in the definition above, systematic investigation, requires some additional discussion because it so often leads to confusion about how systematic evaluation compares and contrasts with research.

Unlike most program evaluation, most educational and social science research focuses primarily on the need to produce credible, generalizable knowledge about the nature of the world around us. Typically, research questions do not address the quality of a specific program but rather gaps and uncertainties in important theories or areas of knowledge. A researcher typically designs a research project to study these uncertainties and gaps and strives for complete control of how the research, including any interventions or treatments, is performed. The primary audience for most research is the researchers' peers. A secondary audience consists of those who might use this generalized knowledge or translate it into practice.

In contrast, program evaluations help stakeholders answer specific questions or make decisions about specific programs and their components. Evaluators use their professional skills to investigate such things as a program's development, processes, theory, viability, outcomes, and impact. They use their skills in the service of stakeholders' needs and to investigate questions about value to specific stakeholders.

Distinguishing research from evaluation projects based on their methodologies is difficult. For example, sometimes evaluations of standardized interventions are conducted using controlled experimental or quasiexperimental designs with randomized control groups or naturally occurring comparison groups. In these approaches, the evaluation manager strives for considerable control over the intervention and manages both the quality of the intervention and its evaluation. Many evaluators with a background in experimental research prefer these approaches because they help isolate the net impact of the program as an intervention. However, not all programs are simple enough or sufficiently controlled and standardized, especially in complex naturally occurring contexts. Even when programs are well-developed and amenable to standardization, implementing an evaluation component can alter the programs, their contexts, and their outcomes in significant and unpredictable ways. This direct evaluation impact on the program may be positive and result in program improvements. However, direct evaluation impact interferes with generalization that research aspires to. In particular, findings about programs directly affected by evaluation processes do not necessarily generalize to replications of the program without similar evaluation components.

Similarly to experimentalists, researchers trained in naturalism, ethnography, and qualitative designs may set about to understand a program in order to increase knowledge about how and why it functions or does not function in its larger context. When such projects focus more on generating dependable knowledge and less on the quality of the program and its value to its stakeholders, they are more akin to research studies than program evaluation.

Sometimes, those who commission evaluations believe that evaluative inquiry and research inquiry are one and the same. With regard to the available tools, instruments, and methodologies, evaluation and research projects do share many similarities. However, they are very different in how they are planned and managed, and in how they generate value. In many program evaluation situations, serious difficulties arise because those in charge do not adequately address these differences. The remaining chapters in this book provide extensive discussion about how to plan, implement, and improve program evaluations. We believe this book is required reading for program or evaluation stakeholders who confuse social science research with program evaluation. For example, Part I, describing evaluation utility, details how evaluation creates value and how orientation to stakeholders' needs is an important defining feature of evaluation as opposed to research. Part II presents the factors affecting evaluation feasibility and also provides important detail about the relationships between program evaluations and the programs they evaluate. Part III, on evaluation propriety, discusses the intense social and human relationships that are the hallmark of programs and their evaluations and the need for attention to and respect for social and human factors, especially customs, cultures, laws, ethics, morality, and human rights. Part IV, on evaluation accuracy, clarifies how social science methods are used in evaluation projects to create value. It describes how evaluation projects rely on methods from a wide variety of sources to accurately address the needs of evaluation users.

One last consideration about how to describe and define program evaluation quality is presented in Part V. Evaluation projects and subprojects can themselves be documented and evaluated so that they can be improved and held accountable. Such "evaluations of evaluations" are called *metaevaluations.* Just as program evaluation is often confused with social science research, *metaevaluation* is often confused with *meta-analysis. Meta-analysis* refers to the practice of reviewing multiple research studies addressing the same phenomena to draw the most supportable generalizable conclusion based on the quality of the research studies. As a primary way of investigating evaluation quality, *metaevaluation* is discussed more completely in Part V, *Evaluation Accountability.* In contrast, meta-analysis, as a specific research technique, is not addressed in this book.

❖ CONTENTS OF THIS BOOK

The chapters in this book are designed to respond to a wide variety of users and their roles. *Applying the Standards,* the section following this introduction, continues with some of the themes introduced here and describes in greater detail factors that will contribute to optimal use of the standards. Subsequent chapters present the attributes of high-quality evaluations and the standards that support achieving evaluation quality. Sections at the end of the book present a glossary, references that serve to document the specific attributes of quality, and an index. Standard statements from previous editions are included in Appendixes A and B.

❖ THE CORE CHAPTERS ON EVALUATION QUALITY: UTILITY, FEASIBILITY, PROPRIETY, ACCURACY, AND ACCOUNTABILITY

The goal of this book is to help users recognize and improve evaluation quality. Each of Parts I through V presents one attribute of quality and its accompanying standards. After an introductory overview to the attribute and the introduction of a case scenario, chapters on individual standards provide clarification and rationales, specific considerations for implementation, and some hazards to try to avoid. To help illustrate how standards are used, the chapter on each standard concludes with an application of the case scenario. Taken all together, the applications tell the story of how evaluation quality is constructed in specific situations.

A major attribute of evaluation quality is utility, addressed extensively in Part I. *Utility* discusses use, usefulness, influence, and misuse. It describes when and how evaluation worth is created, for example, when evaluations contribute to stakeholders' learning, inform decisions, improve understanding, lead to improvements, or provide information for accountability judgments. Utility is supported by eight standards.

Part II presents the factors affecting evaluation feasibility. *Feasibility* discusses the effects of contexts, cultures, costs, politics, power, available resources, and other factors on evaluations. It details which feasibility factors to consider before implementing an evaluation and how to increase or maintain feasibility in different contexts. Feasibility is supported by four standards.

Part III describes propriety: the moral, ethical, and legal concerns related to evaluation quality. *Propriety* considers the rights of stakeholders and other persons and details the responsibilities of all stakeholders, especially evaluation professionals, in an evaluation. Setting thresholds for adequate propriety can be difficult and requires balancing different stakeholders' needs and situations. Social justice considerations may play a significant role, but not all stakeholders have the same values or conceptions of social justice. Propriety is supported by seven standards.

Part IV discusses how to increase the accuracy of findings and conclusions. *Accuracy* discusses reliability, validity, and reduction of error and bias. The eight accuracy standards address quality in data collection, analysis, logic, conclusions, and communication. The chapter is intended for all stakeholders and does not require prior technical skills in statistics, measurement, ethnography, methodology, or research. Accuracy is supported by eight standards.

Part V is called *Evaluation Accountability.* This encompassing attribute of evaluation quality results from balancing utility, feasibility, propriety, and accuracy. Internal and external metaevaluation, discussed extensively in the accountability standards, provide the methodology used to increase and document evaluation quality. Evaluation Accountability introduces three new standards but is also supported by the 27 specific utility, feasibility, propriety, and accuracy standards.

❖ HOW TO CONTRIBUTE TO CURRENT DISCUSSIONS AND FUTURE REVISIONS

Stakeholder contributions are critical to the continued development of the *The Program Evaluation Standards*. The JCSEE is committed to collecting and responding to feedback from those who use or are affected by the use of these standards. We encourage all stakeholders to try out this edition in any situations that seem appropriate. We need to know whether and how the features and content work for you in your evaluation roles. Interested stakeholders can find out more about how to get involved in standards research and development by contacting us at http://www.jcsee.org. We are already planning for the next edition and invite you to be an important part of that process as this current edition is used, evaluated, and revised. Updates will be posted regularly at jcsee.org.

❖ REFERENCES

Joint Committee on Standards for Educational Evaluation. (1994). *The program evaluation standards: How to assess evaluations of educational programs* (2nd ed.). Thousand Oaks, CA: Sage.

❖ Applying the Standards ❖

The overarching purpose of this book is to support evaluation quality through appropriate applications of these standards. In order to make best use of the standards, evaluators and other stakeholders should familiarize themselves with the concepts and rationales that ground the standards and with the implications and nuances related to their use. This section describes factors that influence standards use and serves as preparation for the specific applications presented in the main body of the book.

Many factors influence how standards are applied in specific evaluation situations. Some of these factors result from

- stakeholders' needs, backgrounds, and prior knowledge,
- the evaluation roles of those applying the standards, and
- the complexity and purposes of the evaluation.

In addition, the standards can be applied to improve quality and accountability during all phases of evaluation. For example, they can inform decisions ranging from whether an evaluation is feasible to how much to trust the findings in a final report. Differing evaluation situations, needs, and purposes may require different emphases and balance among the standards.

Because the standards can contribute to the quality of many different parts of an evaluation, stakeholders should identify possible applications of specific standards at key decision points in the evaluation. The Functional Table following this chapter presents lists of standards to consider for specific evaluation tasks. Similarly, at any given time, some features of the evaluation need greater attention because they are at greater risk for poor quality or are more critical to the evaluation. In general, using the standards well requires considerable reflection and attention to the needs of individuals and groups as the evaluation develops.

In later chapters, specific scenarios and applications provide examples of how standards are orchestrated with one another. Because evaluation work often requires complex problem solving in poorly specified domains, there are as many ways to balance the standards as there are unique combinations of evaluation roles, settings, resources, needs, and purposes. Becoming familiar with the standards and then practicing their application reflectively in all phases of evaluation work, especially in conference and collaboration with other stakeholders, is the best way to achieve expertise in their use.

❖ BECOMING FAMILIAR WITH THE STANDARDS

The first step in applying the standards well is acquiring conceptual and practical knowledge about them. The strategies needed to become familiar with standards may differ for different individuals and groups. Based on their own needs, users of the standards should decide which sections of the book to focus on first and which learning strategies to implement. For example, those who know relatively little about program evaluation might choose to review the lists of standard statements and then read the five attribute introductions, the case scenarios, and the individual applications of standards. Such an approach can provide a good introduction to evaluation concepts and standards use. Later, they can select specific standards to study in greater depth. Others might choose to familiarize themselves with individual attributes and standards one by one. For example, a stakeholder with pressing concerns about evaluation feasibility might start first with the feasibility attribute and standards and review them in detail before considering other standards.

One way to learn how to use the standards effectively is to apply them to different evaluation situations and to solicit feedback from knowledgeable others. Discussing applications with peers and other evaluation stakeholders will make the learning more valuable. For example,

- Reviewers of program evaluation proposals or program proposals with evaluation components can read through the standards to outline the specific attributes and standards they want to emphasize. As they prepare to review, they can agree on specific standards to apply so that they achieve greater quality and consistency in their reviews.
- Practicing evaluators using the standards for evaluation design and implementation can introduce their clients and other stakeholders to the standards and educate them in their use. They can attach and explain the standards as part of evaluation contracts and agreements based on discussions with clients about evaluation quality.
- Evaluation sponsors, clients, and other stakeholders can apply the standards to support the quality they want in the evaluations they are commissioning and using. When decisions are being made by groups

of stakeholders informed by the standards, group discussions can help clarify underlying values and lead to more effective evaluations.

- Students and other learners may apply the standards to evaluations in multiple evaluation settings, discuss dilemmas, and balance the standards with one another in different scenarios with different needs, resources, evaluation stakeholders, and other constraints. In this way, they can gain familiarity with the problem-solving methods required to use the standards adaptively and effectively.
- Instructors, teachers, and others who design and implement curricula, instruction, training, or provide evaluation consultations and guidance can review the standards to determine the roles that they want evaluation to play in their development and accountability work.
- Individuals working with specific types of evaluations or specific interest groups can take advantage of online communities or Web-based wikis, blogs, and share groups to collaborate on applications of the standards. Readers can contact the JCSEE at http://www.jcsee.org for additional details and guidance or to help build and become part of such networks.

❖ THREE IMPORTANT PRINCIPLES

Three principles should guide use of the standards. First, to be most effective, the standards require adaptive, responsive, and mindful use. They should not be applied literally and superficially following a simple recipe. Rather, evaluators must discover how to apply them adaptively in each specific situation to achieve overall evaluation quality.

The second principle is complementary to the first. Users should not conclude from the order of the parts of this book (Utility, Feasibility, Propriety, Accuracy, and Evaluation Accountability) that some standards are intrinsically more important than others. The current ordering of standards reflects the historical and conceptual grounding of the standards. In the early years of evaluation work in North America, many researchers conducting evaluations believed that their responsibilities for quality began and ended with assuring evaluation accuracy. The emphasis on evaluation utility during the last four decades grew out of the recognition that accurate but unused evaluations have little if any actual worth. For this and other reasons, the utility standards came first in the original publication of the standards. However, the lack of adequate emphasis on utility several decades ago should not lead to the conclusion that it is the preeminent attribute of evaluation quality.

The other attributes are equally critical. For example, ignoring feasibility can result in squandering resources through failed implementation attempts or in altering and undermining the program that needs evaluation. Propriety emphasizes the primacy of human rights and responsibilities in all program and evaluation work. Lack of attention to propriety can have serious ethical, moral, professional, and legal consequences. Attention to evaluation accuracy provides the factual foundation required for evaluations to be useful. Evaluation accountability is an overarching requirement because it emphasizes the self-reflective nature of evaluation quality and the need to investigate and document the balance among the other attributes of quality in each evaluation situation as the evaluation is implemented in real time and space.

The third important principle is that using the standards effectively requires understanding them in depth. Those who only read the standard statements are not using them as intended. Much attention has gone into the wording of the standard statements, but they are only compact advance organizers for the concepts and issues they represent. Those who apply the standard statements while ignoring clarifications, rationales, suggestions, and applications are missing out on the richness that makes the standards useful. This book strongly encourages readers to review and revisit specific sections as they apply the standards.

❖ INDIVIDUALS' ROLES IN APPLYING THE STANDARDS

Individuals play many roles in evaluations. For example, some are responsible for decisions about whether and how to fund evaluations or when to commission an evaluator or evaluation team to plan and conduct the evaluation. Some individuals have professional evaluation roles, such as evaluation designer, planner, worker, manager, or other staff member. Some are responsible for decisions based on evaluation findings or other uses of the evaluation. Some individuals are directly affected by the evaluation processes and products and experience beneficial or adverse consequences as a result of the evaluation. An increasingly important role is that of metaevaluator, the role taken on by individuals or teams whose duty is to investigate the quality of the evaluation. Metaevaluators are responsible for decisions about evaluation quality and help make recommendations for evaluation improvement and appropriate use. The section on evaluation accountability has much to say about the special roles that metaevaluators play.

Two features are important with regard to the roles of individuals in implementing the standards. First, individuals often have more than one role in an evaluation. For example, an individual may be both a program staff member (an intended decision-maker and beneficiary of the evaluation) as well as an evaluation staff member. Many internal evaluators have such dual roles and responsibilities. Most evaluators and evaluation users have metaevaluative duties in addition to their other roles. Because individuals take on multiple roles over the course of an evaluation, role confusion, bias, and poor communication and execution of responsibilities is an ongoing possibility. Subsequent sections of the book provide discussion and examples of how to clarify and maintain the rights and responsibilities associated with different evaluation roles.

Second, the fact that individuals have different identifiable roles in an evaluation is a great advantage in applying the standards to achieve evaluation quality. Because of their role identities, different individuals and groups will have different insights into how to apply the standards to achieve evaluation quality in any given evaluation setting. Individual backgrounds and cultures can also interact with the roles being played to result in different perspectives about how to apply the standards. Those wishing to increase their expertise in applying the standards can discuss their meaning and application with people in different evaluation roles and from different backgrounds. Practicing evaluators and other stakeholders can also engage in role-playing by imagining themselves in other evaluation roles and reflecting on how individuals in these roles would interpret and benefit from specific standards applications.

❖ HOW PRACTICING EVALUATORS CAN APPLY THE STANDARDS

Practicing evaluators have a special responsibility for standards application because they are responsible for so many features of evaluation quality. For example, they can apply the standards to increase quality as they

- enter the evaluation setting, communicate with clients, and decide whether the program is evaluable;
- educate clients about what evaluation can and cannot do;
- help create and engage in agreements, contracts, and memoranda of understanding;
- identify and interact with stakeholders;
- plan the evaluation, often in collaboration with clients, intended users, and other stakeholders;
- manage evaluation implementation including data collection and analysis, communication, reporting, and follow-through;
- investigate, document, and improve evaluation quality and accountability through metaevaluation; and
- help create follow-through and appropriate use of evaluations.

Professional evaluators also have special responsibilities for education, not only of clients and evaluation users but also of other evaluators. By documenting decisions made during evaluation planning and implementation and how they relate to the standards, evaluators contribute to the transparency and accountability of their evaluations. In addition, such explicit applications of the standards can contribute to future improvements in how the standards are expressed, clarified, and used.

❖ HOW EVALUATION USERS CAN APPLY THE STANDARDS

The primary duty of evaluation clients, sponsors, and other users with regard to applying the standards is to attend to whether the quality of the evaluation is sufficient for its intended uses. All users should review the needs that the evaluation is intended to address and ask how well the evaluation meets these needs. It is not enough to commission an evaluation and then relinquish all responsibility to the evaluator or evaluation team. Users play an important role in quality control by applying the standards to the processes and products in evaluations that are important to them.

The clarifications, rationales, suggestions, and case applications of the standards are intended to help all stakeholders apply the standards with expertise related to their evaluations and their evaluation needs. Evaluation stakeholders can begin by reviewing the standards and deciding which are the most important in judging the quality of the specific evaluations that interest them. They can apply the standards one by one to determine the extent to which the evaluation has incorporated each standard needed for overall evaluation quality. A particularly powerful approach for evaluation stakeholders, illustrated in the case scenarios and applications, is for groups of users to discuss their values with regard to evaluation quality, the relative importance of the standards for this evaluation, and whether the evaluation is addressing the concerns expressed by that standard. When the users do not have adequate information to determine whether a specific standard has been implemented, they can ask for more information from the evaluators, or they can simply see to it that the evaluators pay appropriate attention to implementing all pertinent standards.

Similarly, evaluation stakeholders reviewing an evaluation after it is completed can apply the standards to determine whether the evaluation is of sufficient quality for the intended uses. If the evaluation designers and managers have attended adequately to the standards, including those supporting evaluation accountability, users of the completed evaluation may have all the evidence they need to review the evaluation for its quality relative to their intended uses. However, in some situations the quality of the evaluation will not have been documented, or it will fall short of users' requirements, resulting in the evaluation having less value in meeting users' needs. It is important for all evaluation users, in collaboration with evaluation professionals as needed, to apply the standards rigorously to determine if the evaluation quality is adequate for their purposes before making decisions, drawing conclusions, or acting on the basis of the evaluation findings and recommendations.

❖ BALANCING INDIVIDUAL ATTRIBUTES AND STANDARDS

When individual standards are applied in specific evaluation situations, some balancing of priorities is required. Because most evaluations are designed and implemented with restricted resources, designing and implementing high-quality evaluations that are sufficiently useful, proper, feasible, accurate, and accountable often requires that some standards receive more implementation support than others. The relative value of any particular standard applied to a specific evaluation situation is sometimes hard to determine in advance. In addition, standards are often most effective when implemented in concert. The role of individual standards in an evaluation is less like the links in a chain, where all must be equally strong for the chain to do its job best, and more like the unique chemistry and procedures that allow great cooks to produce great food. While expert cooks review recipes to increase their knowledge and to recall important steps, they also respond and adapt to different ingredients, equipment, and conditions such as ambient temperature, altitude, and humidity. Similarly, the prominence of the individual standards in a specific implementation may depend on factors specific to that setting. Each evaluator and evaluation user should develop a framework that reflects key values and concerns specific to what is being evaluated so that these can be discussed and negotiated. Then the relative support for the implementation of selected standards can be aligned with the values and importance of the specific evaluation goals. Part I, on Utility, provides specific discussions and applications describing ways that this alignment can take place (see, for example, U5 Relevant Information and U6 Meaningful Processes and Products).

Attending to and applying the standards in specific settings is challenging. In some cases, standards exist in dynamic tension with one another because of limited resources. Maximizing the implementation of one standard may jeopardize implementation of another that turns out to be equally important. In many situations, evaluations are better served when scarce resources are distributed so as to achieve satisfactory levels of support for all critical standards rather than to maximize the implementation of just a few. In most situations, evaluators and evaluation sponsors will have to make hard decisions about how to achieve the best balance in applying the standards. In some cases, evaluators and stakeholders may decide to postpone full implementation of some standards until a later time. However, such decisions have to be made with full care and diligence, anticipating both proposed benefits and possible negative consequences. The three applications in Part V, Evaluation Accountability, illustrate some ways to attempt this balance. In addition, the other standards descriptions and applications revisit these challenges repeatedly and provide examples of how to deal with them.

❖ USING THE STANDARDS FOR EVALUATION ACCOUNTABILITY

This book addresses accountability as it relates to both programs and program evaluations. Accountability is complex and refers to multiple facets of programs and their evaluations. For example, both programs and evaluations can be held accountable for

- appropriate resource use,
- effectively meeting intended users' needs,
- all manner of propriety considerations,
- maintaining good records,
- investigating needed improvements,
- taking steps to implement improvements, and
- the alignment of their specific, intended processes and results to needs and intentions.

Most stakeholders recognize the need to hold programs accountable for their processes, products, and benefits as weighed against their costs. They have a commonsense understanding of the role of program evaluation in supporting systematic accountability judgments of program worth. However, they may not have thought as much about how to hold evaluations accountable.

From start to finish, this book emphasizes the importance of evaluation accountability. As part of this emphasis, Part V, Evaluation Accountability, describes how systematic procedures can improve and document evaluation quality. The rationale for this addition seems compelling at this time. Currently too few sponsors, clients, and evaluators attend to the need for evaluations to be fully documented so that they can be metaevaluated. Metaevaluation (the evaluation of evaluations) has been viewed too often as simply another standard in the accuracy attribute.

Accountable evaluations document how specific standards have been selected and implemented and which trade-offs were required to balance effectiveness and efficiency. They also communicate the limitations that evaluations inevitably suffered as a consequence of restrictions on resources supporting design and implementation. Professional evaluators have a special duty to evaluation accountability, but high-quality evaluations are simply not possible without the efforts of key stakeholders, including the sponsors, clients, and actual users. Thus all individuals with an interest in program evaluation should recognize that they have a duty to increase and to document the accountability of program evaluations. These thirty standards provide a powerful framework to assist them.

❖ USING THESE STANDARDS WITH OTHER STANDARDS AND GUIDELINES

The first step in revising these standards was to ask what is required for high-quality reflective evaluation practice in current North American, multicultural, globalized settings. Since the early 1970s, when members of the Evaluation Research Society began work on evaluation standards, many individuals and groups have provided contributions. From the late 1960s through the early 1980s much of the standards development work took place in North America. Since the second edition of *The Program Evaluation Standards* was published in 1994, the number of new national and international organizations supporting program evaluation has increased to the point where it is hard to keep an accurate tally. At this time, the number of national and international evaluation associations and societies is probably approaching 100. Most of these were founded after the American Evaluation Association merged with the Evaluation Network and the Evaluation Research Society to form a single organization in 1986. Many of these national organizations have their own standards and guidelines, often based at least in part on the first or second editions of *The Program Evaluation Standards.*

U.S. and Canadian organizations sponsoring *The Program Evaluation Standards* also support other related standards and guidelines, such as the *Guiding Principles for Evaluators* (American Evaluation Association) and the *Standards for Educational and Psychological Testing* (American Educational Research Association, the National Council on Measurement in Education, and the American Psychological Association, 1999). Governments and NGOs sometimes have their own standards and guidelines as well, such as the U.S. Government Accounting Office's *General Auditing Standards,* which apply standards for program performance assessment. The JCSEE has also developed and published *The Student Evaluation Standards* (2004, in revision) and *The Personnel Evaluation Standards* (1988, 2009) which should be applied to program evaluations in some settings. All of these standards and guidelines, as well as others, have demonstrated value and are available for use by evaluation practitioners and scholars in improving evaluation quality and accountability.

One current JCSEE initiative is to serve as a contact point facilitating comparisons and contrasts between the Program Evaluation Standards and other standards and guidelines. Readers with an interest in this topic or who want to contribute to research on this topic are encouraged to visit http://www.jcsee.org and share in the resources and opportunities as they are posted there.

With regard to using *The Program Evaluation Standards* in conjunction with other resources, the goal must be to increase well-informed reflective practice while striving for the greatest possible evaluation quality in response to stakeholders' needs. In developing each edition of its standards, the JCSEE conducts an extensive review of scholarly publications, evaluation reports, and other guidelines and standards. (See the section on Documentation on page 297 for a list of these resources.) Similarly, this edition encourages all evaluation stakeholders to bring to bear all of their resources as they engage in reflective program evaluation practice and use.

❖ APPLYING THE STANDARDS VIA CHECKLISTS AND INVENTORIES

This edition of *The Program Evaluations Standards* consists of thirty individual standards organized into five general attributes. The sections describing individual attributes and standards provide overviews, clarifications, rationales, considerations, hazards, and case applications. Most evaluators and evaluation users cannot keep in mind every standard and their supporting details and maintain the necessary working memory to actually design, implement, or metaevaluate the evaluation. Checklists of standards, standard implementation guidelines, and possible hazards can be very useful memory aids.

However, when used in isolation checklists can make complex enterprises seem more mundane and rudimentary than they are. Checklists, whether stored in our own memories or written out, are no better than the knowledge and skill that they elicit in actual practice. A beginning pilot will use the same pre- and in-flight checklists as the experienced pilot but is not likely to fly the plane with anything resembling the skill and judgment that come with experience. A checklist is critical, even for the most expert, to ensure that nothing is overlooked, especially when pressures are intense and time is short. While checklists can help prevent disaster and enhance performance regardless of the level of prior preparation, they are no substitute for practice, reflection, skill, and other forms of expertise.

Numerous evaluation checklists summarizing standards and other guidelines are available. The authors of this book strongly support their judicious and informed use. Please visit the JCSEE website for links to checklists related to evaluation standards.

❖ REFERENCES

American Educational Research Association, American Psychological Association, & National Council on Measurement in Education (1999). *Standards for educational and psychological testing.* Washington, DC: Author.

American Evaluation Association. (2007). *Guiding principles for evaluators.* Retrieved June 26, 2007, from http://www.eval.org/Publications/GuidingPrinciples.asp

Joint Committee on Standards for Educational Evaluation. (2009). *The personnel evaluation standards: How to assess systems for evaluating educators* (2nd ed.). Thousand Oaks, CA: Corwin.

Joint Committee on Standards for Educational Evaluation. (2003). *The student evaluation standards: How to improve evaluations of students.* Thousand Oaks, CA: Corwin.

United States Government Accountability Office. (2007). *Government auditing standards, July 2007 revision* (GAO-07–7316). Washington, DC: Author.

❖ The Functional Table of Standards ❖

Applying Standards to Some Common Evaluation Tasks

The Functional Table is designed as a guide for selecting and applying standards in specific evaluation settings. It lists typical tasks associated with conducting evaluations and some standards to consider for each. It provides a way to begin applying the standards and can serve as a guide for which standards to consider first.

The functions listed in the table do not create a road map for evaluation work. As is true in all applications of the standards, each evaluation unfolds within a unique context. The dynamics of a context can

- trigger the emergence of new or more specific tasks to be addressed,
- influence the ordering of the tasks,
- alter the importance of the individual standards listed within each task, and
- change over time in unpredictable ways that influence the tasks and how standards can apply to them.

Thus the Functional Table does not list all aspects of evaluation duties that might be improved by application of the standards. It would be a mistake to use the Functional Table other than as a starting point for reflection about which standards to apply with these tasks. To enhance reflective practice, evaluators and evaluation users should consider keeping a record of their actual evaluation duties and how they apply the standards. This record could include the rationales and the order and applications of the standards that were considered in completing specific tasks. It can serve as an audit trail and help make a case for evaluation quality (E1 Evaluation Documentation and E2 Internal Metaevaluation).

❖ DEVELOPMENT OF THE FUNCTIONAL TABLE

The tasks listed in this Functional Table are the product of a cross-source analysis of enumerated evaluation tasks. In this analysis, task force members compared the tasks listed in the Functional Table of Contents from the second edition (1994) with those currently listed by eight governmental and nonprofit agencies in the United States and Canada. These agencies were randomly selected from a list of those that regularly engage in evaluation or provide evaluation services. Evaluation tasks listed across sources were analyzed for their congruence and salience. The current table reflects this analysis. All of the tasks identified in the second edition of *The Program Evaluation Standards* are included in some form in the table.

The individual standards listed under each task heading were proposed by one or more task force members and retained by consensus of the task force. Other standards might also be pertinent to these evaluation functions. Similarly, in some settings, stakeholders might choose not to apply one or more of the standards listed here.

Deciding Whether to Evaluate

U1 Evaluator Credibility

U2 Attention to Stakeholders

U3 Negotiated Purposes

F2 Practical Procedures

F3 Contextual Viability

P2 Formal Agreements

P3 Human Rights and Respect

P4 Clarity and Fairness

P6 Conflicts of Interests

A4 Explicit Program and Context Descriptions

E1 Evaluation Documentation

Negotiating and Formalizing Agreements, Contracts, and Budgets

U1 Evaluator Credibility

U2 Attention to Stakeholders

U6 Meaningful Processes and Products

U7 Timely and Appropriate Communicating and Reporting

F1 Project Management

F4 Resource Use

P2 Formal Agreements

P4 Clarity and Fairness

P6 Conflicts of Interests

P7 Fiscal Responsibility

E1 Evaluation Documentation

E3 External Metaevaluation

Determining Who Will Evaluate

U1 Evaluator Credibility

U2 Attention to Stakeholders

U4 Explicit Values

F1 Project Management

F3 Contextual Viability

F4 Resource Use

P2 Formal Agreements

P6 Conflicts of Interests

E1 Evaluation Documentation

Negotiating and Developing Evaluation Purposes and Questions

U2 Attention to Stakeholders

U3 Negotiated Purposes

U4 Explicit Values

U5 Relevant Information

U6 Meaningful Processes and Products

F2 Practical Procedures

F3 Contextual Viability

P1 Responsive and Inclusive Orientation

P3 Human Rights and Respect

P4 Clarity and Fairness

P5 Transparency and Disclosure

P6 Conflicts of Interests

A1 Justified Conclusions and Decisions

A2 Valid Information

A4 Explicit Program and Context Descriptions

A7 Explicit Evaluation Reasoning

E1 Evaluation Documentation

Describing the Program

U2 Attention to Stakeholders

F2 Practical Procedures

F3 Contextual Viability

P1 Responsive and Inclusive Orientation

P5 Transparency and Disclosure

P6 Conflicts of Interests

A2 Valid Information

A3 Reliable Information

A4 Explicit Program and Context Descriptions

A7 Explicit Evaluation Reasoning

A8 Communication and Reporting

E1 Evaluation Documentation

Designing the Evaluation

U2 Attention to Stakeholders

U3 Negotiated Purposes

U4 Explicit Values

U6 Meaningful Processes and Products

F2 Practical Procedures

F3 Contextual Viability

F4 Resource Use

P1 Responsive and Inclusive Orientation

P2 Formal Agreements

P3 Human Rights and Respect

A1 Justified Conclusions and Decisions

A2 Valid Information

A3 Reliable Information

A4 Explicit Program and Context Descriptions

A5 Information Management

A6 Sound Designs and Analyses

A7 Explicit Evaluation Reasoning

E1 Evaluation Documentation

Managing the Evaluation

U1 Evaluator Credibility

U2 Attention to Stakeholders

U6 Meaningful Processes and Products

U7 Timely and Appropriate Communicating and Reporting

F1 Project Management

F2 Practical Procedures

F3 Contextual Viability

F4 Resource Use

P4 Clarity and Fairness

P5 Transparency and Disclosure

P6 Conflicts of Interests

P7 Fiscal Responsibility

A1 Justified Conclusions and Decisions

A6 Sound Designs and Analyses

E1 Evaluation Documentation

Collecting Information

U2 Attention to Stakeholders

U5 Relevant Information

U6 Meaningful Processes and Products

U7 Timely and Appropriate Communicating and Reporting

U8 Concern for Consequences and Influence

F1 Project Management

F2 Practical Procedures

F3 Contextual Viability

F4 Resource Use

P3 Human Rights and Respect

A2 Valid Information

A3 Reliable Information

A5 Information Management

E1 Evaluation Documentation

E2 Internal Metaevaluation

Analyzing Information

U4 Explicit Values

U5 Relevant Information

U6 Meaningful Processes and Products

U7 Timely and Appropriate Communicating and Reporting

F1 Project Management

F2 Practical Procedures

F3 Contextual Viability

P1 Responsive and Inclusive Orientation

P4 Clarity and Fairness

P5 Transparency and Disclosure

A1 Justified Conclusions and Decisions

A2 Valid Information

A3 Reliable Information

A5 Information Management

A6 Sound Designs and Analyses

A7 Explicit Evaluation Reasoning

A8 Communication and Reporting

Communicating and Reporting

U2 Attention to Stakeholders

U5 Relevant Information

U7 Timely and Appropriate Communicating and Reporting

U8 Concern for Consequences and Influence

F2 Practical Procedures

F3 Contextual Viability

P1 Responsive and Inclusive Orientation

P3 Human Rights and Respect

P5 Transparency and Disclosure

P6 Conflicts of Interests

A1 Justified Conclusions and Decisions

A7 Explicit Evaluation Reasoning

A8 Communication and Reporting

THE STANDARDS

Part I

Utility Standards

STANDARD STATEMENTS

U1 Evaluator Credibility	*Evaluations should be conducted by qualified people who establish and maintain credibility in the evaluation context.*
U2 Attention to Stakeholders	*Evaluations should devote attention to the full range of individuals and groups invested in the program and affected by its evaluation.*
U3 Negotiated Purposes	*Evaluation purposes should be identified and continually negotiated based on the needs of stakeholders.*
U4 Explicit Values	*Evaluations should clarify and specify the individual and cultural values underpinning purposes, processes, and judgments.*
U5 Relevant Information	*Evaluation information should serve the identified and emergent needs of stakeholders.*
U6 Meaningful Processes and Products	*Evaluations should construct activities, descriptions, and judgments in ways that encourage participants to rediscover, reinterpret, or revise their understandings and behaviors.*
U7 Timely and Appropriate Communicating and Reporting	*Evaluations should attend to the continuing information needs of their multiple audiences.*
U8 Concern for Consequences and Influence	*Evaluations should promote responsible and adaptive use while guarding against unintended negative consequences and misuse.*

❖ UTILITY OVERVIEW

At its simplest, judgments about an evaluation's utility are made based on the extent to which program stakeholders find evaluation processes and products valuable in meeting their needs. A good starting point for understanding evaluation utility is to examine the variety of possible uses for evaluation processes, findings, and products.

Evaluation Uses

Early evaluations investigated accountability by documenting how resources were used or investigating whether claims made about program benefits could be justified. While the need to demonstrate program accountability remains a significant impetus for evaluation, the uses made of evaluations have expanded. Currently, the evaluation community is engaged in important conversations about how evaluations contribute to learning organizations, to program development, and to knowledge building and dissemination. Evaluations often provide information to those seeking to improve programs and influence policy formulation and implementation. For evidence-informed decision making, systematic evaluations often provide powerful inquiry mechanisms and accurate findings.

As evaluation use expanded, evaluators developed conventions for talking about types of use. For example, evaluations can inform judgments about program merit, worth, or significance, and can help to improve or develop a program and its specific components. These uses were described as *instrumental* uses. In contrast, "enlightenment" and other *conceptual* uses resulted when evaluations altered stakeholders' understanding of the program and related phenomena (e.g., its structures, materials, strategies, outcomes, accessibility, inclusiveness, or appropriateness).

The branching out of evaluation to serve different types of use is both supported by and a consequence of increased attention to the needs of stakeholders. Stakeholders' needs vary by group, program type, and context, and are often expressed indirectly through questions such as

- Does our program make a unique contribution to the community/agency/organization?
- To what extent is the program meeting its stated goals?
- How do we think our program should be working?
- What are the discrepancies between the intended program and the program-in-action?
- Are there better ways to do what we're doing?
- How can we adapt this program in light of budget cuts?

- What should be the future direction of our program?
- Are we optimizing use of our human and fiscal resources?
- What does it mean to have a program that is adaptive and responsive?
- Are we doing a good job of reaching and servicing our potential user groups?
- How can we do a better job of advocating for our program?

Important questions addressing stakeholders' needs are at the heart of worthwhile evaluations. Useful evaluations lead to descriptions, insights, judgments, decisions, recommendations, and other processes that meet the needs of those requesting the evaluation.

Increasing Attention to Process Use

In addition to producing useful findings that address stakeholders' information needs, all evaluations include activities with direct benefits to stakeholders, known as *evaluation process uses.* For example, participants and staff who participate in surveys and interviews, or express their ideas in a focus group, may experience greater understanding of their own motivations and those of their colleagues. Just implementing an evaluation, regardless of the information produced, can result in program improvements through attention to program goals and activities. It can also result in greater understanding of the critical role of evaluation in program development, improvement, and accountability.

In some contexts, evaluation processes may account for much of an evaluation's value. For example, evaluations may be conducted in ways intended to help organizations build internal evaluation capacity and integrate systematic evaluative inquiry as a regular mechanism. Stakeholders learn about specifying evaluation goals, developing and refining questions, identifying information sources, debating and selecting methods, managing information and knowledge (informatics), formulating meanings and judgments, and communicating in ways that promote understanding and decisions that are most appropriate given the contexts. The utility of evaluations that focus on process use is measured in part by the degree to which stakeholders identify personal and organizational *value added* as a consequence of their involvement in the evaluation.

At the organizational level, this value can take the form of acquiring the capacity to sustain ongoing evaluative inquiry. This outcome is more likely when participants experience evaluation as a meaningful and productive way to enhance patterns of work and communication. Participatory, collaborative, appreciative, and empowering mechanisms are often at the heart of evaluations where process use is a high priority. These mechanisms can promote stakeholder ownership of the evaluation processes and products and thus enhance process use, as well as use of evaluation findings.

For some organizations, evaluation capacity building means that evaluation stakeholders learn how to work effectively with external evaluators. This organizational learning further facilitates the contributions that external evaluation processes and findings can make to the organization's growth and productivity.

Orientation to Stakeholders' Needs

The utility standards alert evaluators to the needs of sponsors, clients, participants, and staff. However, evaluations can intentionally serve the needs of other selected stakeholders, too, including those who otherwise are silent during conventional forms of program inquiry and decision making. Culturally sensitive interactions between evaluators and stakeholders can promote more inclusive discussions of programs and their values. To enhance use, evaluations can highlight the contribution of diversity to program effectiveness and support an equitable redistribution of authority. Evaluation practitioners who understand the multiple dimensions of use, who are skilled in implementing utilization-oriented approaches, and who are committed to addressing the needs of diverse stakeholders have a solid foundation for promoting evaluation use.

Challenges in Implementing Utility

In attending to utility, evaluators must consider three challenges. First, it may not always be possible for those being served by the evaluation to fully and directly articulate their needs. Early expressions of stakeholders' needs may reflect reactions to immediate and somewhat transitory program pressures and problems. Evaluations that intentionally encourage participants to deliberate about evaluation purposes and implications are more likely to uncover needs embedded in individuals' tacit knowledge of the program. In discussing evaluation purposes and program descriptions, evaluators should encourage processes that unearth these insights.

Second, it is rarely possible to predict exactly how stakeholders will make use of processes, descriptions, insights, findings, judgments, and recommendations. This unpredictability is due, in part, to the complex environments in which programs operate. Given the pressures that programs are subject to, program stakeholders should become adept at using all available resources to help solve problems and improve decisions. Judging evaluation use based on evidence of fidelity to reported findings or recommendations may seriously underestimate the significance of the evaluation.

Third, when an evaluation takes place over any length of time, changes are likely to be occurring within and around the program even as the evaluation proceeds. Changes in program mandates, staff, resources, leadership, users, and the evaluation itself will change the way people prioritize and perform their roles and responsibilities. These changes can threaten the utility of an initial evaluation design. Being alert and responsive to the evaluation context enhances the likelihood that the evaluation will be used.

Ongoing Planning for Utility

Evaluation use can be increased through good planning. However, programs are dynamic systems, made up of multiple interconnected elements, and plans cannot be static. To achieve utility in the face of uncertainties, evaluators and stakeholders are wise to consult standards and other recognized evaluation principles and guidelines as they plan and revisit their plans. Planning for communication in support of evaluation use is especially important (U1 Timely and Appropriate Communication and Reporting). In addition, comprehensive evaluation plans should include attention to all attributes and standards of evaluation quality (F1 Project Management).

Utility in Relationship to Other Attributes of Evaluation Quality

Skilled evaluators are acutely aware that decisions intended to optimize utility also have the potential to affect the other four attributes of quality (evaluation propriety, feasibility, accuracy and accountability). Experienced evaluators who are familiar with the standards use them in concert with one another. They have a deep familiarity with the principles embedded in the standards and call upon them as the demands of the evaluation context unfold. Because of time pressures, they often apply standards on the fly. However, expert evaluators also reflect regularly on the quality of their decisions, using particular standards as touchstones. They maintain documentation of how the standards have interacted with one another and have influenced the evaluation processes, products, and results (E1 Evaluation Documentation).

Although utility is a specific, independent attribute of high quality evaluations, it shares themes with the other attributes of quality. For example, the issue of how evaluation decisions must take into account stakeholders' cultural norms and other background characteristics is a critical theme across all attributes. The connection between utility and accuracy is particularly strong. The two share numerous themes, such as stakeholder and evaluator interactions, communication and reporting, the need for clarity about evaluation purposes and questions, and the necessary collaborations among evaluators and other stakeholders. The utility and accuracy standards have different purposes, however. The accuracy standards focus on information and the quality of procedures used to select, gather, analyze, disseminate, and interpret information. Utility standards focus primarily on the qualities that prepare stakeholders to use the processes, descriptions, findings, judgments, and recommendations in ways that best serve their needs.

Introduction to the Utility Standards

The utility standards presented here help support high quality evaluation use through attention to all aspects of an evaluation. Their goal is to increase the likelihood that the evaluation will have positive consequences and substantial influence, as needs and opportunities appear over the course of the evaluation. The first standard addresses evaluator characteristics (U1 Evaluator Credibility). For example, evaluation use can be enhanced when the technical skills of the evaluators are augmented by a sincere willingness to work with stakeholders. This willingness leads to developing and maintaining the cultural competencies required for trusting professional rapport. Credible evaluators are more likely to be successful in actively engaging the program's diverse stakeholders. They will have better opportunities to be inclusive in their processes and to demonstrate the utility of evaluation to these same constituents (U2 Attention to Stakeholders).

Evaluation purposes may initially appear self-evident. In programs characterized by multiple perspectives, however, the experiences, dispositions, and needs of the various stakeholders are likely to pull the evaluation in many directions. Initially identified purposes should be examined in light of these perspectives and renegotiated when necessary (U3 Negotiated Purposes). Values shape the decisions made within an evaluation. When the values underpinning the evaluation are explicit, stakeholders are better able to review and help increase utility (U4 Explicit Values). In addition, for an evaluation to have utility, the information collected and generated by the evaluation has to be believable and acceptable. The evaluation must seek out credible data sources and when necessary help stakeholders understand the source of that credibility (U5 Relevant Information).

An evaluation's utility is typically tied to its ability to help evaluation participants and users become more confident and competent in working within their programs. Evaluation processes and products become meaningful when participants use them to rediscover, reinterpret, or revise their understandings of both their programs and their roles in them (U6 Meaningful Processes and Products).

Evaluations are often responsible to multiple audiences. Audiences can have differing information needs and unique capabilities for understanding technical information. Evaluation communication, at times in the form of formal reports, should attend to the differing and time-sensitive needs for evaluation information (U7 Timely and Appropriate Communicating and Reporting). Standard U8 Concern for Influence and Consequences reminds both evaluators and the users of evaluation that evidence of utility is not constrained to immediate or straightforward uses of processes and products. What is learned as a result of evaluation is available for consideration and adaptation by stakeholders well after final reports have been completed. The likelihood of negative consequences or purposeful misuse of evaluations can be significantly reduced when evaluative inquiry becomes an integrated feature of program decision making and problem solving.

❖ UTILITY SCENARIO

In order to illustrate how they can be used and applied, each of the utility standards concludes with a brief application based on the scenario below. Each of the eight individual applications provides a coherent introduction to how the standards might function in the context of real-world evaluation dilemmas. The applications are not intended to represent unique best practices. Rather, they illustrate sound responses to important evaluation dilemmas or demands. Evaluation practice is complex. Standards should be used in tandem with practical knowledge, values, and experiences to produce high-quality decision making.

The section below introduces the specific utility scenario and provides some context for the individual applications that follow. It describes the general characteristics of the program being evaluated along with some background information about key people and their roles. The individual applications present specific dilemmas as experienced by these principal players, analyses of how individual standards are related to the dilemmas, strategies used to respond to the dilemmas and implement the standards, and other standards that might come into play given the specific dilemmas. This scenario and subsequent applications are intended to highlight some of the dilemmas that may arise and actions that may be appropriate in evaluation practice.

This scenario is not based on any real evaluation undertaken by the authors. The programs and individuals are entirely constructed to support the application. The dilemmas and actions, however, reflect real experiences.

Evaluation of the Centerville Health for Eco-Educated Residents (CHEERS) Program

The CHEERS Program. CHEERS was founded by a group of eight environmental, social service, education, health care, and business professionals who volunteered their time in support of the following mission:

The Centerville Health for Eco-educated Residents (CHEERS) program promotes the health and well-being of all residents by actively working to reduce environmental stressors, lifestyle-related illness, and isolation within the community. Projects contribute to safe, active, and ecologically responsible community living.

Since its origins, CHEERS has recruited primarily volunteers to operate three community projects: Community in Motion, Safe Walk, and Greening Today.

CHEERS recently applied for and received three years of substantial philanthropic funding. The funder, a nonprofit organization, has a mission of supporting "the development of community identity, action, and welfare." The CHEERS grant will be used primarily to support the program's infrastructure and two proposed projects, Camp Rhea and Play and Leadership (PAL). If CHEERS can demonstrate through yearly evaluations the merit, worth, and significance of the overall program (that is, of all five projects), the program will be eligible for stable long-term funding from this sponsor.

The main characters in the CHEERS program are as follows:

- Suparna Rim has just become the full-time CHEERS program director. Suparna became a volunteer and original board member of CHEERS when she and her husband first moved to Centerville. At that time Suparna chose not to look for a full-time job so that she could spend more time caring for her children. As first one and then the other of her two girls reached school age, Suparna invested more and more time with CHEERS. She was a major author of the proposal for philanthropic funding. Her background as a certified elementary school teacher and 10 years as a youth camp director also contributed to her appointment as program director. As the director, Suparna is accountable to the board of directors for both the operation of the whole program and the implementation of the evaluation.

- Jase Andrews is a long time Centerville resident. He recently retired from his position as the physical and health services director at the Family YMCA. Jase knows the community well and served several terms on the local United Way executive board. Jase was also an original CHEERS volunteer, and he accepted the opportunity to work with Suparna and coordinate existing CHEERS projects enthusiastically.

- Camilla Mendez. The new funding made it possible for CHEERS to hire a full-time administrative assistant. Camilla has lived in Centerville for 15 years and has seen her four children successfully complete high school and her youngest begin studies at the local state university. Over that time she has also seen a significant increase in the number of Spanish-speaking residents in the Centerville community. The fact that she is bilingual made her a valued volunteer for the Greening Today project when it was first launched. Camilla earned a college diploma in business accounting and human resources through part-time studies. For 12 years she was the office manager at a local sporting good store. The administrative assistant position at CHEERS opened just after Camilla's employer retired and sold his business.

Other CHEERS workers:

- Erica is the coordinator of the new Camp Rhea project. She has a recreation management degree and two years experience in municipal recreation.

• Ted is the camp leader at the Camp Rhea Ridgewood community site. He is a second-year education student at the local state university.

• Dakota is the coordinator of the new PAL project. He has just completed his BA in Youth Services and Administration.

• Liying is coordinator of the Safe Walk project. She is a longtime community volunteer who has connections with a wide network of civic leaders. She has coordinated this project for three years.

• Emile is coordinator of the Greening Today project. He is a retired firefighter and local swim team coach.

• Mike is the coordinator of the Community in Motion project. Mike has two more years ahead of him as a part-time student in order to successfully complete his degree in environmental studies. This is Mike's second year of coordinating this project.

Centerville Research and Evaluation Specialists (CRES). This firm is a well-established private consulting agency. The president and two vice-presidents of the firm were all faculty colleagues at the state's largest private university. They took early retirement together to start this firm. Over their 10 years of consulting, they have put together a small team of highly credible evaluators and engage in regular contracts with government, education, and health organizations. The lead CRES evaluator is Jamaal Russo.

• Jamaal Russo is the most recent hire at CRES. He has an advanced degree in urban planning and a graduate certificate in program evaluation from a prominent national university. CRES was Jamaal's first choice of employer in part because of its reputation for high quality work and in part because it emphasized commitment to employment equity and diversity in the workplace. The firm is also located within a day's drive of his extended family members. During his interview, Jamaal was pleased to learn about the CRES mentoring program for new project managers. It will connect him directly to a senior associate and allow him to gradually work his way into a full load of projects and responsibilities.

• Janet Chipperfield, PhD, is in her third year as a CRES senior associate and is now Jamaal's mentor. Janet initially worked as a research and evaluation specialist with the state Department of Education. Earlier, she had coordinated a highly successful evaluation in collaboration with one of the CRES directors while he was still associated with the university. Janet was subsequently recruited by CRES and has been with the firm now for seven years.

The CHEERS Program Evaluation Scenario

CHEERS operates in the fictional midsize city of Centerville (pop. 185,000). Centerville is rooted in a productive but seasonal agricultural economy. Even though the population of first-language Spanish-speaking residents has grown to about 30,000, it would be inaccurate to describe Centerville as a multicultural or multiethnic community. However, a growing trend toward diversity in both the downtown core and in the suburban neighborhoods has been spurred, in part, by the expansion of the state university and a new technology research center. The founding directors of CHEERS are a group of eight environmental, social service, education, health care, and business professionals who volunteer their time. One of the founders of CHEERS is Suparna Rim. Suparna and her husband came to Centerville from New York City eight years ago when Suparna's husband accepted a position in the medical school of the state university. At that time Suparna felt fortunate to spend time with her young children, but as they grew so did Suparna's interest in returning to her professional interests in education and recreation.

During the first three years of the CHEERS program, Suparna shared management responsibilities with the other directors. In Year 4, the success of the program allowed the group to hire one person to coordinate each of the three established projects. At the same time Suparna became the half-time salaried manager of the overall CHEERS program. Suparna's new job responsibilities included assessing community needs, considering new projects that might meet these needs, and exploring funding options for the new projects. The other seven original members became the formal board of directors.

The CHEERS program has become successful and highly visible within the community. It has three core projects:

- *Community in Motion* is coordinated by Mike. He works with about 20 volunteers. These volunteers guide weekly hikes, most often for groups of seniors or school children, in the Central State Reserve on the edge of the city. While exploring the many trails, participants remove litter and look for any signs that areas may be vulnerable to overuse. They report these problems to appropriate authorities and sometimes assist in reclamation projects. Every Sunday afternoon is family hiking day in the reserve. For families new to the outdoors, the volunteers often organize and guide these hikes. CHEERS provides transportation to and from the reserve.

- Safe Walk is coordinated by Liying, who takes primary responsibility for screening and scheduling the approximately 450 volunteers who supervise the 18 neighborhood walking routes for elementary school children. These routes operate both in the morning and afternoon on all regular school days.

- Greening Today is coordinated by Emile and supported by over 30 volunteers. The hotline and website attached to this project provide information on how best to use renewable energy and recycling resources. The project also helps residents establish carpool connections.

Recently, the CHEERS board of directors was awarded substantial philanthropic funding for program support and expansions. Money is now available for office rental, staffing, maintenance of the three original programs and support for the development and implementation of two new related projects.

- Camp Rhea is to be coordinated by Erica. Named after the mythological daughter of earth and sky, this project will operate four nonprofit eco-friendly neighborhood day camps for elementary school children. These environmental education camps will operate on the six professional development days scheduled during the regular school year and also for 8 one-week summer sessions (40 days). Campers will participate in numerous educational and service activities. Neighborhoods have been selected on the basis of residents' needs for family support resources. While preparing the grant application, Suparna negotiated donations of the four new Camp Rhea sites and sponsorships for 210 camper days for the first year of operation. Erica will hire four part-time camp leaders and work with these individuals to hire counselors and select support volunteers.

- Play and Leadership (PAL). The PAL project, coordinated by Dakota, will sponsor four leadership development programs per year for qualified high school students. Teens will be recruited from the neighborhoods where the day camps operate. Those who satisfactorily complete the 40-hour counselor-in-training program will be asked to apply for junior or senior counselor positions in the Camp Rhea day camps. Suparna negotiated agreements with the local school district to award a cooperative education credit for those teens successfully completing the training program and 20 days as a Camp Rhea volunteer counselor. The teens can also be employed, either in lieu of receiving the co-op credit or after the 20-day period is over. Local schools also donated facilities for the leadership training program.

When CHEERS received the good news about the philanthropic award, Suparna was not surprised to learn of the required annual program evaluation. However, she was somewhat dismayed to learn that at least 5% of the annual resources for the first two years must be directed toward professional external evaluation. She remembered that the grant stipulated that second- and third-year funding was contingent upon the sponsor's acceptance and approval of these first and second annual evaluation reports. Should CHEERS be awarded funding for a third year, the sponsors themselves will require and fund a summative external evaluation. A positive judgment of CHEERS's merit, worth, and significance based on evaluated performance in the third year can result in a recommendation for long-term sustainable funding.

With the extra funding and responsibilities, Suparna has become the full-time CHEERS program director, responsible to the board of directors. Suparna's job description includes managing the organization and its budget, overseeing all projects, launching the Camp Rhea and PAL projects, working directly with the two new project coordinators, and overseeing the program evaluations.

The full-time assistant director, Jase Andrews, will have an office with Suparna in a small, newly rented three-room house near downtown. Jase was the former physical and health services director at the Family YMCA and half-time coordinator role for the Community in Motion project before he retired. Suparna lobbied the board of directors to approach Jase to work with them again during the 3-year term of the grant. His knowledge of the original CHEERS projects and the community was seen as a critical asset to the new organizational structure. Suparna was delighted when Jase agreed to return. Jase will monitor the three continuing projects and work directly with the project coordinators.

The grant has also made it possible for CHEERS to hire a full-time administrative assistant, Camilla Mendez. Camilla is ideal for this position because she is both familiar with CHEERS and fluent in Spanish. Camilla's experience comes from being one of the initial volunteers monitoring the Greening Today hotline. In this role she not only developed an in-depth understanding of Greening Today but also learned how to answer general questions about the other projects.

Given the requirements for external evaluation stipulated in the award, the CHEERS board of directors, through Suparna, approached a local, well-regarded research firm, Centerville Research and Evaluation Specialists (CRES), about contracting for the evaluation. Since then, Suparna has met with Janet Chipperfield from CRES and negotiated the agreements necessary to begin exploring CHEERS's evaluation needs and the possible purposes the evaluation might serve.

The lead CRES evaluator for CHEERS is Jamaal Russo. As a new project manager, Jamaal has spent his first two months with CRES shadowing his mentor, Janet, and collecting and analyzing data in four ongoing CRES projects. Soon after receiving the CHEERS evaluation inquiry, Janet scheduled a meeting with Jamaal. She began by telling Jamaal how pleased CRES personnel were with his thoughtful and skillful contributions to ongoing projects. She then expressed confidence in his readiness to undertake his first project as principal evaluator.

The next day, Jamaal is briefed on the CHEERS request for proposal (RFP) and the formal contractual process that will be undertaken. He knows that his firm has a policy that first year managers are restricted to leading only one evaluation at a time. He also knows that, should his proposal to CHEERS be successful, he will be exempt from any new responsibilities on other projects for the first 3 months of that contract. He is reminded, however, that he will be required to debrief Janet regularly on the progress of the evaluation. It will also be his responsibility to make a case at the end of his first year that he is ready for a promotion to full associate and a more lucrative contract and benefits package.

U1 Evaluator Credibility

Evaluations should be conducted by qualified people who establish and maintain credibility in the evaluation context.

❖ RATIONALE AND CLARIFICATION

Participants in evaluations make judgments about evaluator credibility early and often. These judgments are not arbitrary, nor are they beyond an evaluator's control. Evaluators whose intentions are trustworthy, whose actions are principled, whose perspectives are balanced, whose requests are reasonable, and whose efforts generate insights into the program and its context are more likely to be viewed as credible. The perceived credibility of the evaluator can shape stakeholders' willingness both to participate meaningfully in evaluation processes and to endorse evaluation products (descriptions, findings, and recommendations). Without evaluator credibility, the utility of all facets of the evaluation is in jeopardy.

Practicing evaluators come from a variety of methodological traditions, social practices, and ideological orientations. This diversity enables evaluation to be responsive to a wide array of program questions. The fit between the evaluator and the evaluation context directly influences the evaluation's utility.

Credible evaluators assess this fit at the outset of the evaluation and continue to monitor it throughout the process. Any concerns that arise about stakeholders' confidence and trust in the evaluator should be addressed early. Spending time with stakeholders and helping them understand how the background, knowledge, and skills of the evaluator can be applied to their evaluation setting is time well spent.

Concerns over evaluator credibility can arise from the smallest of misunderstandings and if unresolved may gradually erode the confidence stakeholders have in the evaluator's ability to make fair and balanced judgments (P4 Clarity and Fairness and P5 Transparency and Disclosure). If concerted efforts to gain and maintain credibility prove unsuccessful, then evaluators should seriously consider whether to proceed with the evaluation. Evaluators who choose to continue while knowing that they are being judged as unqualified, unresponsive, or biased may discover that their efforts to access complete and relevant information have been blocked and that the evaluation's findings and recommendations—however technically adequate—will be ignored or rejected.

It is not unusual for first impressions of credibility to be based on the evaluator's previous work experience. The importance of working in an area before evaluating it will depend on the evaluation purposes and the extent to which clients and stakeholders can be counted on to provide substantive program knowledge. Inviting stakeholders to participate in the role of program experts allows an evaluator to assert the other competencies that will be critical in assuring utility, i.e., observation, communication, and group process skills; logical reasoning; technical, methodological, and analytic expertise; political astuteness; and sensitivity to culture and context.

In evaluations that require evaluators and stakeholders to work closely together, credibility can be lost or gained based on the quality of these interactions. Stakeholders will also assess the degree of energy and enthusiasm evaluators bring to projects, whether evaluators are committed and conscientious, and whether they demonstrate integrity in making decisions.

Meeting stakeholders' criteria for evaluator credibility may be beyond the capacity of a single person. For this reason it is not unusual for evaluations to be conducted by teams of people who collectively possess the desired traits. The credibility of evaluation teams is influenced by the acceptability of the team and their qualifications, (i.e., knowledge, skills, experiences, and dispositions).

How such teams are constructed may also influence evaluator credibility. Recruiting stakeholders such as program personnel or program users onto the team is often an effective approach. They bring knowledge and experience about the program and its context and can add rich information to descriptions and deliberations. Engaging these same stakeholders in evaluation decision-making can help to demystify evaluation processes. Internal evaluations provide a particularly appropriate context for teams that blend expertise from professional evaluators and program stakeholders. On the other hand, teams formed in this way may not be as useful in contexts where the utility of the evaluation will be judged primarily on the degree of evaluator independence.

Establishing credibility is not the same as becoming liked or being endorsed by stakeholders. A serious mistake for evaluators is adopting a particular stakeholder perspective in exchange for acceptability, appreciation or backing. In contrast, credible evaluators establish functional professional associations with a variety of stakeholders while maintaining independence in thought and action.

The hallmark of credible evaluators and evaluation teams is the ability to address the needs of evaluation users while adhering to professional guidelines and standards, for example, these *Program Evaluation Standards* and other standards developed by the JCSEE, the American Evaluation Association's *Guiding Principles for Evaluators,* and the *Evaluation Quality Standards* from the Development Assistance Committee of the Organization for Economic Co-operation and Development. Credible evaluators typically find ways to continuously combine the acquired wisdom of the profession with lessons learned from their own experiences to customize a coherent and defensible evaluation approach.

Credibility is always context dependent. Credibility is made up of both evaluation expertise and perceived legitimacy. The knowledge, skills, dispositions, cultural competency, and practices that serve evaluators well in one setting may need to be amplified or emphasized differently in the next project.

❖ IMPLEMENTING U1 EVALUATOR CREDIBILITY

The following are important recommendations for implementing this standard:

1. Acquire evaluation credentials, but recognize that credentials alone cannot establish long-term credibility. Recognized credentials include advanced academic degrees, diplomas, and certificates from practitioner-oriented institutes.

2. Become an active member in a community of practice. The growth of regional, national, and international evaluation associations and societies has spawned a variety of formal and informal communities of practice. Go to http://www.jcsee.org for links and suggestions.

3. Stay current with research that informs evaluation. An extensive and evolving body of knowledge is available to guide and inform evaluator deliberations and decision making.

4. Include a statement in proposals and reports describing qualifications and experiences relevant to the program to be evaluated. It is important to inform stakeholders about the importance of fit between their situation and the knowledge, skills, dispositions, and experiences you have as an evaluator.

5. In large-scale evaluations with multiple site evaluators, clarify with clients which individuals will be responsible for the various elements of the evaluation, and provide assurance that each has the expertise or support required to complete the work.
6. Have the evaluation plan reviewed by another evaluator whose credentials are acceptable to the client (E3 External Metaevaluation).
7. Build good working relationships, and listen, observe, and clarify. Making better communication a priority during stakeholder interactions can reduce anxiety and make the evaluation processes and activities more cooperative.
8. Learn about and remain sensitive to cultural norms so that you are aware and respectful of stakeholders' perspectives, daily rhythms, and duties.
9. Keep evaluations moving forward while maintaining sensitivity to stakeholders' concerns. Enthusiasm and sustained efforts help to establish and maintain credible interactions.
10. Become methodologically versatile and match methods to questions rather than restrict the evaluation to a limited methodological comfort zone. Credibility is enhanced by attention to the information needs of evaluation users.

❖ HAZARDS

Some possible hazards with regard to U1 are as follows:

1. Assuming that significant experience in a program or program field is sufficient qualification to be an evaluator in that field
2. Taking on an evaluation project believing that all the knowledge and skills necessary to conduct it effectively can be learned along the way
3. Thinking that credibility is established by going it alone or acquiring the authority to make all decisions related to the evaluation
4. Not considering how you as the evaluator may be contributing to stakeholders' resistance, indifference, or discomfort with the evaluation
5. Working to establish credibility only with those who have formal leadership roles in the program while ignoring those who are informal leaders

Application Number One for the Utility Case Scenario

The scenario that supports this application, including background information about the program, context, and key players, can be read at the end of the Utility Overview on page 9.

Suparna, Jase, Jamaal, and the five project coordinators have scheduled their first evaluation meeting. Jamaal wants to make a good first impression. He has read over their request for evaluation and familiarized himself with the CHEERS materials available on the Internet. He has several goals for the meeting. The first is to listen and clarify rather than promote his own ideas about the evaluation. Listening well should help him with his second goal, to learn how CHEERS personnel are thinking and feeling about both the program and the evaluation. He knows that previous negative evaluation experiences or inaccurate assumptions about what is to come could derail the evaluation. He wants to address any concerns they have and let them know that he is competent and capable of working both with them and on their behalf.

Jamaal remembers that successful first meetings often require detailed planning. During his training, he experienced an activity that he thinks could help him accomplish his meeting goals. He brings along drawing pencils and several sheets of 8 ½" x 11" card stock for the activity. As they arrive and sit down at the spacious work table in the coordinators' office, Camilla, the administrative assistant, promises to hold all calls. Suparna orchestrates introductions and refers to Jamaal as "our evaluator." When his turn to speak comes, Jamaal thanks them for taking time out of their very busy day to meet with him. He assures them that there will be time to find out more about him and ask questions about the evaluation but suggests that before they get too serious, he'd like to do an activity with them. Jamaal then pulls out the drawing pencils and the card stock and asks each of them to sketch an animal that represents their notion of evaluation. He gives them some uninterrupted time to draw. Everyone begins to chuckle and chat as they work through the task. After five minutes, Jamaal has everyone share their sketches and talk about what they represent.

Suparna breaks the ice by showing the group a guide dog. She stresses how important it will be over the next three years to demonstrate accountability. She is hoping the evaluation will lead them to that outcome. Jase has drawn an octopus. He suggests that the evaluation will probably reach into all projects and pull out things they didn't even know about the program. The five project coordinators display sketches of an alligator, an elephant, a ram, a turtle, and an owl. In discussing their sketches coordinators make it clear that their priority is implementing their own projects. They are concerned about the additional time, energy, and resources the evaluation might consume (alligator), the priority that the evaluation will have in the program (elephant), how volunteers will be affected if they are forced to participate in the evaluation (ram), how the evaluation might slow down or interfere with their real work (turtle), and whether they will actually end up with a better understanding of how their projects work, both independently and together, when the evaluation is over (owl).

Jamaal has been taking some notes but works hard to maintain eye contact with those talking. After everyone finishes, he responds carefully to their impressions. He acknowledges the importance of creating an evaluation report that demonstrates the effectiveness and accountability of the entire CHEERS program to the sponsors but introduces the notion of doing this in a way that might be useful for the individual project coordinators as well.

As the discussion continues, Jamaal finds ways to reveal his background in urban development, his credentials and experience in evaluation, and his role in the local firm. To the question of whether he knows the tools he will use to collect data for the evaluation, he responds with an honest "No, not yet." He explains that he is familiar with a number of different methods and instruments that could be used, but no decisions have been made yet. He uses this moment to emphasize that there are several prior decisions to be made about the evaluation before they can select their methods and instruments. He states that Suparna and Jase can make some of these decisions, but that other decisions will require insights from all of them as the project specialists.

This stimulates a few minutes of talk among the coordinators concerning what might be important for them to contribute about their projects. Sensing some real interest in the questions they are raising, Jamaal allows this discussion to continue. His hope is that the coordinators are warming up to the evaluation a bit. Also important, they are learning that he is interested in what they are thinking. Jamaal then makes a commitment to everyone not to let the evaluation activities overwhelm them. While still concerned about their first impressions, Jamaal is pleased to see them laughing and being candid about their expectations.

As the meeting comes to a close Jamaal makes a request. He begins by telling them that he intends to send out summaries of their meetings. He tells them how difficult it is for him to take notes and attend to what they are saying at the same time. He says that from now on he would like to record their meetings. He assures them that the recording can be stopped or erased immediately if confidential or embarrassing topics are discussed too explicitly. He also assures them that he will be the only one in the research firm who will listen to the recordings and that the data will be stored on his fingerprint-protected computer and erased from the portable device within 24 hours. All of them quickly and readily give consent to this request.

The meeting ends with Jamaal asking for their drawings, current program documents, a copy of the successful grant proposal and the evaluation requirements as described by the sponsor. He promises to look over their documents and then send Suparna minutes of their meeting. He asks Suparna if he can copy everyone with the minutes and she enthusiastically agrees. She suggests to her staff that they should also feel free to contact Jamaal with their questions and information. Suparna does not want the staff to feel that they need to go through her (although she would appreciate being copied). On the way out Jamaal meets Camilla, the administrative assistant for CHEERS. Suparna asks that Jamaal copy Camilla with all his correspondence as well.

Back at his office, Jamaal uses his notes to construct his first set of minutes. He also reviews the program, the funding, and the evaluation materials. It is clear that Suparna, Jase, and the coordinators have different needs with respect to the evaluation. He schedules a meeting with his mentor, Janet. She is ideal in this role because she has had experience with both community- and health-related evaluations. Later, as he explains the situation, she nods knowingly and assures Jamaal that he has started off well. She also suggests that when the formal agreement between Suparna and their company is drafted, her name be added as a consultant.

Jamaal decides he needs to show the CHEERS group how evaluation activities can help them. He has learned that the sponsors will want a general program description and individual project descriptions. He also senses that coordinators could benefit from a more formalized description of their project goals, activities, resources, and expected outcomes. He begins a template for a program logic model that could be used to describe each of the projects. He will fill in only information that is explicitly stated in their program documents and the new program proposal and will suggest to Suparna that he work with coordinators at their convenience to complete the logic models accurately. By interacting with Suparna, Jase, and the coordinators so early in the process, he hopes he has opened the door for an evaluation that integrates Suparna's need to demonstrate program accountability with a more collaborative and developmental approach.

Jamaal wants to distribute the minutes within 48 hours. He will begin the routine of listing bulleted highlights in the body of his e-mail and attaching the full document for reference. He also plans to contact everyone individually within a week to see if there is anything they wanted to respond to before moving forward. He will also use those conversations to make sure he is interpreting the documents accurately. Then he will ask Suparna for a meeting so he can introduce his working strategy to her and have an in-depth discussion about what the evaluation could and should accomplish.

Jamaal is satisfied that he got off on the right foot with Suparna, Jase, and the project coordinators. Even so, he still has many questions:

- What is the current status of the evaluation budget, contract, or other agreements and how often do they need to be visited or revisited (P2 Formal Agreements)?
- Do members of the board of directors have specific expectations of the evaluation other than what was described briefly in the funding proposal (U2 Attention to Stakeholders)?
- Does he really understand the significance of the different needs for the evaluation expressed by Suparna and the rest of the program staff, and can he realistically meet all of these needs (P4 Clarity and Fairness)?
- Given the two new projects she is putting into place, will Suparna be willing to consider developmental as well as accountability purposes for the evaluation (U6 Meaningful Processes and Products and P2 Formal Agreements)?
- Given his other responsibilities at the firm (even though these are minimal now), will he have enough time for sufficient interaction with the CHEERS personnel (P1 Responsive and Inclusive Orientation)?
- How can he best lead the evaluation without putting unwarranted demands on the CHEERS team (F2 Practical Procedures)?

Jamaal makes these questions his first entry in his new personal electronic journal entitled *The CHEERS Evaluation.* As he reflects on the first meeting, he is pleased that it got off to such a good start. He was worried about his credibility as the CHEERS evaluator, but he believes that his actions and efforts have paid off in creating the right first impressions and the framework for continued credibility.

❖ SUPPORTING DOCUMENTATION

Cousins, J. B., Cullen, J., Malik, S., & Maicher, B. (2009). Debating professional designations for evaluators: Reflections on the Canadian process. *Journal of MultiDisciplinary Evaluation, 6*(11), 71–82.

Donaldson, S. I., Gooler, L. E., & Scriven, M. (2002). Strategies for managing evaluation anxiety: Toward a psychology of program evaluation. *American Journal of Evaluation, 23,* 261–273

Hurley, C., Renger, R., & Brunk, B. (2005). Learning from a challenging fieldwork evaluation experience: Perspectives of a student and an instructor. *American Journal of Evaluation, 26,* 562–578.

King, J. A., Stevahn, L., Ghere, G., & Minnema, J. (2001). Toward a taxonomy of essential evaluator competencies. *American Journal of Evaluation, 22,* 229–247.

Trevisan, M. S. (2004). Practical training in evaluation: A review of the literature. *American Journal of Evaluation, 25,* 255–272.

U2 Attention to Stakeholders

Evaluations should devote attention to the full range of individuals and groups invested in the program or affected by the evaluation.

❖ RATIONALE AND CLARIFICATION

Stakeholders are those who have a legitimate interest in or are served in some meaningful way by the program and are thus implicated in the program's evaluation. Attention to stakeholders contributes to evaluation use in several ways. In some contexts the utility of the evaluation depends on stakeholders' willingness to use the processes and results of the evaluation. When stakeholders are not engaged by the evaluation, it is unreasonable to expect them to automatically embrace subsequent decisions and recommendations. Early in the evaluation, gathering multiple perspectives about the program-in-action may be invaluable in confirming, revising, or even renegotiating the purposes and boundaries of the evaluation (P1 Responsive and Inclusive Orientation). Reasoned deliberations with stakeholders about the intentions, processes, and values embedded in the program provide important data for understanding the program in context (A4 Explicit Program and Context Descriptions).

In attending to a full range of stakeholders, evaluators learn about the program from those typically positioned both inside and outside program decision-making circles. Interactions with stakeholders may also shed light on any unintended consequences of the program. Evaluations that proceed while ignoring inequities, contradictions, and conflicts narrow the scope of evaluation use (P6 Conflicts of Interests). Evaluations that are flawed from the outset because they are overly narrow waste human potential and miss opportunities for social betterment.

Stakeholders are identified through an analysis of the program's scope. To identify program stakeholders evaluators ask questions such as the following:

- Who has decision authority over the program (sponsors, foundations, communities, governing boards, and legislators)?
- Who has formal or informal authority to shape the dissemination or implementation of findings (program leaders)?
- Who are the program implementers (program personnel, instructional or training staff, administrators, managers, and volunteers)?
- Who are the program users (participants in programs, direct beneficiaries of services)?
- Who are the *indirect* beneficiaries of program services (individuals whose employment or quality of life is contingent on the availability of the program)?
- Who benefits from or is disadvantaged by the fact that resources are invested in this rather than other programs (individuals, groups, and communities)?
- Is there anyone with a particularly valued perspective regarding the program (community leaders, informal leaders, experts, and other authorities)?
- Who will be most interested in using the evaluation findings (individuals, groups, communities, and media)?

Evaluations typically cannot attend equally to all stakeholders. For this reason, the grounds and values used in defining the evaluation boundaries are important to document (P4 Clarity and Fairness and A7 Explicit Evaluation Reasoning).

Once the stakeholders are identified for inclusion, the challenge is to work with them to bring to light assumptions, interests, values, behaviors, and concerns regarding the program. This work can be used to build a program description and can also shed light on the appropriateness of the evaluation questions (A4 Explicit Program and Context Descriptions). Stakeholders who feel respected by the process and who can identify with the information and methods used in the evaluation are more likely to invest in evaluation activities and ultimately use the processes and findings. Attention to stakeholders facilitates realistic expectations for the evaluation. Helping stakeholders understand the evaluation purposes and boundaries, as well as the methodological, logistical, financial, and political constraints of the evaluation may require significant effort. A misunderstanding of these constraints can leave stakeholders with unrealistic expectations for the evaluation and thus jeopardize its utility.

❖ IMPLEMENTING U2 ATTENTION TO STAKEHOLDERS

The following are important recommendations for implementing this standard:

1. Attend to stakeholders in ways that are sensitive to organizational and cultural norms. This will help to
   - o access pertinent information (A2 Valid Information and A3 Reliable Information),
   - o uncover the tensions and values shaping the program (P6 Conflicts of Interests and U1 Explicit Values), and consequently
   - o generate processes and findings that support evaluation use, and therefore
   - o assure that the contexts for evaluation activities are relevant (F2 Practical Procedures).
2. Let the processes supporting the determination of the evaluation purposes help identify stakeholders.
3. Develop strategies for probing the program context for important and less visible stakeholders. Evaluators can play out scenarios of possible findings with sponsors, clients, or program personnel in order to identify individuals or groups who may be directly or indirectly affected by the evaluation and its findings.
4. Consider groups or communities whose perspectives are typically excluded because they are perceived as having only "special interests." These may include those who differ from most stakeholders on the basis of ethnicity, sexual orientation, education, age, gender, ability, religion, health, or immigration status, or those who lack the resources or the authority to lobby for inclusion.
5. Create conditions for stakeholder engagement that are safe, comfortable, and contribute to authentic participation. The effort invested in creating these conditions will depend in part on the amount and quality of information required to proceed confidently in answering the evaluation questions (A2 Valid Information and A3 Reliable Information).

❖ HAZARDS

Some possible hazards with regard to U2 are as follows:

1. Recognizing individuals, groups, or communities as stakeholders, collecting data from them, and then failing to communicate further with them

2. Misjudging the logistics and feasibility of widespread stakeholder involvement
3. Promising stakeholders a level of involvement or representation before the evaluation purposes and questions are finalized
4. Assuming that the values of decision makers reflect those of program personnel and program users
5. Compromising the role of evaluator to become an advocate for a particular stakeholder group
6. Putting undue pressure on individuals or groups of stakeholders to participate more extensively than they want to or have time for

Application Number Two for the Utility Case Scenario

The scenario that supports this application, including background information about the program, context, and key players, can be read at the end of the Utility Overview on page 9.

After the first meeting with the entire CHEERS program staff, Jamaal knows that one deliverable the sponsor expects is a comprehensive program description (A4 Explicit Program and Context Descriptions). He wants to produce a draft of this quickly and effectively to help establish his working style and build his credibility with program staff. He has decided that the description should consist of at least a stakeholder map and logic model for each project as well as one for the overall program.

Jamaal arrives for a scheduled meeting with Suparna and Jase. He has brought with him his copy of the sponsor's evaluation requirements, a template that could be used to develop program logic models for each project, and his tape recorder (which he tested before he left the office).

It is not surprising that both Suparna and Jase are eager to talk about a survey to collect the information that is important to them. Not wanting to curb their enthusiasm, Jamaal agrees that it is time to collect some data but uses the sponsor's evaluation criteria and his draft template of the logic model to talk with them about what it means to build a program description. In doing so, he stresses the roles they will all play in the task. They are in the best position to identify those with whom they work most closely and to describe how and why they work together. Jamaal gives each of them a piece of paper, asks them to put their name in the middle and then to place the names of people or groups around the outside who are a priority in their work lives. Jamaal continues: "The ones who are most important and have the most contact with you should be closer to your name."

When Suparna and Jase are done, they compare maps. Jamaal has them both talk about why they located people and groups where they did so that he can refer to their comments later when synthesizing the two documents. He is pleased that both have identified the board of directors as a critical group. He asks whether either of them have discussed the evaluation with the board members. Suparna reports that at the last meeting she announced the name of the firm that had been hired and specified Jamaal's name. Suparna then suggests that Jamaal attend the next board meeting to introduce the evaluation. Jamaal sees this as an important opportunity. His reading of the program and sponsor's documents has clarified that all agreements with the sponsoring organization have been made under the name of the chair of the board of directors. It will be critical to compare the goals that directors have for the evaluation to the ones articulated by the program staff. It will also be important that the board, Suparna, and Jamaal be in agreement about what information will go to the sponsor and what information will stay in-house for continuous program development and improvement.

As the meeting wraps up, Jamaal asks Suparna if he can arrange to do the same mapping exercise with the five coordinators. He suggests that he may be able to accomplish this with a phone call and a couple of e-mails rather than calling a meeting. He would just like them to know that Suparna has already had the experience and is encouraging them to participate. She agrees to send a note out to everyone as soon as the meeting breaks up.

Over the next week Jamaal works to synthesize what he has learned from the diagrams provided by the program staff. He is using a simple graphics program to create a stakeholder map that will display the many people and groups that now have an investment in the CHEERS program and the interrelationships and communication patterns that exist among these stakeholders. After the program staff is satisfied that it is accurate and complete, he will present it at the next board meeting.

As he reflects on what is emerging, two things strike him. Only on Suparna's map is there any reference to Camilla, the administrative assistant. This seems strange, as his experience so far tells him that she is the first-line contact person for CHEERS. He realizes that he may have been remiss by not inviting her to complete a diagram of her own. He resolves to contact Camilla in the morning and integrate her perceptions into the stakeholder maps. In addition, sketches drawn by the program coordinators responsible for the new day camps (Camp Rhea) and the teen leadership (Play and Leadership) projects have no references to any individuals or groups in the communities that the programs are intended to serve. In fact, a second glance across established projects suggests that interactions with current project users and their community groups are sparse. He wonders whether this reflects a more serious set of issues or is just an omission.

Jamaal is satisfied that the program staff members are now familiar with the concept of stakeholder, even if all the stakeholders have yet to be identified. He is also aware that there are some challenges ahead. For example, they will need to continue working on the stakeholder maps. Jamaal will need to explain clearly why community groups and project users should feature more prominently in these descriptions. He is hoping this adjustment will be self-evident as he has them revisit program and project goals and the needs they are trying to address. He will introduce this critical step in crafting the second part of the descriptive process, the logic models.

Jamaal is aware that he must continue building credibility with all of the program staff. He is trying to do this by keeping the evaluation moving forward as efficiently as possible and taking on tasks that he knows the program staff would be hard-pressed to accomplish given their normal responsibilities. His new questions for his journal address the following issues:

- Has he avoided placing too many demands on staff, so that when Suparna schedules the next meeting they will want to attend (F2 Practical Procedures)?
- Will his draft maps do a good job of representing what he is learning about the CHEERS program (F3 Contextual Viability)?
- Will he be able to effectively represent the needs of stakeholders not yet identified by program staff (P4 Clarity and Fairness)?
- If he has already missed identifying an important stakeholder such as Camilla, is it possible that other stakeholders have been omitted from the draft description (A2 Valid Information)?

In order to create current, accurate, and credible evaluation records, Jamaal considers how to document the processes used to investigate the needs of evaluation stakeholders. He also wants to record the processes used to select the evaluation purposes in support of selected needs. He knows it is likely that internal and external formative and summative metaevaluations focused on utility and conducted either by his firm or the new funder will scrutinize how well the evaluation is aligned with stakeholders' needs (E1 Evaluation Documentation, E2 Internal Metaevaluation, and E3 External Metaevaluation).

❖ SUPPORTING DOCUMENTATION

Fetterman, D. M. (2002). Empowerment evaluation: Building communities of practice and a culture of learning. *American Journal of Community Psychology, 30*(1), 89–102.

King, J. A., Cousins, J. B., & Whitmore, E. (2007). Making sense of participatory evaluation: Framing participatory evaluation. In S. Mathison (Ed.), *Enduring issues in evaluation: The 20th anniversary of the collaboration between NDE and AEA: New Directions for Evaluation, 114,* 83–105.

Mathie, A., & Greene, J. C. (1997). Stakeholder participation in evaluation: How important is diversity? *Evaluation and Program Planning, 20*(3), 279–285.

O'Sullivan, R. G. (2004). *Practicing evaluation: A collaborative approach.* Thousand Oaks, CA: Sage.

Plottu, B., & Plottu, E. (2009). Approaches to participation in evaluation. *Evaluation, 15*(3), 343–359.

U3 Negotiated Purposes

Evaluation purposes should be identified and revisited based on the needs of stakeholders.

❖ RATIONALE AND CLARIFICATION

There are three principal reasons why evaluation purposes should align with stakeholders' needs. First and foremost, stakeholders judge the utility of an evaluation by the extent to which its processes and products add value to their experiences with the program (U1 Meaningful Processes and Products). The challenge for evaluators is to learn what can be addressed given the resources and boundaries defining the evaluation (F3 Contextual Viability and F4 Resource Use). For many stakeholders, including experienced program administrators, identifying evaluation needs is not easily done. The originally expressed purpose for contracting the evaluation should be weighed against the dilemmas, quandaries, and desired evaluation outcomes as expressed by a range of stakeholders (P6 Conflicts of Interests). Maintaining relevant evaluation purposes requires initial and ongoing processes that clarify the needs and changes in needs of evaluation stakeholders.

Second, evaluation purposes guide subsequent decisions about the evaluation design and implementation (P2 Formal Agreements). The extent of the program description, the data collection and analysis strategies, and the methods of communicating and reporting, will all be determined on the basis of the contributions they make to the stated purposes. When appropriate purposes and the needs they address are not clearly understood or emerge too late in the evaluation, the utility of data collection, analysis, and reporting may be jeopardized. Too many midstream corrections, while potentially useful, may be untenable because of the significant resources they are likely to consume (F4 Resource Use).

Third, revisiting the evaluation purposes in the face of critical incidents or at critical decision-making points acknowledges the complexity of program contexts. Programs do not stand still in the presence of evaluation. Needs identified as priorities by evaluation users at the outset of the project may evolve or change completely due to unexpected events such as a new policy, a new manager, or a merger with another project, program, or organization. At these times evaluation purposes may need to be renegotiated and realigned to the new conditions.

Typically, systematic evaluative inquiry serves such purposes as the following:

- Describing the program
- Contributing to the development of programs
- Providing information for program improvement
- Supporting a wide variety of program decisions
- Making judgments about program merit, worth, or significance
- Engaging and educating stakeholders in the processes of systematic evaluative inquiry and knowledge use

Each of these purposes can serve a variety of specific needs. Sometimes, the need is to understand the program and its users in context. To address this need, a program description would have as one of its goals to understand and interpret the lived experiences of stakeholders and bring to light the uncertainties and possible unknowns in the program.

Results that generate evidence of a program's local significance may also be situated within broader political, economic, and social contexts. Using results in this way may address the goals related to learning about the program's accountability, costs versus benefits, and generalizability, or its ability to promote democratic participation, empowerment, or emancipation.

Entire organizations are sometimes evaluation users. More often, organizations are under pressure to be proactive and creative in the face of change. Developing the capacity to engage in systematic evaluative inquiry is a way for organizations to address this need. Building evaluation capacity provides individuals within organizations a greater opportunity to become more adept at evidence-informed decision making, appreciative inquiry, knowledge building, and knowledge management.

It is not unusual for a single evaluation to have multiple and interdependent purposes. For example, an evaluation that recruits an internal evaluation team to conduct an improvement-focused evaluation while training evaluation participants in the principles of systematic inquiry addresses complementary purposes.

Some purposes for evaluation may be obvious from the initial request for proposal or client meeting. For example, a school district may commission an evaluation to assess the success of the implementation of a new outreach program. School districts, accountable to the public for their allocation of funds, will often use evaluation to demonstrate program accountability. Other purposes for evaluation may be quite veiled. Consider the ambiguity in a request from a program's board of directors to evaluate "how the program is working." Are directors looking for a formative evaluation to help the program improve, or is there some internal debate going on about the program's overall relevance? More problematic for evaluators are disguised or unethical purposes, such as when a program manager remains mute about his or her agenda to use an evaluation to discredit program personnel (P3 Human Rights and Respect, as well as the JCSEE's *Personnel Evaluation Standards,* 2009). When they are able to map their purposes onto explicit and significant needs of stakeholders, evaluations are less likely to be manipulated by the political agendas of individuals (P2 Formal Agreements).

❖ IMPLEMENTING U3 NEGOTIATED PURPOSES

The following are important recommendations for implementing this standard:

1. Differentiate wants from needs and be clear about the priorities for addressing specific needs. Significant needs are those, which if left unattended, constrain or jeopardize program operations, decision making, and viability.

2. Probe even the most explicitly stated purposes for the evaluation to be sure that the most important purposes have been named and clarified. Probing may also provide participants with evidence that the evaluator is truly interested in working on their behalf (U1 Evaluator Credibility).

3. Help stakeholders develop ways to talk about evaluation and develop with stakeholders a shared understanding of the evaluation language necessary for negotiating purposes, such as the distinction between formative and summative uses of evaluation. Helping stakeholders to identify and communicate broad purposes underpinning their request for evaluation can launch deeper and more refined discussions about why the evaluation needs to be conducted.

4. Before or during early stages of the negotiation of evaluation purposes, clarify the nature of evaluation work using tools such as needs assessments, program descriptions, logic models, and evaluability assessments. Such activities can bring stakeholders together and help to clarify the purpose for subsequent evaluation activities.

5. Clarify any ambivalence that may exist about reasons for conducting the evaluation (U4 Explicit Values).

6. Look for the expression of competing evaluation purposes among stakeholder groups and help to prioritize these purposes. Stakeholders will not always initially agree on the purposes for evaluation (P6 Conflicts of Interests).

7. Help stakeholders understand the feasibility and value of addressing specific evaluation purposes at specific times in the program life cycle. For example, it would be important to challenge a proposed impact evaluation of a program before it is fully developed and implemented in stable fashion.

8. Communicate the purposes and goals of the evaluation and the needs these purposes are intended to serve in ways that are understandable and meaningful to all Stakeholders (P2 Formal Agreements and U6 Meaningful Process and Products).

❖ HAZARDS

Some possible hazards with regard to U3 are as follows:

1. Assuming that program stakeholders have ratified the purposes expressed in a formal request for evaluation

2. Agreeing to conduct an evaluation where the needs and purposes established by stakeholders conflict with the evaluator's standards of practice (P3 Human Rights and Respect)

3. Agreeing to implement a particular method (e.g., a survey) in advance of clarifying the evaluation purpose or purposes

Application Number Three for the Utility Case Scenario

The scenario that supports this application, including background information about the program, context, and key players, can be read at the end of the Utility Overview on page 9.

Jamaal believes that his efforts to introduce the program staff to stakeholder maps and logic models have been successful. He is confident that the work will continue once the next formal contract between CHEERS and his firm is signed. The descriptive work has triggered an in-depth discussion about whose needs are served by the different CHEERS projects. This leads naturally into a discussion of whose needs are to be served by the evaluation.

As expected, the program staff identifies many different types of information that might be useful in planning and improving the projects. Jamaal introduces the notion of evaluation boundaries. He reminds them of two existing constraints: an obligation to provide the sponsor with specified types of evaluation data and the limited amount of funding in the budget. As a group they revisit the sponsor's evaluation criteria. The criteria are fairly general and specify only that evaluations conducted in the first two years be designed for program improvement as well as to show accountability for the grant money received. These criteria alleviate Jamaal's concern about misguided pressure to demonstrate definitive effects from the two new projects (U8 Concern for Consequences and Influence). The sponsor's criteria allow them time to focus on documenting growth and effectiveness as the projects mature.

Keeping the sponsor's requirements in mind, Jamaal leads the group, including Camilla, in a discussion that explores the processes and information that could really help them do their work. His role during this discussion is to analyze the extent to which these suggestions can be integrated into the evaluation without either overtaxing the participants or the budget (F3 Contextual Viability and P7 Fiscal Responsibility). In the end, several purposes and multiple goals for the evaluation are identified. Jamaal is pleased that the five project coordinators had participated directly in negotiations that would affect their own work. They seem ready to take on some responsibility for learning about their projects, including collecting information about the participants and the experiences of both the volunteers and the clients of the different projects. Camilla is also involved in the negotiations and provides perspectives on data entry and storage (A5 Information Management).

Suparna and Jase seem more assured after Jamaal requests immediate and regular feedback about the impact the evaluation is having on their work lives. Jamaal also wants their opinions about which activities are more or less useful in collecting and analyzing data. Suparna, Jase, and Jamaal plan to regularly revisit the purposes and processes of the evaluation and make improvements in the second year's approach (E2 Internal Metaevaluation).

The last step in the process is to make sure their agreements are formalized (P2 Formal Agreements). This requires the signatures of the chair of the board of directors and Janet from CRES. Jamaal suggests that Suparna and Jase present a summary of the evaluation purposes to the board before forwarding the formal contract for signing (A8 Communication and Reporting). Jamaal agrees to prepare a single-page handout describing the purpose of the evaluation for everyone. He also volunteers to attend the meeting to support them if there are questions. Suparna views Jamaal's suggestion as a good one because it provides an opportunity to demonstrate how she and Jase are managing the evaluation.

Jamaal finds the currently negotiated evaluation purposes to be reasonable. However, the devil is in the details. Later, Jamaal writes in his electronic journal:

- What evaluation questions will best express the purposes and goals that the program personnel have talked about?
- What might a design look like for collecting and analyzing the data to answer these questions?

Jamaal uses his notes to begin drafting some tables to summarize their discussions and help answer these questions for the first year of the evaluation. He plans to distribute them as soon as they are complete.

Projects: Community in Motion, Safe Walk, Greening Today

Draft Evaluation Plan for Continuing Projects

Purpose	*Goals*	*Supporting Procedures*
Program Description	Be able to provide all invested stakeholders with an accurate description of each project	• Construct stakeholder maps • Document each project's context, aims and objectives, operations, resources, users, and intended outcomes. Link project goals to resources, activities, and expected outcomes
Judgments of Program Worth	Establish preliminary evidence that the projects are making a positive contribution to the community	• With project coordinators, develop indicators for measuring program outcomes • Gather outcome evidence on major project goals
Program Improvement	Develop an updated and defensible argument for current project aims, processes, and outcomes	• Compare project intentions to the project-in-action • Document intended program improvements
Evaluation Capacity Building	Support project coordinators in making decisions	• Collaborate with project personnel as feasible on data collection, analysis, and interpretation

Projects: Camp Rhea and PAL (Play and Leadership)

Draft Evaluation Plan for New Projects

Purpose	*Goals*	*Supporting Procedures*
Developmental Evaluation	Design and implement projects that are consistent with program values and expected outcomes Build the confidence and design skills of project personnel	• Document rationales for planning and implementation decisions • Document the dynamics and interdependencies that sustain the program • Support and document the ability of staff and volunteers to be reflective, collaborative, and insightful in advancing their projects
Evaluation Capacity Building	Support project coordinators in making decisions informed by evidence	• Collaborate with project personnel as feasible on data collection, analysis, and interpretation • Provide evidence of positive course corrections based on findings from ongoing systematic inquiry

CHEERS Composite Program

Draft Evaluation Plan for the Program as a Whole

Purpose	*Goals*	*Supporting Procedures*
Program Description	Develop an overall understanding of the CHEERS program	• Identify community contexts where direct and indirect effects of any CHEERS project might be occurring • Consider possible positive and negative side-effects of operating CHEERS projects • Gather effects-based evidence from the community about each CHEERS project • Feed this information back into individual CHEERS projects for consideration
Judgments of Program Merit	Demonstrate fiscal accountability	• Prepare a financial statement accounting for the use of all first-year funds • Summarize funds generated by the projects as well as assets of the program from in-kind services • Connect all project outcomes to CHEERS mission statement
Judgments of Program Worth	Establish the unique contributions of the CHEERS program to the community	• Establish criteria and rationales for comparing CHEERS program to any existing critical competitors
Judgments of Program Significance	Establish the value added by the CHEERS program to the funder's mission	• Compare both program results and program effects to funder's criteria for a successful program

Jamaal knows that the wording of the goals and the supporting procedures still need to be considered carefully. There may even be other goals that need to be added to the framework. In doing this exercise, however, Jamaal now sees even more clearly the scope of the evaluation. He adds a note to his e-journal: "Before we come to an agreement on these, make sure to estimate the time and resources that will be required to accomplish everything we say we want to do."

❖ SUPPORTING DOCUMENTATION

Chelimsky, E. (2006). The purposes of evaluation in a democratic society. In I. F. Shaw, J. C. Greene, & M. M. Mark (Eds.), *The Sage handbook of evaluation* (pp. 27–48). London: Sage.

Mark, M. M. (2006). Introduction: The evaluation of policies, programs, and practices. In I. F. Shaw, J. C. Greene, & M. M. Mark (Eds.), *The Sage handbook of evaluation* (pp. 1–26). London: Sage.

Schwandt, T. A., & Burgon, H. (2006). Evaluation and the study of lived experience. In I. F. Shaw, J. C. Greene, & M. M. Mark (Eds.), *The Sage handbook of evaluation* (pp. 85–101). London: Sage.

Stufflebeam, D. L. (2000). Lessons in contracting for evaluations. *American Journal of Evaluation, 21,* 293–314.

U4 Explicit Values

Evaluations should clarify and specify the individual and cultural values underpinning the evaluation purposes, processes, and judgments.

❖ RATIONALE AND CLARIFICATION

Valuing is at the heart of each decision and judgment made throughout an evaluation. The utility of the evaluation is dependent, in part, on the extent to which program and evaluation stakeholders can identify and respect the value perspectives embedded in each facet of the evaluation.

Making the values that guide evaluation explicit does not have to be problematic or onerous. In many educational and social program contexts, imperatives such as equity, inclusion, fairness, tolerance, and social justice are unambiguous and embedded into program processes and activities. Stakeholders in these contexts are likely to use the same scrutiny in testing out the values underpinning evaluation decisions as they do when managing their own programs. Discrepancies, if they do arise, are typically noticeable and can be readily addressed. There are contexts, however, where the values that are attributed to both the program and evaluation are varied and implicit. Acting on the assumption that the values guiding the evaluation will be easily understood could be a serious detriment to utility.

This standard encourages evaluators and stakeholders to acknowledge the diversity in background and experience that might, at times, make evaluation decisions appear biased or unresponsive. Within the evaluation community, there are a wide variety of value stances regarding optimal purposes, processes, and judgments for evaluation. As evaluators develop self-knowledge of their own values, it becomes easier to be explicit about these during the negotiations that lead to a formal agreement with stakeholders. A clear sense of one's own orientations also makes it easier to monitor and, when appropriate, regulate the effects of these values during a project. Stakeholders' perspectives and behaviors during an evaluation will also vary based on the strength of particular program, social, and cultural norms. Acknowledging and learning about this variability keeps evaluators sensitive to the implications of their own behavior. Evaluators and stakeholders do not have to share a common value system in order for an evaluation to be feasible (F3 Contextual Viability). However, optimizing utility requires openness about the values shaping the evaluation. Evaluations cannot afford to be seen as merely reflecting the vested interests of those who already have significant influence in the program and its evaluation.

There are several choice points within an evaluation where the values of decision makers will influence the evaluation's overall utility. For example, values shape the reasons for selecting some sources and forms of information over others. Evaluators tend to value examined assumptions, reasoned thinking, and information grounded in empirical observations, (A2 Valid Information and A3 Reliable Information). It is important to understand the extent to which stakeholders share these values and will respect the ideas grounded in these processes. In some program contexts, beliefs, traditions, and intuition play a vital role in developing rationales for judgments and decisions. Conflicting values about what constitutes worthy information can cause both evaluators and participants to be alienated from the processes and findings. This alienation can lead to lack of use.

Values also shape the negotiation of evaluation purposes (U3 Negotiated Purposes). When exploring the motivations for engaging in an evaluation, multiple and competing needs among stakeholders can surface (P6 Conflicts of Interests). The decision about whose needs get met could involve a needs assessment, the use of formal priority setting and decision-making strategies such as consensus building, or other less formal strategies. Because none of these options is inherently the right way to proceed, the values and consequences associated with each choice should be made clear. This provides stakeholders with an opportunity to weigh the degree of acceptability associated with each alternative. They then have a basis for considering the utility of each choice.

In addition, values shape the ways in which information is perceived and communicated. For example, difference in values can influence evaluators' descriptions of a community. One evaluator may observe and report, "Children roam unsupervised and in packs." Another evaluator, observing the same phenomena, may report, "For the children, the entire neighborhood is home. Rarely is a child seen playing alone or isolated from the community." Being sensitive to the interpretive potential in language helps evaluators and stakeholders monitor when and how particular values are shaping evaluation activities and judgments.

Finally, values underpin recommendations that emerge from evaluation findings. For example, educational program administrators will sometimes establish in advance of a program evaluation (and probably for defensible reasons) that instructors' annual contracts will be honored regardless of their performance. Evidence about unsatisfactory performance will be accompanied by a recommendation for professional development and improvement rather than termination of employment. This recommendation is neither right nor wrong. What it reflects is a value stance. To avoid misuse of the evaluation findings, this stance should be made clear to all of the evaluation's key stakeholders including the instructors themselves in advance of data collection (A1 Justified Conclusions and Decisions and U8 Concern for Consequences and Influence).

❖ IMPLEMENTING U4 EXPLICIT VALUES

The following are important recommendations for implementing this standard:

1. Learn what stakeholders value about the program, how strongly these values are held, and the degree to which these values converge or conflict.
2. Reflect on the implications of specific, strongly held values for evaluation processes and activities.
3. Facilitate opportunities for individuals and groups to come together to examine evaluation plans. Bring together those program participants who are normally distanced from one another to examine how the scope and strength of their values can lead to individual and organizational learning. This can help to build trust and confidence in later judgments.
4. Remain sensitive to body language and tone of voice. The ability of evaluation participants to communicate their values is, in part, a function of their experience in making their needs and preferences explicit.
5. Respect the contributions of stakeholders regardless of their status within the program structure. An evaluator who attends to all involved stakeholders makes it clear that examining the values at work in the program context is important regardless of who is expressing them.

❖ HAZARDS

Some possible hazards with regard to U4 are as follows:

1. Imposing your own values on the project. Evaluators who work in isolation are vulnerable to mindlessly overemphasizing their own values around the tasks of selecting data, interpreting information, and generating recommendations
2. Ignoring strong negative reactions to proposed evaluation activities. Such reactions should be seen as opportunities to learn about the underlying experiences and values producing the stakeholders' responses
3. Assuming or allowing others to assume that evaluators are objective and able to make value-free judgments
4. Designing the data collection and analysis procedures without considering what criteria (e.g., a performance compared to a reference group, a predetermined standard, or a value stance) will be used to interpret the findings
5. Failing to acknowledge and review the values underlying decision rules in evaluation before data are collected (A7 Explicit Evaluation Reasoning)

Application Number Four for the Utility Case Scenario

The scenario that supports this application, including background information about the program, context, and key players, can be read at the end of the Utility Overview on page 9.

It has been four weeks since Jamaal's first meeting with Suparna, the director, Jase, the assistant director, and the five coordinators from the CHEERS program. In that time he has met with the entire program staff twice and had several e-mail contacts with each of them. He has also met twice with Suparna and Jase, individually and briefly, and supported the two of them at the board of directors meeting. It was reassuring to see the outline of the evaluation purposes and the evaluation questions unanimously accepted. With the formal agreements in place it is time to begin the work of drafting the methods and the schedule for data collection.

Jamaal is concerned about an e-mail he just received from Suparna. It confirms that the signed contract had arrived back in their office and that everything was "good to go!" She writes,

> With so many things to look after in implementing our projects, we are delighted that you will be doing our evaluation for us! Let me know if Jase can be of help. I'm looking forward to meeting you when you have some preliminary results to share with everyone.

In Jamaal's mind the evaluation has been set up as a participatory evaluation, although he realizes now, with some dismay, that the phrase *participatory evaluation* never appeared in the contract (see P2 Formal Agreements). They had talked about collaboration in the various phases, but, as Jamaal had to admit, *collaboration* could be a very ambiguous word (see P4 Clarity and Fairness).

Jamaal's biggest dilemma is that for the evaluation to accomplish all of the negotiated purposes, Suparna, Jase, the project coordinators, and at least some of the volunteers will need to work with him in the data collection, analysis, and decision-making processes. If he cannot establish working groups for each project, the evaluation as drafted in the contract is not feasible within the negotiated budget. He feels he can make this case with Suparna, because he can refer to his written notes from the meeting where they agreed that learning how to conduct evaluative inquiry would be a significant additional benefit of the evaluation. In an e-mail with Liying, the Safe Walk project coordinator, the local library had already been identified as a great place to do some of the planning for data collection.

Now it appears that Suparna is reneging on her commitment to have coordinators directly involved. One thing is clear: proceeding without confronting these different perceptions will not only threaten the evaluation, it may create new and perhaps damaging tensions within the CHEERS office and between Jamaal's firm and the CHEERS staff (F3 Contextual Viability). It is essential that he and the coordinators be clear on the extent to which Suparna values their involvement in the evaluation. Because of the seriousness of this issue, Jamaal decides not to discuss it over the phone (U6 Meaningful Processes and Products). He arranges instead for a half-hour meeting with Suparna first thing the next morning. If this is just a misunderstanding due to a poor choice of words on Suparna's part, he will be in and out in five minutes. However, he is not making that assumption.

Jamaal prepares for the meeting by reviewing the notes from each meeting where the project coordinators showed enthusiasm for being collaborators in the evaluation. He also remembers that it was in his meeting with Suparna and Jase that they had begun talking about adding value to the program through the evaluation. He made notes about that piece of conversation as well. He also rereads the sponsor's goals for the evaluation and drafts some possible data collection strategies for selected evaluation questions. In this way he can get Suparna to assess how meaningful it might be for the coordinators and their volunteers to be the data collectors and analyzers. He hopes that she will recognize how impossible it is for Jamaal to do all of this work given the resources that CHEERS is investing in the evaluation. Putting everything together gives him the comfort of having documentation to work with at the meeting.

As the meeting begins, he realizes he was wise not to assume that this was just an ambiguously worded e-mail. Suparna does not have a vision of the coordinators being directly and continuously engaged in the evaluation. When she realizes how differently she and Jamaal are thinking about things, she calls Jase into the meeting. Jamaal presents his case for the participatory approach. This includes having Suparna and Jase look at his outline of possible data collection strategies. Jamaal stresses that these are only possible activities. The coordinators, he emphasizes, have a much better understanding of the projects and how and when data gathering might work best, which is one of the important reasons why they need to be involved. Without that understanding, he continues, it will be difficult for him to tell how well the data match their purposes. Moreover, a poor fit will ultimately affect the accuracy and utility of the findings (A6 Sound Designs and Analyses). More important for the program, if coordinators get hands-on experience during this evaluation, they can continue examining the value of their projects once the formal evaluation is over. This can increase the usefulness of the process and contribute to their organization's overall development.

Eventually the logic of Jamaal's argument, the time he gave the two of them for reflection, and his encouragement about the benefits sway Suparna to agree to the participatory approach, but not enthusiastically. Never having experienced this approach, she is anxious that direct engagement in the evaluation will jeopardize the ability of the coordinators (especially those connected to the two new projects) to focus on planning and implementation. Any ineffectiveness in these responsibilities may jeopardize the whole program before they even have a chance to qualify for stable funding.

Jamaal responds to Suparna's discomfort. He suggests that another goal be added to the contract, namely that the evaluation be monitored throughout the year for its ability to support project implementation. It should also be metaevaluated at the end of Year 1 to make sure it has accomplished its purposes while not being overly burdensome (E1 Evaluation Documentation and E2 Internal Metaevaluation). He invites Suparna to provide oversight and guidance for this monitoring process, while he takes responsibility for developing the tools and timelines for the evaluation.

Just as the meeting is winding down, Suparna adds one more concern. "I'm afraid that by having our program staff involved in the evaluation, the resulting report won't appear to be objective enough for our sponsor" (A1 Justified Conclusions and Decisions and U8 Concern for Consequences and Influence). Jamaal shows Suparna the statement in the sponsor's guidelines that the evaluation should demonstrate how the program is being improved as well as report outcomes. He then clarifies how evidence of this capacity building in a report can document an important dimension of program improvement.

The next day Jamaal receives a copy of Suparna's e-mail to the project coordinators. In it she reports on the meeting and encourages the coordinators to work with Jamaal to move the evaluation forward (U3 Negotiated Purposes). She also asks each of them to let her know immediately if carrying out evaluation activities is negatively affecting their projects. Jamaal smiles. One good thing about this note is that it demonstrates Suparna's sensitivity to her staff and the challenges they face in managing their projects and learning new skills.

Jamaal becomes even more determined to erase, as much as possible, the line Suparna has drawn between systematic inquiry into their projects and their "real" work. He realizes that he values participatory approaches most highly because of the learning and independence they can lead to. He also feels that he has recognized and dealt with a serious problem. He had not made the meaning and implications of participatory evaluation explicit. He had also made an assumption that Suparna's notion of collaboration was congruent with his own understanding. In addition, he has not yet developed a thorough communication plan that will integrate the evaluation and its processes into the ongoing working of the program.

Jamaal opens his electronic journal and writes,

- Have each of the coordinators articulate what "working on the evaluation" means to them. It is quite possible that each project will look a little different. Involve Suparna and Jase in deciding what information should be common across all projects.
- Consult with Suparna on her monitoring process. Formalize this monitoring process a bit more, so that we have some trustworthy data to work with when we assess the utility of the evaluation processes and products at the end of the year.
- Draft a communication plan for the evaluation. Make sure the plan allows for regular exchanges with Suparna, Jase, Camilla, and the project coordinators.
- Don't assume that when we speak the same words we mean the same thing.

❖ SUPPORTING DOCUMENTATION

Botcheva, L., Shih, J., & Huffman, L. (2009). Emphasizing cultural competence in evaluation. *American Journal of Evaluation, 30,* 176–188.

Datta, L. (2000). Seriously seeking fairness: Strategies for crafting non-partisan evaluations in a partisan world. *American Journal of Evaluation, 21,* 1–15.

Henry, G. T. (2003). Influential evaluation. *American Journal of Evaluation, 24,* 515–524.

House, E. R., & Howe, K. R. (1999). *Values in evaluation and social research.* Thousand Oaks, CA: Sage.

Mertens, D. M. (2007). Transformative considerations. *American Journal of Evaluation, 28,* 86–90.

U5 Relevant Information

Evaluation information should serve the identified and emergent needs of intended users.

❖ RATIONALE AND CLARIFICATION

Evaluations always have the goal of producing information. Observations, descriptions, artifacts, self-reports, and statistical evidence continue to be foundational information for judgments and decision making (A2 Valid Information and A3 Reliable Information). To optimize evaluation utility, however, information must also be relevant. Typically this requires additional decisions about what types of information will be most valued, how much information is necessary for evaluation credibility, and who are regarded by others within the evaluation context as the most trustworthy information sources. In addition, relevant information is not always accessed most easily, and easily accessed information is not necessarily the most relevant. The acceptability of evaluation products such as portrayals, judgments, and recommendations is tied directly to stakeholders' perceptions of the appropriateness and relevance of the information used to construct them.

Information is relevant if it is connected directly to the purposes of the evaluation and the needs of stakeholders. The relevance of the information, just like the purposes of the evaluation (U3 Negotiated Purposes), should be a subject of discussion and negotiation with evaluators and evaluation users. Relevant information may come in diverse forms, including individually constructed program theories, preferences, frequency counts, and survey data. The form that relevant information takes will also differ depending on how well it aligns with the evaluation questions.

Information is also judged more or less relevant depending on the credibility of the data source and the acceptability of the processes used to collect and analyze it. The credibility of those contributing information to the evaluation typically depends on whether their experiences, expertise, and values are held in high regard. A quality evaluation pursues data sources that provide credible and valuable information.

When stakeholders understand and have opportunity to comment on proposed data collection and analysis processes, they are more likely to find the resulting information relevant. Evaluators, as part of their education, typically become practiced in selecting, collecting, analyzing, and communicating information in ways that are congruent with specific evaluation questions. When participants express preferences for less useful but familiar information, it is essential to explore their reasons or rationales. Under optimal conditions, an evaluator may need only to help stakeholders understand the value of the alternative information and analysis procedures and why a specific approach is being recommended.

❖ IMPLEMENTING U5 RELEVANT INFORMATION

The following are important recommendations for implementing this standard:

1. Keep the selection of information bounded by the evaluation purposes and the stakeholders focused on the specific questions (U2 Attention to Stakeholders and P2 Formal Agreements) but be open to renegotiation as needed (U3 Negotiated Purposes).
2. Remain open to unexpected but pertinent sources of information from a variety of sources (P2 Responsive and Inclusive Orientation). Reticent or skeptical stakeholders may not be forthcoming with information, and evaluators should stay engaged and avoid early judgments about whether stakeholders have relevant information to offer.
3. Remain sensitive to the fit between evaluation data and emergent evaluation purposes. Review and make changes as needed.
4. Be prepared to focus on issues where there is the greatest need for information and on the information with the highest relevance.
5. Retain responsibility for the usefulness of information used in the evaluation. In an age of Internet search engines, e-mail, and free access to social networks, the quality and relevance of information

must be assessed with vigilance (A2 Valid Information, A3 Reliable Information, and A5 Information Management).

❖ HAZARDS

Some possible hazards with regard to U5 are as follows:

1. Trusting that a single authoritative source of information can provide all the needed information (A5 Information Management)
2. Treating all information as equally useful: Evaluators must work with stakeholders to weigh the relevance, scope, and accuracy of information (A2 Valid Information)
3. Selecting information based on the pressures applied by different stakeholders: Stakeholders, especially those sponsoring the evaluation may have a preconceived notion of what data should be collected to answer their questions
4. Keeping sources of information confidential when there is no legal or ethical reason to do so
5. Overvaluing information because it is in print and is currently available
6. Being naïve about the strengths and limitations of online data: Much useful information is hidden from general access on protected intranets. Easily available information may be the result of efforts to create social or political influence or present an ideal representation
7. Ignoring attempts to manipulate the evaluation through inclusion of data that are not relevant for the evaluation purposes but can serve positive or negative public relations or other political purposes

---

Application Number Five for the Utility Case Scenario

The scenario that supports this application, including background information about the program, context, and key players, can be read at the end of the Utility Overview on page 9.

The CHEERS evaluation has been in progress now for a full six weeks. Jamaal, the principal evaluator, is working from a signed formal agreement that specifies the various purposes for the evaluation (described in the application accompanying U3 Negotiated Purposes). He refers to a simple organizational chart.

Program Director–**Suparna**	
Assistant Program Director–**Jase**	Administrative Assistant–**Camilla**
PROJECTS	**COORDINATORS**
Community in Motion (ongoing)	**Mike**
Safe Walk (ongoing)	**Liying**
Greening Today (ongoing)	**Emile**
Camp Rhea (new)	**Erica**
Play and Leadership (PAL). (new)	**Dakota**

He has had meetings with those coordinating the three ongoing projects to discuss the kinds of information that would help them demonstrate the achievement of project goals. They are now recruiting volunteers who are willing to help them collect some program observations and user satisfaction data. Jamaal is meeting even more regularly with Erica and Dakota, the two coordinators of the new Camp Rhea and PAL projects. Because this is the first year of implementation, Jamaal is helping these coordinators work with Camilla to track their decision-making processes systematically, especially the adjustments they make in response to unexpected events and conditions.

Jamaal is pleased that the evaluation has generated some excitement about evaluative inquiry among the coordinators. He is also aware that, on its own, evidence that individual projects are getting better at meeting their goals and generating outcomes is unlikely to sway the sponsors to provide more stable funding. For this reason, it is now time to meet with Suparna and Jase to design the evaluation activities targeted at understanding CHEERS as a program of five integrated projects. In their next meeting together they begin by reviewing the goals related to the purposes of describing CHEERS and establishing its value. They review the goals they have already established:

- To develop an overall understanding of the CHEERS program
- To establish the unique contributions of the CHEERS program to the community
- To demonstrate fiscal accountability
- To establish the value added by the CHEERS program to the sponsor's mission

They also address ways to communicate with stakeholders in the CHEERS program to help collect and share useful information.

As a group they review the latest draft of the stakeholder maps to see which individuals, groups, or organizations might be able to assist them in gathering data. As the process continues Jamaal begins to brainstorm those stakeholders not yet added to the map. He proposes options such as senior citizens groups, hospitals, elementary school teachers, school bus providers and staff, other recreational programs for children, community police precincts, the recycling depot, and the municipal transportation management department. Both Suparna and Jase, however, repeatedly veto his suggestions. When Jamaal finally asks why his suggestions are not appropriate, he learns that Suparna and Jase want the stakeholder map to include only those who are positive about CHEERS. Jamaal knows how common it is for program personnel to want only positive information about their programs. He also knows that the evaluation must provide the sponsor with information that will be valued. He is aware of his urgent responsibility to help them understand that positive information about the program is not the same as relevant information and that they might be inaccurate in their assumptions about how others perceive the program. He also notes some accuracy concerns that should be considered as well (A1 Justified Conclusions and Decisions, A2 Valid Information, and A7 Explicit Evaluation Reasoning). Together, they have to consider what might help the sponsor make a positive judgment about the program, not only after the first year, but beyond.

Jamaal approaches this dilemma by suggesting the three of them look over the sponsor's mission and goals. These may provide some sense of the values that will shape judgments about CHEERS (U4 Explicit Values). In doing this they find the sponsor's overarching purpose to be "the development of community identity, action, and welfare." Embedded in the description are statements such as: "We seek to support programs that encourage citizens to participate in and take pride in improvements to their community," "Programs should enable communities to develop a sustainable sense of identity and connection to others," and "Over time, citizens should be able to testify to program services that contribute to their quality of life." The three of them agree that if CHEERS is to become one of the ongoing programs supported by the sponsor, they will need to demonstrate how CHEERS contributes both to the overall mission and to these and other important indicators. Jamaal points out specific phrases in the sponsor's statements such as *sustainable* and *over time*. It will be important to get baseline data on these dimensions so that by the end of the third year, there will be evidence of either prolonged effects or change in effects. It is difficult, Jamaal explains, to show that your program is having an impact if you narrow the contexts where you are willing to look for the impact. It is even more difficult to show improvement if you are not willing to learn about where your program needs improving.

It has been a challenging meeting, but in the end the three of them have come up with a template and examples of how program effects might be demonstrated. Suparna and Jase want an opportunity to think about this on their own and develop the template further.

Project	*Indicators*	*Data Source*
Community in Motion	Attracting a wide variety of senior citizens who participate regularly	Attendance sheets
Safe Walk	Volunteer pool remains stable in number even though there is a turnover in individuals	Volunteer records
	A healthier height/weight ratio for children who almost always walk to school than for those who rarely walk, controlling for out of school activities.	Parents

(Continued)

(Continued)

Project	*Indicators*	*Data Source*
Greening Today	An increase in the amount of materials recycled by the community	Recycling station
Camp Rhea	Baseline data on what children did on nonschool days before this program was available	Parents
Play and Leadership (PAL)	Baseline data on the self-improvement projects these teens engaged in before this program Baseline data on the number and types of co-op credits per year awarded in participating schools	Teenagers' self-reports School district office

Jamaal is not yet convinced that they have the best set of indicators for the evaluation, but they have made significant progress today. More important, Suparna and Jase are now beginning to look at evaluation information differently (A2 Valid Information). Certainly they all want data that demonstrates that CHEERS is worthy of stable funding, if such data exist. It is also reassuring to hear Suparna and Jase talk about how information on these kinds of program indicators can give them a much bigger picture of the program's influence in the community and ultimately provide their coordinators with information for improvement as well.

Jamaal's entry into his e-journal reads, "Make sure everyone understands why we're choosing some types of information over others. Continue to think about documenting evaluation processes" (E1 Evaluation Documentation).

❖ SUPPORTING DOCUMENTATION

Alkin, M. C., & Taut, S. (2003). Unbundling evaluation use. *Studies in Educational Evaluation, 29*(1), 1–12.

Bozeman, B. (2004). The Internet's impact on policy evaluation: Information compression and credibility. *Evaluation Review, 28*(2), 156–174.

Christie, C. A. (2007). Reported influence of evaluation data on decision makers' actions. *American Journal of Evaluation, 28,* 8–25.

Grasso, G. F. (2003). What makes an evaluation useful? Reflections from experience in large organizations. *American Journal of Evaluation, 24,* 507–514.

Leviton, L. C. (2003). Evaluation use: Advances, challenges, and applications. *American Journal of Evaluation, 24,* 525–535.

U6 Meaningful Processes and Products

Evaluation activities, descriptions, findings, and judgments should encourage use.

❖ RATIONALE AND CLARIFICATION

Without attention to how various stakeholders understand evaluation processes and products, evaluators run the risk of not meeting stakeholders' needs. Evaluations may be technically sound and defensible from the evaluators' perspectives without being useful (A1 Justified Conclusions and Decisions).

Evaluation processes and products are meaningful when they are perceived to have significance and value for stakeholders. As a rule, an evaluation's utility is higher when it allows stakeholders to better understand and act on the strengths, limitations, and potential of their program. To support these uses, evaluators strive to design activities that assure appropriate data selection, collection, and analysis (A5 Information Management and A6 Sound Designs and Analyses). Designing activities to assure both accuracy and meaningfulness can help stakeholders to (a) better understand the complexity of their program's operations, (b) feel more confident in making decisions about future directions, (c) develop insights into their own roles and the contributions of other stakeholders, and (d) assess their own contributions to the program and how these might be strengthened. While evaluation products such as descriptions, findings, and judgments also need to be accurate, they will be meaningful when stakeholders judge them to be clear and functional, and to be logical consequences of the evaluation activities

(E1 Evaluation Documentation, A2 Valid Information, and A7 Explicit Evaluation Reasoning).

There are some evaluation contexts in which utility is judged by the extent to which stakeholders become more self-sufficient in evaluative inquiry and in understanding their programs. In these contexts, evaluations are meaningful because they create new knowledge, skills, and attitudes, and encourage stakeholders to continue learning about their programs after the formal evaluation is completed.

Sometimes, despite considerable effort on the part of the evaluator, stakeholders do not engage in the evaluation. This poses a serious obstacle to creating meaningful processes and products. Under these circumstances the evaluation is likely to be neither feasible (F3 Contextual Viability) nor useful. In such situations, the memorandum of agreement should be revisited and the feasibility of purposes reconsidered.

❖ IMPLEMENTING U6 MEANINGFUL PROCESSES AND PRODUCTS

The following are important recommendations for implementing this standard:

1. Know the stakeholders. Evaluators who make the effort to learn about how various stakeholders view and contribute to the program and what are considered challenges and successes within the program are better positioned to build meaningful processes and products.
2. Implement processes that are worth the investment of time and resources needed to support them (F1 Project Management, P3 Human Rights and Respect, and P5 Transparency and Disclosure).
3. Adapt essential processes and products in ways that address diverse stakeholders' needs while not compromising the primary purposes of the evaluation.
4. Regularly revisit stakeholders' evaluation needs and expectations. Doing so engages stakeholders in meaningful ways, thus enhancing opportunities for evaluation use.

❖ HAZARDS

Some possible hazards with regard to U6 are as follows:

1. Using the initial contract to stipulate evaluation activities and then imposing these on stakeholders

2. Assuming that all stakeholders will approach an evaluation eager to participate or learn about their program
3. Not preparing for and providing the time, resources, or experiences necessary to make meaningful participation feasible
4. Proceeding without understanding how stakeholders are thinking about or reacting to the evaluation
5. Allowing participants to attribute their learning to the authority of the evaluator rather than to the evaluation process, leaving them poorly positioned to be able to use or adapt the findings

Application Number Six for the Utility Case Scenario

The scenario that supports this application, including background information about the program, context, and key players, can be read at the end of the Utility Overview on page 9.

CHEERS personnel are preparing to collect data on the five individual projects and the program as a whole. Jamaal has initiated a participatory evaluation design, making it possible for project staff to be directly involved in the creation of evaluation instruments. As a way to understand their own projects and to be able to look across projects, the staff along with Jamaal designs what ended up as a 20-item user satisfaction survey. The survey has two sections. Section 1 contains six items that ask respondents to describe themselves in different ways, how they became acquainted with the project, when they intend to participate, and the ease with which they are able to access information when they need it. Suparna and Jase are responsible for constructing these items. The remaining 14 items are specific to each project. It was agreed that four of these items should explore the roles and influences of volunteers in each program.

Before starting construction of the surveys, Jamaal gives everyone a two-page handout describing some of the challenges they are about to face in survey development. Suparna arranges a Thursday morning half-day meeting when everyone can work together designing the surveys. The morning begins with a review of the key points from the handout. They talk at length about the advantages of asking several questions that can reveal whether the goals of their projects are being achieved rather than asking one question about whether respondents thought the project was achieving its goals. They create some statements about project outcomes with a Likert-type scale accompanying them. The scale is anchored on one end by *strongly agree* and on the other by *strongly disagree.* One dilemma they wrestle with is how many scale points to use. Jase worries that it may be really difficult to get stakeholders to select an extreme response, like *strongly agree.* If respondents only choose *agree* or *mildly agree,* it might make the projects look bad. Jamaal suggests that some statements be positively worded and some negatively worded so that stakeholders will rate agreement with both positive and negatively worded items. They finally agree to implement a 1 to 7 scale, with 7 representing *strongly agree.* They will include a mix of positive and negative statements about the projects and the program. Jamaal shows them some histograms and correlation tables in a file on his laptop to illustrate the kinds of information they could produce with the help of the spreadsheet and chart software. Finally, before writing any items, the work group revisits the three evaluation questions being addressed by the survey. "When you finish constructing an item," Jamaal adds, "ask yourself why it is important to include it in the survey and which of the evaluation questions it is addressing." Everyone had brought something to contribute to lunch, so the group has a productive 4-hour working session. It has been a good beginning, and everyone leaves feeling much has been accomplished, but with more work to do. Jamaal asks that everyone send drafts of their surveys for his review within the week. He promises to meet with them the following week to finalize the items and then run pilot tests on each of the surveys.

The coordinators have agreed to recruit four assistants from their regular volunteer group to help administer the survey. These assistants have agreed to attend a scheduled training session in how to collect data and then to administer the survey to identified participants. At the training session, Jamaal works with the volunteers and illustrates how to use the instructions he has drafted to guide their work. He reviews how to approach potential respondents, provide them with information about the survey, interact while they were filling out of the survey, and preserve the confidentiality of their responses (P3 Human Rights and Respect). He also shows the volunteers the spot on the survey they will need to initial when the survey is submitted. While the respondents will remain anonymous, the volunteers collecting the survey responses will be identified. This information will help them see the distribution of responses at each project site. Jamaal and the coordinators are excited about what they will learn. Because of the design process and stakeholder ownership, Jamaal is confident that the survey will result in meaningful findings.

On the next Thursday morning Jamaal receives an urgent call from Mike, the project coordinator for the Community in Motion project. He was at the CHEERS office and had just finished leafing through the first 17 surveys that had been dropped off. Despite the successful pilot tests, half of the respondents appeared to have had difficulty in answering the items. Many items had comments scrawled across them with none of the options selected. Some were just left blank. Jamaal knows immediately that they have a significant problem (A2 Valid Information and U5 Relevant Information). Jamaal tells Mike he will be right there.

In looking for patterns across these surveys, Jamaal notices that the same two volunteers had administered all of them. Mike immediately wants to remove these two people from his data collection team. Jamaal cautions that this may not be the best solution (U8 Concern for Consequences and Influence). He asks Mike to arrange a meeting with the two people at their earliest convenience.

The meeting takes place 2 days later in a downtown coffee shop. After they order and receive their coffee, it quickly becomes apparent that these two individuals have spent a great deal of time discussing the survey and do not like it. Responding quickly before Mike can, Jamaal asks the volunteers to tell him more. "These items don't let participants tell us about their experiences in the program and what the program means to them," one says. "There isn't even a good question about how the volunteers contribute to the program." They go on to explain that for these reasons, as they gave out the surveys, they encouraged participants not to worry about the questions as they were written and to just describe what they liked or didn't like about the program and focus on the quality of their interactions with volunteers.

Jamaal responds that he hears their frustration. He then reviews the items with the two volunteers just as he had done with Mike during the editing process. Jamaal agrees that there is no single item directly asking about the importance of the volunteers' contributions. He shows them that four items dispersed throughout the survey are designed to work together to yield a better understanding of the significance of those contributions. For example, one of the items asks respondents to indicate how much they agree or disagree with the statement, "I have considered becoming a volunteer for Community in Motion." After identifying all four items and hearing an explanation of what each item can contribute, the two volunteers begin to understand better how the survey is designed and how important it is that respondents answer all of the questions. To Mike's surprise, Jamaal acknowledges that the two volunteers did have a good point. The survey design team has not considered creating items for respondents to talk directly to the staff in their own words. Jamaal suggests to Mike that a new back page be added to the surveys that will ask for any other observations or information respondents would like to offer. Jamaal asks the two volunteers whether this change will make it possible for them to support the survey. They answer *yes.*

Jamaal knows it wasn't the addition of open-ended questions that brought the two volunteers on board. Rather, it was a concerted effort to help make the survey meaningful. He realizes that he had just experienced the shortcomings of assuming that only those working with the data really need to understand how the survey produced the data. He had not anticipated how invested some volunteers would be in the survey. He is disappointed that he overlooked the fact that these volunteers were stakeholders in the evaluation process (U2 Attention to Stakeholders) and that they needed to see the information being collected about the project as significant (U5 Relevant Information).

Back at his own office Jamaal quickly enters a note in his e-journal for tomorrow,

> Write up a summary of today's meeting in the form of a bulletin to send out to all volunteers helping administer the survey. Be sure to include the details of this event. Describe how the evaluation is progressing and consider the implications of these processes for evaluation improvement and accountability (E1 Evaluation Documentation and E2 Internal Metaevaluation).

❖ SUPPORTING DOCUMENTATION

Fjellstrom, M. (2008). A learner-focused evaluation strategy: Developing medical education through a deliberative dialogue with stakeholders. *Evaluation, 14*(1), 91–106.

McNamee, S. (2003). Appreciative evaluation within a conflicted educational context. In H. Preskill & A. T. Coghlan (Eds.), *Using appreciative inquiry in evaluation: New Directions for Evaluation,100,* 23–40.

Patton, M. Q. (2008). *Utilization-focused evaluation* (4th ed.). Thousand Oaks, CA: Sage.

Taylor, J. R., & Van Every, E. J. (2000). *The emergent organization: Communication as its site and surface.* Mahwah, NJ: Erlbaum.

Westley, F., Zimmerman, B., & Patton, M. Q. (2006). *Getting to maybe: How the world is changed.* Toronto, ON: Random House Canada.

U7 Timely and Appropriate Communicating and Reporting

Evaluations should attend in a timely and ongoing way to the reporting and dissemination needs of stakeholders.

❖ RATIONALE AND CLARIFICATION

Evaluations can become irrelevant when they withhold information and results until all activities have been completed. They can become incidental to the very people who stand to benefit most from the findings. Evaluators have a responsibility to make sure that stakeholders have access to important information as it emerges and that the information is available in forms that adequately serve their needs (P5 Transparency and Disclosure).

A recurring theme in evaluation work is that the timelines established at the beginning of an evaluation are not always stable. The work of stakeholders and evaluators is vulnerable to pressures that arise from changing conditions around and within a program's context. These changes sometimes present stakeholders with unanticipated opportunities for action or demand that decisions be made based on the best possible information available at the time. Evaluations that communicate their approaches, activities, and products in a continuing fashion allow stakeholders to construct timely understandings of how the evaluation is proceeding and what it is finding. These understandings create the potential for unanticipated use as the evaluation proceeds. They also help the evaluation respond to changes in timelines and needs.

Communication and reporting mechanisms that respond to the explicit time requirements of sponsors and program decision makers can enhance both the evaluator's credibility and the evaluation's overall utility (U1 Evaluator Credibility). Expectations for communicating and reporting to the evaluation sponsors are usually formalized in the evaluation contract (U3 Negotiated Purposes and P2 Formal Agreements). Evaluators should consider these as minimal expectations and should not assume these provisions will be comprehensive enough to optimize evaluation use. During a project, evaluators may need to communicate with a variety of stakeholders at times and in ways that give assurances about the merit, worth, and significance of the evaluation. A plan detailing the ongoing processes and products needed for communication with stakeholders will help to enhance evaluation utility (as well as feasibility, propriety, accuracy, and accountability).

To design an effective plan requires an in-depth understanding of the program and the cultures and contexts in which information will be shared and used (U2 Attending to Stakeholders). For some stakeholders, communications that are overly technical or formal can be easily dismissed as obscure or too academic. For others, reports that do not use the technical language of measurement or research paradigms will be regarded as untrustworthy and inconsequential. There may also be contexts, especially when process use is a high priority, where written summative reports of evaluation findings may not be required at all. Evaluators need to be proactive in developing a repertoire of methods and resources for communicating and reporting (A1 Justified Conclusions and Decisions and A8 Communication and Reporting).

❖ IMPLEMENTING U7 TIMELY AND APPROPRIATE COMMUNICATING AND REPORTING

The following are important recommendations for implementing this standard:

1. Be sensitive to the contextual and cultural patterns that shape both when and how information is best shared. In practice this may mean
   - translating materials when necessary;
   - accommodating visually and hearing impaired audiences;
   - including multiple types of media and reviewing them for inclusiveness;
   - selecting meeting venues where stakeholders are comfortable;
   - adapting to conceptions of time, such as what it means to be on time or to spend the right amount of time;
   - sharing the responsibility of communicating and reporting with community members who have credibility.

2. When possible, embed communication and reporting into existing program structures through such mechanisms as bulletin boards, intranet lists, and meeting agendas, but avoid so much information that everything is ignored.
3. Supplement formal with informal and interactive communications as part of a carefully designed communications plan.
4. Be sensitive to the broader social implications of the evaluation by planning when and how to interact with community members, social networks, and the media.
5. Plan time for explaining technical language in reports, for follow-up discussions and activities, and for helping with interpreting findings and applying them to decisions.
6. Make written reports functional and responsive to decision makers' needs for relevant evaluation information without overwhelming them. For example, write executive summaries that stand on their own and clearly respond to the users' information needs.

❖ HAZARDS

Some possible hazards with regard to U7 are as follows:

1. Relying on individuals internal to the program to arrange meetings with influential stakeholders for data collection and then ignoring them once access to information has been secured
2. Using reports primarily to underscore the technical ability of the evaluator or to demonstrate accountability for the resources used in the evaluation
3. Delivering reports to stakeholders and assuming they will be distributed appropriately
4. Assuming without confirmation that distributed reports are read and understood
5. Not taking into account the resource demands of communication and reporting when estimating the cost of a project (F1 Project Management and F4 Resource Use)
6. Assuming that evaluators should do all or most communication and reporting

Application Number Seven for the Utility Case Scenario

The scenario that supports this application, including background information about the program, context, and key players, can be read at the end of the Utility Overview on page 9.

When Jamaal accepted the responsibility as the evaluator for the CHEERS program, he realized that the communication networks within the program were complicated. The staff had decided to use the smallest room of their three-room downtown space as the office for Suparna, the program director, and Jase, the assistant program director. This room could be accessed through a door off the entrance hall, but it also connected through an inside door to a larger room that was the office of Camilla, the program administrator. Camilla's office space was an ideal reception room because its wide access to the entrance hall allowed Camilla to see people immediately as they entered the building. In this office, each of the five CHEERS projects had its own bulletin board where information about the project and volunteer activities were posted. There was also a board reserved for administrative notices. Across the hall from Camilla's office was the largest room. Here each of the five project coordinators had their workstations. The room also contained a bookcase, shelves, and a 6-foot worktable that everyone used for meetings and lunch. At the beginning of the evaluation, Suparna invited Jamaal to work in this room whenever he wanted.

Jamaal made a deliberate decision early on in the evaluation to track the flow of information about the evaluation through the organization. He didn't know how, but he had a feeling that understanding how the staff networked might be of great help to him down the road (F1 Project Management). It was somewhat surprising to learn in conversations with Camilla that she was the hub for much of the formal information exchange. If Suparna or Jase needed to get something out to project coordinators, the task was often given to Camilla. Even when Suparna or Jase sent out messages themselves, Camilla was usually blind-copied. One of her assigned duties was to maintain the official records of communication for the CHEERS program. Camilla told Jamaal that she read only a small portion of the e-mail she processed, but she had developed a system of folders on her computer that would give Suparna a paper trail if she ever needed one. Jamaal realized that he might also be able to enlist Camilla's help in documenting the paper trail for the evaluation so as to improve its quality and demonstrate accountability (E1 Evaluation Documentation, E2 Internal Metaevaluation, and E3 External Metaevaluation).

In talking about this process to Suparna, she admitted sheepishly that this system was more of a management necessity for her than a deliberate choice. Her favorite form of communication was the monthly staff meeting where she, Jase, and the five project coordinators would update each other on new developments. Camilla attended, took minutes, and then put them into an electronic file for reference. When Jamaal learned about these staff meetings, he asked if he could attend and have the evaluation added as a regular agenda item. Suparna was pleased to comply. She seemed even more pleased about his interest in the operations of the program team.

In each of his first three staff meetings, Jamaal found himself only partially understanding the discussions of some of the agenda items. Not wanting to slow the meetings down, he did not ask for clarification unless the discussion concerned the evaluation. Finally, after the third meeting he asked Suparna if he could review some of the correspondence around the recent decision to try to raise the profile of CHEERS in the city. Suparna laughed. "I don't think you'll find much. This was one of those things we just chatted about to each other here in the office."

It was at this moment that Jamaal realized that despite staying current with the formal business of the program, he was missing some of the most important conversations—the informal ones the staff shared as they moved around the office. While he had been diligent in sending regular electronic updates about the evaluation to the directors and coordinators, he was likely missing out on information about how his updates were being received and how the program was evolving even as the evaluation continued.

Because this was Jamaal's first experience as lead evaluator for Centerville Research and Evaluation Specialists (CRES), he was allowed to dedicate the equivalent of 2 days per week to this project. With the program description, stakeholder maps, and logic models up to date, much of Jamaal's work now was with staff to collect and analyze data. He had just finished analyzing the focus group data collected from volunteers in each of the established projects. Thanks to Camilla, he was now ready to begin entering user-satisfaction data from the surveys. Almost all of this work was done on his office laptop, which he backed up regularly on his thumb drive and nightly on his external drive at home (A5 Information Management).

In light of what he has learned about the importance of the CHEERS informal networks of communication, Jamaal suggests to Suparna that he work in the CHEERS office every Thursday morning. Thursdays are good because all of the staff members are usually in the office for at least some time that morning. He explains to Suparna this might be a good way for everyone to keep up to date on the progress of the evaluation. He explains that he will be ready to post some of the themes from the volunteer focus groups, and the quotes supporting these themes, next week. Jamaal is also hoping that this will be a better way for him to learn about the context in which CHEERS is operating.

After 6 weeks of this new working arrangement, Jamaal is pleased with his ability to keep Suparna, Jase, and the five project coordinators up to date on the evaluation. Camilla has arranged for him to have some space on the administrative bulletin board in her office. Each Thursday when he arrives, he posts an update from the previous week and a description of what he is working on that day. When it is time to remove a posting, he puts it in a file as part of the evaluation documentation (E1 Evaluation Documentation). With each passing week, he notices that people are becoming more relaxed about coming to talk to him while he is working. He is also being invited to join in coffee breaks.

One Thursday when he arrives, the office is abuzz. Suparna has been notified that in response to their efforts to raise the profile of CHEERS in the city, an influential blogger for the local paper wants to do a feature article on CHEERS, including how it is being funded and evaluated. Suparna and Jase call Jamaal into the office. They want to know whether some of the products that Jamaal is helping them create for their sponsor can be modified to help them manage the interview. They already know from Jamaal's postings that a prominent theme from the volunteer focus group data is the increased depth of connection volunteers feel for Centerville and its neighborhoods because of their regular associations with program participants. Jamaal had posted this theme and the quotes from the focus group that supported this theme several weeks ago. Jamaal has also shown them graphically how program users responded to questions about their experiences in each of the three established projects. Suparna and Jase both want to learn how to talk about this information better before the scheduled interview.

While helping Suparna and Jase prepare for such an event is not part of the formal agreement, Jamaal realizes that this is an opportunity for the evaluation to make a significant contribution to stakeholders. Over the next 2 weeks, Camilla, Suparna, and Jase organize materials describing each of the projects. Stakeholder maps and logic models feature prominently. They also spend time with the project coordinators looking over newer evaluation data that Jamaal has organized for them. While the complete data analysis will not be ready for at least another 3 months, Jamaal coaches them on things they can discuss with confidence now. Jamaal also agrees to be in the office for consultations when Suparna, Jase, and the interviewer arrive back from the various site visits. He suggests that Camilla keep track of the inquiries about the various projects she receives in the 2 weeks before the blog is posted, then compare these to the inquiries received in the 2 weeks following the posting. Because he has some questions about how to maintain his role as evaluator distinct from that as an adviser on public relations, Jamaal schedules a quick meeting with Janet, his mentor at CRES, to be sure how he should proceed (A8 Communication and Reporting, P6 Conflicts of Interests, P3 Human Rights and Responsibilities, P1 Responsive and Inclusive Orientation, and F4 Resource Use). He also wants to be sure that the evaluation findings are not misused (U1 Evaluator Credibility and U8 Concern for Consequences and Influence).

The Thursday after the blog appears, the CHEERS office is still reveling in the positive publicity they received. Camilla has posted the video and write-up and has them bookmarked on the reception room computer. Jamaal arrives with his laptop, posts his weekly report, and sits down to work. He is pleased that he organized data in ways that could be easily accessed and shared with the program staff when this opportunity arose (A5 Information Management). By having a good understanding of both the data and the program context, he could respond more easily to this unexpected opportunity (U3 Negotiated Purposes). Engaging the staff in preparing for the publicity was also a way to demonstrate to Suparna in a concrete way the "value added" nature of participatory evaluation (U1 Evaluator Credibility). By working directly with the program staff in analyzing and understanding the meaning of the preliminary data, Jamaal had also helped them avoid the hazard of overstating their accomplishments (A8 Communicating and Reporting).

Jamaal opens up his electronic journal and writes, "This group is teaching me a lot about the potential for evaluation use."

❖ SUPPORTING DOCUMENTATION

Alkin, M. C., Christie, C. A., & Rose, M. (2006). Communicating evaluation. In I. F. Shaw, J. C. Greene, & M. M. Mark (Eds.), *The Sage handbook of evaluation.* London: Sage.

Bozeman, B. (2004). The Internet's impact on policy evaluation: Information compression and credibility. *Evaluation Review, 28*(2), 156–174.

Lawrenz, F., Gullickson, A., & Toal, S. (2007). Dissemination. *American Journal of Evaluation, 28,* 275–289.

Rolfsen, M., & Torvatn, H. (2005). How to 'get through': Communication challenges in formative evaluation. *Evaluation, 11*(3), 297–309.

Torres, R. T., Preskill, H. S., & Piontek, M. E. (2004). *Evaluation strategies for communicating and reporting: Enhancing learning in organizations* (2nd ed.). Thousand Oaks, CA: Sage.

U8 Concern for Consequences and Influence

Evaluations should promote responsible and adaptive use while guarding against unintended negative consequences and misuse.

❖ RATIONALE AND CLARIFICATION

The concept of evaluation use includes the full range of consequences that can result from engaging in evaluation. Evaluation influence has emerged as a structure for identifying the intentions and timing of these consequences. Together evaluation use and influence provide evaluators and program stakeholders with a framework for understanding the scope and import of their work.

Systematic evaluation has the capacity to validate programs and catalyze beneficial changes in program contexts, policies, and practices. Systematic evaluations are most meaningful when they also contribute to individual, organizational, or social betterment. Sponsors will sometimes emphasize one of these ideas more than the others in stating their evaluation goals. Often the three are interdependent, and the evaluator can initiate communication about these complementary purposes. In either case, promoting evaluation use that is aligned with the negotiated purposes of the evaluation remains the primary concern of evaluators.

Evidence of nonuse can arise early in an evaluation in the form of resistance, avoidance, and passivity. If these behaviors are allowed to persist, the influence of the evaluation is threatened, not just for those expressing lack of interest but also for those in the program connected to these people. In such contexts it becomes critical to learn about the compelling forces that are shaping stakeholder thinking, opinions, attitudes, values, and behaviors. Understanding these may help in the design of more appropriate evaluation activities or lead to a reconsideration of evaluation purposes (U3 Negotiated Purposes).

Even in contexts in which the intended and direct consequences of evaluation become immediately evident, unintended consequences, both positive and negative, and even misuses can occur. The potential for these occurrences requires evaluators to be forward looking. For example, an evaluation may provide accurate and trustworthy information to a managerial group about a program's functioning. The report includes recommendations for program restructuring and downsizing which are implemented almost immediately. The recommendations, however, are used specifically as a rationale for releasing the most recently hired program staff, all members of a visible minority. It is hard to know whether this is an example of unintended consequences or misuse. Had the evaluator and stakeholders anticipated and assessed the consequences of such recommendations, different and perhaps better choices might have been possible.

It is not unusual for the intended uses of the evaluation to be adapted once activities are begun and findings are materializing (P1 Responsive and Inclusive Orientation). Adaptation is a logical consequence when stakeholders are considered active, sense-making participants. This orientation emphasizes paying close attention to stakeholders' reactions to what they are learning and experiencing. Feedback from participants identifies whether the meanings being constructed are based on intended and accurate messages. Learning about, supporting, and, when appropriate, challenging the meanings that stakeholders are constructing for themselves about the evaluation and its findings are necessary skills for the evaluator (A2 Valid Information and A7 Explicit Evaluation Reasoning). Evaluations that provide opportunities for stakeholders to test their assumptions and fine-tune their understandings will minimize the likelihood of unintended immediate or long-term negative consequences.

Most programs exist as complex systems, emerging and adapting in response to forces within and around them. In such contexts, evaluation is only one strategy that programs use to answer questions, make decisions, and solve problems. Systematic evaluation collects and analyzes data in response to questions identified by stakeholders as important, and guides stakeholders in using the resulting information in ways that are logical, meaningful, ethical, and transparent (P5 Transparency and Disclosure and P3 Human Rights and Respect). While evaluators are not directly responsible for the use and influence of an evaluation once their work is completed and they are no longer in contact, their professional behaviors and decisions during the evaluation can affect what follows. Ongoing reflection on the fit between one's practices and the full set of evaluation standards can promote responsible adaptive evaluation use

(E1 Evaluation Documentation, E2 Internal Metaevaluation, and E3 External Metaevaluation).

❖ IMPLEMENTING U8 CONCERN FOR CONSEQUENCES AND INFLUENCE

The following are important recommendations for implementing this standard:

1. Identify both formal and informal communication mechanisms that connect stakeholders, so that individuals, groups, and organizations can integrate and channel their learning along established pathways of influence.
2. Assess formally and informally the consequences of evaluation activities for stakeholders as soon as possible after they are completed.
3. Be assertive and appropriately engage stakeholders who appear to be sabotaging the evaluation (F3 Contextual Viability). At times, the personal or political agendas of stakeholders may run counter to the purposes of the program and its evaluation (P6 Conflicts of Interests).
4. Selectively revisit previous evaluation sites for evidence of linkage between the evaluation and subsequent policies or practices. Learning about such relationships makes it possible for evaluators to review the long-term uses associated with their approaches and helps to refine professional practice (E1 Internal Metaevaluation).

❖ HAZARDS

Some possible hazards with regard to U8 are as follows:

1. Losing sight of the negotiated purposes for evaluation and the needs these purposes are intended to serve, so that consequences and influences are negatively affected (U3 Negotiated Purposes)
2. Assuming that a technically excellent evaluation is sufficient for positive use and effective influence
3. Presuming to know the only legitimate ways stakeholders should use the evaluation findings
4. Failing to determine in a timely manner that evaluation findings have the potential to jeopardize human rights or principles such as truth,

social justice, equity, and democratic participation (P3 Human Rights and Responsibilities)

5. Failing to examine the relationship between one's habitual evaluation approaches and the underlying contributions these may or may not be making to evaluation use (E2 Internal Metaevaluation and E3 External Metaevaluation)

Application Number Eight for the Utility Case Scenario

The scenario that supports this application, including background information about the program, context, and key players, can be read at the end of the Utility Overview on page 9.

Jamaal is amazed to realize that the first year of his first professional evaluation project is drawing to a close. Data collection is done, and most of the analyses are completed. He has drafted an outline for a report that will, he thinks, more than satisfy the sponsors of the Centerville Health for Eco-educated Residents (CHEERS) program. With Camilla's help, he has collected considerable documentation in preparation for a formal internal metaevaluation and review of plans for next year's evaluation (E1 Evaluation Documentation and E1 Internal Metaevaluation).

Next week, he will go over the report draft with Suparna and Jase before they present it to the board of directors. On this Friday afternoon, Suparna calls Jamaal and asks if he can accompany her to one of the new project sites. It is a professional development day for elementary teachers, hence a holiday for students. All four community Camp Rhea sites are operating. Erica, the project coordinator for all four campsites, has asked them to come and observe the Ridgewood site specifically.

Erica, with Jamaal's guidance, has been working systematically with her camp leaders in documenting "the dynamics and interdependencies that sustain the program." This was stated as one of the formal purposes of the developmental evaluation being conducted in the two new CHEERS projects. After becoming more aware of the goals and logic for the developmental evaluation, Ted, the leader of Camp Rhea, has not only done some additional thinking but has also initiated some action. As he would explain to his colleagues later, "I was seeing how the connections we had made with the schools had really contributed to acceptance of this camp by my community." Ted's reasoning was that if some connections between camp and the community were good, then more connections may be better. He wants to test the effects of more involvement.

Based on his understanding of the project goals and the outcome assessments already developed for the evaluation, Ted has recruited two second-year education students from the local state university to work with his 8 senior counselors and 80 kids. In exchange for volunteering their time, Ted will verify that the students have completed their minimum 40-hour service-learning practicum requirements. Fortuitously, the two practicum students also have a minor area specialization in performance arts. Ted is thrilled with their response to his challenge to contribute to the camp's mission as a high-activity program with a focus on environmental education. During the morning activities rotation, the practicum students lead each group of campers, along with their counselors, in a planned 45-minute exercise involving intense dramatic movement. Ted is excited about this activity session because it engages campers in the kind of physical activity recommended for children. Mixing drama activities and sports appears to be a more inclusive way to promote physical well-being.

In the afternoon rotation, as a follow-up to the educational video and science activity, each group has a half hour of help from one of the practicum students in creating a short skit, a song, or an advertisement to promote that day's environmental theme. For the last 40 minutes of the day, the two students act as hosts of *Camp's Got Talent,* in which each group performs for the rest of the campers.

Suparna and Jamaal arrive in time for the final camp circle and the presentations. It is an activity that reinforces many important educational ideas while provoking much laughing and cheering. Both Suparna and Jamaal notice that many parents and caregivers are arriving early to pick up their children, possibly in hopes of seeing their children perform. Erica and Ted welcome parents and invite them to come and sit around their campfire circle rather than stand in the doorway.

After the children leave, there is praise all round for these innovations. Suparna pulls the two university students aside while Erica and Jamaal sit down with Ted. "It just seemed like such a good way to build another partnership," Ted explains. "You and Erica have been stressing from the beginning that this year's evaluation is about learning what works. I am trying to build on what we talked about during our evaluation meetings. Our meetings gave me the confidence to see if this kind of partnership might be able to contribute something to the way the program was developing."

Suparna and the students rejoin the three of them, and together they begin considering the possibilities of practicum students volunteering for the Camp Rhea camps. Their practicum coordinator has enthusiastically approved this placement. The students claim they are having great fun working with the kids, the counselors, and Ted. They even suggest that Suparna allow them to promote the Camp Rhea camps as a practicum site for the next school year.

After the practicum students leave, Suparna and Erica both congratulate Ted on his willingness to be proactive. Erica remarks that a partnership with the school of education seems to be "a perfect fit—at least for this site." Ted replies that he had learned more about how to plan for his program by watching how outcomes were being assessed. Suparna promises that she will call the university on Monday to set up a formal meeting with the practicum coordinator. At the very least, she wants to learn more about this practicum and how it can support Camp Rhea in the future. Erica and Ted plan to interview the two students after the last camp session to see if they can identify what has made this a good experience for them. Jamaal offers to help them develop the protocol for the interview. "We need to learn what the elements are that have given you such good chemistry here!"

Neither the CHEERS staff nor Jamaal predicted that Ted would take this kind of initiative. During his graduate training, Jamaal had heard of both immediate and long-term instrumental and conceptual uses stemming from evaluation reports. He had not imagined, however, seeing such effects stemming from the evaluation process. He wonders whether Ted's action might also be considered a form of process use. Whether or not Ted's actions will lead to a new staffing structure for the Camp Rhea project, Ted's camp has benefitted from his interpretation of the developmental evaluation process.

Back at the office, Jamaal tries to pinpoint his personal contribution to this unexpected effect. Ted obviously trusted that Jamaal's proposals for the evaluation were both important and realistic (U1 Evaluator Credibility). Ted must have also felt that the evaluation activities he was engaging in were worthwhile (U1 Meaningful Processes and Products). The rest, Jamaal thought, all had to do with the potential inherent in the Camp Rhea project and with Ted's qualities as a person and camp leader.

Jamaal opens his electronic journal and writes, "Remember that a commitment to doing professional evaluation can have unexpected and positive spin-offs. And sometimes, if you're lucky, you get to see them."

Epilogue

The CHEERS scenario continues in the last Part of this book, Evaluation Accountability, where internal and external metaevaluations are planned and described.

❖ SUPPORTING DOCUMENTATION

Cousins, J. B. (2004). Commentary: Minimizing evaluation misuse as principled practice. *American Journal of Evaluation, 25*(3), 391–397.

Henry, G. T., & Mark, M. M. (2003). Beyond use: Understanding evaluation's influence on attitudes and actions. *American Journal of Evaluation, 24*(3), 293–314.

Kirkhart, K. E. (2000). Reconceptualizing evaluation use: An integrated theory of influence. In V. J. Caracelli & H. Preskill (Eds.), *The expanding scope of evaluation use: New directions for evaluation, 88,* 5–23.

Sridharan, S. (2003). Introduction to special section on "What is a useful evaluation?" *American Journal of Evaluation, 24,* 483–487.

Zuckerman, B., & Preskill, H. (2001). Throwing a curveball in the game of evaluation: Deception and the misuse of findings. *Advances in Developing Human Resources, 1*(1), 55–68.

Part II

Feasibility Standards

STANDARD STATEMENTS

F1 Project Management	*Evaluations should use effective project management strategies.*
F2 Practical Procedures	*Evaluation procedures should be practical and responsive to the way the program operates.*
F3 Contextual Viability	*Evaluations should recognize, monitor, and balance the cultural and political interests and needs of individuals and groups.*
F4 Resource Use	*Evaluations should use resources effectively and efficiently.*

❖ FEASIBILITY OVERVIEW

Evaluations are feasible when they can take place with an adequate degree of effectiveness and efficiency. Working to increase feasibility adds value to evaluations in three ways. First, attention to feasibility highlights the logistical and administrative requirements of evaluations that must be managed. Good evaluation project management increases the likelihood that evaluations will be successful.

Second, attention to feasibility brings the world of possible evaluation procedures into the world of practical procedures for a specific evaluation. Evaluators must ask the question, "Can I use these procedures in this program evaluation at this time?" For example, procedures that are feasible at the beginning of the evaluation may not be as feasible later due to changes in the program, its services, or the situation in which the services are provided. Because feasibility depends on the specific context of the evaluation at a given point in time, planning for feasibility must be a responsive and iterative process that continues throughout the evaluation.

Third, adequate feasibility serves as the precondition for other attributes of quality. While attention to feasibility does not ensure utility, propriety, accuracy, or accountability, it can result in better resource use and more effective and efficient activities that support the other attributes of quality. More efficiency can free up resources to address additional needs, such as creating greater cultural competence or securing additional information. Thus, the effective and efficient use of resources allows for greater evaluation quality and impact.

Key Concepts

Four key concepts are germane to the discussion of evaluation feasibility: *evaluability, context, values,* and *accountability.* To create feasible evaluations, evaluators and stakeholders need to develop a shared understanding of these concepts (A2 Valid Information). The first concept, *evaluability,* describes the degree to which it is possible to evaluate a specific program at a specific time and place. Program evaluability depends on a number of factors, including

- the presence of program goals,
- performance indicators that correlate with program goals,
- agreement on the purposes and uses of the evaluation,
- identification of appropriate procedures for conducting the evaluation,
- adequate resources for conducting the evaluation, and
- a context in which the evaluation can provide value.

Evaluability assessments help to ensure that programs are ready to be evaluated before evaluations are launched.

The second concept guiding discussions of feasibility is *context,* defined as the cultural, political, economic, governmental, and geographical circumstances and environments in which the program occurs. Context includes all of the variables that shape the program, such as program history, purpose, laws and regulations, funding, organizational structure, and the needs of the program sponsor, managers, and clients. Context is also defined by the needs, values, and norms of stakeholders and the cultures in which the program occurs. With multisite programs, important segments of the context may differ significantly for each site, especially when sites are separated by major boundaries, such as linguistic groupings, socioeconomic levels, degree of urbanization, or state and national divides.

The third concept, *values,* refers more broadly to the systems of concepts and qualities that stakeholders use to prioritize and judge aspects of their lives (U4 Explicit Values). Different stakeholders and stakeholder groups may be guided by very different values. In most evaluation contexts, values often lie under the surface until they are explicitly investigated or come into conflict naturally. If left unaddressed or suppressed rather than managed, conflicts in values can impede the design and implementation of programs and evaluations and exert other negative effects on evaluation feasibility.

In general, recognizing and positively addressing different stakeholders' values is a key step in increasing evaluation feasibility (as well as utility, propriety, accuracy and accountability). Stakeholders' values are critical influences on how they think about the need for and the quality of programs and the program evaluations. Stakeholders' values influence their expressed needs and the services and products they think will address those self-identified needs. When it comes to programs, stakeholders' values not only define program quality along specific characteristics or dimensions but also dictate how much they want of any particular type of quality. Similar dynamics are in play with regard to stakeholders' values and their assessment of the worth of the evaluation.

Often stakeholders' values are expressed through actions and reactions rather than through systematic study and analyses. For example, the level of engaged program participation may be an indicator of the program's value to clients. The value that community members have invested in specific programs is often demonstrated through voting to use tax dollars to fund them or providing monetary or nonmonetary support to the organizations that support them. Evaluators' values are often made visible in the decisions they make concerning how to frame and conduct an evaluation, how to use resources, which stakeholders to include, and which performance indicators to adopt (U4 Explicit Values).

Taken all together, the values, interests, and views of different stakeholders, whether in harmony or in tension, affect all aspects of evaluation, including feasibility. For example, the value or perceived value of a program and its services is sometimes visible in decisions concerning whether an evaluation is allowed to be undertaken; whether evaluators will have access to people, data, and other resources; how fully the results are reported and to whom; and whether the results are used (U4 Explicit Values).

The fourth concept, *accountability,* relates to resource use. Accountability is supported by the effective and efficient use of evaluation and program resources, including time, money, and people, to create value (Evaluation Accountability Overview). By demonstrating accountability for resources, evaluation teams increase the potential and actual feasibility in many evaluation settings.

Introduction to the Feasibility Standards

The feasibility attribute includes four standards. Standard F1 Project Management focuses on using good management processes as a strategy for controlling evaluation scope, time, and budget. The consistent use of effective project management strategies increases the likelihood of evaluation feasibility.

Standard F2 Practical Procedures focuses on the processes that are necessary to create evaluation feasibility given the usual and customary ways that a program and its contexts operate. The feasibility of a specific evaluation is increased through evaluation procedures that are responsive to the ways that a specific program and its contexts actually operate.

Standard F3 Contextual Viability alerts evaluators and stakeholders to important context factors, especially stakeholders' cultural and political needs and values. It recognizes that all evaluations occur in a cultural context and that all evaluations are political in nature. It focuses on the importance of engaging evaluation stakeholders without any unnecessary and differential burdens as a consequence of not attending to important needs, values, and perspectives. For example, conducting interviews at a time or location convenient for the interviewer but difficult for stakeholders can seriously undermine the feasibility of that evaluation component.

Standard F4 Resource Use emphasizes the need to secure adequate resources and maximize their effective and efficient use to increase the likelihood of a valuable evaluation. However, the benefits derived from an evaluation cannot always be calculated in dollars. Even though the degree of actual effectiveness may not always be clear, this standard requires that the value of resources be considered during all phases of the evaluation and compared to the expected uses and benefits of the evaluation.

❖ FEASIBILITY SCENARIO

To illustrate how the feasibility standards can be used, each of the chapters presenting the individual standards concludes with a brief application based on the scenario below. The individual applications provide a coherent introduction to the standards in the context of real-world evaluation dilemmas. The applications are not intended to represent the one set of best practices or to be emulated exactly. Rather, they illustrate sound responses to important evaluation issues. After considering the specific applications, evaluators and other stakeholders might think of appropriate alternative actions. Evaluation practice is complex, and the standards work in tandem with evaluators' and users' knowledge, values, and experiences to affect decision making.

The section below introduces the specific feasibility scenario and provides some context for the individual applications that follow. It introduces the general characteristics of the program being evaluated along with key people and their roles. The applications will present specific dilemmas as experienced by the principal players and will illustrate

- how individual standards are related to the dilemmas,
- ways to respond to and implement the standards, and
- how other standards might come into play given the specific dilemmas.

The scenario selected here describes the evaluation of a fictional school district's use of resources to further student achievement. The programs and characters in the scenario and applications are not based on any specific, actual evaluations but are typical of what evaluators face across a broad spectrum of real-world situations.

Evaluation of Carr County School District

The state legislature has a 10-year plan to review each of its 225 school districts, including Carr County, for the purpose of improving student achievement and use of resources. The state Office of Evaluation is responsible for conducting the evaluations and providing the state legislature a formal report with findings and recommendations. Carr County and other districts will also receive copies of their reports. The primary people involved in the evaluation include the following Carr County School District personnel:

- William Masson, the school board chairman, is a lifelong resident of Carr County. He earned a BS in finance and a JD in law at the state university. He is now serving his third term as school board chairman, a position to which he was elected by other members of the school board.

- Mike Ruck, the superintendent, earned a BS in physical education and an MS in administration and supervision at the state university. He served as a football coach and physical education teacher for 10 years, an assistant principal for 2 years, and a principal in the middle and high schools for 10 years. Ruck is now in his second term as the elected school superintendent for Carr County.

• Kathleen Torry, a deputy superintendent, earned a BA in elementary education and an MS in student personnel and counseling from the state university. She is a lifelong resident of Carr County. She has served as a classroom teacher for 5 years and a school counselor for 5 years. She is now in her third year as deputy superintendent for Carr County.

• Steven George, a middle school principal, earned a BA in history and education and an ME in educational leadership. He has served as a classroom teacher in both the private and public schools for a total of 5 years. Prior to coming to Carr County, he served for 2 years as an assistant middle school principal in a contiguous county. He is now in his second year as a principal in Carr County.

• Rebecca Todd, an elementary school principal, earned a BA in elementary education. She has served as a classroom teacher for 12 years. Most of those years were spent teaching fourth grade. She served as an assistant principal in Carr County for 10 years. She is now in her sixth year as principal.

The evaluation team is composed of the following people:

• Roberto Perez, the project director, has a BA in mathematics and education and a PhD in organizational behavior. Roberto is bilingual in English and Spanish. Following the completion of his undergraduate degree, Roberto joined the Peace Corps and worked in South America. He has also served as a classroom teacher. He has been conducting education related evaluations for more than 20 years and directing evaluations for the past 5 years. The Carr County School District evaluation is one of several school district evaluations that he is responsible for directing. Roberto's primary responsibility is helping to administer the project scope, budget, and evaluation schedule. He is also responsible for assigning roles to team members, monitoring the progress of the evaluation, determining project methodology in conjunction with the evaluation manager and team, and overseeing internal formative and summative metaevaluation (E2 Internal Metaevaluation).

• Mary Weber, the evaluation manager, has a PhD in research and evaluation. She has taught graduate-level courses in program and personnel evaluation in the United States, Mexico, and Germany. While living and working in Mexico and Germany, Mary was able to hone her evaluation and language skills and speaks Spanish and German fluently. She has more than 20 years of evaluation experience and has conducted a variety of education-related studies, including school district evaluations. During the past 5 years Mary has developed her evaluation competencies by working in diverse contexts while serving as an evaluator for school systems located in the southwestern United States. As manager for the Carr County School District evaluation, Mary is responsible for determining the scope of the project and the project methodology in conjunction with the project director and the team. She is also responsible for day-to-day monitoring of the evaluation and some of the fieldwork. She will collaborate with Roberto on the internal formative and summative metaevaluation (E2 Internal Metaevaluation).

• Beatrice Alford, a staff evaluator, has participated in multiple evaluations, including several other school district evaluations, during the last 7 years. She completed an MS in research and evaluation and has good evaluation skills. She keeps up to date in evaluation theory and practice by attending at least one professional workshop or conference a year. Beatrice has a reputation of completing assignments quickly, thoroughly, and effectively. In addition to being an excellent writer, Beatrice is skilled at conducting interviews and focus groups.

- Fred Cox, a staff evaluator, earned a BS degree in psychology, an MS in social psychology, and a Graduate Evaluation Certificate from the state university. During the last 5 years, he has participated in several other school district evaluations. Like Beatrice, he keeps up to date in evaluation theory and practice by reading journal articles and attending at least one professional workshop or conference a year. He completes assignments thoroughly, quickly, and effectively. Fred is skilled at conducting interviews and focus groups and is bilingual in English and Spanish. His excellent language skills are the result of his academic training, extensive travel, and volunteer work in migrant farm worker communities.

- Mark Kelley, a staff evaluator, earned an MS degree in educational policy and evaluation. This is his second professional evaluation experience. Prior to joining the state Office of Evaluation, he completed a one-year evaluation internship with a federal government agency. As an intern, he participated on one evaluation team. Later as a staff member of the agency, he participated in planning, design, fieldwork, and report writing for one previous evaluation.

- Juan Mendoza, an evaluator, earned an MS degree in educational policy and evaluation. As a degree requirement, Juan completed a six-month internship with the internal evaluation office for a state agency. As part of the internship, Juan conducted interviews with agency staff, assisted with the development of a survey instrument, and completed a preliminary analysis of the survey responses. The Carr County School District evaluation is his first professional evaluation experience. Juan, a lifelong fluent speaker of Spanish, is also fluent in English. He is enthusiastic about being part of the team and acquiring more skill in evaluation.

To help determine the fiscal and human resources required to conduct an evaluation of the Carr County School District, the state Office of Evaluation requested demographic data for the district from its Office of Information Services. In summary, the data revealed that slightly more than 20% of Carr County's children are of school age (5–17 years old) while an additional 6% are under the age of 5. By contrast, 13% of the county's residents are 65 years of age or older. Approximately 74% of the county's adult residents are high school graduates, and 8% have graduated from college. The district had an enrollment of 7,029 students in the previous academic year, and operates 13 schools: 7 elementary schools, 5 middle schools, 2 high schools, and 1 adult education center.

Carr County has a civilian workforce of 20,850 people. The county's primary sources of employment are service industries, health care, and manufacturing. The annual summary produced by the state Office of Demographic Research reveals that the majority of residents are white (65%). People of Hispanic or Latino origin constitute the second largest group at 26% of the population. In addition, 8.8% of the county's residents reported being Black or African American. A small percentage of the residents reported themselves to be multiracial. The racial/ethnic composition of the student population for Carr County mirrors these percentages.

The state Office of Evaluation allocated $60,000 for the evaluation of Carr County School District, based on the number of schools and population figures. The evaluation team will have 3 months to complete the evaluation and deliver the final report to the state legislature and school district.

The Evaluation Team

The state Office of Evaluation has assigned evaluation responsibility for the Carr County School District to a team of six persons. Roberto will serve as the project director. The Carr County School District evaluation is just one of several that he is responsible for directing. Mary, the evaluation manager, is responsible in consultation with Roberto for determining the scope of the project methodology, team assignments, and the day-to-day project monitoring. She will also conduct some of the fieldwork.

In addition to Roberto and Mary, two members of the team, Beatrice and Fred, have participated in multiple evaluations, including several other school district evaluations, during the last 2 years. The other two team members, Mark and Juan, are just entering the evaluation profession and have little experience on an evaluation team.

Roberto and Mary have discussed Mark and Juan's limited evaluation experience but appreciate their excellent communication skills and their eagerness to learn. One concern is that in previous assignments, Beatrice and Fred have been unwilling to mentor new team members. In fact, they tend to be very impatient with staff members that do not perform at their quick pace. As the evaluation manager, Mary has allocated some of her time for mentoring Mark and Juan and monitoring their work products.

Roberto and Mary agree that the evaluation budget and time frame are adequate for conducting this evaluation if everything goes well. However, Roberto and Mary also know that very few evaluations go exactly as planned. They have agreed to hold back 10% of the budgeted resources for surprises and unexpected tasks.

The first meeting between the team and the school district includes School Board Chairman Masson, District Superintendent Ruck, Deputy Superintendent Torry, the principal from each of the district's schools, the chairperson for the district advisory council, and the six members of the evaluation team. After introductions and words of welcome, Mary presents the scope of the evaluation, the expected evaluation methodology, and the schedule and time frames. She notices immediately that the school district administrators look stressed and unhappy. After she finishes her presentation, School Board Chairman Masson reports that the school board views the evaluation as another attempt by the state to take over management of the district. They believe that the state wants to replace the locally elected school board members and superintendent with other school administrators selected by political leaders. Despite knowing that the evaluation was scheduled as part of the state's ten year plan, School Board Chairman Masson also expresses his annoyance at the lack of local involvement from the beginning of the planning process. Superintendent Ruck speaks up to express his concerns about the potential disruption and inconvenience the evaluation will cause. He advises the evaluation team that they would need to schedule all district interviews and requests for records or data through his office. Some members of the team began to wonder silently about completing the evaluation within the given time frame if the district delays access to data or people.

F1 Project Management

Evaluations should use effective project management strategies.

❖ RATIONALE AND CLARIFICATION

Effective project management helps to structure the evaluation and make optimal use of resources. Evaluators with project management skills consider and capitalize on all types of diverse resources for increased evaluation feasibility. Project management can help make evaluations in difficult contexts more systematic and responsive and thus more effective and efficient.

Implementing effective project management strategies can reduce the learning curve for new evaluators and increase feasibility by helping the evaluator answer questions about where, how, and when to proceed with key project phases and procedures. For established evaluators, project management strategies can lead to positive processes and challenge established habits that may undermine feasibility.

Well-managed evaluation projects identify and focus on specific goals and objectives. They include realistic time frames, well-considered budgets and activities selected specifically to assist in meeting goals and objectives. They balance scope, time, budget, risk, and communication. They also identify and recruit qualified staff with the knowledge and skills necessary for successful project implementation and completion.

Successfully managed evaluations have to be nimble. A change in one aspect of an evaluation is likely to lead to other changes. This in turn may affect the feasibility of the evaluation by altering resource availability. For example, an increase in project scope is likely to increase the resources needed for staff to perform the additional work. The additional work will put new stresses on the resources needed for other goals and adversely affect the feasibility of the original evaluation design. Delays could result in lost opportunities for the evaluation to support critical decisions, having an impact on future aspects of the program as well as the evaluation.

To be effective, evaluation project managers need essential knowledge and skills in the following component processes:

- Planning
- Scheduling
- Project staffing
- Monitoring
- Communicating
- Procurement
- Risk assessment

Effective planning will help to identify the work to be completed and increase evaluation feasibility by reducing waste. Effective planning is responsive and iterative, and continues throughout the evaluation. It foresees unexpected evaluation needs and reserves resources to address any needed changes. Its ultimate goal is to increase evaluation effectiveness and to minimize delays in completion and implementation of the evaluation's recommendations.

Scheduling helps to define the evaluation project and to ensure that there are sufficient resources to perform the work. The level of detail in schedules depends on the size of the project, time available for completion, the number of people serving on the team, evaluator experience, and the number of interrelated tasks. For example, the schedule for a project involving multiple people or a team with limited experience may require dedicated time for training and team meetings and more detail to ensure that the required products and due dates are adequately described.

Staffing an evaluation with individuals possessing the skills necessary to perform work in specific contexts increases the likelihood of a timely and successful completion of the project. In addition, the use of culturally competent staff may contribute to the effectiveness and efficiency of the evaluation because of their greater skill in understanding the values, customs, and norms existing in a context. With inexperienced staff, time and other resources may be required for training, delaying project completion. Additional monitoring of resources may be required to ensure that completed work meets the goals of the evaluation. However, sometimes investing in training and developing human resources on the existing evaluation team is the most feasible plan of action.

Project monitoring is essential for controlling time and costs. It is needed to recognize unexpected problems, such as when a previously trustworthy procedure no longer works in a new situation, and to direct resources to solving those problems. Like the scheduling process, the complexity of monitoring the evaluation may be affected by the number of persons serving on the evaluation team, team members' evaluation experience, and the number of interrelated tasks. Skillful communication contributes to the effectiveness of all project management processes. Coherent and strategic communication with clients and stakeholders is important in establishing the purposes of the evaluation, clarifying evaluation goals, keeping everyone advised of evaluation progress, resolving problems, and helping the evaluator stay abreast of any program changes that might impact the feasibility of the evaluation (U7 Timely and Appropriate Communicating and Reporting). Effective communication strategies within the evaluation team can contribute to a better understanding of the work to be completed and the value of each team member's contributions. Communication at all levels can assist in identifying and resolving project management issues in a timely manner before the evaluation is delayed.

In some evaluations, purchasing supplies, arranging for needed materials and facilities, hiring local assistance, and other procurement tasks are essential for evaluation feasibility. Inattention to procurement can result in evaluations experiencing serious delays when needed resources are not available.

Well-managed program evaluations catalogue and manage the potential risks that can render the evaluation infeasible or less effective and efficient. They revisit the risks to evaluation quality on a regular basis and develop strategies to cope with them. Some specific risks to feasibility are discussed and illustrated in F3 Contextual Viability and F2 Practical Procedures. In addition, a well-managed evaluation project would review all the standards for their contributions to identifying and reducing the risks to evaluation feasibility, propriety, utility, accuracy, and accountability.

In summary, effective project management enhances evaluation feasibility and is essential for utility, propriety, accuracy, and accountability. The skill with which the management processes are executed will affect the successful implementation and completion of the evaluation. Successful evaluation project management also requires reflective application of the standards through documenting and metaevaluating the evaluation, discussed in more detail in the Evaluation Accountability chapter (E1 Evaluation Documentation, E2 Internal Metaevaluation, and E3 External Metaevaluation).

❖ IMPLEMENTING F1 PROJECT MANAGEMENT

The following are important recommendations for implementing this standard:

1. When possible (especially for multiple sites and large teams), develop a formal management plan detailing evaluation
   - purposes, goals, and objectives;
   - strategies;
   - resources;
   - activities;
   - product;
   - time estimates and time lines;
   - communication strategies;
   - purchasing needs;
   - risks;
   - costs; and
   - quality constraints and requirements.

The details of the management plan can be expanded or contracted depending on the size of the project and the needs of the evaluation team.

2. Prepare project checklists, especially when numerous details and tasks need attention.
3. Review the evaluation stakeholders' needs and evaluation purposes, goals, and objectives when developing the management plan.
4. Identify who is responsible for implementing and controlling the quality of each major component in the management plan. Arrange for reporting or other communication to monitor and track implementation.
5. Remain flexible and review the plan for needed changes when the program or the evaluation constraints and demands change.
6. Be sure that the management plan is communicated to everyone who can help implement or improve it.

❖ HAZARDS

Some possible hazards with regard to F1 are as follows:

1. Developing a management plan that is not flexible enough for the iterative nature of evaluation and the inevitable changes in project scope, time, budget, or risks

2. Assuming that a management plan is not required since all persons assigned to the evaluation are experienced evaluators with the same understanding of the project
3. Assuming that all team members are committed to the management plan and that monitoring evaluation activities and products will not be required (E2 Internal Metaevaluation)
4. Proceeding toward accomplishment of initially defined plans in the face of information which suggests that the original goals may no longer serve the needs of clients and identified stakeholders (P1 Responsive and Inclusive Orientation and U3 Negotiated Purposes)
5. Completing tasks singly without recognizing connections and opportunities for efficiencies
6. Completing tasks in an excessively linear fashion without recognizing interrelations among tasks
7. Not involving stakeholders in developing, reviewing, improving, and implementing the plan (E2 Internal Metaevaluation and P1 Responsive and Inclusive Orientation)
8. Failing to formulate and document the plan, unless inadequate resources prevent doing so (E1 Evaluation Documentation)

Application Number One for the Feasibility Case Scenario

The scenario that supports this application, including background information about the program, context, and key players, can be read at the end of the Feasibility Overview on page 75.

Following the initial meeting between the evaluation team and the school district personnel, Roberto, the project director, Mary, the evaluation manager, and the other team members meet to discuss how to deal with the lack of cooperation expressed in the initial meeting with the school district. School district officials seemed to be antagonistic to the evaluation. Roberto and Mary think that strategies related to effective evaluation project management, especially communication, need to be addressed to help create a feasible situation for this evaluation to be implemented (U7 Timely and Appropriate Communicating and Reporting and A8 Communication and Reporting). Mary is concerned about establishing a satisfactory relationship to reduce the hostility that seemed to be expressed in the initial meeting. Roberto and Mary are aware that communication with the district administration will be critical for maintaining access to people and data and achieving project goals. Establishing and maintaining communication with teachers, parents, and other stakeholders will be equally important because the robust informal communication network could influence stakeholders' willingness to participate in the evaluation.

Mary expresses a concern about whether they will be able to complete the project on time if the district is slow in responding to their requests for data and human sources of information. If the district delays their access, they will need to be sure that they are as effective and efficient as possible to make up for the delays. Having an accurate understanding of the overall project and how to complete the individual tasks will take on even greater importance. To keep the project on schedule, each member of the team will need to understand how the various tasks and procedures interrelate and whether some tasks need to be deleted, moved up in the schedule, or delayed until data are available. Excellent communication within the team will be required for the timely completion of the project.

A related responsibility for Mary is evaluation monitoring. As evaluation manager, Mary is responsible for monitoring the work of all team members to ensure the project is progressing as scheduled and the work products are providing the needed information. Monitoring will help Mary and the team to identify any real or potential problems and needed changes in the scope of work. Given the limited experience of Mark and Juan, Mary wants to schedule extra time to mentor both of them. This will be in addition to her responsibility for regular monitoring of all team members' work products for quality and timeliness.

Mary asks others on the team if they have questions. Juan and Mark express some confusion with the schedule and their assignments. Both are concerned about the specific work required, the time line for completing certain tasks, and how their work relates to the assignments of Beatrice and Fred. Beatrice and Fred express related concerns. While they think they understand their project assignments, they are concerned that any confusion or misunderstanding could result in delays or create the need for additional resources that compromise the timely completion of the project. In response to these concerns, Mary suggests that the team expand the management plan to include enough detail to provide clarity about the work to be completed and how the various assignments fit into the total project. Mark and Juan are relieved. Even Beatrice and Fred, experienced evaluators accustomed to working with brief management plans, view a detailed plan as a good tool for keeping the team on schedule and a good way to communicate procedural information and product due dates. The revised management plan will include more details about how, where, when, and by whom various tasks are to be performed. Beatrice and Fred view the expanded management plan as a reminder of the processes they should follow and as a check on their skills. While they think fewer details are needed to define their assignments, they can see how the management plan will be useful in clarifying the project calendar and work products. Juan and Mark agree that the detailed management plan will be helpful to them in developing an understanding of the overall project and how their work interrelates with the assignments given to Beatrice, Fred, and Mary, as well as other parts of the project. Mary is hopeful that regularly scheduled team meetings will be useful in establishing communication within the team, building project commitment, and identifying problems. They all agree that a detailed management plan will assist them in managing the project scope, time, and budget to support project feasibility and will help to monitor what the actual evaluation activities have been and to provide documentation for any future assessments of their work (E1 Evaluation Documentation).

Mary considers how she might help Mark and Juan as they grow in understanding of the roles that solid management plans can play. She jots down some notes about what she wants to tell them concerning how effective project management supports evaluation feasibility and evaluation accountability. As she writes down her thoughts, she also makes notes about how the management plan will change in the face of some identified risks to the evaluation, such as potential difficulty in getting the needed information.

By the time of their next meeting, the management plan has been expanded to include additional scheduled meetings between the team and the school district. Mary and the team view these additional meetings as an opportunity to advise district administrators of project progress, improve communications, establish evaluation and evaluator credibility, and move toward a positive working relationship. The meetings will also be valuable in helping the team stay abreast of any changes or additional risks within the district that might affect the evaluation. In addition, these meetings could be useful in building team commitment and identifying problems and issues before they become barriers to evaluation.

Mary jots down some more notes to share with Juan and Mark later:

> The absence of effective and efficient project management may result in insufficient resources for necessary procedures that support feasibility, accuracy, utility, or propriety of the evaluation. Wasted resources may prevent essential data collection procedures or data analyses later. When evaluations are not completed on time, the usefulness of the information may be lost. For example, the legislative committee that needs this information for a proposed new law or budget deliberation will not have the information they need to make the best decision.

She also makes a note to be sure that Mark and Juan each have a copy of *The Program Evaluation Standards.*

❖ SUPPORTING DOCUMENTATION

Compton, D. W., & Baizerman, M. (Eds.). (2009). *Managing program evaluation: Towards explicating a professional practice: New Directions for Evaluation, 121.*

Project Management Institute. (2004). *A guide to the project management body of knowledge (PMBOK® guide)* (3rd ed.). Newtown Square, PA: Author.

Stufflebeam, D. (2001). Evaluation checklists: Practical tools for guiding and judging evaluations. *American Journal of Evaluation, 22,* 71–79.

Thomsett, M. (1990). *The little black book of project management.* New York: American Management Association.

F2 Practical Procedures

Evaluation procedures should be practical and responsive to the way the program operates.

❖ RATIONALE AND CLARIFICATION

Evaluation procedures aligned with and not in conflict with normal program and context activities are referred to as *practical procedures.* Such procedures contribute to enhanced feasibility and also support greater utility, propriety, accuracy, and accountability. They increase the likelihood of stakeholder participation in the evaluation and acceptance of evaluation procedures and results.

Procedures are the specific actions and processes undertaken in all phases of the evaluation from initiation to closing. They are the tools that bridge the gap between evaluation questions and the cultural and political context. Procedures include the actions performed to establish the evaluation's purposes and goals and to determine the evaluability of the program. They also include actions taken to identify the program's cultural and political context, to identify stakeholders' needs, to select purposes and goals, and to document all aspects of the program and its context, including its outcomes, through information collection and analysis (U3 Negotiated Purposes and A4 Explicit Context and Program Descriptions). Procedures are involved in all aspects of data selection, including deciding what information will be collected, how and when it will be collected, whether the collected data is accurate, and how it will be analyzed (A5 Information Management and A6 Sound Designs and Analyses). Procedures also determine how evaluation results are prepared and reported. Evaluation procedures should support utility, propriety, accuracy, and accountability, but they must also be feasible.

Practical procedures are responsive to cultural and other background influences. Culturally responsive procedures guide decisions about the best approaches to use with those who contribute to the evaluation and about the best formats for a given evaluation context. For example, a survey instrument for the visually impaired might be administered in audio, Braille, or another format compatible with assistive technology devices. The diversity of the stakeholders in some contexts might require the availability of data collection instruments in multiple languages or at a range of readability levels. Data collection procedures that are responsive to contextual diversity increase evaluation feasibility and help ensure valid interpretations (A2 Valid Information).

Although many procedures can appear value neutral to the majority culture, they should be designed to balance the interests and values of diverse stakeholder groups (P1 Responsive and Inclusive Orientation). For example, conducting focus groups or interviews with parents during the school day may appear value neutral while actually precluding contributions from parents who work during the day and cannot take time off from their jobs. Similarly, conducting interviews only after school may limit contributions from those with other responsibilities, such as after-school child care. Participation in focus groups may also be constrained by the languages in which they are conducted or the lack of planning to accommodate transportation or other family situations. Similarly, data collection procedures such as surveys or interviews may exclude persons who are difficult to reach because of limited access to telephone or e-mail.

❖ IMPLEMENTING F2 PRACTICAL PROCEDURES

The following are important recommendations for implementing this standard:

1. Review related laws and regulations, program goals, budget documents, and program reports in order to learn enough about the program and its context to be able to select procedures that are responsive to the cultures and other context factors.
2. Seek access to insider knowledge about the customary ways that programs operate, especially when actual operations are different from formal descriptions (A4 Explicit Program and Context Descriptions).
3. Regularly seek information about changes in program conditions or practices that would reduce the feasibility of the evaluation, such as a change in program goals or denial of access to necessary data. Changes in the program may require the development of new procedures if established procedures are no longer feasible.

4. Become familiar with key stakeholders' understanding of the program's purposes, goals, and procedures based on their own experiences, which may be different from descriptive information provided by program staff or written descriptions.

❖ HAZARDS

Some possible hazards with regard to F2 are as follows:

1. Failing to conduct an evaluability assessment prior to conducting an evaluation, resulting in wasted evaluation resources
2. Failing to develop a thorough understanding of the cultural and political context in which the program operates before selecting evaluation procedures
3. Designing an evaluation that does not facilitate adequate input from key stakeholders
4. Selecting procedures that are practical for only one group of stakeholders
5. Assuming that the values of and constraints surrounding a program are the same for all stakeholders
6. Assuming that all evaluators have the necessary competencies to work and interface with any cultural context
7. Utilizing evaluation methods that are familiar to the evaluator without considering the appropriateness for the program structure and cultural context
8. Selecting procedures based solely on convenience, time, or money available for the evaluation while ignoring the cultural context and/or the diversity of the program
9. Failing to consider the disruption to the program or staff that may result from specific evaluation procedures, especially those that require staff effort or interfere with their normal duties

Application Number Two for the Feasibility Scenario

The scenario that supports this application, including background information about the program, context, and key players, can be read at the end of the Feasibility Overview on page 75.

The evaluation team is meeting to review progress reports and to discuss issues and problems that surfaced during their initial interviews. Mary is particularly interested in whether the evaluation procedures are adequately addressing the questions in the context of this district. The evaluation management plan, initially developed by Roberto and Mary with input from the team, includes procedures for collecting information from a wide range of district stakeholders, especially school board members, administrators, teachers, parents, and community leaders. The team will conduct in-depth individual interviews with district administrators concerning the district's administration, operation, and resource use (which will also be verified by district records). Focus groups are a preferred data collection method for other stakeholders and will allow input from a large number of teachers, parents, and other stakeholders over a short period of time.

At today's meeting, Beatrice and Mark recount for Mary, Fred, and Juan their interview with Deputy Superintendent Torry. According to the deputy superintendent, scheduling focus groups only during the day will limit the participation of teachers without a free period. To participate, those teachers must arrange for someone to cover their classrooms. Fred and Juan report that they received similar information from several school principals. Some parents and other stakeholders will also not be able to participate during the workday. In addition, Mr. George, the middle school principal, told the team last week that approximately 26% of the district's parents speak little or no English. Conducting focus groups only in English will create additional barriers for non-English-speaking stakeholders regardless of the time of day.

In response to the new information, the team focuses on how to maintain evaluation feasibility and support the accuracy, propriety, utility, and accountability of the evaluation. They amended the data collection strategies from the original management plan (F1 Project Management). Beatrice and Juan will conduct some focus groups during the day for teachers, parents, and community stakeholders. Fred and Mark will moderate additional focus groups in the evening for those not able to attend a daytime focus group. Mary and Fred will moderate two additional focus groups for Spanish-speaking parents and for teachers and other stakeholders who are more comfortable communicating in Spanish. The team will continue conducting face-to-face interviews with school board members, the district management team, and school principals.

Mary considers all that is going on in the evaluation and realizes that the forces in play are complicated. She jots down some notes to remind herself what to emphasize for Juan and Mark.

> Commitment to practical procedures is a responsive process (remind Juan and Mark to review P1 Responsive and Inclusive Orientation). For example, today we revised the data collection procedures based on the new information gained from interviews with district administrators about the availability of teachers and stakeholders. To minimize disruption in the classroom and not place an unnecessary and differential burden on teachers or stakeholders, we plan to conduct focus groups both during the day and evening. To be responsive to the needs of non-English-speaking stakeholders we will expand the number of focus groups to include two sessions specifically for Spanish-speaking stakeholders.

At her next opportunity, Mary plans to discuss these issues with Mark and Juan and ask if they think that the team has done enough to ensure the practicality of the procedures, or if not, what else needs to be done.

❖ SUPPORTING DOCUMENTATION

Fitzpatrick, J., Sanders, J., & Worthen, B. (2004). *Program evaluation: Alternative approaches and practical guidelines* (3rd ed.). Boston: Allyn & Bacon.

Johnson, E., Kirkhart, K., Madison, A. M., Noley, G., & Solano-Flores, G. (2008). The impact of narrow views of scientific rigor on evaluation practices for underrepresented groups. In N. Smith & P. Brandon (Eds.), *Fundamental issues in evaluation* (pp. 197–218). New York: Guilford Press.

SenGupta, S., Hopson, R., & Thompson-Robinson, M. (2004). Cultural competence in evaluation: An overview. In M. Thompson-Robinson, R. Hopson, & S. SenGupta (Eds.), *In search of cultural competence in evaluation: Toward principles and practices: New Directions for Evaluation, 102,* 5–19.

Weiss, C. (1998). *Evaluation* (2nd ed.). Upper Saddle River, NJ: Prentice Hall.

Wholey, J. S. (2004). Evaluability assessment. In J. S. Wholey, H. P. Hatry, & K. E. Newcomer (Eds.), *Handbook of practical program evaluation* (2nd ed., pp. 33–66). San Francisco: Jossey-Bass.

F3 Contextual Viability

Evaluations should recognize, monitor, and balance the cultural and political interests and needs of individuals and groups.

❖ RATIONALE AND CLARIFICATION

Contextual factors exert considerable influence on all aspects of evaluations. Economics, status, power, cultural values, and other group and individual factors may interact dynamically with the evaluation to determine its feasibility. These interactions may either support or hinder the evaluation.

Two important categories of such influences are political interests, for example, those related to economics and power, and preexisting systems of values, such as religious or cultural values. Political influences exist at many levels, from the internal dynamics of the local agency or organization to the community, state, and national levels. Typically these influences control the resources, regulations, and other factors that directly affect the program and its evaluation. The second domain of factors affecting contextual viability consists of the background values that individuals and groups bring to the context for the evaluation. These factors may not be directly apparent or recognized, but they can exert both direct effects and indirect influences through individual and group political activities. Culturally competent evaluators will be eager to interact with and learn from individuals and groups about the existing cultural landscape, including cultural politics. Such interactions have the potential to improve the conditions for feasibility and increase evaluation utility, propriety, accuracy, and accountability.

Two primary strategies that evaluators use to improve feasibility in context are to investigate these political and cultural influences and to engage in dynamic communication with individuals and groups. However, sometimes awareness and interaction will be insufficient to overcome preexisting forces and values in opposition to the evaluation. Individuals and groups may engage in direct activity to hinder the evaluation. They can attempt to reduce funding for the program or its evaluation, reduce or eliminate sources of evaluation information, interfere with use of evaluation processes and products, or otherwise interfere with evaluation procedures. At other times, less vocal individuals and groups wait unrecognized and uninvolved in the background. Before the evaluation is completed, they direct attention to the fact that their input was not sought and that their interests have not been included, thus weakening any support for the evaluation. Existing political and cultural conflicts also present special challenges for feasibility because they make communication, understanding, and shared sense-making more difficult. Individuals and groups who stand to benefit from the evaluation may work against one another and undermine the evaluation without directly intending to do so.

Fortunately, individuals and groups often see the value that high quality evaluations can provide. They come together to support the evaluation. Ideally, this alignment takes place without evaluators having to work hard to facilitate it. However, evaluators should always take seriously the possibility that support can erode quickly. Special interests that were not evident in the normal operation of the program may emerge once the evaluation begins. When individuals and interest groups begin to perceive what could happen as a result of the evaluation, they may exert pressures to ensure that the evaluation does not harm them. In other words, preventing the possibility of any harm may be more important than staying open to possible benefits.

Specific procedures can help ensure evaluation feasibility in the face of all these challenges. Early on, the evaluators must learn what individuals or groups value and do not value about the program and its evaluation. They should be alert to opportunities to enlist stakeholder and interest group support. Evaluators should inform themselves as far in advance as possible about developments that could threaten individual and group interests and the success of the evaluation. When individuals or groups pose a threat to feasibility, evaluators should attend to and involve them (P3 Human Rights and Respect, P4 Clarity and Fairness, and P5 Transparency and Disclosure). Evaluators should be sure that the interests of only a few do not dominate to the point that others are not heard, are alienated, or refuse to participate in the evaluation. Individuals and groups that are recognized and believe they can contribute to a fair and useful evaluation are less likely to withhold information or try to block the evaluation. Even when they come from quite different political and cultural perspectives, stakeholders are more likely to endorse an evaluation as long as they are certain that their voices will be heard and that they have the opportunity to directly contribute to the evaluation processes and decision making (P1 Responsive and Inclusive Orientation).

❖ IMPLEMENTING F3 CONTEXTUAL VIABILITY

The following are important recommendations for implementing this standard:

1. Understand the program's cultural, political, and economic contexts by reviewing program materials, budget documents, organizational charts, reports, and news media accounts and by interviewing program staff, program recipients, and key stakeholders.
2. Recognize which individuals and groups have different opinions about the value of the program and its evaluation, and give them repeated opportunities to be heard. Identify key opinions through interviews with program staff and other stakeholders, reviews of prior reports, and program-related documents.
3. Identify and establish communication with key stakeholders to further a balanced understanding of the purposes, benefits, and limitations of the program and the evaluation.
4. Be aware of stakeholders who are not currently involved and encourage them to have a positive impact on the evaluation by providing needed information.
5. Attend to the needs of key stakeholder groups in an equitable manner. Culturally and politically viable evaluations should be inclusive and responsive to the needs of stakeholders.
6. Consider an advisory group to help identify factors that can affect evaluation feasibility. Care should be taken in selecting members of the advisory group to ensure that it is representative of and acceptable to a broad range of stakeholders.
7. Ensure that the evaluation will have access to required data. Access to data may be limited or denied by stakeholders who feel threatened by the evaluation or who do not understand the importance of the data to the evaluation.
8. Keep the evaluation on schedule, or, if that is not possible, negotiate new deadlines. When evaluation processes are delayed and initial results are not made available on time, stakeholders' concerns may increase and the continued feasibility of the evaluation may be in jeopardy.

9. Consider increasing communication with stakeholders and interest groups through the development of a project-related website and the posting of project-related information such as a summary of background information, project status reports, minutes of advisory group meetings, and schedules for upcoming meetings. The project website might also include opportunities for stakeholder inquiry or feedback.

❖ HAZARDS

Some possible hazards with regard to F3 are as follows:

1. Ignoring the program's cultural and political contexts because they seem complicated and difficult
2. Failing to develop an understanding of the multitude of social and political forces associated with the evaluation, such as funding issues, program support, and stakeholder needs and values
3. Responding to the needs of one group of key stakeholders only, thus creating the appearance that the needs of one group are of greater importance than those of other groups
4. Failing to develop culturally competent evaluators to help create effective participation by key stakeholders
5. Jeopardizing evaluation feasibility by failing to provide appropriate mechanisms for key stakeholders to have input in the evaluation

Application Number Three for the Feasibility Scenario

The scenario that supports this application, including background information about the program, context and key players can be read at the end of the Feasibility Overview on page 75.

The evaluation team is conducting its weekly meeting. Agenda items include reviewing the management plan and discussing what progress is being made. The team senses that the plan may need to be updated to reflect the results of interviews with district personnel and the outcome of the first focus group with teachers, parents, and community stakeholders. The importance of maintaining evaluation feasibility and evaluator credibility in the district continues to weigh heavily on the team (U1 Evaluator Credibility). The feasibility and accuracy of the evaluation may be affected negatively if stakeholders will not participate in interviews or focus groups. Currently, rumors are circulating through the district grapevine about the program and service cuts that will result from evaluation findings.

From the beginning of the evaluation, an ongoing issue for the team has been communication with the district. The team is planning additional briefings with the superintendent in response to the distrust of the evaluation expressed by the district personnel at the first meeting. The original plan for just two scheduled meetings at entrance and exit now includes scheduled biweekly meetings to provide updates on the progress of the evaluation and to help build a positive working relationship. At today's team meeting, the focus is again on communication, especially the rumors that are circulating concerning the evaluation. Earlier this week, Mr. George, the middle school principal, reported to Beatrice and Mark during an interview that according to what he had heard, the evaluation team will recommend elimination of some district programs and services including the district's popular middle and high school guitar program.

Beatrice and Mark express their wish that the team rectify the false information making its way through the district's rumor mill. Fred and Juan report they had heard a similar story during their interview with Ms. Todd, an elementary school principal. Fred has an idea about what they could do and relates a similar experience he had during another evaluation in which the team conducted town hall meetings for the purpose of countering false information. After much discussion about the value of town hall meetings and alternate procedures, the team decides to conduct one town hall meeting during the day and a second in the evening to provide information and answer questions about the evaluation. In addition, the team plans ways to reach out to stakeholders not able to attend the public meetings. Beatrice and Mary propose a website for educating Carr County and other districts about the evaluation processes and dispelling the rumors spreading rapidly among other school districts. The website will provide the team a venue for addressing frequently asked questions such as why the Carr County School District is being evaluated. They will post helpful advice, too, such as how to schedule a meeting with a member of the evaluation team or encouraging non-English-speaking parents to provide input in their native languages. The team will also post open meeting schedules and invitations and provide space for comments.

Later, Mary sits down to make notes about things to discuss with Juan and Mark. She notes:

> All evaluations are influenced by the individuals and groups with an interest in the evaluation. In an attempt to maintain evaluation feasibility and to balance the cultural and political interests operating in Carr County School District, we amended the work plan to include town hall meetings and the creation of a website for the posting of evaluation updates. We were concerned that if we did not balance the false information circulating through the district's informal grapevine that personnel and other stakeholders would mistrust us and not participate in the evaluation.

She also made a note to have Mark and Juan review again the four feasibility standards and apply them to the current school district situation. As she reviews her notes, Mary realizes that she should increase the detail in her notes and add them to the evaluation documentation (E1 Evaluation Documentation).

❖ SUPPORTING DOCUMENTATION

Brandon, P. R. (1998). Stakeholder participation for the purpose of helping ensure evaluation validity: Bridging the gap between collaborative and non-collaborative evaluations. *American Journal of Evaluation, 19,* 325–337.

Chelimsky, E. (1995). The political environment of evaluation and what it means for the development of the field. *Evaluation Practice, 16,* 215–225.

Datta, L.-E. (2000). Seriously seeking fairness: Strategies for crafting non-partisan evaluations in a partisan world. *American Journal of Evaluation, 21,* 1–14.

Hood, S. (2005). Culturally responsive evaluation. In S. Mathison (Ed.), *Encyclopedia of evaluation* (pp. 96–100). Thousand Oaks, CA: Sage.

House, E. R., & Howe, K. R. (1999). *Values in evaluation and social research.* Thousand Oaks, CA: Sage.

F4 Resource Use

Evaluations should use resources effectively and efficiently.

❖ RATIONALE AND CLARIFICATION

An effective and efficient evaluation does not consume more resources than necessary to achieve its goals. Effectiveness means achieving the best evaluation possible with the available resources. Efficiency means using resources carefully with as little waste as possible. Achieving the best balance of efficiency and effectiveness requires coordinated attention to both. An emphasis on efficiency alone might result in too large a reduction in quality through attempts to reduce costs. An emphasis on effectiveness alone might result in poor decisions about resource management. Simultaneously balancing effectiveness and efficiency in resource use can help ensure that evaluations will be worth their costs and that sponsors get their money's worth.

Even for experienced evaluators, the right balance of efficiency and effectiveness may be hard to achieve. For example, an evaluation team may be worried about low response rates and engagement levels but still decide to rely on web-based surveys instead of telephone interviews to reduce costs. The risk in this situation is that only certain types of respondents will log on to the survey. In addition, the respondents may be multitasking or for other reasons not paying sufficient attention to the questions (A2 Valid Information). The resulting low response rate and poor attention will produce less valuable information. The point is not that telephone methods are uniformly superior to Web-based methods; they clearly are not. The point is that achieving the right balance of effectiveness and efficiency requires diligent attention to all the pertinent forces at play in each situation.

Achieving a balance in effective and efficient resource use requires planning, good problem-solving, monitoring, and accountability. Sometimes it is necessary to give up some efficiency to gain effectiveness and vice versa. Even with careful planning, uncertainty plays a role in decisions about how to balance effectiveness and efficiency. In many situations, evaluators make decisions with consequences that are not immediately apparent. The benefits from effective resource use can occur at many points in time. Benefits sometimes take place during the evaluation, for example, when the evaluation addresses and contributes to program improvements from one year to the next. Sometimes the evaluation helps potential beneficiaries gain useful information about the program, such as how to qualify for services that they need. Evaluation benefits may also take place after the evaluation is over, for example, when evaluation results are used in later funding cycles to obtain renewed support for the program. Documenting program outcomes may be especially valuable to the program staff whose jobs depend on the program's success. Future program participants will benefit as well if the program is renewed and continues to serve their needs (U2 Attention to Stakeholders, U5 Relevant Information, and U6 Meaningful Processes and Products).

Documenting all the benefits from evaluations is often quite difficult if not impossible. Some benefits are intangible and valued differently by different stakeholders or may come to fruition after systematic monitoring of benefits has stopped. For example, when stakeholders in the evaluation experience high quality evaluation processes, they may learn more about how to use evaluation to improve their performance or other aspects of the organization. The ensuing contributions to organizational learning and to the capacity of the organization to use information for better decision making can have considerable value but be difficult to recognize or identify concretely.

Even when recognized and identified, benefits may be hard to assess. In many situations, evaluators make decisions with consequences that are not immediately apparent. Involving key stakeholders, especially clients and those closest to the program and evaluation, can help evaluators anticipate the ways that specific choices will play out. At minimum, sharing decision making about tough choices regarding effectiveness and efficiency can lead to wider responsibility and ownership for the evaluation. It can also support greater evaluator credibility (U1 Evaluator Credibility and U8 Concern for Consequences and Influence).

An additional challenge to decisions about effectiveness and efficiency is that sometimes one stakeholder's direct cost is another stakeholder's direct benefit. For example, depending on who pays and who benefits, a health insurance program for state employees may be viewed as an unnecessary cost by some policymakers and as a cost-efficient benefit by others. Respondents in an evaluation of the program may therefore view the costs and benefits of their evaluation participation quite differently.

Costs are the total value of all resources used in the evaluation. These include time and human resources (the evaluators, staff, participants, and volunteer workers); financial amounts actually charged; and infrastructure support (equipment, facilities, software, and communications). In addition, costs include the foregone opportunities such as services not provided, materials not purchased, or salaries not paid because money, time, and personnel were applied to the evaluation. For example, the effort and time spent participating in evaluation data collection rather than preparing for class or actually teaching students is an important opportunity cost.

In summary, evaluators should identify the benefits and costs of evaluation, including costs to others, as they strive for balanced effectiveness and efficiency (E1 Evaluation Documentation). Evaluation benefits and effectiveness grow naturally from addressing purposes, goals, and objectives, and from meeting users' needs effectively (U3 Negotiated Purposes, U5 Relevant Information, and U8 Concern for Consequences and Influence). Reflective evaluators monitor whether evaluation uses actually take place, what the actual benefits are, and how they compare to costs (E1 Evaluation Documentation and E2 Internal Metaevaluation).

❖ IMPLEMENTING F4 RESOURCE USE

The following are important recommendations for implementing this standard:

1. Identify all of the important costs related to the evaluation including human resources, equipment, materials, training, and travel, and compare them to the resources available. Remember that volunteers and other negotiated resources may supplement appropriations and fixed resources.
2. Weigh the costs against evaluation quality expected and select the most efficient alternative only when the trade-off with regard to effectiveness is acceptable.
3. Select evaluation procedures producing the greatest benefit if the costs are unaffected or justifiable. Select the least costly approaches when the benefits appear to be equal.
4. Discuss with key stakeholders the benefits and costs of the evaluation so that different views of benefits and costs may be revealed.
5. Take care not to favor the needs of one group of stakeholders over another solely on the basis of costs. Cost-benefit determinations must be considered along with propriety considerations (P1 Responsive and Inclusive Orientation).

❖ HAZARDS

Some possible hazards with regard to F4 are as follows:

1. Failing to consider the benefits as well as the cost when considering stakeholder participation in evaluation procedures

2. Focusing solely on the total cost of the evaluation rather than on the costs of selected procedures and components
3. Failing to recognize that increasing culturally competent practices in evaluation can be a cost-reduction strategy
4. Failing to document the evaluation costs that accrue to the program itself as a result of the evaluation, such as program staff time required to participate in interviews or respond to data requests
5. Failing to utilize existing data and systems when they are well-aligned with the evaluation purposes
6. Collecting data that do not align with the evaluation purposes or stakeholders' needs

Application Number Four for the Feasibility Scenario

The scenario that supports this application, including background information about the program, context, and key players, can be read at the end of the Feasibility Overview on page 75.

Throughout their planning for the evaluation of the Carr County School District, the evaluation team has focused on the effective and efficient use of resources. For example, the team's deliberation and final selection of data collection procedures is focused on whether specific procedures such as surveys, face-to-face interviews, or focus groups are practical for the evaluation context, will increase feasibility, and will support the accuracy, propriety, utility, and accountability of the evaluation.

To help the team compare the costs of the three potential data collection strategies, Mark and Juan prepare a table listing the likely costs related to each procedure. Under project costs, they include the resources which would be required by the team to develop and conduct each method. These costs included the team's travel time, transportation costs, lodging and per diem, meeting space and materials, recording equipment, expenses related to advertising the meetings, and data analysis. In reviewing the table, Mary notices that Juan and Mark have listed each of the items as a cost to the project, but they have not recognized that some of the items will result in a cost to the district or other stakeholders. After they discuss this issue, Juan and Mark expand the table to show which of the items will be a cost to others as well as the evaluation. To help Mark and Juan get a better understanding of the concept of cost to others, Mary inquires whether there will be any costs for the school district related to mailing, such as processing address labels or e-mail addresses. Juan knows that the team will need to obtain address labels from the school district if the team conducts a mailed survey so in the Cost to Whom column he lists the district as well as the project. Mary also mentions the participation of teachers and stakeholders in focus groups. Juan remembers that Superintendent Ruck told the team that teachers who participate in a focus group during the day will be required to arrange for someone to cover their classroom, unless they can use a planning period. Juan adds teachers to the Cost to Whom column. Mark also adds focus group respondents to the Cost to Whom column since their participation will result in costs if they have to take time off from work, hire a babysitter, or pay for transportation. A focus group will also represent an opportunity cost to participants because they will forego the opportunity to do something else of value.

When Mark and Juan present the information to the team, Fred raises several questions related to project costs that are not addressed in the table. Fred wants to know what value focus groups bring to the project and if the value is worth the additional time and costs to the project and to focus group participants. He raises similar questions about the value of conducting face-to-face interviews with every school administrator. Fred also wants to know if the cost in evaluation time and personnel to conduct and analyze the information is an effective and efficient use of resources. Mary reminds the team that the selection of procedures should not be based on costs alone but should be weighed against other factors such as the benefits from a useful, proper, accurate, and accountable evaluation. Mary asks the team to consider whether a more expensive procedure that allows participation by stakeholders with a different perspective should take precedence over a less expensive procedure. Mary also wants the team to consider the value of more expensive alternatives, such as the use of culturally competent evaluators to conduct focus groups for Spanish-speaking stakeholders, the conduct of focus groups in the evening for working parents who might have a different opinion about the value of after-school programs than parents with more flexible daytime schedules, or the conduct of individual interviews of parents of homebound children.

After the meeting, Mary sits at her desk and stares out the window. Trying to mentor Juan and Mark is leading to insights and changing her reflections about the evaluation. She has always been a reflective practitioner who needs time to think about the evaluation work to avoid missteps. However, trying to reflect from the perspective of Juan and Mark has also been beneficial to her. She noticed in the last meeting that Mark and Juan are developing additional trust in their own ideas and reflections about the evaluation. She thinks about the learning they demonstrated in the last meeting. For example, they understood that efficiency and effectiveness do not always complement each other in evaluation. The use of an online survey in Carr County School District might be the most efficient data collection procedure; however, it would not be the most effective use of resources or support contextual viability. The team's decision to use face-to-face interviews and focus groups for this evaluation, while more costly to the evaluation, probably represents a more effective use of resources. She expects the interviews to produce more in-depth information about the district's programs and services. The focus groups should allow a wider and more varied group of stakeholders to participate in the evaluation process.

Mary's thoughts go back to her mentoring of Juan and Mark. In many ways, this has not been a model evaluation. The stakeholders in the school district were really not well integrated into the original planning for the evaluation. Mary begins to jot down the standards that were not attended to in the original planning. For example, it appears that the purpose for the evaluation was conceptualized in response to needs at the state level. Did anyone consider the needs of the school district leadership and personnel? Mary makes a note to call Juan and Mark's attention to U2 Attention to Stakeholders and P1 Responsive and Inclusive Orientation. She also wonders whether the information they are collecting will be relevant to plans and decisions at the district level. She jots down U5 Relevant Information and U8 Concern for Consequences and Influence. She wonders whose values are driving the decisions that were made about the design and methods for the evaluation and thinks about U4 Explicit Values.

Without a doubt, they still have obstacles ahead. If they cannot repair some of the damage that was done and get their local stakeholders to see value to them from the evaluation, the accuracy of the evaluation may be in jeopardy. Mary notes: P4 Clarity and Fairness, A1 Justified Conclusions and Decisions, and A2 Valid Information.

Mary considers the evaluation team's responsibilities. She knows that evaluations like this one still go forward to fulfill statutory obligations, even when they begin in precarious circumstances with less than adequate attention to the needs of all stakeholders or to conflicts of interests. Even in these difficult circumstances, she and the team are responsible for the quality and accountability of their work. She thinks about the most recent version of *The Program Evaluation Standards* and its focus on evaluation accountability. She resolves to talk tomorrow with her team about the need to conduct rigorous formative metaevaluation of their evaluation. It might lead to improvements, and if nothing else, it would give the stakeholders who have felt excluded from the evaluation's design an opportunity to be heard. Perhaps they need the perspective of a third party as well. She thinks about a colleague who is a practicing evaluator in a neighboring state and has an interest in metaevaluation and evaluation accountability. She picks up the phone to give her boss a call. Maybe he would like to authorize an unbiased external metaevaluative consultation for improvement purposes. The budget has 10% to cover unexpected problems, but that will not go far if there are other emergencies. Nevertheless, she thinks that a few hours from an external metaevaluator reviewing the current evaluation situation would be money well spent.

❖ SUPPORTING DOCUMENTATION

Davidson, E. J. (2005). *Evaluation methodology basics: The nuts and bolts of sound evaluation.* Thousand Oaks, CA: Sage.

Henry, G., & Mark, M. M. (2003). Beyond use: Understanding evaluation's influence on attitudes and actions. *American Journal of Evaluation, 24,* 293–314.

Hood, S. (2001). Nobody knows my name: In praise of african american evaluators who were responsive. In J. C. Greene & T. A. Abma (Eds.), *Responsive evaluation: New Directions for Evaluation, 92,* 31–43.

Kirkhart, K. (2000). Reconceptualizing evaluation use: An integrated theory of influence. In V. Caracelli & H. Preskill (Eds.), *The expanding scope of evaluation use: New Directions for Evaluation, 88,* 5–23.

Nelson-Barber, S., LaFrance, J., Trumbull, E., & Aburto, S. (2005). Promoting culturally reliable and valid evaluation practice. In S. Hood, R. Hopson, & H. Frierson (Eds.), *The role of culture and cultural context: A mandate for inclusion, the discovery of truth, and understanding in evaluative theory and practice* (pp. 61–85). Greenwich, CT: Information Age.

Part III

Propriety Standards

STANDARD STATEMENTS

P1 Responsive and Inclusive Orientation	*Evaluations should be responsive to stakeholders and their communities.*
P2 Formal Agreements	*Evaluation agreements should be negotiated to make obligations explicit and take into account the needs, expectations, and cultural contexts of clients and other stakeholders.*
P3 Human Rights and Respect	*Evaluations should be designed and conducted to protect human and legal rights and maintain the dignity of participants and other stakeholders.*
P4 Clarity and Fairness	*Evaluations should be understandable and fair in addressing stakeholder needs and purposes.*
P5 Transparency and Disclosure	*Evaluations should provide complete descriptions of findings, limitations, and conclusions to all stakeholders, unless doing so would violate legal and propriety obligations.*
P6 Conflicts of Interests	*Evaluations should openly and honestly identify and address real or perceived conflicts of interests that may compromise the evaluation.*
P7 Fiscal Responsibility	*Evaluations should account for all expended resources and comply with sound fiscal procedures and processes.*

❖ PROPRIETY OVERVIEW

Propriety refers to what is proper, fair, legal, right, acceptable, and just in evaluations. Propriety includes three overlapping domains:

1. The evaluators' and participants' ethical rights, responsibilities, and duties
2. Systems of laws, regulations, and rules
3. The roles and duties inherent in evaluation professional practice

These domains are important in their own right and also complement the other evaluation attributes: utility, feasibility, accuracy, and accountability.

Ethics

Ethics encompasses concerns about the rights, responsibilities, and behaviors of evaluators and evaluation stakeholders. All people have innate rights that should be respected and recognized (P3 Human Rights and Respect). For instance, the Universal Declaration of Human Rights, adopted by the General Assembly of the United Nations in 1948, proclaims that every individual and organization must strive to protect and respect rights and freedoms of all.

For some citizens, free speech, religious freedom, and other fundamental human rights are constitutionally guaranteed. However, constitutionally guaranteed rights are not universal in all societies and are not universally implemented across all levels of societies, even when constitutionally guaranteed. Some evaluators may falsely assume that their experienced rights are the norm in every evaluation context where they practice. Such unwarranted assumptions can lead to serious problems. At minimum, evaluators should understand individuals' basic rights in the specific evaluation settings where they practice. For example, they should be knowledgeable about stakeholders' experienced rights related to privacy, informed consent, confidentiality, access to information, and participation (or not) in evaluations. In addition, they should be aware of how their understanding of ethical principles and ethical realities influences their evaluation practices in these settings. In settings where the experienced rights of stakeholders are severely diminished, evaluators must act with the greatest care as they determine if proper evaluations are possible (F3 Contextual Viability).

Ethical issues are not confined to one specific time in the evaluation process, nor are they only relevant to the evaluator. They require responsive evaluation processes from the design through dissemination stages and are important to users of the evaluation and other stakeholders across these stages. Ethical issues are also intimate, personal, and reflexive. At various stages in the process, proper evaluations require repeated reexamination of individual and group values. Evaluators, clients, sponsors, users, and other stakeholders have responsibility for acknowledging unique entr e and access issues, as well as particular community mores, habits, and customs that determine suitable conduct in the evaluation process. Stakeholders should also be sensitive to the roles of both the tacit and explicit processes in local and global community contexts. By definition, tacit processes are ones that few if any are aware of unless they can be examined and made explicit. Tacit along with explicit processes are important in part because they control how individuals or groups gain permission to participate; receive and access documents; respond to evidence and needs for evidence, and understand and implement privacy, confidentiality, and anonymity.

Legal Contexts for Evaluation

Laws and rules that regulate the conduct of people and organizations set the context for evaluations. Evaluations should be consistent with local, state, and federal laws. When local, state, or federal laws conflict with one another, or when laws in one stakeholder jurisdiction conflict with those in another, evaluations may require legal counsel to proceed. Evaluations in settings where adherence to laws or regulations can lead to violations of human rights are particularly difficult. The propriety standards can be helpful in these situations (Especially P2 Formal Agreement, P3 Human Rights and Respect, P5 Transparency and Disclosure, P6 Conflicts of Interests, and P7 Fiscal Responsibility). Legal counsel is recommended in situations where the evaluator, the stakeholders, or the propriety of the evaluation may be in jeopardy.

Many evaluations are also governed by specific regulations. For instance, institutional review board requirements regulate research with human subjects. Evaluators based in institutions of higher education, as well as those receiving federal funding in the United States, follow appropriate codes and regulations that relate to the treatment of human subjects[1]. These regulations have been promulgated by sixteen federal agencies that conduct, support, or regulate research involving human subjects.

When evaluators are adequately aware of legal and regulatory requirements and culturally determined norms and customs, they will be better positioned to delineate roles and responsibilities and ensure participants' rights

---

1. For example, Title 45 Part 46 of the Code of Federal Regulations, adopted in 1991 by the Federal Policy for the Protection of Human Subjects.

in the evaluation process (P2 Formal Agreements and P3 Human Rights and Respect). Formal agreements can take several forms. For example, memoranda of agreement (MOA) are binding agreements (written documents or other culturally determined ways of enforcing obligation) that guide the conduct of participants and people involved in the evaluation. Proper evaluations ensure that MOA and other binding agreements exist in valid formulations for the cultural contexts of the involved parties.

Professionalism in Evaluation

Professionalism in the service of propriety requires dynamic knowledge of appropriate standards and principles combined with an understanding of contextual elements that further stakeholder benefit, dignity, and self-worth. Professional evaluators have a duty to employ best standards of evaluation practice and processes (P1 Responsive and Inclusive Orientation, P3 Human Rights and Respect, and P6 Fiscal Responsibility).

In addition to this work of the Joint Committee on Standards for Educational Evaluation (JCSEE), a major contribution to professional guidelines for evaluators in North America is the American Evaluation Association's (AEA) *Guiding Principles for Evaluators.* Three of the five principles presented there are particularly relevant to propriety: Respect for People, Honesty and Integrity, and Responsibilities for General and Public Welfare. These three offer guidance for decision making based on the best interests of respondents, program participants, clients, and other evaluation stakeholders. The *Guiding Principles,* in combination with the Propriety Standards, honor a diverse range of concerns, including support for the broader societal and social justice issues beyond those of powerful and influential stakeholders, whose interests may overshadow those of the less enfranchised, powerful, or privileged. Other national organizations sponsoring members on the JCSEE also produce standards and guidelines that contribute to professionalism in evaluation. Additional information is available in the documentation for these standards as well as at http://www.jcsee.org.

The Program Evaluation Standards are North American standards but address evaluation professionalism as it becomes increasingly global in scope. In part, this global perspective results naturally from collegial exchange, the training of evaluators from other contexts in North America, and North American evaluators' practice and experiences in other areas of the world. In addition, other regions and nations have developed or adopted professional guidelines and standards that help describe the responsibilities of professional evaluators. For instance, the Australasian Evaluation Society, the African Evaluation Association, the European Evaluation Society, and the numerous country level societies and organizations have developed modifications of these or their own guidelines and standards. Just as with the *Program Evaluation Standards* and the *Guiding Principles,* these standards and guidelines specify professional responsibilities for evaluators.

As described in these standards and guidelines, professional responsibilities include operating with dynamic knowledge of basic human needs and liberties. Professional evaluators should anticipate and prevent procedures, data, or processes threatening the legal, ethical, or other human rights of those parties involved in evaluations (P1 Responsive and Inclusive Orientation, P3 Human Rights and Respect, and P6 Conflicts of Interests). In particular, professional evaluators should be able to understand and address the needs of the least powerful in society without jeopardizing their safety and well-being (P6 Conflicts of Interests). They should also be prepared to consider how, how intensely, and in what settings they should advocate for the disadvantaged and powerless. Professional principles related to inclusion, dialogue, and deliberation between and among evaluators and stakeholders are especially relevant in settings where evaluation can be a method for democratizing public decisions. In the final analysis, professional principles and the actions of professionals should also withstand the critical examination of those whose lives they affect.

Summary

In summary, propriety standards help ensure that ethical, legal, and professional considerations guide respectful and equitable conduct and just and fair interactions in evaluations. The ethical, legal, and professional considerations embedded in the propriety standards emphasize that the welfare of stakeholders is paramount. Propriety considerations encourage evaluations that serve all stakeholders, protect their rights and dignity, and identify and eliminate damaging conflicts of interest, especially where values are in conflict. The core worth of propriety standards depends on how well they are implemented in evaluations and their contexts.

❖ PROPRIETY SCENARIO

In order to illustrate how the propriety standards can be used, each of the following individual standards concludes with a brief application based on the scenario below. The individual applications provide a coherent introduction to the standards in the context of real world evaluation dilemmas. The applications are not intended to represent best practices. Rather, they illustrate sound responses to important evaluation dilemmas or demands. Reviewing the circumstances in the scenario below, evaluators and evaluation users will think of other appropriate and alternative actions depending on the specific standards that are emphasized. Evaluation practice is complex, and the standards work in tandem with evaluators' and users' knowledge, values, and experiences to affect decision making.

The section below introduces a specific case scenario as the context for the individual applications. It includes the general characteristics of the program being evaluated and the principal players and their roles. The individual applications will present specific dilemmas as experienced by these principal players, analyses of how individual standards are related to the dilemmas, strategies used to respond to and implement the standards, and other standards that might come into play given the specific dilemmas. This scenario and subsequent applications are selected to highlight dilemmas and reflective practices typical for many programs and program evaluations across a wide variety of fields and applications.

Evaluation of the Helping Ourselves Promote Engagement (HOPE) Program

A pilot social program, Helping Ourselves Promote Engagement (HOPE), is initiating an evaluation to address its core practices and program efforts over the last two years. The HOPE program operates in a large metropolitan area (River City) with a proud and distinguished history of hardworking citizens and economic accomplishment. The diverse population, largely of European ancestry, is dispersed in a host of neighborhoods in the urban region. A growing population of African Americans is predominately the result of in-migration from other states spurred by changes in working-class employment patterns in the last half of the twentieth century. Other ethnic and racial groups live in the larger region, but in very small numbers.

Some key individuals in the HOPE program and its evaluation are as follows:

- Jonah McArthur, the HOPE executive director, is a lifelong resident of the community. He worked his way through college and over time has completed both an MSW and an MBA. His family includes a wife, two birth children, and three foster children, all attending public schools. His wife teaches elementary school, and both have extended family in the greater region. Jonah is a creative and flexible thinker and very skilled socially. He is the main facilitator of the small and large group processes at the heart of the HOPE program and uses various modes of art (poems, music, photographs, and other visual media) to initiate dialogue in those groups addressing the environment, economic disparity, ethnic and racial discrimination, and the other specific topics.

- Kwame Jones completed his PhD in sociology with a specialty in social research methodology at the state university of an adjoining state. Other than the time he spent in college on the East Coast and his graduate study, he is a lifelong resident of River City. He feels especially grateful to have found his ideal job in his former hometown. Now that he is a tenured professor of applied social science methodology at the university, he has the autonomy to pick and choose the evaluation work that he wants. He is very committed to mentoring and coaching the next generations of evaluators now in graduate school because he deeply believes that communities and societies can improve through well-designed and evaluated programs that serve the public good. While he is quite competent in quantitative methodologies, over the years Kwame has specialized more and more in qualitative, naturalistic, and interpretive methods. In complex communities, these skills seem to help him get closer to the factors that most need to be understood.

- Dawn Williams is a graduate student in the university's applied social research methodology program. She has taken one graduate course in program evaluation and is planning to take several more. Professor Jones is her academic advisor and research assistantship supervisor. In addition, she expects that he will direct her dissertation research project next year after she completes her comprehensive exams this semester and is admitted to candidacy. Dawn grew up in a major metropolitan area, which she misses, but has found that River City also fascinates her and has its own endearing cultures.

- Nina Sarapova has an MS in quantitative methods from the state university and is a multiyear employee of River City Research Incorporated (RCRI). She is a trusted employee, a no-nonsense, direct colleague who always says things the way she sees them, and is very diligent and hardworking. She has an adult daughter in another state and has lived in River City for the last 10 years. Nina doesn't really differentiate research from evaluation and is largely unaware of professional issues in evaluation that are not also present in research. Her primary interests are in constructing high-quality data collection instruments and in generating findings that provide defensible answers to research questions.

- Hanna Berkowitz has a PhD in educational psychology and research from the state university, where she specialized in mixed methodologies. She had a research assistantship in the survey research center at the university and conducted her PhD ethnographic field work in a Catholic school not far from Nairobi. Hanna is gracious, but energetic and driven. She is clearly ambitious but enjoys working with Nina and respects her experience and advice.

- River City Research Incorporated (RCRI) is the creation of two university professors who established it more than 20 years ago to meet the needs of the local region for high quality, nonmarketing research for various civic and industrial purposes. Over the years as demands for their services have increased, the firm has added staff and developed its own strong reputation for high quality research services.

The broad aim of the HOPE program is to promote ethical and civic leadership in diverse urban and suburban communities. In particular, HOPE is designed to encourage a more engaged and reflective public, one that is committed to creating and connecting communities and neighborhoods across differences and diversity. To do this, HOPE solicits racially and ethnically diverse volunteers from churches, civic and community groups, public agencies, schools, and other organizations. These volunteers participate in group meetings over a seven-session period. Afterwards, participants make a commitment to participate in some new and demonstrable civic or social activity. These activities are intended to contribute to a new spirit of engagement and civic discourse addressing troubling issues in the city and region.

The HOPE program is especially relevant because of increasing social, racial, ethnic, and economic tensions that have beset the metropolitan area and region as the economy has declined over the last several years. This trend is defined by an unemployment rate higher than the national average, complaints by civic leaders about escalating gang violence, perceptions of privilege and inequity based on racial discrimination in workplaces, and growing gentrification in urban neighborhoods of color. The decreased social cohesion and declining social capital appear to be hurting the city's and the region's ability to keep or attract families, businesses, and cultural assets. This is taking place at a time when the number of people in the area is remaining constant and the availability of human resources for civic action should be at an all-time high. The broad diversity of perspectives and abilities in the area should provide powerful resources for community development. Regardless of their problems, with adequate leadership these communities have the potential for growth and transformation.

Based on facilitative discussions at initial meetings with leaders, Jonah comes to understand that the primary concern to be addressed by a HOPE program evaluation is the many possible intended and unintended effects on participants and their communities. He also hopes the evaluation can help guide his decision making on how best to sustain these dialogues and further develop the program within the city and beyond. Jonah decides to test the waters to see what ideas practicing evaluators might have about how to conduct the evaluation. He wants to solicit evaluation proposals from a diverse group of practicing evaluators, so he drafts a request for proposals with an emphasis on documenting how the program is working; what changes, if any, have occurred in participants; and the extent to which the program has been influential in participants' communities.

After receiving comments, recommendations, and proposals from a host of potential evaluators, Jonah and the board of directors evaluate the proposed evaluations and hire a team of evaluators made up of people from the nearby regional university and a local research firm, River City Research Incorporated (RCRI). Professor Kwame Jones, PhD, will lead the team with the assistance of a graduate student, Dawn Williams. Two additional colleagues on the evaluation team, Nina Sarapova and Hanna Berkowitz, represent RCRI. This is the first time that either the university team or the local research firm team has collaborated with an external team in an evaluation project. However, Hanna and Kwame have met at a social occasion at the university and all three have considerable professional respect for one another.

P1 Responsive and Inclusive Orientation

Evaluations should be responsive to stakeholders and their communities.

❖ RATIONALE AND CLARIFICATION

Responsive evaluations attend to and engage with the needs and characteristics of stakeholders and their contexts. Responsiveness is not just an orientation to individuals or groups but also requires attention to the setting and context features that help shape the evaluation and its purposes (U3 Negotiated Purposes). Inclusiveness is complementary to responsiveness and refers to the breadth of involvement of stakeholders. Inclusive evaluations recognize all, not just a small group of, stakeholders and their needs, backgrounds, and contexts. Thus an evaluation that is responsive to a few stakeholders and context features might not be adequately inclusive. Similarly, an evaluation could recognize many stakeholders and context features at an overly superficial level and not be adequately responsive.

Responsive and inclusive evaluation processes have wide-reaching ethical and moral consequences and can also serve to increase utility, feasibility, accuracy, and accountability. Because they require some degree of independent effort and resources, responsiveness and inclusiveness exist in dynamic tension. In any specific situation, evaluators and stakeholders must make decisions about the degrees of responsiveness and inclusion to achieve. They might come to different conclusions about the right balance based on the purposes of the evaluation, resource availability, or other factors. If evaluations were only concerned about the practical value of responsiveness and inclusiveness, then decisions about this balance would be based on what was necessary to achieve the optimum blend for feasibility, utility, accuracy, and accountability. For example, some settings and purposes might require limiting one or the other to achieve feasibility.

Standard P1 calls attention to the moral and professional duty for a responsive and inclusive evaluation orientation. In other words, attending to stakeholders and their contexts is not just a practical value but is also a moral and professional duty. This standard recognizes that in a democratic society, stakeholders should be included and attended to regardless of their politics, status, or power. Evaluations should be as inclusive as possible because it is one of the basic values of a democratic society. At the same time, as an evaluation orientation, Standard P1 recognizes practical limitations imposed by circumstances. It does not require that all stakeholders receive equal attention or be included to an equal degree. Rather it emphasizes systematic and transparent attention to who is included, to what extent and how they are included, and who receives the most attention (P5 Transparency and Disclosure). There is a minimum level of responsiveness and inclusion required for this moral imperative to be met, but that level may differ from situation to situation. Reflection and care are necessary to determine how to implement this requirement in each particular case.

Responsive and inclusive evaluation designs, practices, and procedures also help evaluators develop fair and equitable relationships with stakeholders. They lessen the danger that powerful stakeholders' questions and interests will dominate while the perspectives, needs, or interests of others are ignored. It is the moral duty of the evaluator to design evaluations that provide multiple opportunities for participants to be involved, contribute, and be heard within the limits imposed by resources or other legitimate contextual constraints (U2 Attention to Stakeholders).

Additionally, this standard presumes a social justice perspective that furthers the development of democratic and other adaptive institutions and procedures. As human resources for a society, all stakeholders serve important functions. When evaluations are inclusive and responsive, they empower stakeholders to function as skilled participants in democratic institutions even beyond the actual evaluation itself. This process use of evaluation is not just valuable because it increases utility but also because it is a moral good. In addition, stakeholders may become better and more informed participants and consumers of evaluation. They may become better equipped to ask and answer questions, make better-informed decisions, and contribute to their communities and societies at large.

Responsive and inclusive evaluations also address relationships between and among stakeholders and between the evaluators and evaluation users or other stakeholders. Such evaluations deliberately serve the welfare of others without regard to status. Over time, responsive and inclusive processes may reveal important aspects of culture, power, and control embedded in the evaluation context. Thus, intended and actual participants, their communities, and their organizations will grow to expect these evaluations to attend to their values, interests, and contexts, leading perhaps to greater expectations for democratic quality in other interactions.

Deliberative and democratic designs presume that the interests of all stakeholders and groups of stakeholders and the procedures that address them are dynamic. In keeping with this dynamism, sometimes inclusive procedures must be frequent and intense. For example, one open meeting or town hall may not be enough. Repeated opportunities and venues may be required for stakeholders to recognize the sincerity of the evaluators in seeking input. In addition, evaluators can adjust their schedules to the needs of stakeholders through open opportunities for dialogue and interaction. In the final analysis, a responsive and inclusive orientation helps stakeholders make their own judgments and interpretations in the context of awareness of and attentiveness to the full community of stakeholders and their needs and perspectives.

Responsive and inclusive evaluations do not appear arbitrary or capricious to stakeholders (F3 Contextual Viability and F2 Practical Procedures). They do not exacerbate oppression, discrimination, power differences or other imbalances. Instead, whenever possible, they attempt to interrupt such forces so as to contribute to improved democratic functioning and social betterment. When the inclusive and responsive evaluation orientation is well articulated and implemented, stakeholder groups and communities find that their involvement, experiences, and input are more likely to translate via equitable democratic processes into the evaluation purposes, questions, methods, analyses, and findings. They can then accept these for their moral quality as well as their practical value (U3 Negotiated Purposes, U6 Meaningful Processes and Procedures, and A1 Justified Conclusions and Decisions).

❖ IMPLEMENTING P1 RESPONSIVE AND INCLUSIVE ORIENTATION

The following are important recommendations for implementing this standard:

1. Identify stakeholders broadly, gather useful information from them, and include them in decisions about the purposes, questions, and design of the evaluation, so that they recognize the opportunity to participate as both a right and responsibility.

2. Be open to contradictory views, interests, and beliefs regarding data, knowledge, and contexts that are influenced by the culture, prior history, and situations at the local level of the program.

3. Respect and attend to the local settings and maintain an understanding of the program that is fully in tune with the program settings in which participants live and function (F2 Practical Procedures).

4. Make deliberate attempts to build meaningful relationships and contribute to the evaluation process by including groups that have been historically disenfranchised, for example, on the basis of gender, race, culture, ethnicities, sexual orientation, economic status, or disability.
5. Get to know the stakeholders and the local settings, history, significant events, culture, and other factors affecting the program and its evaluation.
6. Strive for an appropriate balance of responsiveness and inclusiveness given stakeholders' needs and the available resources in the evaluation setting.

❖ HAZARDS

Some possible hazards with regard to P1 are as follows:

1. Designing evaluations that intentionally favor certain stakeholders in powerful positions or that discriminate against certain participants and groups
2. Allowing the needs of the evaluation staff and team to interfere with effective responses to the interests of other stakeholders
3. Always favoring a specific evaluation method or approach without proper regard for the needs of the actual stakeholders in the current setting and the purposes of the evaluation (A5 Information Management and A6 Sound Designs and Analyses)
4. Not attending adequately to context or culture in evaluation designs and practices (A6 Sound Designs and Analyses)
5. Encouraging thinking and models that focus on the deficits or liabilities of individuals and their cultures rather than on their assets or strengths (U6 Meaningful Processes and Products and A2 Valid Information)
6. Ignoring or minimizing the political vibrancy and inherent value of stakeholder positions and value judgments (F2 Practical Procedures and F3 Contextual Viability)

Application Number One for the Propriety Case Scenario

The scenario that supports this application, including background information about the program, context, and key players, can be read at the end of the Propriety Overview on page 110.

The HOPE evaluation team develops a time line to conduct the evaluation and begins with a series of internal evaluation team meetings to clarify the intent of the evaluation. The purpose of the HOPE evaluation is to document the effects of the program on participants and their communities (U2 Attention to Stakeholders). As meetings of the evaluation team occur, the aims of the evaluation appear more complicated and potentially more far-reaching. Considering the recent escalating social, racial, ethnic, and economic tensions in the regions' neighborhoods and communities, the team is especially interested in ensuring that there is sufficient stakeholder and community ownership of the evaluation. As discussions among team members unfold, they approach agreement that the evaluation should address how programs like HOPE can encourage dialogue across communities. They hope the evaluation might serve as a catalyst to bring divergent community groups together in ways that can encourage productive dialogue rarely realized in the region.

In order to understand the program better, the internal evaluation team arranges for occasional meetings with Jonah, the HOPE executive director. Jonah's participation is central to developing a working knowledge of the program and its logic. As potential evaluation questions are developed within the team, they are frequently vetted with Jonah in an attempt to gain a better understanding of agency needs and expectations (U3 Negotiated Purposes). In response to a suggestion by Jonah, Kwame and Dawn agree to become participant-observers in group sessions during the next 7-week period. This will give the team an inside view of group dynamics and the range of topics explored, as well as more familiarity with the concerns and intentions of individual members of the group. It will also be a way to establish rapport between the stakeholders and the evaluation team.

In keeping with good ethnographic and fieldwork principles, the team tries not to overstep perceived boundaries as participant-observers or evaluators. Since they intend to write up their evaluation work for eventual presentation and publication, the team is careful to implement the research requirements and protections for research participants established by their local university's institutional review board (IRB).

As a result of e-mail correspondence with Jonah about evaluation purposes and possible questions (U3 Negotiated Purposes), the team of evaluators settles on two evaluation questions that resonate with Jonah and his executive board. The first question asks to what extent HOPE is making a difference in the lives of participants and their communities. According to Jonah, HOPE wants to know what changes occur in the lives of participants who attend dialogue sessions, what relationships are created, and if participation occurs beyond the sessions. Kwame recalls one pivotal meeting early on when Jonah stood up and wondered, "Do our practices and activities make a difference or are we, too, part of the problem?"

The second evaluation question is how the core practices of the program address conversations and discussions about civic and social engagement. Here, HOPE staff members and the board are interested in knowing if the unique practices that they are using involving art, self-reflection, and other group practices made the participants more accepting of social change. Do these unique practices spark dialogue beyond the group and really provide opportunities for reflection to citizens and groups who want to make a difference in their communities?

Jonah and Kwame schedule a meeting to be sure that these questions reflect the needs of most stakeholders in the program, not just those who designed it. In addition, Kwame is concerned that their evaluation processes may not have been inclusive enough because, at least initially, too few community members were involved in reviewing the questions. Kwame and Jonah discuss the potential conflicts of interests that Kwame and the evaluation team have with regard to trying to collect information that is responsive to the needs of clients and stakeholders but that also provide information for professional presentations and publications (P6 Conflicts of Interests). In particular, some members of the evaluation team who bring solid methodological skills have much more experience with research projects than evaluation projects. For example, in one meeting both Nina and Hanna seemed not to be able to differentiate how methods need to be responsive to stakeholders in evaluation settings as distinct from research settings. Kwame resolves to discuss these matters with stakeholders and members of the evaluation team.

Kwame is confident that they have been sufficiently responsive and inclusive for the beginning stage of an evaluation. He believes that the purposes of the evaluation have been well formulated (U3 Negotiated Purposes and U5 Relevant Information). However, the evaluation is just getting started, and they will need to monitor their responsiveness and inclusiveness on a regular basis and maintain procedures that engage stakeholders regularly. Jonah and Kwame discuss how they want to do this. Kwame agrees to discuss this further with the evaluation team.

❖ SUPPORTING DOCUMENTATION

Frierson, H., Hood, S., & Hughes, G. B. (2002). Strategies that address culturally responsive evaluations. In J. Frechtling (Ed.), *The 2002 user-friendly handbook for project evaluation.* (NSF 02–057). Arlington, VA: National Science Foundation, Directorate for Education and Human Resources.

Greene, J. C. (2006). Evaluation, democracy, and social change. In I. F. Shaw, J. C. Greene, & M. M. Mark, (Eds.), *The Sage handbook of evaluation* (pp. 102–122). London: Sage.

Greene, J. C., & Abma, T. A. (Eds.). (2001). *Responsive evaluation: New Directions for Evaluation, 92.*

House, E. R., & Howe, K. R. (1998). The issue of advocacy in evaluation. *American Journal of Evaluation, 19,* 233–236.

Mertens, D. M. (2005). *Research and evaluation in education and psychology: Integrating diversity with quantitative, qualitative, and mixed methods* (2nd ed.). Thousand Oaks, CA: Sage.

Stake, R. E. (1971 October). Program evaluation, particularly responsive evaluation. Keynote address at the conference "New Trends in Evaluation," Institute of Education, University of Göteborg, Sweden.

Stake, R. E. (1986). *Quieting reform: Social science and social action in an urban youth program.* Urbana: University of Illinois Press.

P2 Formal Agreements

Evaluation agreements should be negotiated to make obligations explicit and take into account the needs, expectations, and cultural contexts of clients and other stakeholders.

P2 Formal Agreements

❖ RATIONALE AND CLARIFICATION

In general, formal agreements are part of the fabric that binds us as societies to the rule of law. Such agreements can facilitate greater stability, efficiency, and predictability. They provide protection from unfounded allegations and encourage explicit identification of the responsibilities of all involved parties. They often regulate the use of resources, fiduciary responsibilities, and other obligations.

Formal evaluation agreements are binding contracts between evaluators and parties for whom the evaluation is conducted. They specify obligations, such as what is to be done, how, by whom, and when. They are useful for focusing and planning the actual evaluation and for holding all parties accountable. Formal agreements often specify communication, management, and reporting plans that outline for clients and evaluators the details of the evaluation. The process of developing written agreements provides evaluators and clients the opportunity to review and clarify their respective rights, responsibilities, and expectations.

When they are developed with mutual respect and confidence, formal evaluation agreements serve to aid communication, provide the basis for understanding, clarify the interests of involved parties, and regulate evaluation processes. Clearly articulated formal agreements are also likely to aid the design, scope, and cost calculations for the intended evaluation (F1 Project Management).

Typically, formal evaluation agreements are written. However, oral obligations and agreements can also be legitimate. In certain cultural contexts where oral agreements are expected or in particular circumstances where only oral obligations are possible, credible witnesses or shared recordings can vouch for the negotiated stipulations.

Evaluation agreements can range from the simple to the quite complex. They can vary with regard to the number and the roles of people who are involved, for example, sponsors, staff members, clients, participants, and other stakeholders. The formality of agreements among parties involved in evaluations can range from the very formal (legally binding contracts describing the rights and duties of contractors, employees, or human subjects) to the less formal (written promises, discussions among two or more parties captured in minutes, or e-mailed assurances). Where evaluations entail multiple formal and informal agreements, it is important that they be compared to one another and that no conflicting obligations are left unexamined and unresolved.

In certain evaluation settings, formal agreements may stipulate unusual or unique evaluation conditions. For example, in situations where the evaluation information has actual market value and belongs to a firm or is protected from widespread distribution for legal or ethical reasons, the contract may stipulate that the results not be disclosed to anyone other than the sponsors or clients who commissioned the evaluation.

In general, formal evaluation agreements make ethical, legal, and professional stipulations and obligations explicit. In many settings they are also legal documents. However, evaluators should also view formal agreements as an opportunity to increase evaluation quality more broadly. Formal agreements and their negotiations are part of the communications that support other attributes of evaluation quality: feasibility, utility, accuracy, and accountability (for example, U8 Concern for Consequences and Influence and A8 Communication and Reporting). Formal agreements require communication processes and result in tangible products. The process of building formal agreements over time can also contribute to the credibility and perceived professionalism of the evaluator (U1 Evaluator Credibility). They can help clarify differences in assumptions and cultural influences that might otherwise remain below the surface. Evaluators should use the opportunity to strengthen trust in communications by renegotiating agreements whenever it is needed, especially when the scope of work is altered. Renegotiated agreements can help clarify any changes in evaluation purposes and questions; data collection and analysis procedures; stakeholder, client and evaluator roles; resources; and other issues (U3 Negotiated Purposes). They can help strengthen the overall communication capacity in the evaluation.

❖ IMPLEMENTING P2 FORMAL AGREEMENTS

The following are important recommendations for implementing this standard:

1. Establish evaluation contracts and memoranda of agreement through stakeholder consultation and participation. Agreements should identify the key evaluation procedures and products that meet the needs of evaluators, clients, and key stakeholders.
2. Develop agreements that conform to federal, tribal, state, or local requirements, statutes, and regulations.
3. Negotiate agreements and revisit them over time as needed. Consider several iterations to ensure that the elements in the agreement have been fully reviewed and understood by stakeholders.
4. Design agreements that respond to the unique features in the local context or culture of a particular program. Be sure to find out how formal agreements are documented so that all parties are clear about expectations and obligations.
5. Be sure that agreements are used to monitor and track specific duties and responsibilities.
6. View the formal agreement process as an opportunity to improve the overall quality of communication processes and products.
7. To the extent possible, monitor and review all formal and informal agreements to determine whether they create conflicts and incompatibilities.
8. Consider explicit mention of *The Program Evaluation Standards* and other guidelines as principles to regulate the conduct of the evaluation so that those documents can serve as references for any disputes that arise related to interpretations of the agreement.

❖ HAZARDS

Some possible hazards with regard to P2 are as follows:

1. Neglecting or omitting key elements in formal evaluation agreements
2. Neglecting or omitting key stakeholder groups in the development of agreements
3. Altering agreements without the full engagement of evaluators, clients, and other key stakeholders

4. Assuming the evaluation proposal constitutes the expectations of clients and other contracting parties and is a formal agreement without the requisite review, discussion, and approval
5. Changing design, scope, or cost of the evaluation study without prior review and approval from key clients, sponsors, or other important stakeholders
6. Discounting the role that agreements play in ensuring trust and mutual respect between the evaluator and contracting individuals and agencies
7. Not making all agreements available to all, except when such openness is restricted by laws, regulations, or other standards
8. Hiding important public issues with regard to agreements or treating them as covert rather than open
9. Being careless or inattentive to the evaluation agreement process and the written document when addressing proprietary or private information and thus infringing on stakeholders' privacy, property, or other rights

Application Number Two for the Propriety Case Scenario

The scenario that supports this application, including background information about the program, context, and key players, can be read at the end of the Propriety Overview on page 110.

As planning for the HOPE program evaluation is becoming more concrete, negotiating and finalizing agreements is added to the agenda for the upcoming evaluation meetings. In particular, Kwame and Jonah want to be explicit about who will be doing what, when, and how. They want to describe roles, duties, responsibilities, and obligations for Jonah, Kwame, Dawn, Nina, and Hanna. Based on initial meetings, they settle on a shared working relationship in which the university-based evaluation specialists, Kwame and Dawn, agree to draft an evaluation work plan for review and approval by Jonah. Nina and Hanna will have primary responsibility for survey development and implementation and for securing existing data. Where appropriate, all four evaluators will share in interviewing participants and staff, but Kwame and Dawn will conduct the in-depth, *in situ* interviews. Part of the planning process entails specification of the resources, including financial support, needed for each specific step in the evaluation. Together Kwame and Jonah review each Program Evaluation Standard and ask if and how the steps to address it should be specified in the evaluation plan or the formal agreement.

In addition to the meetings between the external team of evaluators, occasional meetings at the outset take place with Jonah. Rather than a joint Memorandum of

Agreement between HOPE, the university, and the research team, Jonah prefers to be invoiced for completed services and products as specified in the evaluation plan presented to the board of directors. Kwame agrees that they can start out that way initially but is of the opinion that they will need at least a preliminary formal agreement soon.

In previous meetings, Jonah, the board, and the evaluators have discussed and clarified the two general guiding evaluation questions:

1. Is HOPE making a difference in the lives of participants and their communities?
2. How do the core practices of the program address conversations and discussions about civic and social engagement?

The evaluation team has begun discussing how the questions might be expanded into specific subquestions that could be addressed by sources of information and various methodologies. They are preparing a short specific menu of options and suggestions for Jonah and his board to weigh and consider. In addition, the evaluation team has asked Jonah to suggest methods for engaging other groups of stakeholders in the evaluation planning before any formal agreements are signed in preparation for evaluation implementation.

After several meetings among the involved parties, Jonah reports that a national philanthropic sponsor has taken interest in the work of the agency and the HOPE program. The sponsor intends to help fund the program and its evaluation but wants the evaluation to address the full scope of learning that takes place among participants in the HOPE program. In a follow-up e-mail, the foundation evaluation officer indicates that

> because of the work we do with grantees like your organization who create such complex learning experiences for participants in local areas, we like to think about how learning is documented and how this learning affects larger communities. This information would be helpful to us as we think about our own evaluation and grantee portfolio.

The evaluation team meets to reshape this statement of interest into a third question:

3. How can we best evaluate the complex, embedded learning experiences taking place in the HOPE program?

When she reads this question, Dawn is intrigued. She remarks, "This is a different type of question." She continues with a string of her own questions: "Won't this require us to be more self-reflective about our own work? Can we do this and focus on the first two questions? Do we have the resources or time to even consider this additional question?" Kwame replies that these are excellent questions to ask about how the foundation's needs can be met and how they will affect their evaluation plan.

They begin by considering the implications of the third question on their initial time lines, resources, and budget. Through their previous negotiations, team members had planned and reached agreement on a small-scale evaluation funded with the scant resources available locally. The working relationship between the team members had led to a feasible and equitable design that they were planning to implement after it was fully developed and vetted by additional stakeholders. Now there are some obvious questions among the evaluation team members about how much weight to give the third question and how to answer it in a complete manner. They agree to e-mail Jonah requesting a meeting within the week to develop a more formal working contract specifying expectations and budgets for team members from both the university and RCRI.

As Kwame reflects on the way the evaluation is taking on its own organic life and the enthusiasm that their new sponsor is demonstrating for the program and for evaluation, he is pleased that Dawn agreed to participate in this project. She is a very talented student. He wanted her to experience a dynamic evaluation and to learn how interaction with stakeholders guided by specific program evaluation standards can lead to ongoing improvement and ultimately solid evaluation quality. He decides that the best procedure to produce good evaluation work and high-quality learning for Dawn is to begin with the propriety standards, followed quickly by attention to utility and feasibility in concert with one another. He wonders if his focus on Dawn's learning is a compatible interest or conflicting interest with other evaluation goals (P6 Conflicts of Interests). He is a bit concerned that RCRI is focused more clearly than he and Dawn are on billable hours, and wonders what that will do for the evaluation budget (P7 Fiscal Responsibility). Kwame knows that they need to step up their efforts to map out who the stakeholders are and reach out immediately in a representative way that puts them in contact (P1 Responsive and Inclusive Orientation and P4 Clarity and Fairness). He is concerned about involving more stakeholders as soon as they can, not only because it is the right thing to do but also because it is critical for utility, feasibility, accuracy, and accountability (for example, U2 Attention to Stakeholders, F3 Contextual Viability, A1 Justified Conclusions and Decisions, and E2 Internal Metaevaluation). Before he leaves to teach his graduate evaluation class, Kwame smiles to himself. He really does like his job.

❖ SUPPORTING DOCUMENTATION

Alkin, M. C., Christie, C. A., & Rose, M. (2006). Communicating evaluation. In I. F. Shaw, J. C. Greene, & M. M. Mark (Eds.), *The Sage handbook of evaluation* (pp. 337–354). London: Sage.

Fitzpatrick, J. L., Sanders, J. R., & Worthen, B. R. (2004). *Program evaluation: Alternative approaches and practical guidelines* (3rd ed.). Boston: Allyn & Bacon.

Guba, E., & Lincoln, Y. (1981). *Effective evaluation.* San Francisco: Jossey-Bass.

Stufflebeam, D. L. (2000). Lessons in contracting for evaluation. *American Journal of Evaluation, 21,* 293–314.

Worthen, B. R. (1987). *Evaluating educational and social programs: Guidelines for proposal review, onsite evaluation, evaluation contracts, and technical assistance.* Boston: Kluwer-Nijhoff.

P3 Human Rights and Respect

Evaluations should be designed and conducted to protect human and legal rights and maintain the dignity of participants and other stakeholders.

P3 Human Rights and Respect

❖ RATIONALE AND CLARIFICATION

Standard P3 addresses the obligation to respect and protect the rights and welfare of participants and communities. It mandates interactions with participants, communities, and other parties that are respectful and to the extent possible maximize benefit and minimize harm. It emphasizes the importance of adhering to applicable federal, state, local, and tribal regulations and requirements, including work with ethics committees, Institutional Review Boards (IRBs), and local/tribal constituencies that authorize consent to work in and with respective communities. This standard also holds evaluators to a higher degree of commitment to human rights and respect in evaluation than may be required by lawmakers, external agencies, or review boards.

Protecting the rights and welfare of stakeholders and their communities requires understanding their cultural and social backgrounds and values as important features of their respective organizations or communities. Evaluations can incorporate tailored approaches to address stakeholders' and stakeholder groups' concerns, establish rapport, collect data, and communicate findings. In all cases, evaluation processes and activities should fit communities' expectations for human respect and dignity. When community expectations are in conflict, evaluations should help resolve the resulting difficulties.

The protection of human and legal rights and respect for the dignity of participants should be an integral part of evaluation processes and products. For example, procedures should encourage just and fair interactions with and among stakeholders. Participants should be made aware of their rights, such as their rights to participate, withdraw, or challenge decisions that are being made at any time during the evaluation process. In addition, as a general courtesy in practice, evaluators should be knowledgeable about social manners and mores that exist in institutional or community contexts, especially those that are new to them, so that their practices reflect an attention to and valuing of these communities. Social manners, mores, and ways of expressing respect and individual rights are sometimes bounded by the cultural contexts of participants, the organization, or the community. Culturally competent evaluators are aware of and constantly learning about these cultural influences.

Ethics committees, IRBs, and local or tribal community-enforced boards play important roles in evaluation and research. These committees, boards, and representative groups exist to ensure that evaluation and research studies involving humans (and animals) are carried out with consideration of ethical issues that may arise. They review and regulate methods and require adherence to specific, approved procedures involving individuals contributing to evaluation and research. Depending on jurisdictional issues, evaluators should also be prepared to complete more than one formal application as required by different committees and boards to gain approval for their evaluation procedures.

In addition to consulting with IRBs or ethics committees, evaluators should make explicit their own moral principles and codes of conduct. They should develop and cultivate moral and professional dispositions that demonstrate integrity, respect, and trust throughout the evaluation process. Evaluators have the responsibility to ensure that these moral groundings extend to participating institutions, colleagues, culturally different communities and groups, and other evaluation stakeholders. Applying *The Program Evaluation Standards* and other guidelines can help communicate evaluators' commitments to propriety.

Ethical behavior is further influenced by the decisions evaluators make in the evaluation process. For instance, evaluators can develop strategies for reducing and managing ethical conflicts in the design and conduct of the evaluation. In addition to preventing physically and emotionally harmful research, evaluators have an ethical responsibility to ensure that evaluations produce benefit where possible. They should serve the well-being of individuals, communities, and other stakeholders. As public stewards, evaluators are responsible for the well-being of individuals and communities in the evaluation process. Proper evaluation practices and procedures respect and promote the dignity of diverse groups, cultures, and traditionally underserved populations.

Other professional associations have also produced standards, practice guidelines and principles that address professional and ethical treatment of humans in evaluations and studies. One particularly useful set of guidelines for evaluators, the *Guiding Principles,* addresses the rights of and respect for humans in at least three of its five principles:

- Principle C: Integrity/Honesty
- Principle D: Respect for People
- Principle E: Responsibilities for General and Public Welfare

Evaluators who display honesty, integrity, and respect for people ensure that these principles are embedded in the entire evaluation process and that concern for the security and self-worth of respondents, participants, and communities are a critical part of evaluation practices and procedures. They also facilitate honesty, integrity, and respect among stakeholders in their interactions with one another.

❖ IMPLEMENTING P3 HUMAN RIGHTS AND RESPECT

The following are important recommendations for implementing this standard:

1. Consult human subjects committees and IRBs in advance of conducting evaluations to ascertain pertinent ethical and legal issues and concerns.
2. Monitor the interactions of evaluation team members and stakeholders to ensure respect even in the face of differing opinions.
3. Ensure that ethical commitments such as respecting the dignity and humanity of persons are evident in all evaluation processes and products.
4. Acknowledge and respect the unique cultural values and ways of implementing respect, politeness, and courtesy among diverse participants. Sometimes what appears to be respectful from one cultural perspective may appear disrespectful from another.
5. Develop culturally sensitive and congruent methods that support the well-being of communities and participants.
6. Inform stakeholders of their rights in an atmosphere of respect and cooperation so as to enhance interactions among involved parties.
7. Assure that communication and interpersonal contacts throughout the process are not threatening or harmful.

❖ HAZARDS

Some possible hazards with regard to P3 are as follows:

1. Avoiding and ignoring the interplay of age, sex, ethnicity, cultural or religious backgrounds, or language differences in developing mutual respect and understanding in the evaluation process
2. Neglecting to consult with appropriate parties where legal or cultural expectations require unique attention to the protection of rights and respect
3. Assuming that all individuals, participants, and communities in the evaluation process observe the same notions of respect, care, and dignity
4. Not developing the cultural competence necessary to determine what is acceptable and not acceptable evaluation practice in cultures other than one's own
5. Assuming that just because an action or behavior is acceptable in a culture or political context, it is to be tolerated in the evaluation, such as contradicting important features of the Universal Declaration of Human Rights or the human subject protections required by IRBs

Application Number Three for the Propriety Case Scenario

The scenario that supports this application, including background information about the program, context, and key players, can be read at the end of the Feasibility Overview on page 110.

As part of the HOPE evaluation, the university team of evaluators, Kwame and Dawn, anticipate they will need to initiate a process to have their formal study, including the new third evaluation question, approved by the university's institutional review board (IRB). This is the standard practice where evaluators intend to publish and present findings to larger audiences. It is clear from team meetings that HOPE program staff members are not expecting participants to complete informed consent forms. RCRI does not require that a process of informed consent be initiated either. Jonah, in agreement with RCRI perceives the evaluation more as an administrative tool to initiate continued funding and to understand HOPE outcomes. After an additional meeting in which distinctions and purposes between research and evaluation are clearly articulated and understood, Jonah and the evaluation team all agree to assist the university team in the IRB process, including deciding on the necessary informed consent procedures. It may be the case that the IRB chairperson will find the evaluation studies exempt from full review or that they will be viewed as quality control and administrative functions rather than as research. Nevertheless, they agree it is better to proceed cautiously and err on the side of consideration of all respondents' rights.

To investigate the three evaluation questions, the team prepares for participant interviews and focus groups to gather information about the changes that have occurred in the lives of program participants and whether any changes can be attributed to the program's core practices. Focus groups and interviews with volunteers from previous dialogue sessions are scheduled over a 4-week period.

The first focus group includes members of a church group from a pivotal neighborhood. The Slippery Breeze Interfaith Church Network is a group of diverse congregations in a part of the city undergoing gentrification. This neighborhood once thrived with local shops and vibrant communities, but now encroaching new development is reshaping the identity of the church. Not only do Slippery Breeze members represent different faith groups, they are one of the more multiracial and multicultural religious groups in the region. A focus group sampling Slippery Breeze members who had participated in HOPE will stimulate and document dialogue about key topics in the larger community.

At the initial meeting with Slippery Breeze participants, evaluation team members notice uneasiness and reticence. They proceed with their usual introductions that include the purpose of the study, its risks and benefits, and expectations about compensation, confidentiality, and participants' right to withdraw. After a bit, one elderly church member raises his hand, stands up, and describes an occurrence which had taken place with members of his community who participated in a research study from the university. To a series of nods from other church members, the elderly gentleman recalls a number of discomforting and trust-undermining experiences that had taken place. He describes how they had experienced university researchers as especially self-serving and unconcerned with the well-being of the community they studied.

Kwame asks for more details. A fuller story slowly emerges. As it turned out, the Slippery Breeze community had been discovered by a university researcher who had approached them with an impassioned plea that they contribute to "our greater scholarly understanding" of how emergent, multiracial communities worked. In a series of studies conducted by the researcher and his graduate students, increasingly invasive questions were asked of them, and they were treated as if they had an obligation to provide answers. Some of the Slippery Breeze leaders asked to review any reports written about them and asked if and how they would be identified. Not only were their e-mails ignored, but the researcher did not return their phone calls once the data were collected. The community in general had felt used by the researchers.

At this point, some people in the group demand more assurance that their needs will be respected and ask for clarification of their rights and how these would be guaranteed. They demand that the team of evaluators prepare a summary for their church members, be available to answer questions about their study in a meeting of interested members of the church congregation, and let them decide whether to use their real names or pseudonyms in descriptions and presentations. In response, the evaluation team agrees to provide research summaries as needed, allow for church members to react to findings and allow revised and second opinions about findings and what they mean. The issue of whether to include real names as opposed to pseudonyms will need to be investigated and discussed in the context of modifications submitted for IRB approval.

Later, back at the university, Kwame asks Dawn what she had learned from observing this turn of events. She wonders if they had been negligent in not contacting the Slippery Breeze community quickly enough, but then adds that they had gotten to it about as quickly as they could. As she muses aloud, she wonders what other groups might be concerned about their rights in the evaluation. Are there other local community organizations or organizers who needed to be contacted? What shall they do with regard to the investors who have been pouring money into this area? Should any business organizations be made aware of the evaluation? Will they be interested in contributing to HOPE or in controlling and redirecting it? Kwame and Dawn plan to sit down later and review the full list of communities and issues they know about to decide best how to recognize their obligations for serving overarching social betterment in the communities served by HOPE.

In addition, Dawn mentions that she is becoming mildly concerned that they and their RCRI colleagues are not discussing their responsibilities as evaluators on a regular basis. Kwame decides to call their attention to *The Program Evaluation Standards* and the *Guiding Principles* again and try to include them in discussions of their obligations as members of a professional evaluation team. Kwame is not overly concerned because they are all committed to professionalism and evaluation excellence. However, he understands Dawn's concern because both Nina and Hanna have much more experience with research than with evaluation projects.

❖ SUPPORTING DOCUMENTATION

Australasian Evaluation Society. (2006). *Guidelines for the ethical conduct of evaluations.* Retrieved May 1, 2007, from http://www.aes.asn.au

American Association of University Professors. (2001). Report: Protecting human beings: Institutional review boards and social science research. *Academe, 87*(3), 55–67.

American Evaluation Association. (2007). *Guiding principles for evaluators.* Retrieved June 26, 2007, from http://www.eval.org/Publications/GuidingPrinciples.asp

Centre for Social Research and Evaluation. (2004). *Guidelines for research and evaluation with Maori.* Ministry of Social Development, New Zealand.

Morris, M. (2003). Ethical considerations in evaluation. In T. Kellaghan & D. L. Stufflebeam (Eds.), *International handbook of educational evaluation* (pp. 303–328). Dordrecht, Netherlands: Kluwer.

National Commission for the Protection of Human Subjects in Biomedical and Behavioral Research. (1979). *The Belmont report: Ethical principles and guidelines for the protection of human subjects of research.* Washington, DC: U.S. Department of Health, Education, and Welfare.

Oakes, J. M. (2002). Risks and wrongs in social science research: An evaluator's guide to the IRB. *Evaluation Review, 26,* 443–478.

Simons, H. (2006). Ethics in evaluation. In I. F. Shaw, J. C. Greene, & M. M. Mark (Eds.), *The Sage handbook of evaluation* (pp. 243–265). London: Sage.

Schwandt, T. (2001). Ethics of qualitative inquiry. In *Dictionary of qualitative inquiry* (2nd ed., pp. 73–77). Thousand Oaks, CA: Sage.

Thomas, V. G., & McKie, B. K. (2006). Collecting and utilizing evaluation research for public good and on behalf of African American children. *Journal of Negro Education, 75*(3), 341–352.

P4 Clarity and Fairness

> *Evaluations should be understandable and fair in addressing stakeholder needs and purposes.*

❖ RATIONALE AND CLARIFICATION

Fairness and clarity refer to two separate but interactive components of evaluation propriety. Fair evaluations follow principles and procedures that help to ensure stakeholders' rights. In addition, fairness is closely tied to the distribution of benefits experienced by specific stakeholders and the extent to which these are justified. However, fairness does not require that all evaluation stakeholders be treated in exactly the same way or receive similar benefits from the program or the evaluation (see also F4 Resource Use). Rather, fairness requires adaptive and accommodating attention to individuals' and groups' needs compared to costs while ensuring that everyone's rights are supported.

Fairness and unfairness exist on a continuum. Fairness, as described above, is equitable support for individuals' and groups' rights, including the right for their needs to be explicitly considered. Unfairness is closely tied to *unjustified* disadvantage, loss, and harm that occur when one or more individuals or groups experience reduced support for their specific rights or needs, sometimes in order for others to receive greater support and attention to their wants, needs, or rights. Unfairness is exacerbated when the rules guiding these decisions are not transparent and clear. For example, to be fair, evaluations must justify any differential valuing of any stakeholders' evaluation needs over the needs of other stakeholders. In extreme cases, evaluations can be unfair to all stakeholders and groups because everyone's rights are inadequately supported and no one's needs are met. In other cases, evaluations can be differentially unfair for specific individuals and groups. Any degree of unfairness may happen through ignorance, as might be the case when the cultural contexts or other context features are not understood. The goal for high-quality evaluations is to be as fair as possible to as many evaluation stakeholders as possible, given the contexts and constraints.

One persistent concern about evaluation fairness is how to respond to social and political forces as they influence programs, contexts, and evaluations. For example, in some contexts the existing political and cultural rules are designed to benefit some groups in ways that lead to unfairness. In other contexts, political forces promote compensation to address prior unfairness through redistribution of resources. Those striving for distributive justice recognize that unfairness is often created when the wants of individuals in more powerful groups receive greater attention than the needs of those in less-empowered groups. Fair evaluations can help clarify how groups and individuals define and address wants and needs and apply resources to them. In such complex environments, evaluations can steer toward fairness by focusing on the rights of all individuals with a stake in the evaluation. They can create a framework in which to discuss the extent to which stakeholders are treated fairly by programs and policies.

In addition, evaluators and other stakeholders can always raise the issue of fairness in an evaluation, regardless of the political systems, existing programs, and policies. In this way, evaluation can bring about discussions of social betterment without exercising undue, inappropriate, or unfair emphasis on the needs of one group or another. Contributing to fairness for stakeholders who have previously been treated unfairly is also a core concern for proper evaluations, as is avoiding unfair treatment for anyone that results from evaluation procedures and products. In fair evaluations, these two concerns go hand in hand.

Fairness does not require that all stakeholders have their needs met by the evaluation, only that their needs be considered with transparency and clarity and that their rights be protected. Because different stakeholders are often served by different evaluation processes and products, evaluators should provide sufficiently clear information about how specific needs and purposes are chosen (U3 Negotiated Purposes). In this difficult and complex mix, maintaining fairness for all requires skill and dedication. Evaluators should always consider ways to create greater benefit for all rather than assuming some must be ignored in order for others to have their needs met.

Finally, fairness is related to the other attributes of evaluation quality in direct and indirect ways. Lack of attention to feasibility can create unfairness, for example, when resources are used in ways that unnecessarily disadvantage stakeholders and groups (F4 Resource Use). Lack of use or misuse of evaluations can also unfairly benefit or harm specific individuals or groups as well (U8 Concern for Consequences and Influence). Similarly, inaccuracy in evaluations can create moral, legal, and ethical consequences that contribute to unfairness (A1 Justified Conclusions and Decisions and A2 Valid Information). In general, unfair evaluation procedures and products need immediate improvement (E2 Internal Metaevaluation and E3 External Metaevaluation).

The second emphasis in this standard is clarity and shared understanding so that fairness will be recognized and furthered. Clarity refers to careful monitoring and communication of evaluation procedures supporting fairness, especially with regard to stakeholders' needs and evaluation purposes. Clarity and shared understanding require attention to implemented procedures as well as stakeholders' perceptions. For example, political or fiscal self-interest can lead either to real unfairness or the mere perception of unfairness. Both the reality and the perception can be damaging to the evaluation. Similarly, monitoring may reveal factors outside of the evaluators' control that could negatively affect fairness. These factors can be described and disclosed to help clarify what their impact has been and what can be done about them (F3 Contextual Viability and U4 Explicit Values).

Maintaining clarity and mutual understanding about rights, needs, and purposes in the support of fairness requires ongoing communication with different stakeholders and groups throughout all phases of the evaluation (U7 Timely Communicating and Reporting and A8 Communication and Reporting). Monitoring for clarity about stakeholders' needs and evaluation purposes should focus on different possible ways that the evaluations might be unfair, ruling out or addressing each one. It is not possible to prove that an evaluation is completely fair, but by questioning and examining the relative degree of fairness and unfairness across all relevant stakeholders and groups with regard to all processes and procedures, evaluation unfairness can be identified and in many cases addressed and ameliorated.

In striving for fairness and clarity, evaluators must be aware of the roles they play and use their positions positively. In their contacts with all stakeholders, evaluators must not abuse their authority to guide evaluation processes, deceive the public about these processes, promote their own agendas, or be unfair in or outside the evaluation.

❖ IMPLEMENTING P4 CLARITY AND FAIRNESS

The following are important recommendations for implementing this standard:

1. Guard stakeholders' rights and ensure that they are supported by evaluation policies, processes, and products.
2. Maintain communication strategies that further fairness and clarity.

3. Encourage frequent communication among evaluators and stakeholders across all phases of the evaluation to help prevent misunderstandings about evaluation fairness.
4. Commit to addressing issues of inequity and social justice in programs and contexts to the extent that they have an impact on the rights of stakeholders in the evaluation.
5. Consider the role of the evaluation in addressing unfairness in the program or context and the possibility that the evaluation may contribute to unfairness if it does not do so.
6. Facilitate understanding of decision making and power structures within programs and contexts and their impact on stakeholders' rights.
7. Recognize that evaluation resources seriously limit the extent to which evaluations can meet stakeholder needs and develop fair and transparent rules to clarify how decisions are made about which needs and purposes to serve.

❖ HAZARDS

Some possible hazards with regard to P4 are as follows:

1. Ignoring the rights of less vocal groups of stakeholders because they are silent or hard to discover
2. Making decisions about which stakeholders' rights and needs to address without clarifying or communicating the bases for such decisions
3. Ignoring obvious violations of stakeholders' rights in programs because no evaluation questions address the rights of stakeholders
4. Agreeing to covert evaluations when the results of those evaluations can be used to undermine stakeholders' rights
5. Allowing political pressure to distort or inappropriately influence any aspect of the evaluation planning, implementation, or results such that the rights of stakeholders are undermined, including their right to have decisions made based on accurate information and findings

Application Number Four for the Propriety Case Scenario

The scenario that supports this application, including background information about the program, context, and key players, can be read at the end of the Propriety Overview on page 110.

Kwame sets up an appointment with Jonah, asking for an hour of his time to revisit the process and information needs of stakeholders. They have spent time on this before with regard to evaluation utility, but since his exchange with the Slippery Breeze community, he has some concerns. It was clear that the Slippery Breeze focus group participants were unclear about the uses and purposes of the evaluation. They were apparently in the dark and thinking that this was just another research study. If they thought that this was faculty research, then they must not have had the opportunity to learn that the evaluation was designed to address their and other program stakeholders' needs. As stakeholders, they should have had the opportunity to say what their needs were with regard to evaluation processes and products. Perhaps, for example, they would have liked to volunteer to help with the evaluation in order to develop evaluation capacity in their church if they had known that such needs could be raised during evaluation planning sessions. Kwame is also worried that other HOPE participants may not know enough about the evaluation and its purposes. Perhaps the evaluation team should have considered more questions related to community needs and not have been so quick to focus on outcomes in the absence of needs. A little tweaking of the surveys and interviews might accomplish both purposes at the same time and address more of the participants' needs as well as the requirements of staff and potential sponsors.

Based on what they have already formally agreed to, the evaluation plan has taken shape. It includes a number of mixed-method data collection strategies:

- Literature and document reviews of programmatic materials
- Participant observations of dialogue groups in session
- Surveys of current and former participants
- Ethnographic case portraits of selected participants
- Face-to-face and telephone interviews with current and former participants, including those who began but did not complete the series of dialogue groups

As part of the shared data collection that took place, the university team of Kwame and Dawn has already started ethnographies of participants who are interested in providing more detailed cases of their experiences in making change happen in their local communities.

Kwame recently met Roderick, who expressed interest in talking about his experiences in carrying out a meaningful social change project as part of participation in HOPE. Roderick has participated regularly in dialogue sessions where Kwame was functioning as a participant-observer.

Roderick has also taken on a facilitator role during previous postdialogue sessions and is adept at encouraging other participants even after the initial sessions are completed. After seeing Roderick in successive postdialogue sessions, Kwame considers him a prime example of engaged participation by a community member. He suggests that they get together for an interview. Roderick agrees enthusiastically, and they begin a series of meetings that will take place once a week for 2 months. The plan is to continue the meetings once a month thereafter for as long as a year, if the meetings continue to be fruitful.

Meeting at various neighborhood establishments and coffee shops, Roderick reveals information about his background and motivation to participate in the HOPE program, how the program is making a difference in his life, and how much the HOPE program core practices matter to him. By sharing stories and backgrounds with one another, Roderick and Kwame develop a relationship that might extend beyond the HOPE program and evaluation. They talk about creating opportunities to collaborate and share work, bringing their families together for dinner, and other topics of interest.

In the enjoyment of their conversations, Roderick gradually forgets about the initial consent forms and the fact that they are engaged in an ethnographic work. However, Kwame is well aware of his responsibilities and wants to be sure that the information he is collecting is accurate. One way to increase the validity of Roderick's information is to share the written case portrait with him so that he can respond to it and clarify any misleading information (A2 Valid Information and A5 Information Management). After two months of meetings, Kwame e-mails a copy of his write-up to Roderick and suggests that they discuss it at a subsequent meeting.

Following the e-mailed delivery of the case write-up, Kwame receives an unsettling voice mail message from Roderick. In a tone that Kwame has not heard before, Roderick expresses disappointment, if not anger, about the write-ups. He declares: "I don't know what your agenda is, but this statement does not accurately reflect who I am." Taken somewhat aback and worried that he has seriously misunderstood what Roderick was communicating and that their relationship might be in jeopardy, Kwame ponders what to do. He does not want to rush to call Roderick until he has thought a little about this predicament.

The next day, Kwame calls Roderick suggesting that they meet. He suspects that he has seriously confused his roles with Roderick and that he should immediately give Roderick the opportunity to clarify what his needs are with regard to their meetings. Roderick says that he was in some ways more confused and surprised than offended, once he had an opportunity to think about it. He would like very much to meet, but suggests it can wait until their next regularly scheduled coffee shop appointment in 2 days.

At the coffee shop, Roderick and Kwame greet each other as if things were the same, but this time, Kwame does not record anything or make notes. He tells Roderick again about the purposes and processes of the evaluation and asks Roderick if he were conducting the evaluation, what he would want to know. Roderick asks for more detail about what an evaluation is and why people do them. They spend almost 30 minutes talking about the role of evaluation in the HOPE program. They discuss how evaluation might help Roderick know how effective his own efforts are. Roderick wants to know why these interviews with him are important to the evaluation. Roderick is excited and engaged again, and he and Kwame agree to a new approach in the future. For the first part of the visit, Kwame and Roderick will talk about his actions and clarify how he is engaging in the change efforts. Roderick understands that Kwame will send him the summaries so that they can be made more accurate and that they will often need amendment and clarification at Roderick's hands (A2 Valid Information).

Later, Kwame breathes a sigh of relief that his relationship with Roderick is intact. He realizes that he is actually seeing process use in action (U6 Meaningful Processes and Products and U8 Concern for Consequences and Influence) as Roderick comes to understand evaluation and the ways it might help him in his own efforts to create positive change. Kwame looks forward to discussing this turn of events with Dawn and others in his evaluation seminar next week. He also plans to discuss this thoroughly with the full evaluation team. He is looking forward to seeing Roderick learn more about evaluation and how it can help him assess needs and be more effective as a change agent in the HOPE community.

❖ SUPPORTING DOCUMENTATION

Cronbach, L. J., Ambron, S. R., Dornbusch, S. M., Hess, R. D., Hornik, R. C., Phillips, D. C., et al. (1980). *Toward reform of program evaluation.* San Francisco: Jossey-Bass.

Fraser, D. (2004). National evaluation standards for Australia and New Zealand: Many questions but few answers. In C. Russon & G. Russon (Eds.), *International perspectives on evaluation standards: New Directions for Evaluation, 104,* 67–78.

House, E. R., & Howe, K. R. (1999). *Values in evaluation and social research.* Thousand Oaks, CA: Sage.

Mark, M. M., Greene, J. C., & Shaw, I. F. (2006). The evaluation of policies, programs, and practices. In I. F. Shaw, J. C. Greene, & M. M. Mark (Eds.), *The Sage handbook of evaluation* (pp. 1–26). London: Sage.

Morris, M., & Cohn, R. (1993). Program evaluators and ethical challenges. *Evaluation Review, 17*(6), 621–642.

Scriven, M. (2003). Evaluation theory and metatheory. In T. Kellaghan & D. L. Stufflebeam (Eds.), *International handbook of educational evaluation* (pp. 15–20). Dordrecht, Netherlands: Kluwer.

P5 Transparency and Disclosure

Evaluations should provide complete descriptions of findings, limitations, and conclusions to all stakeholders unless doing so would violate legal or propriety obligations.

❖ RATIONALE AND CLARIFICATION

Disclosure refers to open communication with all stakeholders and stakeholder groups concerning the information that they have a right to know. Evaluations should also disclose information that may benefit stakeholders when the disclosure does not violate legal, ethical, or professional codes. When legal, ethical, and professional codes are in conflict about what can be disclosed, transparency requires that these conflicts also be disclosed. Transparency and disclosure in action are candid and complete, involving careful, negotiated, and coordinated interaction with key stakeholders and participants in the evaluation.

Disclosure in the service of transparency requires that roles, values, purposes, and expectations are clearly presented during all evaluation cycles. Proper transparency and disclosure prevent unfairness that could result when individuals do not have access to the information they need and thus are not able to decide or act with the requisite knowledge and understanding that should be available to them. Transparency and disclosure also extend to reporting all major sources of support for evaluations, including monetary and in-kind support (F4 Resource Use and P7 Fiscal Responsibility).

Maintaining high standards of disclosure and transparency also provides other benefits. First, transparent evaluations are able to withstand critical examination and scrutiny by stakeholders or clients who might otherwise have reason to believe important information has been withheld. Second, transparent evaluations are completed and communicated in an atmosphere of honesty and candidness where participants have multiple opportunities to provide direct and open comments in all stages of the evaluation. Last, transparent evaluations expose limitations of methodology, logic, design, and analysis. Such a climate of transparency can lead to greater acceptance, credibility, use, and accuracy (F3 Contextual Viability, U1 Evaluator Credibility, U8 Concern for Consequences and Influences, A1 Trustworthy Conclusions and Decisions, and A7 Explicit Evaluation Reasoning).

However, not all information and procedures can or should be disclosed. Disclosure should not threaten legal or ethical rights at all or other aspects of evaluation quality unnecessarily (F2 Practical Procedures and U1 Evaluator Credibility). Evaluators should also be sensitive to people's rights not to have information disclosed without careful consideration when disclosure could lead to embarrassment or distress.

Evaluators must also attend to any further disclosure and dissemination that takes place once information is shared. Those who receive information are responsible for understanding and implementing confidentiality, privacy, and respect for human rights (P3 Human Rights and Respect). Often evaluators will need to contribute to stakeholders' understanding of their rights and responsibilities with regard to transparency and disclosure. Evaluators should communicate the responsibilities and obligations that come with receipt of the information.

Often, rules for disclosure are regulated by federal or state statute and organizational regulations, especially with regard to student information.[2] In addition, IRB scrutiny often extends to the way information is reported or disclosed as well as the manner in which individuals are advised of their rights and responsibilities (P3 Human Rights and Respect).

Standard P5 is also supported by and works in concert with a number of other standards, including U2 Attention to Stakeholders, U5 Relevant Information, U7 Timely Communicating and Reporting, A8 Communication and Reporting, and P2 Formal Agreements. As communication plans are developed in conjunction with utility, feasibility, and accuracy considerations, propriety should also receive adequate attention.

❖ IMPLEMENTING P5 TRANSPARENCY AND DISCLOSURE

The following are important recommendations for implementing this standard:

2. For example, the Family Educational Rights and Privacy Act, FERPA, http://www2.ed.gov/policy/gen/guid/fpco/ferpa/index.html

1. Ensure that credible, complete, and honest information is provided to stakeholders and clients.
2. Ensure disclosure of all major sources of support, both monetary and in-kind, for the evaluation.
3. Maintain open lines of communication with and be accessible to identified stakeholders throughout the evaluation process so that transparent disclosure is available to them.
4. Consult with persons or groups who will be affected by the evaluation well in advance of reporting or presentation of findings so that the evaluation process is both open and constructive for all parties involved.
5. Recognize that disclosure and transparency of evaluation findings may create risks and potential harm for some participants and that evaluators have a duty to reduce that risk where possible (P3 Human Rights and Respect).
6. Find culturally appropriate ways throughout an evaluation to disseminate information to stakeholders and other audiences in need of that information.

❖ HAZARDS

Some possible hazards with regard to P5 are as follows:

1. Violating stakeholders' privacy and confidentiality rights in an effort to be accurate or thorough during information collection
2. Failing to understand, determine, or negotiate the control and release of evaluation results in ways that protect stakeholders
3. Revealing sensitive or embarrassing information without cause or compensatory benefit
4. Allowing those who might suffer consequences from the disclosure of accurate evaluation findings to interfere with disclosure under the guise of protecting stakeholders' privacy
5. Treating evaluation results as if they are research and publishing or presenting them at conferences when the necessary IRB oversight and approvals have not been secured

Application Number Five for the Propriety Case Scenario

The scenario that supports this application, including background information about the program, context, and key players, can be read at the end of the Propriety Overview on page 110.

At the next meeting of the evaluation team with Jonah and the board of directors, Kwame presents the current evaluation design and updates the group on where they are and what has been accomplished. With regard to Question One, concerning the effect of the HOPE program on participants and their communities, the team has started implementing multiple evaluation methods:

- Multiple ethnographic interviews focusing on a selected number of participants who have completed the discussion rounds. The interviews explore participant backgrounds, motivations for attending HOPE, and the role of HOPE in their lives. Ethnographic interviews are being audio-recorded
- Recorded telephone interviews conducted in a semi-structured format, lasting an average of 10 to 20 minutes, primarily with participants who had not completed the series of discussion groups
- Focus groups conducted to further ascertain participant understanding of the HOPE experience. Aligned to the three central evaluation questions, focus group questions center on the impact of HOPE and how HOPE is distinct from other group experiences
- Surveys before and after the dialogues, and plans for a follow-up survey in one year. The survey administered after participation focuses on programmatic practices, while the preliminary and 1-year surveys focus on changes in individual perspectives related to participation in HOPE
- Participant observations as part of the ethnographic evaluation process. Kwame and Dawn have enrolled in discussion rounds and are observing and documenting HOPE group activities and developing relationships with current participants for purposes of follow-up ethnographic interviews

Jonah and the board members appreciate the full scope of approaches and anticipate the analyses. From their perspectives, everything in the program seems to be going well, and they are eager for the data to confirm their impressions.

At the end of the meeting, Jonah asks a casual question that turns the positive mood sour. In passing, he asks Kwame how many program participants they can afford to interview. Kwame explains the full sampling approach, which also includes potentially negative cases from those who had not completed the minimal number of group discussions. The evaluators decided to include these cases to shed light on why some community members dropped out. Jonah becomes concerned that these interviews will not show HOPE in a positive light. He asks why he was not made aware of this use of funds sooner. Kwame reminds him that the he and the board members had supported stratified sampling of interview participants but admits that the decision to sample from all participants, including those with negative experiences, might not have been as clear to Jonah and the board as Kwame assumed it was.

In the ensuing weeks as Kwame and Dawn complete the analyses of the interview data, they are thinking about how to address Jonah's concerns. The completed analyses confirm Jonah's apprehension that those who dropped out have negative things to say. These interviews are in stark contrast with the other interviews and reveal skepticism about the program's contributions to positive change or other potential benefits.

Kwame decides to discuss this issue with Jonah at the next opportunity. Jonah is disappointed because he wanted the program evaluation results to be displayed in program brochures and marketing announcements for future groups. He states that he is not comfortable with releasing the negative results. The evaluation team, however, feels a professional obligation to include the telephone interview findings in the final evaluation report. Kwame and Jonah meet on two more occasions to discuss this issue without fully resolving their concerns. At the end of the second meeting, Kwame brings Jonah a draft report contextualizing the findings so that they are put in perspective and not exaggerated in any way. In addition, he points out to Jonah that these "negative" results provide an opportunity to improve the program by reaching out to the few community members who have become somewhat alienated during their participation. Jonah begins to see the possibility of good coming out of results he has viewed as only negative. As he and Kwame continue to discuss the results and how they can be useful to him and other stakeholders, he begins to entertain the possibility that reporting the few negative comments will be beneficial in part by adding to the credibility of the many positive comments.

❖ SUPPORTING DOCUMENTATION

Bustelo, M. (2006). The potential role of standards and guidelines in the development of an evaluation culture in Spain. *Evaluation, 12*(4), 437–453.

Chelimsky, E. (1999). The political environment of evaluation and what it means for the development of the field. *Evaluation Practice, 16*(3), 215–225.

Chen, H.-T. (2002). Designing and conducting participatory outcome evaluation of community-based organizations' HIV prevention programs. In Evaluating HIV Prevention Programs [Supplement], *AIDS Education and Prevention, 14*(3), 18–26.

Davis, J. E. (1992). Reconsidering the use of race as an explanatory variable in program evaluation. In A.-M. Madison (Ed.), *Minority issues in evaluation: New Directions for Program Evaluation, 53,* 55–65.

Fitzpatrick, J. L., & Morris, M. (Eds.). (1999). *Current and emerging ethical challenges in evaluation: New Directions for Evaluation, 82.*

Morris, M., & Cohn, R. (1993). Program evaluators and ethical challenges. *Evaluation Review, 17*(6), 621–642.

Newman, D. L., & Brown, R. D. (1996). *Applied ethics for program evaluation.* Thousand Oaks, CA: Sage.

Patton, M. Q. (2002). A vision of evaluation that strengthens democracy. *Evaluation, 8*(1), 125–139.

Picciotto, R. (2005). The value of evaluation standards: A comparative assessment. *Journal of Multidisciplinary Evaluation, 3,* 30–59.

P6 Conflicts of Interests

Evaluations should openly and honestly identify and address real or perceived conflicts of interests that may compromise the evaluation.

❖ RATIONALE AND CLARIFICATION

Conflicts of interests are inevitable. In general, conflicts of interests occur within, between, and among individuals and groups when they have competing needs, wants, or duties demanding different courses of actions and uses of resources. In evaluations, conflicts of interests emerge in and affect all groups of stakeholders, including evaluators. In any specific evaluation, conflicts of interests typically include, but extend beyond, simple personal or financial interests. For example, different individuals or groups may try to influence when evaluations are commissioned, which purposes and questions are addressed, who can serve as evaluators or evaluation staff, when data are collected, which methods are used, who can provide or later access information, who has primary access to findings, and how findings are interpreted.

Because conflicts of interests are unavoidable, evaluations should try to manage rather than suppress them. Often how conflicts of interests are managed is much more important than their mere existence. High quality evaluation processes identify, limit, or otherwise manage situations where conflicts can compromise evaluation quality. Trying to avoid or ignore conflicts of interests can derail the evaluation. Unrecognized conflicts can silence important perspectives and voices in the evaluation. This oversight can lead to overly narrow or poorly chosen evaluation focuses and questions that disenfranchise and ignore important potential program and evaluation beneficiaries. Conflicts may also be ignored, not because they go unrecognized, but because planners believe them to be too unwieldy, costly, or controversial to address. However, working to identify and manage conflicts of interests provides an opportunity to understand the specific and unique elements affecting the evaluation, the evaluator, and the program (F3 Contextual Viability).

A serious concern with all conflicts of interests is that they could potentially lead to unethical, illegal, or unprofessional behavior. Many conflicts of interests create some degree of risk that if left unaddressed may lead to serious threats to evaluation quality on multiple subdimensions of propriety. However, conflicts of interests can also damage other attributes of evaluation quality, utility, feasibility, accuracy, and accountability, when they are not recognized and managed. Transparent and well-disclosed evaluations will help to make conflicts of interests visible and open to monitoring and management (F3 Contextual Viability and P5 Transparency and Disclosure).

The pluralistic nature of evaluation contributes to conflicts that stem from competing values and claims. Evaluators and evaluations are by their nature embroiled in hotly contested debates about the nature of methodologies, paradigms, and traditions that provide evidence for findings, applications, and use. What is considered good, successful, and of high quality is routinely debated. Evaluators who are too closely aligned with one approach to evaluation may experience a conflict of interests when they insist on their preferred approach even in the face of evidence that a different approach is warranted.

Most evaluations, especially ones that are funded, involve inherent conflicts of interests for the evaluator. For example, regardless of whether an evaluator is external or internal to the organization housing the program, evaluators benefit from the evaluations. They receive salary, professional recognition, and potential acclaim and may have access to resources related to professional presentations, publications, and professional development. In addition, the evaluation work that they do contributes to their present and future credibility and employability (U1 Evaluator Credibility). Sometimes, evaluators must bring bad news. When the evaluations they manage produce unwelcome findings, they can experience considerable loss of future income possibilities, damaged reputations, and general aggravation. In such settings the proper course of action is adherence to evaluation accuracy, utility, propriety, and feasibility while documenting and examining evaluation accountability (E1 Evaluation Documentation, E2 Internal Metaevaluation, and E3 External Metaevaluation). Then the evaluation findings can speak for themselves with an authority that is somewhat buffered from acknowledged conflicts of interests.

External evaluators also experience conflicts of interests and are no less biased or more objective than internal evaluators. Both internal and external evaluators experience demanding conflicts of interests. These must be made explicit and managed so that the quality of the evaluation remains intact and is well documented. Internal and external evaluations are discussed more fully in Part V of this book under Standards E2 Internal Metaevaluation and E3 External Metaevaluation.

The processes needed to manage conflicts of interests often illuminate larger issues embedded in role confusions and conflicts throughout the evaluation. Therefore, when evaluators work toward compromise, facilitation, deliberation, and understanding of the inherently conflicting processes and positions that underlie evaluations, the evaluation itself can manifest greater quality along a number of dimensions and better serve the rights and needs of stakeholders and society at large.

❖ IMPLEMENTING P6 CONFLICTS OF INTERESTS

The following are important recommendations for implementing this standard:

1. Whenever they occur, attend to real, potential, or suspected conflicts of interests in a spirit of mutual and deliberate understanding and learning.
2. Ensure that conflicts of interests are openly and productively discussed throughout the entire evaluation process.
3. Build and sustain openness and transparency in the evaluation process to deal with conflicts of interests involving values, positions, status, or other factors.
4. Acknowledge that stakeholders' views, interests, and value judgments may contrast significantly and be in conflict with other stakeholders' views, interests, and judgments (F3 Contextual Viability).
5. Recognize that evaluators and stakeholders can have different perceptions and opinions about the occurrence and severity of conflicts of interests.
6. Be especially alert for conflicts that may be more obvious during the later stages of the evaluation when results are presented.
7. Notice the unique positions that internal and external evaluators occupy with regard to specific conflicts of interests and don't assume that one type is necessarily more objective or less subject to conflicts of interests.

❖ HAZARDS

Some possible hazards with regard to P6 are as follows:

1. Assuming as an evaluator that you have no conflicts of interests
2. Deciding not to raise the issue of a conflict of interests because dealing with it would be too messy
3. Disqualifying information or personnel on the basis of a preexisting conflict of interests without fully exploring whether the conflict has undermined accuracy
4. Failing to consider the impact of conflicts of interests on all dimensions of evaluation quality, including utility, feasibility, propriety, accuracy, and accountability
5. Missing opportunities to help stakeholders recognize and deal with difficult conflicts of interests that might interfere with the benefits they can receive from the evaluation
6. Failing to report serious conflicts of interests as potential limitations of the evaluation

Application Number Six for the Propriety Case Scenario

The scenario that supports this application, including background information about the program, context, and key players, can be read at the end of the Propriety Overview on page 110.

Early on, as soon as the evaluation design was conceptualized and the information collection instruments were prepared, Kwame initiated the application to his university's institutional review board (IRB). Nina and Hanna did not typically initiate IRB applications, and after some initial differences of opinion, they were comfortable supporting Kwame and Dawn by providing the instruments they had been developing and helping describe the methods they proposed. The IRB proposal described the research questions, purpose, and significance of the study; the research design, procedures, and methods of analysis; how subjects would be recruited; and informed consent procedures, confidentiality, and other matters pertaining to interactions with participants. After some queries and clarifications, the IRB approved the study, and the team began collecting, storing, and analyzing the information.

Once data collection had begun, Kwame began to reflect on some of the conflicts that were emerging. First there was the matter with the Slippery Breeze focus group members, where it appeared that previous researchers had been less than responsive to their concerns and needs. Then there was Kwame's experience with Roderick, where he realized that he had missed the opportunity for the evaluation to meet some of Roderick's needs via process use. Kwame decides that they need to consider any potential conflicts of interests more carefully.

He begins by examining his own possible conflicts of interests. First of all, as a university professor, he has obligations to his students and to his wider profession. He realizes that his annual salary and his progress through the tenure and promotion system have depended in large part on his ability to publish peer-reviewed research on evaluation related work. A significant portion of his attention in the HOPE evaluation has focused on publishing results of the studies. He can justify doing so because those who would read the journal articles are potential beneficiaries. However, he wonders if his own vested interests in publication have distracted him from putting primary emphasis on identifying the needs of all stakeholders, including the Slippery Breeze community and participants like Roderick.

He also recognizes the importance of funding to pay for a month of his summer salary and to compensate Dawn as a research assistant. Dawn had been a stellar performer so far, but he wonders if she would have been hired in a competitive process that sought to employ the best staff possible for the available funds. He wonders if his desire to train future evaluators also presents a conflict of interests.

In addition, during data collection, he realized that several respondents were very much invested in seeing the HOPE program continue. He wonders again if their emotional investment in the program led them to minimize any potential weakness and ignore problems, thereby making the outcomes and their learning and accomplishments seem more positive.

His reflections carry him to other examples. Originally, Jonah, the executive director, was more interested in how the HOPE program might be improved, but as the stakes riding on a good evaluation report increased, he seemed to become more concerned about the analyses and what would be included in any public reports. His concern about the negative results from the telephone interviews reflected his conflicts. On the one hand, he wanted to know truthfully about program weaknesses that could be improved. On the other hand, he wanted evaluation results that would support an additional year of funding for the program and his own position. At times he seemed to move in the direction of wanting a marketing study rather than an evaluation.

Most recently, Dawn has interviewed participants from one particular neighborhood group who have been frequent participants in the dialogues because they have their own political agenda that diverges from that of the HOPE program. Rather than trying to address community engagement for social improvement, they are building a local political interest group supporting a council member who is prodevelopment. In addition, this group wants to use the evaluation report for their own political purposes, as soon as they can get their hands on it. Kwame knows that he and Dawn are not quite sure how to handle their interview data.

Kwame also experiences conflicts with regard to publishing in scholarly journals. As they complete their analyses, the evaluation team prepares for the first presentation to Jonah and the board of directors. Kwame is interested in drafting journal articles, too, but is having difficulty finding the time.

Given the pressures to deal with various anxieties and concerns expressed by Jonah and the board, Kwame decides that he needs to deal with the evaluation situation before spending too much time on publications. He and the team suggest to Jonah, who eventually approves the plan after some persuasion, that they recruit a dialogue group of interested participants whose sole purpose is to design reports of findings that can serve the needs of previous and current HOPE participants. The meeting with participants will take place a week after the executive director and board of directors have an opportunity to read and digest the findings. The meeting will be open to all participants, staff, and the board of the HOPE program. The team of evaluators and executive director agree that the evaluators will facilitate the meeting and encourage open and productive dialogue about the findings. In addition, the executive director and board of directors can be present at the meeting and publically agree or disagree with presented or proposed conclusions and interpretations.

Kwame is not sure if he will comment on conflicts of interests in the open meeting. Whether he does or not will depend entirely on the situation. However, as he prepares for the meeting, he is sure that he will continue to examine and try to manage those conflicts that could result in reduced evaluation quality or lead to unethical, unprofessional, or otherwise improper behavior.

❖ SUPPORTING DOCUMENTATION

Greene, J. C. (2005). Evaluators as stewards of the public good. In S. Hood, R. Hopson, & H. Frierson (Eds.), *The role of culture and cultural context in evaluation: A mandate for inclusion, the discovery of truth, and understanding in evaluative theory and practice* (pp. 7–20). Greenwich, CT: Information Age.

Kushner, S. (2000). *Personalizing evaluation.* London: Sage.

Mabry, L. (2003). In living color: Qualitative methods in educational evaluation. In T. Kellaghan, D. L. Stufflebeam, & L. Wingate (Eds.), *International handbook of educational evaluation* (pp. 167–188). Dordrecht, Netherlands: Kluwer.

Mabry, L. (1999). Circumstantial ethics. *American Journal of Evaluation, 20,* 199–213.

Madison, A. M. (2000). Language in defining social problems and in evaluating social programs. In R. K. Hopson (Ed.), *How and why language matters in evaluation: New Directions for Evaluation, 86,* 17–28.

Mark, M. M., Greene, J. C., and Shaw, I. F. (2006). The evaluation of policies, programs, and practices. In I. F. Shaw, J. C. Greene, & M. M. Mark (Eds.), *The Sage handbook of evaluation* (pp. 1–26). London: Sage.

Morris, M. (Ed.). (2008). *Evaluation ethics for best practice: Cases and commentaries.* New York: Guilford Press.

Moskowitz, J. M. (1993). Why reports of outcome evaluations are often biased or uninterpretable. *Evaluation and Program Planning, 16*(1), 1–9.

P7 Fiscal Responsibility

Evaluations should account for all expended resources and comply with sound fiscal procedures and processes.

❖ RATIONALE AND CLARIFICATION

Fiscal responsibility in evaluation refers to the obligations and duties for sound management of all evaluation resources so that they are used effectively, appropriately, and without waste. In addition, fiscal responsibility includes monitoring the actual uses made of resources following best accounting and auditing practices and making monitoring reports available for oversight purposes. Evaluators managing funds have a fiduciary responsibility to sponsors and must document how funds are used in ways that are accurate and transparent to those who fund and audit the evaluation. Violations of fiscal responsibility suggest serious legal and moral failure. In addition, lack of fiscal responsibility can have severe practical consequences, such as lost credibility, reduced use, and evaluation failure. A lack of fiscal responsibility can easily undermine all other aspects of the evaluation.

Responsibility for fiscal resources involves all the steps that good management entails, including planning and oversight (F1 Project Management and F4 Resource Use). Evaluators should be able to enumerate the specific estimated costs and benefits of alternative evaluation procedures to clients, program deliverers, administrators, and other stakeholders. Evaluators are also responsible for making sure that costs are sufficiently explained and clear to clients and stakeholders.

Evaluators apply values when they determine, estimate, and allocate fiscal resources. These value judgments are necessary when evaluators specify the alternatives, costs, benefits, and other pertinent issues that are critical to the allocation and expenditure of resources. Evaluators are responsible for ensuring that the underlying values and perspectives are sufficiently explained and transparent to constituencies (P5 Transparency and Disclosure). Attending to these issues in all stages of the evaluation helps to maintain positive relationships between evaluators and those for whom the evaluation is conducted.

As discussed in detail with regard to feasibility and utility, resources should be used effectively and efficiently (F4 Resource Use, U2 Attention to Stakeholders, and U8 Concern for Consequences and Influences). Standard P7 highlights the duty to produce value through efficient resource use as a professional, legal, and ethical obligation. This duty complements and emphasizes sound and systematic resource use in the service of feasibility, utility, accuracy, and accountability.

❖ IMPLEMENTING P7 FISCAL RESPONSIBILITY

The following are important recommendations for implementing this standard:

1. Consult with clients about anticipated and unanticipated occurrences that threaten the financial viability of the evaluation.
2. Provide opportunities for evaluators, clients, and sponsors to revisit the fiscal resources and processes periodically throughout the evaluation process.
3. Maintain accurate and clear fiscal records detailing exact expenditures (E1 Evaluation Documentation).
4. Arrange for sound accounting practices and hire consultation when necessary to ensure that formal accounting practices are followed.
5. Align actual evaluation tasks with the charges that are incurred so that the budget narrative is clear.
6. Keep records indicating what specific evaluation tasks, such as survey data collection, interview analyses, and reports, actually cost in personnel and other resources.

❖ HAZARDS

Some possible hazards with regard to P7 are as follows:

1. Using resources in ways that are not approved in the budget
2. Not planning for increases in costs over time or because of unexpected problems

3. Failing to have budgets planned and approved before beginning evaluation implementation
4. Assuming that cost estimates are always accurate without asking for second or third opinions
5. Assuming that the lowest bid is the most cost-effective without evaluation of whether it will provide the needed quality
6. Failing to monitor others with access to resources, especially financial assets, to be sure that all funds and resources are accounted for
7. Neglecting financial management because of other pressing evaluation management needs
8. Allowing clients, sponsors, or others with power over the evaluation to convert employees supported by evaluation funds to other tasks that are not part of their job descriptions

Application Number Seven for the Propriety Case Scenario

The scenario that supports this application, including background information about the program, context, and key players, can be read at the end of the Propriety Overview on page 110.

The budget and financial background for the HOPE evaluation has been a complicated one. For various political and quality issues, Jonah and the board of directors prefer to have both the local research firm, RCRI, and the university involved in the evaluation. In addition, because of changing focuses, new evaluation goals, and new funding sources after the evaluation was underway, the dollars available for the evaluation have changed over the course of their first year.

Kwame has exact budget lines for some of his evaluation time, and he bills according to his per hour dollar cost as a university professor, including what is required for fringe benefits. He is able to donate pro bono some hours paid for by university resources because he is engaged in institutionally supported community service as well as research. Furthermore, because he is mentoring and coaching Dawn, he is engaged in teaching, also supported by his budgeted salary line at the university. Sponsors are not paying for all of the hours that Kwame spends on the evaluation, because the university views this mixture of teaching, research, and service as part of its mission and supports faculty to do this kind of work. Each year, Kwame must report to his university supervisors his objectives and accomplishments in each of the three areas. The expectation for Kwame is that he will spend 60% of his time on teaching, 25% on research, and 15% on service. In addition, before engaging in external work, such as the HOPE evaluation, he makes sure to confer with his department chair to clarify that such work is still part of what is expected of him.

Kwame is meticulous about recording the time he spends on tasks. As a novice evaluator, he had no idea how to budget or how much time and money would be needed for specific tasks. Over the years, as he made his notes, his ability to estimate in advance what specific evaluation services and products would cost has become more and more acute.

In the HOPE evaluation, Dawn is funded directly from the evaluation funds. Dawn's efforts are probably worth much more that the dollars spent on her. It is easy to justify her expense because she has been so efficient and productive. However, for various reasons in the past, other graduate research assistants have been less able to produce. Normally, all graduate assistants receive a minimum amount as negotiated at the departmental level. Most work a specified number of hours each week, depending on their appointment level, either quarter-, third-, or half-time. In evaluation work, Kwame supervises the research assistants to allow for ebb and flow in the evaluation work as well as their course work. For example, he allows research assistants to take time off during the weeks before and during final exams. However, he requires that they have banked those hours already or that they have to work extra hours in the future.

Kwame knows he is a good and supportive mentor, and in some cases he has to cover for his graduate students when their reports are substandard or while they are still learning new evaluation tasks and methodologies. Sometimes he works after hours, on weekends, and during vacations to compensate for what he estimates to be the actual value the graduate students needed to produce for the dollars they received. With Dawn, it had been the opposite. She seems to be indefatigable. She is so eager to learn and has such great anticipation skills that she is often working on evaluation matters ahead of time. Kwame also keeps meticulous notes about the extra work that Dawn does. He has learned over the years that effort management and reporting is just as important as tracking the actual dollars spent because effort and dollars need to align. In addition to documenting every expense for accountability purposes, he keeps track of his and others' hours spent on specific tasks.

One of the most difficult financial challenges in the HOPE evaluation is balancing the effort and finances in the evaluation allocated and attributed to the two partners in the team, the university, and RCRI. For example, Kwame and Dawn can rely on the university to provide computers, phones, and other support. For this evaluation infrastructure, they pay a lump sum to the university central office equal to 10% of the total budget that they receive for the evaluation. At RCRI, the situation is strictly pay-as-you-go. Every expense needs to be itemized and planned. The money that Nina and Hanna receive for the evaluation goes directly to and is managed by their internal financial unit. They simply receive salaries and are allowed approved expenses with documentation.

The difficulty in planning for the two evaluation units as one team is that their actual costs to do the same or similar tasks can be different. These differences make it difficult if not impossible to plan and budget for the evaluation without agreements up front. Initially the two partners agreed to allocate roughly equal amounts of available funding for each unit. Then they could each plan to do roughly half of the work and tweak the budgets if needed later. Second, they agreed to have each unit cost out its own expenses, effort, and personnel needs. Third, both RCRI and the university engaged in separate formal agreements with the sponsors and clients. The also considered but rejected a collaboration where one or the other assumed the full budgeted amount from the sponsor and the second entered into a subcontract for services with the first. Perhaps in a future collaboration they might try such an arrangement, as both the university and RCRI had served many times as fiscal agents for research and evaluation projects and subprojects.

At a later date, after the evaluation is completed, Kwame's fiduciary responsibilities continue. Every 5 years, selected faculty members undergo external audits in preparation for accreditation requirements. Small samples of programs are selected by external auditors who review fiscal expenditures and relevant resource uses. Kwame and the HOPE program evaluation are identified by the external auditors for scrutiny. Even though Kwame is on leave from the university to complete a new research project resulting in a book for publication, he will be required to return for face-to-face or telephone consultation with the external auditing team.

As the time for the audit approaches, Kwame prepares for the interview from his home office where he reviews the fiscal records and program folders from the HOPE evaluation. At the appointed time, the phone rings and he is greeted by two members of the auditing team. One is from the external auditing group and one is from the university's auditing department. They introduce themselves cordially and review the purpose of the call and the audit. They describe the stages of auditing that they are undertaking with regard to planning, review of data, fieldwork, and reporting. As part of the fieldwork portion of the audit, Kwame is expected to answer questions about selected transactions and items during the analytical review process.

While the written transactions and recording of resources are clearly spelled out in financial statements and internal departmental budget reports, questions emerge from the external audit about funding for graduate students and the purchases of equipment, gifts, and other related materials. "Why," the external auditor asks, "did you have to hire additional graduate students for analyses and pay them above and beyond the normal graduate student rate set by the university? What assumptions were you making in considering the uses of the graduate students?"

Kwame recalls earlier questions about this very issue over a year ago when the internal auditing office flagged the appointment of the graduate students. Specifically, he recalls how he had detailed conversations with his university's sponsored research office and the budget analyst for the funding agent regarding the anticipated need to hire additional advanced graduate students and purchase more equipment. Originally, he had not planned to have more than one graduate student. However, he needed to hire two additional students for responsibilities that he had not foreseen as additional funded evaluation projects came his way.

In addition to more graduate assistants, the extra evaluation projects required administrative staff to take duties that Kwame normally would have assumed. Kwame lobbied to hire two postdoctoral students with specialized skills to complement and supplement the skill sets of existing staff members. These needs resulted in additional exchanges with the human resources (HR) office, the sponsored research office, and several of his evaluation sponsoring organizations. Ultimately, HR authorized the additional positions, but the required paperwork was extensive and final approval required departmental and dean's level signatures.

Fortunately, Kwame has filed all the e-mails and other correspondence in which he provided a revised budget summary and explanation of the HOPE and other program evaluations. He provides complete answers to the external auditors' questions. Upon the conclusion of the external audit consultation, Kwame returns to his mail thankful again that he made the time to plan and document financial details and effort allocations and to keep all records of discussions and negotiations (E1 Evaluation Documentation).

❖ SUPPORTING DOCUMENTATION

Fitzpatrick, J. L., Sanders, J. R., & Worthen, B. R. (2004). *Program evaluation: Alternative approaches and practical guidelines* (3rd ed.). White Plains, NY: Longman.

Levin, H. M. (2004). Cost effectiveness. *Encyclopedia of evaluation* (p. 90). Thousand Oaks, CA: Sage.

Levin, H. M., & McEwan, P. J. (2001). *Cost-effectiveness analysis: Methods and applications.* Thousand Oaks, CA: Sage.

Posavac, E. J., & Carey, R. J. (2003). *Program evaluation: Methods and case studies* (6th ed.). Upper Saddle River, NJ: Prentice Hall.

Sanders, J. R. (1983). Cost implications of the standards. In M. C. Alkin & L. C. Solmon (Eds.), *The costs of evaluation* (pp. 101–117). Beverly Hills, CA: Sage.

Scriven, M. (1983). Evaluation costs: Concept and theory. In M. C. Alkin & L. C. Solmon (Eds.), *The costs of evaluation* (pp. 27–44). Beverly Hills, CA: Sage.

Part IV

Accuracy Standards

STANDARD STATEMENTS

A1 Justified Conclusions and Decisions	*Evaluation conclusions and decisions should be explicitly justified in the cultures and contexts where they have consequences.*
A2 Valid Information	*Evaluation information should serve the intended purposes and support valid interpretations.*
A3 Reliable Information	*Evaluation procedures should yield sufficiently dependable and consistent information for the intended uses.*
A4 Explicit Program and Context Descriptions	*Evaluations should document programs and their contexts with appropriate detail and scope for the evaluation purposes.*
A5 Information Management	*Evaluations should employ systematic information collection, review, verification, and storage methods.*
A6 Sound Designs and Analyses	*Evaluations should employ technically adequate designs and analyses that are appropriate for the evaluation purposes.*
A7 Explicit Evaluation Reasoning	*Evaluation reasoning leading from information and analyses to findings, interpretations, conclusions, and judgments should be clearly and completely documented.*
A8 Communication and Reporting	*Evaluation communications should have adequate scope and guard against misconceptions, biases, distortions, and errors.*

❖ ACCURACY OVERVIEW

Accuracy is the truthfulness of evaluation representations, propositions, and findings, especially those that support judgments about the quality of programs or program components. In general, accuracy is achieved through sound theory, methods, designs, and reasoning. Evaluations should strive for as much accuracy as is feasible, proper, and useful to support sound conclusions and decisions in specific situations.

One goal of the accuracy standards is to point out the specific components of an evaluation that should be accurate. The eight accuracy standards focus on what it means for specific components to be accurate and how to increase their accuracy. Accuracy of the following evaluation components is especially important:

- Findings, interpretations, conclusions, extrapolations, and decisions (A1 Justified Conclusions and Decisions and A2 Valid Information)
- Reasoning, including the theoretical frameworks that support the reasoning (A5 Information Management, A6 Sound Designs and Analyses, and A7 Explicit Evaluation Reasoning)
- Concepts and terms (A2 Valid Information and A8 Communication and Reporting)
- Information and analyses (A2 Valid Information, A3 Reliable Information, A5 Information Management, and A6 Sound Designs and Analyses)
- Descriptions of programs, program theoretical frameworks, and their contexts (A4 Explicit Program and Context Descriptions)
- Communication and reporting (A8 Communication and Reporting)

Taken together, the accuracy standards also point out how to minimize three factors that can undermine accuracy in evaluations. These limiting factors are

1. Inconsistencies
2. Distortions
3. Misconceptions

No evaluation can remove all systematic and random sources of inaccuracy completely, but the central goal of the accuracy standards is to minimize the presence and impact of these undermining factors as much as possible.

Inconsistencies

Because accurate evaluations require reliable information, they implement practices to increase consistency in information management. Standard A3 Reliable Information directly addresses how to increase and document reliability, not just in outcomes assessments but also in all procedures related to selecting, collecting, and analyzing evaluation information. In general, reliability is increased through reductions in random errors.

Distortions

A second major factor that undermines accuracy is distortion of information and communication caused by omissions, inattention, incompetence, bias, or misconduct. Accurate evaluations prevent, or when that is not possible, investigate and report all known distortions (E1 Evaluation Documentation). There are many potential causes of distortion, such as collecting or entering the wrong information, losing information, not securing information, mislabeling or misclassifying information, inappropriate analysis procedures, inadequate design implementation, ignoring conditions for information collection that deviate from the proposed methods, lack of attention to cultural and other background influences on information, and poor reporting. Good training of evaluation staff can increase the levels of required competence to help avoid distortions. In particular, Standards A5 Information Management, A6 Sound Designs and Analyses, and A8 Communication and Reporting provide many suggestions for preventing and, when that is not possible, monitoring and reporting the impact of distortions (E1 Evaluation Documentation and E2 Internal Metaevaluation).

Misconceptions

Misconceptions in evaluation stem from two different types of conceptualization problems. First, a concept or set of concepts may be illogical or incomplete. Such misconceptions are not supported by the evaluation evidence and information but can result from preexisting ideas, emotional appeals, or other attempts at persuasion. The validation techniques related to A1 Justified Conclusions and Decisions, A2 Valid Information, A7 Explicit Evaluation Reasoning, and A6 Sound Designs and Analyses are often sufficient to expose and correct this type of misconception.

The second type of conceptual challenge is probably best described as *different ways of thinking.* Differences in how people think do not necessarily indicate misconceptions. On the contrary, documenting different stakeholders' conceptualizations about the program can contribute greatly to understanding the program with accuracy. However, these different perspectives, while normal and important for full understanding, are often ignored, marginalized, or viewed as a conflict to be resolved as quickly as possible. Said another way, one stakeholder's dearly held concept, fact, belief, or value that provides the starting point for understanding the evaluation evidence is sometimes another stakeholder's eschewed misconception, falsehood, or superstition. The misconception occurs when only one out of many ways to construct a domain of knowledge is immediately viewed as the only way. To deal with this challenge effectively requires reflection on the part of the evaluator and key users about the differing perspectives and their value in specific contexts. It requires commitment to multiple perspectives, not only to achieve utility, feasibility, and propriety but also to achieve accuracy (see for example, U4 Explicit Values, F3 Contextual Viability, and P4 Clarity and Fairness).

During the last two decades, the evaluation community has explored ways of dealing with different ways of thinking, in particular those that are the result of different cultural experiences and different languages. Generally, most evaluators agree that the best approach does not reside in adopting one type of design and information collection methodology over another. Rather, multimethod techniques can explore different perspectives addressing the important issues and evaluation questions. To use multiple methods and designs well, evaluations must align the designs and methods that fit best with the users of and contexts for the evaluation (A2 Valid Information, A5 Information Management, and A6 Sound Designs and Analyses; see also U3 Negotiated Purposes and U5 Relevant Information). A key requirement for addressing this issue is accurate communication (Standard A8 Communication and Reporting).

The accuracy standards require frameworks for discussing the specific languages, concepts, cultures, and backgrounds that are privileged in any specific evaluation, especially those that receive the most attention and resources (A2 Valid Information). In addition, evaluators must monitor how different stakeholders' values affect accuracy.

The goal of the accuracy standards is to increase the truthfulness of evaluation findings and conclusions, especially those that support judgments about the quality of programs or program components. However, because accuracy is not demonstrable in an absolute sense, different stakeholders left to their own selective opinions may come to very different judgments about an evaluation's accuracy. Therefore, it is important to communicate how an evaluation creates accuracy in each specific program and evaluation context (E1 Evaluation Documentation, E2 Internal Metaevaluation, and E3 External Metaevaluation).

The best foundation for accuracy is robust and nuanced attention to these standards and the sound methodologies that they advocate. Through ongoing communication, individual evaluations informed by the accuracy standards can serve to educate users about ways to increase accuracy. If accuracy is suitably supported and communicated, evaluation findings and conclusions are more likely to be viewed as trustworthy, increasing the likelihood of appropriate use (U6 Meaningful Processes and Products).

❖ ACCURACY SCENARIO

The next section describes an evaluation scenario, including the program being evaluated and the principal players and their roles. Later on, specific applications of the scenario at the end of each standard illustrate

- how that specific standard is related to selected dilemmas,
- strategies for implementing the standard in this scenario, and
- how other standards come into play in this scenario.

This scenario and subsequent applications are related to real world evaluation practice but are not based on any specific evaluation. They highlight dilemmas and reflective practices typical for many programs and program evaluations across a wide variety of fields and applications. In practice, the standards work in tandem with evaluators' and other stakeholders' knowledge, values, and experiences to result in sound decisions in specific settings. These applications are not meant to specify one set of best practices but are intended to support increased reflection about what constitutes excellent evaluation practice in specific situations.

Teacher Quality Enhancement: An Evaluation of Professional Development Programming

One of the pressing problems facing most organizations is how to help skilled workers keep up with new developments in their fields. In this evaluation scenario, a large midwestern state has received a significant amount of federal money and has appropriated state matching funds to enhance teacher quality. The 5-year budget (with the possibility of renewal for another 5 years) has been allocated to addressing the specific needs of these Goal Areas:

1. Math Learners
2. Science Learners
3. English Language Learners
4. Teaching American History
5. Reading
6. Technology Acquisition and Integration

Each of these Goal Areas has its own budget and its own steering committee. All address the needs of preservice or in-service teachers, but the expected long-term outcome is improved academic achievement for all students. A key feature of the program is the collaboration between the state Department of Education (SDE), local area educational associations, institutions of higher education that provide teacher preparation, and individual school districts. Some of the programming is directed at preservice teachers still enrolled in teacher preparation programs. Other programming is directed at practicing, in-service teachers.

Multiple external subcontractors are evaluating different Goal Area programs. Even though they have separate subcontracts, the independent evaluators are in collaboration with one another in order to share resources and improve overall evaluation and program quality. Each year, the independent evaluators must produce preliminary evaluation reports in October and final evaluation reports in May. Typically, they share drafts with one another and the program directors prior to posting the reports. The evaluators are in frequent communication with steering committee members and other possible evaluation users. At biannual conferences, the evaluators meet with the steering committees to discuss and update evaluation purposes, questions, methods, and findings from previously collected information. Executive summaries and full reports are available at the Goal Area websites, and all participating organizations and individuals are encouraged via e-mail and websites to read and comment on the evaluation purposes, uses, methods, and findings. In focus group interviews and discussions, evaluation findings are reviewed in order to further problem solving and dissemination as well as gather new information and refocus the evaluations for the subsequent year. Evaluators prepare and report annual internal metaevaluations.

The main focus of these applications will be the English Language Learner Goal Area, specifically the Summer Institute. Some key personnel in the Summer Institute program evaluation are as follows.

- Huseyin Ozturk, PhD, is the lead evaluator for the English Language Learner Goal Area focus. He has been a tenured professor of evaluation at the state university for more than 10 years and teaches graduate courses in statistics, assessment, and evaluation. Although his training is in quantitative methods, he apprenticed for several years with an ethnographer at the university and is committed to mixed methods. He conducts one or two external evaluations each year and encourages interested graduate students to work on the external evaluations with him as part of a practicum that he offers. Although Huseyin was born in Turkey and lived there until he was 22, he attended English and American language schools that are native to his country. He speaks three languages fluently: Turkish, French, and English. After completing his PhD and marrying a Wisconsin native, he became a naturalized American citizen and speaks English well. He says, "My children are Midwesterners through and through, so I am, too."

- Consuela Mendez is a former middle school language arts teacher with an advanced degree in educational supervision. Her specialty is second language acquisition. She administers the English Language Learner (ELL) Goal Area half-time and chairs the ELL steering committee, responsible for planning and program decisions. As the ELL coordinator, she is also a member of the state Teacher Quality Enhancement (TQE) Program Advisory Board, chaired by the state Department of Education associate director, Dr. Helga LaFayette. Consuela was born and schooled in Puerto Rico before coming to the continental U.S. to attend college on the East Coast. She met her husband in college, and the two of them moved to the Midwest to find good jobs. She is a fully literate, bilingual speaker of Spanish and English.

• Helga LaFayette, PhD, is an associate director for curriculum at the state Department of Education and directs the TQE grant. She is responsible for several ongoing programs at the SDE, including the TQE program. She has been in the state capital since leaving her teaching job 15 years ago to return to graduate school and has been associate director for the past 4 years. She is deeply committed to increasing children's learning in schools and is well connected and attentive to both the governor's office and the state legislature.

• The ELL Goal Focus Steering Committee members are for the most part district curriculum directors and full-time lead teachers. Because participating on the steering committee typically requires a small buyout from their district or local area education association, most of them participate for only 1 year. They are a lively group, full of humor, and enjoy one another's company. They provide a voice for teachers' and students' interests, at least as they understand them.

• Graduate students on the evaluation team have taken two required courses in program evaluation and participated in previous evaluations. They include one East Asian female, an African American female, a White female, and a White male. Only the East Asian student speaks a language other than English. Two have been previously employed full time as public school teachers, and one has taught extensively in Africa. They are all pursuing research PhD degrees but in different fields: one in language development, one in sociology, and two in educational statistics and measurement.

The team evaluating the programming in the English Language Learner Goal Area includes four graduate students under Huseyin's direction. Huseyin reports to Dr. LaFayette and to Consuela, the Goal Area project director. Based on his previous work for the SDE, Huseyin submitted a formal proposal describing his approach to evaluating the English Language Learner Goal Area programming. He referred to *The Program Evaluation Standards* and emphasized his team's commitment to evaluation utility, propriety, feasibility, accuracy, and accountability.

During Year 1, Huseyin and his team were selected as external evaluators in a competitive process, negotiated the final budget, and engaged in a formal memorandum of agreement and subcontracting process. They participated in ongoing collaborative discussions of the purposes and uses the evaluation would serve, investigated who the intended users and audiences might be, and arrived at specific evaluation questions. In general they dealt with many dilemmas and problems related to utility, feasibility, propriety, accuracy, and accountability. Many of the issues are ongoing and are part of the mix that the evaluation team will continue to address throughout the cycles of evaluation. Some of the problems that form the background for the application of the individual accuracy standards are as follows.

• Legislators who supported appropriations for the Teacher Quality Enhancement programs are eager to see demonstrated growth in language, math, and science test scores for all students, and especially for English Language Learners (ELLs). Standardized tests are available with demonstrated reliability and validity for some types of interpretations, but the reliability and validity indices may not be generalizable to this situation. For example, it is not clear that the measures are aligned with the outcomes expected from the Summer Institute. In addition, it is not clear how to isolate effects from other confounding factors in any of the possible feasible designs (F2 Practical Procedures). It is unknown what percentage of students will be motivated to do their best when they take tests. Lastly, too little is known about the measures' reliability and validity for interpretations about the academic growth of ELLs.

- The sponsoring agencies have sent mixed signals about whether they are more interested in investigations of knowledge and skill growth for teachers, students, or both. They clearly want the evaluation team to track the allocation of resources and program implementation. They want to know how participation changes teachers and their instructional methods.

- Even though the program is statewide and other states are implementing similar programs, some SDE officials, especially liaisons to the governor's office, want to see randomized field trials. However, they also want to see most of the funding go to the actual programming rather than to research and evaluation.

- The budgeted amount for evaluations is relatively small, given the multifaceted, statewide scope of the program, and has been distributed over multiple evaluation teams.

- Many advisory team members and program staff are most interested in whether individual teachers actually use specific curricula, presentations, workbooks, and workshop products. For example, one subcomponent of the ELL Goal Area programming is a week-long Summer Institute open to teacher educators, practicing teachers, school administrators, and preservice teachers (teacher education students). The Summer Institute consists of miniworkshops staffed by 14 consultants, each responsible for a different focus (math, science, history, ELL, and reading) and a different age group (elementary or secondary). The consultants use different approaches and materials. Consuela and many advisory committee members want to know which of the miniworkshops benefit participants and actually result in changes in classroom instruction.

This scenario description captures just a small part of the complexity that most evaluation situations entail. To anyone first encountering this situation, it may seem quite challenging. A key question that unifies the accuracy standards is what to do about complexity. How much detail and complexity has to be understood or captured for the evaluation to be accurate? When are summaries, whether narrative or statistical, accurate with regard to what they include and what they omit?

The following eight standards and applications address these questions and illustrate how the standards can help guide evaluation problem solving. In the applications, Consuela, Huseyin, and others use the standards to think about program evaluation dilemmas, trade-offs, and complexities as they go forward with planning, implementing, and using program evaluations.

A1 Justified Conclusions and Decisions

Evaluation conclusions and decisions should be explicitly justified in the cultures and contexts where they have consequences.

❖ RATIONALE AND CLARIFICATION

The accuracy of findings, interpretations, and conclusions is the central goal supported by the accuracy standards. The process of justifying their accuracy requires that evaluators and evaluation users judge

- the quality of information
- the soundness of the logic that leads from information to the findings, interpretations, and conclusions
- the plausibility of alternative interpretations

Standard A1 acknowledges that accuracy in evaluation contexts is not established in a universal sense. Ideas and meanings expressed in specific languages can change over time, places, individuals, and groups. For conclusions to be accurate in a practical sense such that their consequences are justified, they must be understood within the contexts where the languages and concepts that support them can be applied. Part of the rationale for Standard A1 is to call attention to this practicality while emphasizing the key importance of sound methods in specific contexts.

Often evaluation conclusions address whether a program resulted in specific outcomes. In order to justify conclusions about outcomes and impacts, evaluators must attend to supporting methods and research designs (A5 Information

Management, A6 Sound Designs and Analyses, and A7 Explicit Evaluation Reasoning).

From one year to the next, a program may experience variability in funding, policy spaces, resources, participants, or needs. Nevertheless, it is not unusual to find evaluation users drawing conclusions about last year's version of the program and applying them in decisions about this and next year's versions. In addition, program contexts for replications are difficult if not impossible to control due to the many factors and influences involved. Nevertheless, evaluation users often build projections based on a program in one setting and apply them to another setting with a generally similar program or proposed program. This type of conclusion necessitates assumptions, including generalizations about the original context and program. Justifiable conclusions require a rigorous evaluation of these assumptions (A4 Explicit Program and Context Descriptions and A7 Explicit Evaluation Reasoning).

Accurate evaluations rely on many practices common to other domains of inquiry. However, because conclusions and their consequences are justified within cultures and contexts, it is important to include more diverse perspectives than are often employed in any one research paradigm. Moreover, it is critical to identify and report all important assumptions and the interpretive frameworks that are applied. Being explicit about assumptions (A7 Explicit Evaluation Reasoning) allows evaluations to be fine-tuned and also sheds light on the justification for the findings, conclusions, and consequences that follow. Thus stakeholders' values and perspectives are important not only for utility, feasibility, and propriety, they are also critical for accurate conclusions and decisions about the program (see U4 Explicit Values, F3 Contextual Viability, and P1 Responsive and Inclusive Orientation).

❖ IMPLEMENTING A1 JUSTIFIED CONCLUSIONS AND DECISIONS

The following are important recommendations for implementing this standard:

1. Clarify which stakeholders will draw conclusions and make decisions so that their knowledge frameworks and methodological preferences can become part of the accuracy dialogue and reasoning leading to conclusions (U2 Attention to Stakeholders).
2. Clarify the responsibilities of the evaluation team members and other key stakeholders for crafting accurate interpretations, conclusions, and recommendations.
3. Be sure that findings, interpretations, and conclusions reflect the constructs and program theoretical terminology as defined by those

who will draw conclusions and make judgments (A2 Valid Information and A4 Explicit Program and Context Descriptions).

4. Identify how different users define accuracy in evaluation findings and conclusions, and use communication strategies to clarify differing conceptions about accuracy (A8 Communication and Reporting).
5. Make effective choices about the breadth and depth of information addressing different evaluation questions so as to increase the likelihood of accurate findings and conclusions (A5 Sound Information Methods and A7 Explicit Evaluation Reasoning).
6. Ensure that adequate representations of the program and the evaluation context clarify (a) the conditions in which initial interpretations and conclusions are made and (b) how these conditions relate practically and theoretically to other important interpretations and conclusions (A4 Explicit Program and Context Descriptions).
7. In implementing all eight accuracy standards, maintain the perspective that their value lies in supporting sound conclusions and decisions in the cultures and contexts where the conclusions and decisions have consequences.

❖ HAZARDS

Some possible hazards with regard to A1 are as follows:

1. Assuming that findings and conclusions that are accurate from the evaluation team's perspective will result in accurate conclusions and decisions by stakeholders
2. Ignoring different cultural or other conceptual perspectives and assuming that technically adequate methods are the most important or only factor necessary for justified conclusions and decisions
3. Assuming that social science research methodology will transfer intact to evaluation settings and result in justified findings and conclusions
4. Assuming that conditions and factors will not change much from the time of information collection to the time for decision making. The impact of changing conditions on conclusions is especially problematic in many volatile organizational and community settings
5. Using technical social science terms to arrive at findings and conclusions without translating them for stakeholders and decision makers who must arrive at judgments and decisions
6. Assuming that the accuracy of evaluation information will be the only or the most important factor in the contexts where decisions take place

Application Number One for the Accuracy Case Scenario

The scenario that supports this application, including background information about the program, context, and key players, can be read at the end of the Accuracy Overview on page 161.

Dr. Helga LaFayette, the Teacher Quality Enhancement (TQE) program director at the state level, has a general orientation meeting for the evaluation teams and specific project managers. Consuela, her program staff, and many steering committee members and liaisons for the governor's education committee and the legislature also attend. In addition to "meet and greet," a key purpose of the meeting is to discuss how the separate evaluations will be conducted and coordinated. The evaluation teams are already engaged in ongoing discussions of the purposes and uses of their specific evaluations. They are weighing the most important uses of information and the feasibility and propriety of various approaches and methods. The meeting includes breakout sessions for specific Goal Area teams, such as the English Language Learners (ELL) group, to discuss intended evaluation uses and purposes.

For the ELL evaluation component, Huseyin and Consuela put together an initial list of decision makers (in the broadest sense) who will act on evaluation information. They catalogue the kinds of decisions that these individuals are likely to make. With regard to ELL, Huseyin and Consuela discuss the decisions that will be made based at least in part on evaluation information.

- Consuela, her staff, and the steering committee, in consultation with Dr. LaFayette, will decide whether to invest resources in and repeat the Summer Institute and other subcomponents of the ELL Goal Area in future years.
- Consuela, her staff, and the steering committee will decide which aspects of the Summer Institute and other subcomponents to maintain, drop, or improve.
- Educators and administrators statewide will decide if they want to support or participate in the professional development activities of the ELL Goal Area.
- National leaders in Congress, advised by their staff members, will decide whether to continue appropriations for the TQE program at the national level.
- TQE program officers at the national level will make decisions about accountability for the money expended by this specific state's TQE program.
- SDE staff will decide how accountable the expenditure of federal and state funds has been.

Huseyin and Consuela know that this short list is just a beginning and that over the course of Year 1, it will become longer and much more detailed, identifying specific individual users and the decisions that they will likely need to make.

Consuela expresses appreciation for the wide reach of the TQE evaluation, specifically for what Huseyin and his team are doing with regard to the ELL component. However, Huseyin is quick to point out that the evaluation team's primary responsibility is to support the quality of evaluation findings related to the specific questions that she and the steering committee choose. He emphasizes that many decisions will also be based on other factors in addition to evaluation findings: for example political and economic factors.

The evaluation team is committed to the accuracy of evaluation findings in support of policy decisions. Huseyin assures Consuela that the evaluation team will report clearly and try to ensure that the findings are neither ignored and neglected, nor misinterpreted, misapplied, or misused (see also U3 Negotiated Purposes, U5 Relevant Information, and U8 Concern for Consequences and Influence). The team will be vigilant about accuracy of evaluation findings used to justify policy decisions. It will also communicate with users about the role of accurate evidence in justifying minor decisions, such as which of the 14 workshops in the Summer Institute need improvement. Evidence-based decision making is an important goal, but they know they cannot ensure that all decisions will be justified based on evaluation findings alone.

At a subsequent meeting, Huseyin and Consuela discuss the information and degrees of accuracy needed for specific Year 1 evaluation questions. A federal program officer has mentioned that the first-year evaluation does not have to produce information about whether the program has had an impact on students. However, the governor's office is always talking about student achievement as the only outcome of interest. Consuela and the sponsors are most interested in gauging the impact of the program on teachers, both for improvement and accountability. In particular, Consuela wants to know if participants in the Summer Institute

- become more knowledgeable about the needs of ELLs in their districts
- are more confident in their knowledge about academic and social needs of ELLs
- exhibit sustained motivation to change their in-class and out-of-class teaching with regard to the needs of ELLs

Consuela also wants to know if teachers feel that their participation in the Summer Institute was a good use of their professional development time and if it has helped energize and motivate them for the coming school year.

Consuela is aware that teachers have found the school climate challenging in recent years and that burnout, especially of midcareer teachers, is a potentially serious problem. For economic reasons, burned-out teachers do not always quit their jobs. It's important to find ways for them to become excited and re-engaged so that they again find meaning in teaching and helping students. Consuela believes that for most teachers, feeling that they can make a difference in their students' lives is the key to their engagement. Many teachers have been inadequately prepared to deal with the most pressing needs of some of the ELLs. While there are a number of important outcomes to discuss, Consuela is particularly interested in assessing one specific short-term outcome: whether teachers express greater self-efficacy with regard to their responsibilities for ELLs' academic outcomes.

Huseyin and Consuela engage in discussions about evaluation methods that will lead to accurate assessment of teacher outcomes from the Summer Institute. They begin a conversation about what makes interpretations of information valid for their intended purposes and about the technical characteristics that the evaluation team is committed to, including multiple methods and approaches. Huseyin wants to be sure that he and Consuela are on the same page with regard to assumptions about the quality of information (A2 Valid Information), the designs for data collection (A6 Sound Designs and Analyses), and what is needed to reason to specific conclusions (A7 Explicit Evaluation

Reasoning). He wants to know if the focus should be on improving next year's ELL program implementation and whether different goal areas might get more or less funding based on evaluation results. Reliability and information management will need attention later in the process (A3 Reliable Information and A5 Information Management). All of these issues will be addressed in various formal and informal communications (A8 Communication and Reporting). Huseyin and Consuela set a time to continue this discussion about how to get the accuracy needed so that findings and conclusions regarding the evaluation questions are explicitly justified.

❖ SUPPORTING DOCUMENTATION

Charmaz, K. (2000). Grounded theory: Objectivist and constructivist methods. In N. K. Denzin & Y. S. Lincoln (Eds.), *Handbook of qualitative research* (2nd ed., pp. 509–535). Thousand Oaks, CA: Sage.

Cronbach, L. J. (1982). *Designing evaluations of educational and social programs.* San Francisco: Jossey-Bass.

Greene, J. C. (2006). Evaluation, democracy, and social change. In I. F. Shaw, J. C. Greene, & M. M. Mark (Eds.), *The Sage handbook of evaluation* (pp. 118–140). London: Sage.

Mark, M. M., Henry, G. T., & Julnes, G. (2000). *Evaluation: An integrated framework for understanding, guiding, and improving policies and programs.* San Francisco: Jossey-Bass.

Rogers, P. J., & Williams, B. (2006). Evaluation for practice improvement and organizational learning. In I. F. Shaw, J. C. Greene, & M. M. Mark (Eds.), *The Sage handbook of evaluation* (pp. 76–97). London: Sage.

Weiss, C. H. (1998). *Evaluation* (2nd ed.). New Jersey: Prentice Hall.

Wholey, J. S. (2004). Using evaluation to improve performance and support policy design making. In M. C. Alkin (Ed.), *Evaluation roots* (pp. 267–275). Thousand Oaks, CA: Sage.

A2 Valid Information

Evaluation information should serve the intended purposes and support valid interpretations.

❖ RATIONALE AND CLARIFICATION

Validity in its various emphases is an integrating theme across all the Accuracy Standards. For example,

- Standard A3 Reliable Information describes the supporting role of consistency in establishing dependable scores from which valid inferences may be drawn.
- Standard A4 Explicit Program and Context Descriptions requires that the terminology be justified and validated for describing programs and their contexts and that the scope be adequate for the purposes.
- Standard A5 Information Management describes the methodological steps that need to be taken to protect validity during data selection, collection, and storage.
- Standard A6 Sound Designs and Analyses introduces the role of design and analyses in valid interpretations, for example, the validity of conclusions about causality, and the need to investigate threats to validity by examining alternative explanations.
- Standard A7 Explicit Evaluation Reasoning discusses the role of logic and reasoning in the validity of findings and conclusions.
- Standard A8 Communication and Reporting emphasizes that ongoing interactions and formal and informal sharing of ideas are required to achieve validity in interpretations.

The specific purpose of Standard A2 Valid Information is to emphasize the fundamentally interpretive and conceptual nature of validity. At a general level, valid interpretations are important because they form the basis for an accurate understanding of the world. However, different people sometimes interpret experiences in very different ways. In evaluation settings, differences in interpretations of language, experiences, and other information should be made explicit and examined. Any incomplete or poorly differentiated concepts can produce misconceptions that undermine accuracy.

Fortunately, in most evaluation settings, many shared understandings are foundational and widely accepted. They become the nearest thing to shared, universal truths. For example, most people appear to share dependable understandings for concrete objects tied to our senses, such as *water* or *fire,* even though figurative uses of the terms may vary widely. People also share an understanding of common procedures that are essential for human functioning and therefore widely transmitted in most cultures. For example, most evaluators and stakeholders usually agree completely about the procedures for *counting* (i.e., they agree on what *to count* means as a simple procedure).

However, reaching agreement about the exact meanings of terms in evaluations often takes additional communication and definition. In addition to conceptual meanings, exact meanings also include how we make the terms operational in practice. For example, in a program evaluation where we want to count participants accurately, we might have to further clarify what we mean by *participant.* Does *participant* mean all those who register for the workshop, only those who show up the first day, or only those who complete all activities? Are the participants only those who meet all the target criteria for recruitment and enrollment? Is the unit of participation the individual or the group? In short, which types of participants will we count? *Participants* as a term must be defined and made operational in order for us to agree on how to count accurately.

Some concepts are especially hard to define universally because they are constructed quite differently in different languages, cultures, or fields of scholarship. Reaching agreement about how to define terms representing abstract concepts (not concrete sensory objects) is especially difficult. Many such terms are required to evaluate programs: for example, such concepts as *motivation, achievement, cooperation, collaboration, assertiveness, aggression, punishment, self-reliance, health, well-being, value-added, at risk, prevention, community outreach, experiment, translational research, model,* and *theory.*

Most of these abstract concepts are defined in the context of various theories that guide programs and evaluations. For example, cultural systems usually define what *cooperation* is and how it functions. An evaluation of increased cooperation in translational and clinical research must first define what cooperation means for this purpose. Similarly, much of the conceptual foundations for programs have their basis in program theory, described more fully in A4 Explicit Program and Context Descriptions. Absent attention to theory, different participants, staff, and evaluators may begin and end the evaluation with different theories about how and why a program does or does not work. In evaluation, too, conceptualizations are heavily rooted in theoretical foundations. Because different stakeholders have conceptual systems based on different experiences and backgrounds, an acceptable validity framework requires discussion of conceptual differences and some degree of consensus terminology, descriptions, and examples.

Standard A2 recognizes that the accuracy of evaluation information depends on the validity of its interpretation in specific contexts. Interpretations of information validated for one setting and set of purposes cannot be transferred automatically to other purposes or settings. Procedures to investigate and increase the validity of interpretations should attend to the settings and purposes of the information.

Standard A2 also focuses on the scope and the sufficiency of information. Evaluation information should provide sufficiently focused evidence with the right breadth and depth for such purposes as documenting the program's underlying theories, components, and related phenomena. Scope also refers to different sources of information and methods for collecting information, grounded in different understandings and perspectives related to the evaluation purposes. A variety of information types can contribute to judgments about the validity of interpretations because the information is not dependent on just one method or perspective (see A5 Information Management).

In summary, establishing the validity of evaluation information for specific conclusions and decisions requires (1) communication about stakeholders' differing understandings of reality, (2) investigating the alignment of key terms and ideas to one another theoretically and operationally, and (3) arriving at one or more adequate definitions for all terms required for the evaluation purposes. Doing this in ways that are effective, fair, and transparent also contributes to feasibility, propriety, and utility.

The validity of interpretations is always dependent on systems of thought and how they relate to the purposes of the evaluation (U3 Negotiated Purposes). Sometimes compound and complex definitions will be needed in order to address all of the evaluation purposes accurately in the contexts that stakeholders inhabit. Evaluators must involve clients, sponsors, and other stakeholders to be sure that the scope of the interpretations (an accuracy consideration) is aligned with their needs (a utility consideration).

❖ IMPLEMENTING A2 VALID INFORMATION

The following are important recommendations for implementing this standard:

1. Clarify stakeholders' conceptual understandings, terms, and language through focus groups, town meetings, or other procedures to identify problematic areas in specific evaluations.
2. Demonstrate cultural competence with regard to information validity, and attend to key terms and their meaning in all relevant cultural groups. Culturally competent approaches to validity recognize the importance of indigenous systems of thought from all involved cultures.
3. Clarify and be explicit about key terms and propositions from formal theories and research (*etic* perspectives) and key terms and understandings that are indigenous to the setting (*emic* perspectives).
4. Address information validity concerns in an ongoing fashion through the cycles of evaluation. Because validation processes involve communication and learning, determining which terms to use and which systems of thought to prefer, privilege, and adopt may continue for the duration of the evaluation

❖ HAZARDS

Some possible hazards with regard to A2 are as follows:

1. Adopting technical terms from one or more social sciences without investigating their fit to the evaluation setting and without facilitating adequate understanding of their meanings and references by key stakeholders or respondents
2. Ignoring differences in the underlying meanings or values attached to terms and assuming that because one common term is involved it means the same thing to all stakeholders or that there is necessarily only one true meaning
3. Inadequately operationalizing key terms, so that they mean different things for program implementation than for program outcomes. In this context, *operationalizing* a concept means applying specific methods to concretely define, implement, or assess that concept (for example, *aggressiveness* or *achievement*)
4. Privileging representations from the most powerful groups only while ignoring other less powerful stakeholder groups

5. Adopting just one approach or set of approaches when different terms or definitions from different groups would represent a more appropriate and complete representation of the program or its context
6. Not preparing sufficiently detailed explanations, communications, and educational efforts to build bridges from one perspective to another, thus failing to create more broadly accurate information for this setting
7. Assuming that one discipline, approach, or perspective is intrinsically more meritorious without careful attention to its worth in specific situations

Application Number Two for the Accuracy Case Scenario

The scenario that supports this application, including background information about the program, context, and key players, can be read at the end of the Accuracy Overview on page 161.

At the joint meeting of the evaluation and steering committees, Consuela and Huseyin go to the whiteboard to lead a brainstorming session about important words that are vague, unclear, or that might cause trouble. As an example, they ask what the term *English Language Learner* (ELL) really means and how ELLs should be counted. Someone volunteers that ELLs are students who do not have adequate English competency to be able to learn in the typical classroom. Mary Jane Smith, a language arts teacher with a wicked wit, quips "This definition fits 75% of my students who were born in America!" Others comment that ELLs are those who don't speak English as their first language, leading Huseyin and Consuela to both laugh along with the others who remember that English is Consuela's second language (after Spanish) and Huseyin's third (after Turkish and French).

One of the steering committee members, LaTonya Williams, has helped Consuela write a series of state mini-grant proposals to support the needs of ELLs. She recollects some of the scholarship describing variability in ELLs. Students who immigrate to the Midwest speaking a different first language exhibit a wide variety of important characteristics. A few have attended English language schools in their home countries. A few have not attended schools of any kind on a regular basis. Some have developed extensive literacy in their first language. Others do not have basic literacy skills in any language. Some are quite accomplished academically. Especially in math, some are much more advanced than the average student in their current U.S. schools. Others do not have basic academic learning skills, study habits, or background knowledge. ELLs' families are variable, too, with some being able to support their children's learning formally and informally and others not able to do this nearly so well. Consuela and LaTonya point out that these differences are important and ask if all ELLs share any characteristics in common. Many steering committee members agree that all ELLs, even those most fluent in English, might have very different cultural knowledge, especially about such things as standardized testing, the place of individual homework and group work, the role of the teacher, how to relate to other students, local customs, sports allusions and metaphors, and the role of religion in daily life and in the school. LaTonya points out that even though many ELLs would be different from majority students on these dimensions, they would also likely be different from one another, too.

Huseyin asks, "If the long-range goal of the ELL project is to improve academic outcomes for ELLs, how do we identify the subgroups of ELLs that can benefit? Should we count and assess the outcomes for all ELLs, regardless of their background characteristics?" Many people try to talk at once, but Mary, the social studies teacher on the steering committee, catches everyone's attention. "I think we can classify different types of ELLs without too much trouble. What I'm really worried about is what outcomes we plan to measure. I sure hope we don't just rely on our annual standardized test scores!"

Huseyin writes the expression *ELL Outcomes* on the whiteboard, and asks the group, "What does this mean to you?" Someone responds, "Well, it's not just academic outcomes, if we really want to help these kids!" Consuela and Huseyin distribute one of the logic models from the grant proposal so everyone can review the listed outcomes, and the group continues this dynamic conversation about what these mean and how they should be assessed. Someone raises the issue that the governor's office and the legislature probably will want one single, simple-to-explain outcome measure without any complexity or wiggle room, and that their job will be to figure out how to define which ELL types to lump together. The spirited discussion continues, and Huseyin makes a mental note to contact various groups of stakeholders and provide them with an online survey to clarify how they define the critical terms that are surfacing. He knows that he must include parents, legislators and other policymakers, teachers, administrators, and maybe local community leaders. He wonders whether he should survey students, and if so how.

Collecting information about how these terms are understood is the first step, but it is just the beginning. He begins to put together a plan for communicating these different conceptualizations among stakeholders. Because planning and communication are so important for all dimensions of evaluation quality, he begins to alternate between accuracy and utility considerations, all the time reviewing propriety and feasibility issues. He stops after a while, refocuses on accuracy, and makes some notes.

- How can we clarify the key conceptual differences in stakeholders' understandings of the ELL program, its context, and its outcomes?
- How can we select accurate conceptual definitions that are aligned with the purposes and uses the evaluation will serve?
- Once we illustrate differences in definitions, should we choose some limited number to guide us and, if so, which ones and how many?
- How can we be sure that the definitions guiding the actual program and its context are also theoretically and operationally the same as those guiding assessments and documentation?
- If we define different groups of ELLs for assessment and analysis, how do we avoid just grouping them into the ethnic or language groups and really focus on concepts that are important in our theories of ELLs' needs, especially what they need for best academic learning?
- Much of the ELL Summer Institute is dedicated to augmenting what stakeholders know and believe about ELLs. Perhaps conceptual change in how participating teachers define these concepts is an important outcome in its own right?

❖ SUPPORTING DOCUMENTATION

Brandon, P. R. (1998). Stakeholder participation for the purpose of helping ensure evaluation validity: Bridging the gap between collaborative and non-collaborative evaluations. *American Journal of Evaluation, 19,* 325–337.

Guzman, B. L. (2003). Examining the role of cultural competency in program evaluation: Visions for new millennium evaluators. In S. I. Donaldson & M. Scriven (Eds.), *Evaluating social programs and problems: Visions for the new Millennium* (pp. 167–182). Thousand Oaks, CA: Sage.

Kane, M. T. (2006). Validation. In R. L. Brennan (Ed.), *Educational measurement* (4th ed., pp. 17–64). Westport, CT: Praeger.

Kirkhart, K. E. (2005). Through a cultural lens: Reflections on validity and theory in evaluation. In S. Hood, R. K. Hopson, & H. Frierson (Eds.), *The role of culture and cultural context: A mandate for inclusion, the discovery of truth, and understanding in evaluative theory and practice* (pp. 21–39). Greenwich, CT: Information Age.

Kvale, S. (2002). The social construction of validity. In N. K. Denzin & Y. S. Lincoln (Eds.), *The qualitative inquiry reader* (pp. 299–325). Thousand Oaks, CA: Sage.

Madison, A. M. (2000). Language in defining social problems and in evaluating social programs. In R. K. Hopson (Ed.), *How and why language matters in evaluation: New Directions for Evaluation, 86,* 17–28.

Messick, S. (1995). Validity of psychological assessment. *American Psychologist, 50*(9), 741–749.

Scriven, M. (1997). Truth and objectivity in evaluation. In E. Chelimsky & W. R. Shadish (Eds.), *Evaluation for the 21st Century* (pp. 477–500). Thousand Oaks, CA: Sage.

A3 Reliable Information

Evaluation procedures should yield sufficiently dependable and consistent information for the intended uses.

❖ RATIONALE AND CLARIFICATION

Reliability is defined as the consistency of information and information collection procedures and is important as a cornerstone for validity. However, in spite of its importance, an adequate degree of reliability is only one condition needed (for others, see A5 Information Management and A6 Sound Designs and Analyses).

The enemy of reliability is random error, and freedom from random error is equally important for both qualitative and quantitative information summaries. Standardized measures, observations, rich descriptions, ratings, interview transcripts, and other types of qualitative and quantitative information all require attention to consistency and dependability. Similarly, all evaluation information, not just outcome measures, should be adequately reliable. Evaluators should consider investigating the reliability and replicability of the methods forming the bases for all important information summaries, including descriptions of programs, program components, and contexts.

Specific techniques can help estimate the consistency of qualitative and quantitative information. The basis for most of these techniques is some form of documented replicability. For example, two reviewers can write descriptions of the same performances at two different times and compare them for consistency. An evaluation team interested in reducing inconsistencies in testing can review the impact of standardized instructions and maintaining similar conditions at the two different times. Individual raters can re-evaluate a sample of responses at two different times to estimate their consistency.

Random errors can also show up in tests and other assessments as specific item or task errors. For example, some multiple-choice items may be confusing or ambiguous and produce guessing or inconsistent interpretations. For a set of items measuring the same factor, the greater the consistency in individuals' responses across items, the greater the overall internal consistency reliability.

The consistency reflected in qualitative and quantitative information summaries is often influenced by cultural and other background factors. A qualitative or quantitative procedure resulting in a given level of reliability in one specific setting may produce quite different levels in another group or setting. Evaluators must consider how to investigate and describe situations where assessments are differentially reliable depending on specific characteristics in the setting, especially characteristics related to who and what is being assessed. Evaluators should investigate the generalizability and dependability of reliability estimates across all participant groups involved in the evaluation when these differences are important for evaluation purposes.

The measurement of educational outcomes and psychological characteristics is highly technical and requires special expertise. This expertise is needed, for example, to investigate criterion referenced test score dependability, individual test score reliability, group test score reliability, and cut score or decision reliability. Measurement experts apply theoretical and applied statistical foundations from classical test theory, item response theory, and generalizability theory to specific evaluation reliability problems. When evaluation teams or evaluation users need this expertise for specific evaluation purposes, they should be sure that it is present or available through consultation.

Not all inconsistency is the result of unreliability. Sometimes inconsistencies may actually be the result of different understandings and perspectives. For example, different raters or observers may produce consistently different scores or interpretations not because of random error but because of systematic differences in the ways they conceptualize the categories used for interpretation or scoring (see A2 Valid Information). Different raters may judge and interpret a particular concept from fundamentally different understandings, perspectives, or theories. They may be consistent with themselves but inconsistent with one another. It is important to know what has caused differences in raters' performance in order to effectively interpret the differences and increase the accuracy of the ratings. For example, if two raters evaluate student writings differently, the evaluation team must discover whether the discrepancies result from different dimensions of quality being applied to the writing (a validity issue) or from fatigue, lack of training, or other sources of random error (a reliability issue).

The desirable degree of reliability for any information summary depends in large part on the evaluation settings, purposes, and uses. In general, information used for high stakes decisions should exhibit the greatest consistency, especially when only one source or type of information is used. In some situations less than optimum reliability is inevitable, and evaluators must decide what constitutes an acceptable degree of reliability. One additional complication in program evaluations is that methods for estimating the reliability for decisions based on aggregated or group means differ from those used for decisions about individuals. In addition, achieving a high degree of reliability sometimes requires considerable resources, reducing capability to meet other evaluation goals. Regardless of the degree of reliability achieved, evaluators should describe the procedures used to support consistency and provide appropriate reliability estimates for key information summaries (E1 Evaluation Documentation).

❖ IMPLEMENTING A3 RELIABLE INFORMATION

The following are important recommendations for implementing this standard:

1. List plausible sources of error for each source of information included in the evaluation, and attempt to reduce the influence of error by applying cost-effective remedies.
2. Consider building in replications of information sources, scoring procedures, observations, and analyses to increase reliability or provide needed information about reliability and validity (A2 Valid Information and A5 Information Management).
3. Have access to experts who can design, evaluate, and communicate the technical concerns and procedures related to reliability.
4. Integrate concerns about reliability in the overall concern about valid and justifiable conclusions and decisions. The greater the importance of evaluation information, the greater the importance its accuracy and thus its reliability will be.
5. Bear in mind the feasibility, propriety, and utility of procedures before assuming that procedures designed to increase reliability will be sufficiently effective and efficient, given the evaluation situation.

❖ HAZARDS

Some possible hazards with regard to A3 are as follows:

1. Confusing reliability and validity: assuming without further investigation that a highly reliable set of scores will be valid for the intended interpretations and conclusions

2. Concluding that the reliability for a set of scores from a measure used in one setting or at one time will necessarily hold for other places, times, or respondents. While previous demonstrations of reliability with similar respondents in similar administrations are good predictors of future reliability, this assumption needs investigation and confirmation
3. Investing too many resources in increasing and documenting reliability at the expense of other subcomponents of evaluation quality, such as information scope, breadth or depth, or the validity of information more generally (see A5 Information Management, A2 Valid Information, and U5 Relevant Information)
4. Failing to educate information users about the limited but essential role of reliability in accuracy
5. Failing to address the dependability of criterion-referenced measures when used for outcomes assessment
6. Only investigating the reliability of tests and outcomes assessments and not considering the quality of program and evaluation documentation and descriptions, for example (A4 Explicit Program and Context Descriptions and E1 Evaluation Documentation)

Application Number Three for the Accuracy Case Scenario

The scenario that supports this application, including background information about the program, context, and key players, can be read at the end of the Accuracy Overview on page 161.

Consuela picks up the phone and calls Huseyin. She is upset because of a conversation with the governor's legislative aide and the governor's office liaison. Several important legislators are now complaining that the Year 1 evaluation does not use well-established standardized tests to measure improvements in student performance. Consuela tells Huseyin that these important stakeholders are concerned about the lack of reliability in the evaluation instruments they used.

Huseyin has only a few minutes to talk with Consuela. He suggests that they schedule a time as soon as possible to talk again, and they are able to set aside an hour the next day. After they hang up, he reflects on the situation. At the beginning of the evaluation proposal process, he had collected for his own purposes a list of possible information sources (see A5 Information Management and U5 Relevant Information). He catalogued the information sources in a table. The rows listed the possible sources and types of information (including both those already available and those requiring development). The columns listed specific dimensions of quality in the information and the procedures used to collect, analyze, and summarize the information (A6 Sound Designs and Analyses). He organized the table so that the columns were clustered according to usefulness of the information, accuracy of the information, cost (and other feasibility issues), and propriety issues. For example, under usefulness, he had notes about whether and how different sources addressed one or more specific evaluation questions and who might use the information for which identified purposes (U5 Relevant Information). Many of the sources of information already existed, such as workshop blurbs for the Summer Institute, or were illustrative surveys from his evaluation files, such as teacher burnout assessments.

In deciding which sources of information to include in the Year 1 evaluation, the evaluation team had discussed many of the issues regarding usefulness of the information with Consuela, steering committee members, and other selected stakeholders (U2 Attention to Stakeholders). However, Huseyin and the evaluation team had kept the discussions about technical quality to themselves because these topics seemed to require expertise that others did not possess. Huseyin concludes after the phone call that he must quickly work with Consuela and others to develop a strategy for discussing the technical quality of the information the evaluation relies on (A8 Communication and Reporting and U7 Timely and Appropriate Communicating and Reporting).

One problem he is aware of is that most stakeholders and even some members of the evaluation team don't really understand how reliability and validity work together. Some think that reliability is a major component of validity or can be used as a proxy for validity when validity is hard to demonstrate. Consuela and others need his explanations of how the sources of information are being evaluated for accuracy in addition to usefulness and feasibility. They also need to be aware of how additional sources of information will be used in subsequent years of the evaluation, supporting summative decisions about the quality of the program at the end of Year 3.

Huseyin creates a chart addressing information accuracy, much like the chart he had prepared previously addressing the utility of information. He lists each information method and evidence that addresses its reliability, depending on the method and the type of reliability information that is available. He wants to emphasize that the evaluation team is investigating reliability in this evaluation setting—not just relying on reliability established in other contexts. He also outlines the steps he and the evaluation team are taking to reduce random error. He writes out, for example, the way that they have conducted observations of classroom teaching in the past. They followed similar steps in planning how to assess classroom teaching in Year 3.

According to the current plan, the team will create an observation rating sheet addressing key teaching outcomes supported by the program and its workshops. Then, five observers (program or evaluation staff members with different cultural and linguistic backgrounds) will practice using the observation form in volunteering classrooms and for classes that were broadcast using fiber-optics- or Web-based conferencing equipment. In order to be sure that the observation form is sensitive to variations in teacher and student backgrounds, Huseyin intends to test it in classrooms where the teachers have demonstrated a variety of skills with different groups of ELLs. The observers will conduct their observations using the same approaches, get plenty of sleep the night before, not multitask during the observations, and write up their notes as soon as possible. They expect interobserver agreement indices greater than .80 for pairwise comparisons of individual observers across several anchored dimensions of quality. Given previous power analyses in other evaluations, they believe this process will be sufficiently reliable to find important differences in classrooms.

Huseyin also prepares information for Consuela about how criterion-referenced tests will be used to investigate progress toward proficiency. The tests will be conducted in Years 2 and 3 of the evaluation, will be used at each grade level, and will compare the classrooms of teachers participating in the Summer Institute with those of nonparticipating teachers. He illustrates how parallel forms of the criterion-referenced tests will be administered a week apart in selected schools and grade levels to produce a dependability estimate. Huseyin attaches these drafts to an e-mail to Consuela in advance of their next phone call.

When they talk, Huseyin and Consuela discuss how best to communicate with the legislative and executive stakeholders as well as others who might be concerned about the accuracy of information in the evaluation (A8 Communication and Reporting). She expresses appreciation for the information attached to the e-mail, and she and Huseyin develop a communication strategy to report about the quality of evaluation instruments from Year 1 and proposed for Years 2 and 3. They discuss the costs of trying to increase or provide additional information about reliability (F4 Resource Use and P7 Fiscal Responsibility). Consuela suggests that Huseyin list out the different kinds of reliability and replicability estimations and put them on a one-page handout for interested legislators and their aides (some of whom have engineering, accounting, or other technical degrees and good quantitative skills).

Consuela also discusses with Huseyin the importance of not focusing on the legislators alone. She has also heard that some parents and teachers are alleging that the district testing program is not reliable or valid for their ELLs. Huseyin is reminded yet again that demonstrating the accuracy of the evaluation is very important—not just to help justify conclusions and decisions (A1 Justified Conclusions and Decisions) but also to help maintain credibility with important stakeholders (U1 Evaluator Credibility). As they respond to the legislators, he also wants to maintain clarity about purposes so that they don't waste resources needed for critical evaluation tasks (U5 Relevant Information, U6 Meaningful Processes and Products, F2 Practical Procedures, and F3 Contextual Viability).

❖ SUPPORTING DOCUMENTATION

American Educational Research Association, American Psychological Association, and National Council on Measurement in Education (1999, in revision). *Standards for educational and psychological testing.* Washington, DC: American Educational Research Association.

Brennan, R. L. (2001). *Generalizability theory.* New York: Springer-Verlag.

Brown, J. D. (1990). Short-cut estimators of criterion-referenced test consistency. *Language Testing, 7,* 77–97.

Haertel, E. H. (2006). Reliability. In R. L. Brennan (Ed.), *Educational measurement* (4th ed., pp. 65–110). Westport, CT: Praeger.

Miller, M. D., Linn, R. L., & Gronlund, N. E. (2009). *Measurement and assessment in teaching* (10th ed.). Upper Saddle River, NJ: Pearson.

Shepard, L. (2006). Classroom assessment. In R. L. Brennan (Ed.), *Educational measurement* (4th ed., pp. 623–646). Westport, CT: Praeger.

Yen, W. M., & Fitzpatrick, A. R. (2006). Item response theory. In R. L. Brennan (Ed.), *Educational measurement* (4th ed., pp. 111–154). Westport, CT: Praeger.

A4 Explicit Program and Context Descriptions

Evaluations should document programs and their contexts with appropriate detail and scope for the evaluation purposes.

❖ RATIONALE AND CLARIFICATION

Describing programs with sufficient scope and detail can provide evaluation users with a shared perspective. In the absence of dependable description and documentation, stakeholders must rely on their own sometimes limited experiences and assumptions about the program and its contexts. Standard A4 calls for evaluations to clarify exactly what is being evaluated and how it is contextualized.

A key factor influencing program descriptions is program complexity. Programs are often composed of many components interacting in unpredictable or emergent ways. Descriptions of what is being evaluated may focus on any or all of the following:

- Program designs
- Policies, regulations, and administrative procedures
- Resources, infrastructures, and other inputs such as curricula, materials, and assessment instruments
- Goals and proposed activities, processes, participation, and outcomes
- Actual processes, actions, and performances, especially of learners, other participants and stakeholders, staff, leaders, other personnel, and groups or organizational units
- Program impact theory, especially as it directs the identification of needs or growth possibilities, qualified participants, specific goals, and key output, outcome, mediating, and moderating variables

- Proposed and implemented process theories as they clarify service delivery and management activities
- any subcomponents or elements of the above

In addition to differing with regard to the number and complexity of their components, programs also differ with regard to how standardized and replicable they are. When the program is a standardized treatment intervention, Standard A4 emphasizes documenting whether the treatment as implemented conforms to the treatment as specified (treatment fidelity). For treatment fidelity to be established, the actual implemented program must be monitored and described in sufficient detail for comparison to the prescribed program.

In contrast to fully standardized programs, developing and responsive programs may change based on participants' characteristics, needs, or other factors. In such cases, it is necessary to describe in detail the program as it is actually implemented in real time in order to know what its key components are. How the program is actually experienced by key stakeholders is the key source of information for describing such programs. Documenting their experiences is necessary to describe what actually resulted in any observed outputs and outcomes.

An important subcomponent of all programs is their program theory, which describes how they work. Program theories have a number of important uses. They describe how the identified and selected problems, needs, or areas for growth and change are defined. They specify the causal models and intervention hypotheses that explain how intended beneficiaries will change via program activities and indirect (mediating and moderating) influences. They define the key constructs in the program and in outcomes assessments. Program theories also describe how the activities will be managed and how the services will be delivered to reach the intended beneficiaries of the program or project.

Program theories often grow out of preexisting traditions and beliefs. Sometimes program theories incorporate scientific models and scholarship. Often program theories remain implicit and unarticulated. Discovering and describing program theories may be difficult and expensive in time and other resources. When program theory has not been expressed, evaluators must decide how important its revelation is in a specific situation. Program theory evaluations (program theory as the object to be evaluated) are important in some contexts, especially when a key purpose is enlightenment, understanding, or long-term influence (U5 Relevant Information and U8 Concern for Consequences and Influence). Because many clients and users are not aware of program theory, it may be hard in the beginning to decide how many resources to invest in portraying it accurately. A number of evaluators endorse program theory as the best foundation for scientific program evaluation.

Sometimes evaluations compare two or more parallel programs or program components to inform judgments about their relative quality. In the case of comparative evaluations, it is important to describe the two programs or components in balanced and equally sufficient detail. Regardless of program or component complexity or degree of standardization, comparative evaluations are appropriate when they address evaluation needs and purposes.

❖ DESCRIBING CONTEXTS

Standard A4 also calls for describing the contexts surrounding programs and program components. First, it is important to identify any other programs, projects, or factors in the context that may affect the evaluated program's quality, implementation, or performance and results. Factors in the context may amplify or dampen the functioning of the program, either directly or indirectly. For example, the availability of staff to implement the program may depend on context factors (F3 Contextual Viability). Community support or lack of it may be the result of context factors. Volunteers and other interested supporters in the context may have a considerable influence on how the program is implemented and its success. In addition, independently of their direct impact on the program, contextual factors may have positive or negative effects on the participants in the program or may affect program recruitment or retention. If left uninvestigated and undocumented, these factors can lead to false conclusions about the boundaries of the program and the extent to which its processes and outcomes depend on the context.

Second, accurate descriptions of the contexts convey to evaluation users the situations to which evaluation findings can be extrapolated. An evaluation study always takes place in bounded times and locations. Accurate context descriptions increase the likelihood that extrapolations to other contexts and situations will be appropriate. Whether an evaluation user is judging the future value of the program for continued implementation in the same or in a different place, accurate descriptions lay the foundations for trustworthy predictions about results from future implementations.

As mentioned earlier, sometimes only one program component or subcomponent is the object of evaluation. When specific program components are evaluated, then the rest of the program becomes part of the context. Once the evaluation begins, it too becomes part of the context of the program or project (E1 Evaluation Documentation and F2 Practical Procedures). For example, when program personnel become aware of evaluation processes and results, they may change their attitudes and behaviors, especially if decisions based on the evaluation will affect the resources available to them or their job opportunities or responsibilities. Any such changes, whether subtle or substantial, require ongoing investigation and documentation in order for the program and context descriptions to be accurate.

Often users want the results of evaluated programs to be generalizable to new implementations that are not being evaluated. If the impact of the evaluation as part of the context of the program is not documented, users will not be as informed about whether future unevaluated or differently evaluated programs will produce similar processes, products, and results.

Contexts and programs in general are experienced differently by different people, especially people who do not share common linguistic, experiential, cultural, economic, educational, or social backgrounds (A2 Valid Information). Accurate context and program descriptions depend on sufficiently broad and deep information to build satisfactorily inclusive analyses and descriptions for the specified evaluation purposes. Ultimately the degree of accuracy in program and context descriptions rests not on some abstract notion of accuracy in a written report based on an "objective" methodology but rather in the accuracy of the representations of the program and its context in the cognitive structures of intended evaluation users and other stakeholders and evaluation audiences. Accurate descriptions help educate stakeholders by depicting the program as experienced by participants, program staff, and other stakeholders. Such descriptions based on valid information help create a community of understanding across cultural and other backgrounds. They support shared sense-making. This does not mean that prior beliefs, theories, assumptions, or understandings will necessarily be revised or adjudicated. Nor does it mean that all such perspectives are equally valid. It does mean that accurate descriptions aim to capture and represent the most important subtleties and differences without automatically endorsing one perspective only.

❖ IMPLEMENTING A4 EXPLICIT PROGRAM AND CONTEXT DESCRIPTIONS

The following are important recommendations for implementing this standard:

1. Take advantage of a wide variety of approaches and media including
   a. written and oral descriptions and documentation
   b. pictures, video, and other media
   c. films and plays
   d. forums and community events
   e. other techniques that increase shared understanding and sense-making about the contexts and programs as experienced (A8 Communication and Reporting and U6 Meaningful Processes and Products).

2. Rely on concepts, terms, and information types that are sufficiently accurate and address the soundness of the reasoning from analyzed information to conclusions about the program and its context.
3. Choose the right level of specificity in descriptions by listing the components, subcomponents, and elements to be evaluated and the levels they occupy in the program or project.
4. When describing programs, projects, and their subcomponents, consider program theory.
5. When describing programs, projects, and their subcomponents, document goals and intentions as well as the intended, unintended, and actual outcomes. Think about effects on the wider context, too, if they are related to the program or its components.

❖ HAZARDS

Some possible hazards with regard to A4 are as follows:

1. Assuming that proposed program descriptions accurately depict the program as implemented
2. Trying to capture all features of a program and its context. Overlooking significant context features is all too easy, but trying to be too inclusive can waste resources
3. Ignoring key informants with different background characteristics, such as languages, cultures, and prior knowledge, in compiling program and context descriptions
4. Relying too heavily on staff or evaluators' unsubstantiated impressions
5. Not attending to the other standards when describing programs and contexts: accurate descriptions require the same attention to information and analysis quality as do outcomes and impact assessments (A2 Valid Information, A3 Reliable Information, A5 Information Management, and A6 Sound Designs and Analyses)
6. Relying on a one-time snapshot view without updating the descriptions as changes occur or as new perspectives are needed to better meet the evaluation purposes
7. Assuming that the evaluation does not interact with or change the program and its context and not describing such changes
8. Assuming that written descriptions will communicate to all stakeholders equally well without engaging in communication strategies to reach shared understandings (A8 Communication and Reporting)

9. Underestimating the resilience of deeply entrenched beliefs about the contexts and programs that may not change in the face of new information and descriptions, especially if the evaluations are not viewed as trustworthy (U1 Evaluator Credibility and U5 Relevant Information)
10. Not taking treatment fidelity investigations seriously and assuming that confounding influences in field studies can be managed as easily as in a laboratory or other controlled setting
11. Ignoring the importance of program theory when it is not made explicit
12. Forgetting that the context is to be described as experienced by key stakeholders

Application Number Four for the Accuracy Case Scenario

The scenario that supports this application, including background information about the program, context, and key players, can be read at the end of the Accuracy Overview on page 161.

Recently Huseyin and the evaluation team have met to discuss how to go about describing and documenting the program components that they are evaluating and their contexts. They know, for example, that the legislators and the governor's education officers are most interested in knowing about the impact of teacher professional development on students' standardized test scores. However, no one has mapped out the logic of how the program components work separately or in concert to affect ELLs standardized test scores. They want to build logic models, but first they have to decide at which of the various levels they want to work to describe the resources, activities, outputs, and outcomes. The graduate students on the evaluation team find the complexity and number of components and subcomponents daunting.

Huseyin has a theory about the critical role of complexity in accurate communication. He thinks that communication is often undermined by a failure to acknowledge the complex, multilevel, and multifaceted nature of programs and contexts. Decision makers often want to reduce complex outcomes to one measure or one factor, to see the program as if it were one standardized treatment, and to ignore other contextual factors that interact with the program to affect activities and outcomes.

At the same time, evaluators and stakeholders can get lost in complexity and be immobilized, never prioritizing what the most important factors, questions, information types and sources, and uses of the evaluation are. This is a topic for Huseyin to address with the graduate students who are members of the evaluation team. Their job will be to help create a sufficient understanding of the complexity in the ELL program and its context to situate the specific evaluation purposes, questions, and sources of information in the most feasibly accurate way.

Huseyin outlines for the evaluation team the six levels of organizational complexity needed to identify context and program components, from the macrolevel (federal agencies, such as the U.S. Department of Education responsible for grant funding) to the microlevel (the fourteen individual 2-hour workshops at the Summer Institute). He shares a one-page overview as a way of discussing with the team how to focus the description of the ELL program and its context. Part of the context consists of the larger grant-funded program and the other Teacher Quality Enhancement Goal Areas. Huseyin and the evaluation team know that they cannot possibly describe and document in detail every subcomponent of the Year 1 ELL Goal Area. Since Consuela and the steering committee have identified the Summer Institute as the focus in Year 1, they turn their immediate attention to how to document what actually takes place at the Summer Institute.

The ELL steering committee is giving the 14 outside consultants (the miniworkshop trainers) a great deal of control and autonomy. Huseyin has asked each consultant for advance copies of materials, lecture notes, activities, and handouts that the participants will experience. So far, only four of them have responded. Evaluation team members have searched the Web for additional information. Three of the consultants have sites with a general description of the lectures and materials that they have used elsewhere to train ELL teachers. The team agrees that much of what goes on in the workshops will not be documented or described in the normal course of implementation. They believe that the only dependable way to get the full experience and the materials, handouts, and activity guides that participants actually use is to be in the rooms as participant observers.

The evaluation team uses a logic model to outline what will go into their description of the Summer Institute and comes up with the following:

- the contexts that participants come from as well as the contexts for the Summer Institute
- goals for the Summer Institute, including how well it will meet ELLs' needs and teachers' professional development needs
- the costs, resources, inputs, activities, and outputs that constitute the Summer Institute from the perspective of staff, participants, and evaluation team observers
- intended or desired outcomes
- possible unintended outcomes, including unexpected costs
- program theories about how the Summer Institute functions, what needs it meets, and how it is supposed to produce results

The Summer Institute is a fairly complex residential event, taking place at three different sites around the state during specific weeks, and enrolling a total of 300 in-service and preservice teachers and administrators. The evaluation team divides up into three teams of two, with each team responsible for observing on one of the sites. They will attend individual sessions, evening events and celebrations, and keynote addresses. Two of the venues are on liberal arts college campuses so as to lessen the cost of housing. The evaluation team members will also stay in the college dorms at those sites. Referring to the expanded logic model, the evaluation team begins to work on structured observational forms to use for the various events and miniworkshops and to build a file system to store the documents that they will collect. Each team selects one person to control the quality and ensure the safety of the documents that they collect at the Summer Institute event they attend (A5 Information Management).

❖ SUPPORTING DOCUMENTATION

Bhola, H. S. (2003). Social and cultural contexts of evaluation: A global perspective. In T. Kellaghan, D. L. Stufflebeam, & L. A. Wingate (Eds.), *International handbook of educational evaluation, part one: Perspective* (pp. 397–415). Dordrecht, Netherlands: Kluwer Academic.

Chen, H.-T. (2005). *Practical program evaluation.* Thousand Oaks, CA: Sage.

Donaldson, S. I. (2007). *Program theory-driven evaluation science: Strategies and applications.* New York: Lawrence Erlbaum.

Frechtling, J. A. (2007). *Logic models in program evaluation.* San Francisco: Jossey-Bass.

Stake, R. E. (1995). *The art of case study research.* Thousand Oaks, CA: Sage.

Weaver, H. N. (2001). Organization and community assessment with First Nations people. In R. Fong & S. Furuto (Eds.), *Culturally competent practice* (pp. 178–195). Needham Heights, MA: Allyn & Bacon.

Yin, R. K. (2009). *Case study research: Design and methods* (4th ed.). Thousand Oaks, CA: Sage.

A5 Information Management

Evaluations should employ systematic information collection, review, verification, and storage methods.

❖ RATIONALE AND CLARIFICATION

Evaluations can rely on a wide variety of methods to provide information that users need. This information may come through language, performances of all kinds, music, numerical data, and other symbol systems and media. Standard A5 emphasizes the need for information management that maintains accuracy. It also discusses similarities and differences among information types and methods. It attends to issues of how much information to collect, what kinds of information to collect, how to store information, and how to think about methods from the perspective of accuracy.

Historically, evaluators have clustered information collection methods and types into two categories, quantitative and qualitative. This distinction is in many ways a simple one. Quantitative methods impose numerical scoring procedures either prior to data collection or during analysis. In contrast, qualitative approaches allow respondents to create their own responses without preimposed scales or numerical models.

With regard to creating accurate representations for evaluation purposes, there are advantages to both approaches. Using numbers to summarize clearly defined concepts and relationships can provide efficiency, clarity, focus, and standardization. Imposing units and forced choices prior to data collection often helps ensure that respondents will stay focused and provide structured information. In addition, scores are produced directly and can be standardized in ways that allow their dependability to be investigated more easily.

In contrast, qualitative methods produce open responses reflecting individuals' own experiences, feelings, thoughts, and values. Sometimes real-life phenomena are complicated, poorly understood, and confounded with one another. Less restrictive, qualitative information collection procedures such as interviews, narratives, observations, journals, or town meetings allow respondents to report their experiences using their own structures and concepts. Responses are often analyzed and summarized using interpretive, evidence-based approaches that seek to maintain the unique perspectives of respondents.

In some situations, qualitative information can be analyzed into categories or scores. Numeric scaling and classification models can be imposed on qualitative information as part of the analysis process. For example, interviews or performances can be quantitatively scored, using validated rubrics, guidelines, or scales, either during or after information collection. Sometimes the quantification methods are designed to impose preestablished scales. At other times the categories emerge from the body of responses.

There are many reasons to use a mixture of qualitative and quantitative approaches depending on contexts, program characteristics, and evaluation purposes. In practice, mixing designs such as case studies, naturalistic designs, quasiexperiments, and randomized field trials with qualitative and quantitative information types is a common practice to increase evaluation accuracy. Evaluations, particularly if they extend over multiple years, often rely on mixed methods to get the optimum balance of breath and depth. Mixed methods can also serve such accuracy goals as validation, triangulation, exploration, expansion, confirmation, and complementarity (A6 Sound Designs and Analyses).

❖ STORING INFORMATION

Accurate evaluations require quality information storage. There are two primary issues with regard to storing information. First, since information is often transformed in the analysis process, both the original and processed versions need to be documented and maintained. Storing original information for adequate lengths of time will facilitate additional or competing analyses should new questions or purposes arise. Second, access to the information in its original and analyzed forms is required as long as authorized users need it (U2 Attention to Stakeholders). The information should be stored in ways that prevent direct and indirect alterations, distortions, destruction, or any reduction of potential information value or propriety (P3 Human Rights and Respect and U5 Relevant

Information). Information storage requires meticulous attention to detail and protection from any diminishing of the scope and representativeness of the original information.

In summary, Standard A5 focuses on the methods used to ensure accurate information selection, balance, collection, and storage. It goes hand in hand with A3 Reliable Information, A2 Valid Information, and A6 Sound Designs and Analyses. Similarly, documenting the quality of information collection and storage procedures is a key component of E1 Evaluation Documentation and E2 Internal Metaevaluation.

❖ IMPLEMENTING A5 INFORMATION MANAGEMENT

The following are important recommendations for implementing this standard:

1. Identify and implement sound methods in the context of how well they serve the selected evaluation purposes, goals, and objectives (U3 Negotiated Purposes).
2. Catalogue the possible sources of information, and, once the characteristics of each source are identified, select the sources most likely to provide the most accurate information given the purposes.
3. Consider the many potential sources of information, including existing documents (such as proposals, project plans, previous studies and evaluations) and people (such as staff, designers, participants, and other observers).
4. Choose methods that provide information with the appropriate balance of breadth and depth needed for the evaluation purposes and questions.
5. Align key concepts used to describe evaluation purposes, program implementation, and outcomes assessments.
6. Review the methodologies for collecting new information or making use of old information to be sure that information collection is systematic, replicable, and adequately free of mistakes (E1 Evaluation Documentation and E2 Internal Metaevaluation)
7. In new evaluations, be open to procedures that have worked well in previous, similar evaluations or research studies. Durable methods yielding reliable and valid information for one evaluation may be applicable to similar evaluation settings with similar questions and concepts.

8. Select evaluation team members and consultants for the breadth and depth of their skills and knowledge about information collection possibilities and procedures, especially about how to make these procedures technically sound in specific evaluation situations.
9. Plan, evaluate, and communicate accurately the potential advantages, disadvantages, scope, and limitations of different methods, so that sound choices can be made.
10. Accept that there is often no one best approach when it comes to creating technical quality and that different evaluation teams in collaboration with clients and other stakeholders might come to somewhat different decisions about the best methodologies in specific situations.
11. Strive to have information selection and collection procedures that have been "owned" and adopted by those who sponsor, commission, and will use the evaluation information to ensure that they are invested in methodological quality.
12. Avoid strong a priori or absolute preferences for qualitative or quantitative methods in evaluation team members because these create greater difficulty in adapting methods to stakeholder needs and questions.
13. Be careful to clarify sponsors', clients', and other stakeholders' concerns when responding to preferences for qualitative or quantitative methods.
14. Prevent information storage problems and maintain accuracy by avoiding storage mistakes, sabotage, or other corrupting influences (including water, fire, vermin, or computer system failures).
15. Address in detail the steps taken to reduce flaws and support quality, and document all reasonable concerns about possible sources of flaws that could not be prevented or were not investigated or documented (A8 Communication and Reporting and E1 Evaluation Documentation).

❖ HAZARDS

Some possible hazards with regard to A5 are as follows:

1. Relying on the most convenient, most available, or least expensive methodologies or information, even though their quality in this setting is unknown

2. Expecting the information to be accepted without questions about its accuracy: when interpretations do not go the way stakeholders expect, some stakeholders may attack the methods and inaccurately criticize information quality
3. Waiting until after information collection to try to create stakeholder ownership of methods and appreciation for methodological quality
4. Assuming that respondents will provide high quality information naturally and without effort: respondents often provide flawed information because they do not understand the importance of the information
5. Assuming that attitudes, strategies, and approaches that are sufficient to produce accurate research information will work in all evaluation settings

Application Number Five for the Accuracy Case Scenario

The scenario that supports this application, including background information about the program, context, and key players, can be read at the end of the Accuracy Overview on page 161.

Huseyin and the evaluation team members know that development of an evaluation management plan is important for all aspects of quality in an evaluation: utility, feasibility, propriety, accuracy, and accountability (F1 Project Management). In thinking about information selection, collection, and storage methods, Huseyin and the team make lists of their goals with regard to meeting all of these attributes of high quality evaluation work. They share these lists, based extensively on *The Program Evaluation Standards,* with Consuela and the steering committee.

In previous meetings, the evaluation team has worked to clarify the purposes of the evaluation and what information would best meet the needs of stakeholders. They have spent time investigating and discussing stakeholder values and what dimensions of quality in the program were most important to the intended evaluation users (U2 Attention to Stakeholders, U3 Negotiated Purposes, U4 Explicit Values, and U5 Relevant Information).

As professional evaluators, they know that they have additional responsibilities when it comes to accuracy. They know that the evaluation stakeholders look to them as the experts on methodological quality. The stakeholders depend on and defer to them on this topic to a greater degree than they do on some other issues. They realize that they cannot assume that things will necessarily go according to plan. There are numerous opportunities for accuracy to be undermined.

Huseyin and the team meet and discuss how to get accurate data describing the Summer Institute, especially the background and needs of participants (and other important aspects of the context for the Summer Institute), and the immediate outcomes for participants in the Summer Institute. Huseyin is aware that they could exhaust their entire budget just collecting data to describe the individual workshops and participants' experiences. He wants to be sure that the desire for thoroughness in detail does not interfere with the breadth and scope needed to describe the Summer Institute accurately and capture its immediate and long-term participant outcomes.

Huseyin has used both qualitative and quantitative approaches in evaluation work for approximately a decade and is competent and comfortable with both approaches. The team has members who are more experienced in one or the other, but one of Huseyin's main criteria for team membership is comfort with mixed methodologies in response to evaluation purposes. He worries when evaluation team members believe in the superior accuracy of one approach prior to the consideration of users' needs and other situational factors. With regard to clients and users, Huseyin believes that their preferences must be taken into consideration for reasons of utility, feasibility, and propriety. However, he likes to make decisions about accuracy trade-offs based on which methods are most appropriate for the evaluation questions being addressed. In subsequent meetings with clients and other decision makers, they can discuss the pros and cons and reach conclusions that foster accuracy along with utility, feasibility, and propriety.

The evaluation team now has received lists of the knowledge, skill, and performance goals that the steering committee wants the participants to achieve. They also have the list of the outcomes that some of the external consultants believe that their miniworkshops will produce. After much discussion, the evaluation team decides tentatively on the multiple methods and the documentation that they will collect during the Summer Institute. Huseyin assigns each member of the team to provide leadership on specific tasks. All team members can be called upon by the task leader to help with any task. Regular meetings of the full group will help to keep the workload balanced and assure that everything is ready on time (F1 Project Management). Huseyin has developed lists of other evaluation consultants and colleagues he can call on for specific help when outside expertise is needed or timeliness is critical. The specific tasks are as follows:

- Draft Likert-type surveys of changes in skills, knowledge, motivations, and self-efficacy related to specific desired outcomes of the Summer Institute. Teams will draft a larger pool of items, but the surveys must be shortened to no more than 50 items by the time of the Summer Institute. Approximately 5 to 10 of the items can be answered in respondents' own words. Different surveys will be needed for participants in different strands but there will be a core of shared items on each survey.

- Draft focus group and individual interview protocols that allow key samples of individuals to report in their own words how they experienced the Summer Institute, how well the Summer Institute matches their home contexts and needs, and what its strengths and limitations are, especially with regard to improvements for Year 2.

- Draft a combined forced-choice and open-ended Web survey to collect information from participants once the school year is underway. Respondents will report changes in curricula, instruction, and student interactions that they attribute to the Summer Institute. They will also report on the activities of their school- or district-based horizontal and vertical work teams.

- Finish the checklist and protocol for participant-observers (members of the evaluation team, volunteers, or paid consultants) to summarize their experience in the miniworkshops at the Summer Institute. Individual observers will be responsible for collecting all handouts and materials as well as collecting or summarizing slides and other features of the workshops.

- Establish a data management plan that specifies who actually will administer the surveys; when they will be administered; how the originals will be collected, stored, transported, and kept safe; how interview tapes or audio files will be managed and stored; whether they will be transcribed or not; and how observations will be captured and stored.

- Consider methods to improve and document the accuracy of the evaluation methods (E1 Evaluation Documentation and E2 Internal Metaevaluation).

- Update the plan for information integrity and safety, and sign it with all evaluation team members acknowledging their responsibilities.

Once evaluation team members make progress on these tasks, they will create a Web-based discussion page (Wiki) where Consuela, steering committee members, miniworkshop leaders, and other stakeholders can provide suggestions. Team members realize that perhaps only a few stakeholders will actually contribute because of time constraints, but all who so desire will have an opportunity to participate. Consuela and the steering committee members are invited via e-mail to visit the draft methods pages and provide suggestions, either directly on the pages or via e-mail. They are also encouraged to invite other stakeholders. Huseyin makes sure that Consuela and the steering committee members get reports on the evaluation team's work via e-mail and phone conferences.

He reflects on the feasibility of the Year 1 evaluation, based on all that the team must do to collect, analyze, and report even this amount of information. He worries that the emphasis on the Summer Institute may come at the cost of not knowing much about other components. He is not sure whether this is wise or a mistake, but an evaluation focus on the Summer Institute continues to be recommended by the clients and stakeholders.

❖ SUPPORTING DOCUMENTATION

Angrosino, M. V., & Mays de Perez, K. A. (2000). Rethinking observation: From method to context. In N. K. Denzin & Y. S. Lincoln (Eds.), *Handbook of qualitative research* (2nd ed., pp. 673–702). Thousand Oaks, CA: Sage.

Caracelli, V. J., & Greene, J. C. (1997). Crafting mixed-method evaluation designs. In J. C. Greene & V. J. Caracelli (Eds.), *Advances in mixed-method evaluation: The challenges and benefits of integrating diverse paradigms: New Directions for Evaluation, 74*(2), 19–32.

Creswell, J. W. (2003). *Research design: Qualitative, quantitative, and mixed methods approaches* (2nd ed.). Thousand Oaks, CA: Sage.

Denzin, N. K., & Lincoln, Y. S. (2000). Introduction: The discipline and practice of qualitative research. In N. K. Denzin & Y. S. Lincoln (Eds.), *Handbook of qualitative research* (2nd ed., pp. 1–28). Thousand Oaks, CA: Sage.

Eisenhart, M. (2006). Representing qualitative data. In J. L. Green, G. Camilli, & P. B. Elmore (Eds.), *Handbook of complementary methods in education research* (pp. 567–581). Mahwah, NJ: Lawrence Erlbaum.

Ercikan, K., & Roth, W. M. (2003). What good is polarizing research into qualitative and quantitative? *Educational Researcher, 35*(5), 14–23.

Fitzpatrick, J. L., Sanders, J. R., & Worthen, B. R. (Eds.). (2004). *Program evaluation* (3rd ed.). Boston: Pearson.

Mertens, D. M. (2005). *Research and evaluation in education and psychology: Integrating diversity with quantitative, qualitative, and mixed methods* (2nd ed.). Thousand Oaks, CA: Sage.

Patton, M. Q. (2002). *Qualitative research and evaluation methods* (3rd ed.). Thousand Oaks, CA: Sage.

Schwarts, R., & Mayne, J. (2005). Assuring the quality of evaluative information: Theory and practice. *Evaluation and Program Planning, 28,* 1–14.

A6 Sound Designs and Analyses

Evaluations should employ technically adequate designs and analyses that are appropriate for the evaluation purposes.

❖ RATIONALE AND CLARIFICATION

Every evaluation requires an overall design that is responsive to features of the program and program components, context factors, and the purposes of the evaluation. All sound evaluation designs must address two features needed for evaluation accuracy: logistics and logic.

The concern for logistics emphasizes that many specific details supporting evaluation accuracy must be considered and effectively managed. It underscores the need to support adequate accuracy in the context of political, cultural, and other forces. In its attention to logistics, Standard A6 is related to other standards, such as Standard F1 Project Management and Standard A5 Information Management. However, Standards A5 and A6 emphasize logistics to support accuracy, whereas Standard F1 addresses logistics in the service of feasibility.

The second feature of sound designs and analyses, accurate logic, refers to the role of evaluation designs in creating a framework for reasoning (A7 Explicit Evaluation Reasoning). Sound designs are needed to draw specific kinds of conclusions. These designs are formal, in the sense that they are systematic, well-documented, and informed by scholarship, so that when implemented as planned, many threats to valid conclusions have been systematically anticipated. When they are well-documented, both as intended and as actually implemented, evaluation designs can be audited and metaevaluated for quality (see E1 Evaluation Documentation, E2 Internal Metaevaluation, and E3 External Metaevaluation).

Accurate analyses are also required for sound reasoning to conclusions. Accurate analyses allow information to be aggregated and reduced, described, summarized, and understood, and its limitations to be made explicit in the context of specific evaluation questions and uses. Without technically adequate analyses, sound reasoning is undermined.

A key issue for all evaluation designs in complex settings is what to do about naturally occurring complexity. Complexity here is defined as the interdependency of multiple variables and influences in the program, the evaluation, and their contexts (A4 Explicit Program and Context Descriptions). When logistically possible, sound designs can help disentangle the influences of different factors to provide clarity about changes that have resulted from the program or specific components of the program as opposed to other context factors.

For example, sound naturalistic designs, including ethnographies, case studies, and other nonexperimental approaches allow evaluators to observe, describe, and explain the influences of complexity in the program and its contexts and to arrive at rich understandings of program components and the outcomes that resulted from the particular mix in the situation. In contrast, experimental and quasiexperimental designs, such as randomized field trials, experimentally manipulate the occurrence of certain factors while removing, controlling, or estimating the effects of other factors through design and statistical models. Findings from these approaches estimate the outcomes attributable to specific programs or their subcomponents. Both naturalistic and manipulated designs can include well-selected qualitative and quantitative information. Both types find regular use in natural and social science as well as in evaluations.

Some high-quality, well-implemented evaluation designs are better at facilitating valid conclusions about net effects as compared with total effects. The key distinction is the extent to which changes in clients or other targeted individuals and groups can be attributed to the program or program component in isolation or in controlled combinations (net effects) rather than to an undifferentiated mix with other factors in the context (total effects). Whether and how an evaluation can result in adequately defensible conclusions about net or total effects depends in large part on the implemented designs and the quality of the reasoning for a specific program in a specific context (A7 Explicit Evaluation Reasoning).

It is beyond the scope of this section to outline the full set of concerns and techniques that adequate naturalistic and experimental designs incorporate.

Crafting evaluation designs requires expertise acquired through graduate training, mentorships and apprenticeships, and peer-reviewed practice, for example, through focused external metaevaluation (E3 External Metaevaluation). In general, there are many factors that can create the impression that participants have changed as a result of the program (a net effect or impact) when in fact the change is the result of something else. Said another way, not all changes are the result of the program, because the program is just part of a complex and perhaps unspecifiable causal model. The role of evaluation designs is to prepare adequate frameworks for investigating what has resulted from the program or program components and to identify likely threats to sound conclusions about program effects.

In general, evaluation designs must address many factors, such as assumptions and requirements for accurate modeling, differential motivation in participants, historical events, selection and self-selection effects, differential attrition, and when and how to collect information. As is nearly always the case with program evaluation, the extrapolation from observations of existing programs to future situations is difficult when important features are different in the future situation. Evaluators can review possible threats to the validity of evaluation inferences and conclusions. Specific evaluation designs must be responsive to the alternative explanations that are most plausible in each particular evaluation situation (see the accompanying documentation for further reading). Standard A6 calls for responsiveness to assumptions required for accurate conclusions regardless of whether the proposed and implemented designs include naturalistic, quasiexperimental, experimental, or mixed approaches.

One last concern is the impact of evaluation designs on the program and its context. Most implemented evaluation designs are interventions that can create tensions in programs and their contexts. The stakes are especially high when programs are altered from the way they would be if the evaluation designs were not present (compare F2 Practical Procedures). For example, the degree of control needed to implement a randomized field trial may distort programs and their contexts so that they no longer represent real-world conditions to which the results should generalize. Even with naturalistic designs, tensions and influences exist between the observer and the observed. For example, knowledge on the part of program participants and staff that they are being observed and evaluated often leads to different behavior and interactions. They may feel and act differently simply as a result of ongoing evaluation processes, beginning with the evaluator's entry into the setting. All of these concerns raise the question whether findings about evaluated programs can generalize to nonevaluated or differently evaluated repetitions of that same program. This question is also pertinent to the next standard, A7 Explicit Evaluation Reasoning.

❖ IMPLEMENTING A6 SOUND DESIGNS AND ANALYSES

The following are important recommendations for implementing this standard:

1. Select designs based on how well they serve the selected evaluation purposes and questions and the reasoning needed to move logically from information to interpretations and conclusions.
2. Secure adequate expertise (through team membership or external consultation) to implement sound designs in evaluation settings where implementation may be challenging.
3. Consider which designs are in contention, given the purposes and constraints, and identify the advantages and disadvantages of each with regard to accuracy (and feasibility, propriety, and utility).
4. Choose designs to facilitate the reasoning frameworks that can result in justifiable conclusions, given the evaluation purposes and questions (A7 Explicit Evaluation Reasoning and A1 Justified Conclusions and Decisions).
5. Look at the designs used in other evaluations as a starting point. Durable designs for one evaluation may generalize to similar evaluation settings with similar evaluation questions and needs for similar reasoning frameworks.
6. Be ready for decisions about designs that entail compromise and a degree of uncertainty.
7. Consider modifying designs to increase accuracy from year to year, especially as needed in response to unexpected events, needs, and purposes.

❖ HAZARDS

Some possible hazards with regard to A6 are as follows:

1. Choosing off-the-shelf, high-status designs with the best reputations among certain groups of researchers without considering whether and how they will produce the most accurate evaluation information for trustworthy interpretations and conclusions in specific settings
2. Not preparing for disappointing evaluation findings and the inevitable attempts to impeach the interpretations by criticizing the

selected design or the quality of design implementation (E2 Internal Metaevaluation)

3. Not considering feasibility, propriety, and utility issues before selecting randomized field trials or other experimental designs. While these designs are sometimes invaluable in specifying the causes of specific outcomes and estimating net effects, in some situations, they are difficult to implement or unfair (P3 Human Rights and Respect, P1 Responsive and Inclusive Orientation, F2 Practical Procedures, and F3 Contextual Viability)
4. Making design choices in consultation with administrators at higher levels without conferring with the staff who will manage the implementation
5. Not modifying, augmenting, or changing designs when such action is needed, especially if the program, program components, or the evaluation questions change over time (U3 Negotiated Purposes)
6. Viewing the evaluation design as serving one purpose rather than several
7. Failing to implement a well-chosen design by not ensuring that the design is implemented correctly. Design implementation in evaluation is almost always a lower priority for the program staff even though their efforts are often essential for adequate implementation of the design

Application Number Six for the Accuracy Case Scenario

The scenario that supports this application, including background information about the program, context, and key players, can be read at the end of the Accuracy Overview on page 161.

Huseyin is meeting with Consuela and the steering committee prior to the Summer Institute. One key evaluation question to be answered after the Year 1 implementation is what program features need to be maintained, dropped, or improved in Years 2 and 3. Consuela and the steering committee members have observed that the Department of Education is committed to long-term improvement in teachers' knowledge, skills, and performance in support of increases in students' academic outcomes. Evaluation team members wonder if the efforts to improve instruction for ELLs might not also have a positive impact on many other groups of students whose backgrounds or other characteristics make them somewhat different from the typical students of the past. A new member on the steering committee, Rebecca Swanson, comments: "I wonder if what's good for ELLs might not be good for everyone?" Some steering committee members are worried that a focus on all students' academic outcomes will distract from the unique needs of ELLs, especially the ELLs who have not had the opportunity to develop academic skills in any language.

The main evaluation agenda item for today's meeting is presenting the evaluation design to the steering committee one last time for their input. Huseyin notes that their conversations often comingled two different issues: formative evaluation for improvement purposes and summative evaluation for accountability purposes. He knows that the design should probably serve both purposes.

As Consuela turns the meeting over to him, Huseyin describes the nested case study design to be used to investigate and document the Summer Institute. They are treating the Summer Institute as the overarching case and each of the fourteen workshops as nested cases within the larger case. Evaluation team members will provide participant observations, collect PowerPoint slides and handouts from the consultants, and collect survey information from participating teachers and administrators about what they experienced, what needs improvement, and how they benefited. Teacher outcome items on the survey address perceived burnout, self-efficacy, and self-perceived knowledge and skill growth and attitude change. In the fall, the evaluation team will also collect Web-based follow-up surveys on reported classroom and instructional changes, small focus group interviews, and limited classroom observations. This information will serve a number of formative purposes for the design of the Year 2 program and summative, accountability information about the processes, outputs, and results of the Year 1 Summer Institute.

After he has finished his presentation, Consuela and the steering committee alert Huseyin to a looming problem. Staging and implementing the Summer Institute is expensive. Even though they all are committed to it and believe in it, they are not sure that it provides a cost-effective, long-term solution to teacher preservice and in-service development, especially when grant funding is no longer available. They are interested in long-term sustainability built on the infrastructure developed during the grant funding cycles. They want to try out a less costly, nonresidential approach to see if similar benefits are possible.

Further discussion and communication reveals that some steering committee members are adamant that having teachers and administrators congregate for a week of workshop participation is the best way to go, even if it is expensive. Teachers need the time with other teachers to discuss and learn. They believe that much of the benefit to teachers is a result of the time spent interacting with and learning from one another.

Other steering committee members are of the opinion that the Summer Institute benefits only teachers from certain districts who have discretionary time in the summer, who don't have small children, and who don't have to work a second summer job. They think that the residential Summer Institute probably will not reach many of the teachers who need it. They want to consider an alternative summer program that will rely on Web-based materials, is located in teachers' home school districts, can be accessed from home or school computers, and will build on teams of teachers, administrators, preservice teachers, and teacher educators in preexisting clusters in local areas. One steering committee member even argues that in the long run, this local delivery mechanism will create more actual changes in classroom and out-of-classroom support for ELLs because it will not require transfer from external workshop settings to the local situation. "What teachers experience at residential workshops is a vacation from school!" she says. "They forget all about it before they can implement it back home. In my experience, there are no long-term impacts!"

Huseyin reports to his evaluation team members the next day. They are excited about traveling to the Summer Institute sites and glad there are no changes in their design and methods. Huseyin brings up the issue of residential versus in-district approaches to the implementing of content from the Summer Institute. The team members ask with some trepidation if this comparison is supposed to take place in Year 1. Huseyin says, "No, maybe in Year 2 or 3. However, we need to begin to think about the evaluation design right now." He says that what they have described has the possibility to be a natural experiment and that they might be able to implement a randomized field trial or certainly a quasiexperiment.

Team members agree that they will need to continue with ongoing case studies of the two approaches. They expect serious innovation in the next 2 years, regardless of whether the delivery site is residential or in the schools. They are delighted to be included early in the process because with sufficient planning, it may be possible to use some random, stratified, and matched assignment to the different approaches. They may actually be able to produce solid findings for their conclusions about effectiveness as well as costs attributable to the two different approaches independent of confounding factors, such as preexisting teacher skill or motivation. To manage this design will require close coordination with Consuela and others implementing the two comparisons.

There are some challenges. The state will probably have to pay a larger share of the in-school costs, unless the Teacher Quality Enhancement program officer approves the modification. They also know that since these are developing projects, the comparison may be unfair if one approach is better developed than the other, so they hope to repeat the design for at least two consecutive summer replications. Current funds are used in part to reimburse teachers for their expenses while in residence. How would a similar benefit be built into the nonresidential approach, if at all? Moreover, random assignment to the residential and nonresidential programs might not work at all. One part of the rationale for the nonresidential program is to serve those who for various reasons cannot participate in a residential Summer Institute.

The evaluation team also talks about adding a third comparison—teachers who do not participate in any ELL program facet. However, it's hard to see how such a group can be comparable in motivation if it consists of teachers who choose not to participate. Noninterested teachers may be unmotivated, or they may be very motivated but so experienced with ELLs that they don't believe participation is worth their time. Consuela has mentioned previously that teachers who are already very skilled should be excluded because they don't fit the profile of intended participants in the Summer Institute. Huseyin thinks that if more people want to participate than can be accommodated, perhaps they can assign them to three groups: the residential Summer Institute, the lower-cost, localized approach; and a wait list of teachers who cannot be accommodated in Year 2 but who get priority in Year 3. Once again, he's delighted that his relationship with Consuela resulted in her sharing this evaluation issue as soon as she became aware of it. They put the item on the agenda for the next meeting after the Summer Institute. Discussion of the new design possibilities for Years 2 and 3 will be a lot of fun as soon as data collection for Year 1 is completed.

❖ SUPPORTING DOCUMENTATION

Cook, T. D., & Sinha, V. (2006). Randomized experiments in educational research. In J. L. Green, G. Camilli, & P. B. Elmore (Eds.), *Handbook of complementary methods in education research* (pp. 551–565). Mahwah, NJ: Lawrence Erlbaum.

Davidson, E. J. (2000). Ascertaining causality in theory-based evaluation. In P. J. Rogers, T. A. Hacsi, A. Petrosino, & T. A. Huebner (Eds.), *Program theory in evaluation: Challenges and opportunities: New Directions for Evaluation, 87,* 17–26.

Denzin, N. K., & Lincoln, Y. S. (Eds). (2002). *The qualitative inquiry reader.* Thousand Oaks, CA: Sage.

LeCompte, M. D. (1993). *Ethnography and qualitative design in educational research* (2nd ed.). San Diego, CA: Academic Press.

Maxwell, J. A. (2004). Causal explanation, qualitative research, and scientific inquiry in education. *Educational Researcher, 33*(2), 3–11.

Pawson, R., & Tilley, N. (1997). An introduction to scientific realist evaluation. In E. Chelimsky & W. R. Shadish (Eds.), *Evaluation for the 21st century* (pp. 405–418). Thousand Oaks, CA: Sage.

Shadish, W. R., Cook, T. D., & Campbell, D. T. (2002). *Experimental and quasi-experimental design.* Boston: Houghton Mifflin.

Tedlock, B. (2000). Ethnography and ethnographic representation. In N. K. Denzin & Y. S. Lincoln (Eds.), *Handbook of qualitative research* (2nd ed., pp. 455–486). Thousand Oaks, CA: Sage.

A7 Explicit Evaluation Reasoning

Evaluation reasoning leading from information and analyses to findings, interpretations, conclusions, and judgments should be clearly and completely documented.

❖ RATIONALE AND CLARIFICATION

Standard A7 in concert with the other accuracy standards emphasizes that systematic evaluations must go beyond informal, implicit, or intuitive models for reaching conclusions. Standard A7 calls attention to the need for sound and explicit reasoning as the basis for evaluation findings, conclusions, and judgments.

Logic with regard to evaluation conclusions often takes the form of if-then sequences. With regard to evaluation questions, the *if* parts of the statements describe the assumptions, evidence, and criteria that must be met and the *then* parts of the statements describe the conclusion based on evidence. For example, when the purpose is to describe a program and its components that have been under development during the evaluation period, the following line of general reasoning is appropriate, if somewhat rudimentary. "If the descriptions of the program from our stakeholders are adequately representative and are truthful, and if we have collected adequate descriptions from all important subgroups (have sufficient scope), then we can conclude that our documentation is (more) likely to portray the program accurately."

In addition, before they can best support accurate conclusions about the program, evaluations should identify stakeholders' values and the kinds of decisions, conclusions, and judgments that will follow. Then evaluation designs can specify how to collect and analyze information to inform the values and support the reasoning leading to conclusions about quality (A5 Information Management and U5 Relevant Information).

The reasoning needed to support causal findings, that is, whether a program or its components were responsible for specific net outcomes (alone or together with other causal factors), must also address possible alternative causal explanations and why the chosen conclusion is more reasonable and plausible. Some approaches set about to demonstrate that alternative causal models and conclusions are false in order to determine one that is not falsifiable. Specific sources of alternative explanations (threats to causal conclusions) are discussed thoroughly in the documentation at the end of this standard.

Investigations of program effects and their costs and benefits also require explicit reasoning (F4 Resource Use). Assumptions about how to value outcomes must be made explicit. Users who start from different assumptions about what constitutes a benefit can then determine whether and to what extent the reasoning is congruent with their different values (U4 Explicit Values, F4 Resource Use, and P6 Conflicts of Interests).

Standard A7 also emphasizes that evaluation reasoning itself needs to be evaluated for accuracy. When the reasoning is made explicit, stakeholders can decide from their own informed positions how sound it is for their intended uses. In part, Standard A7 calls for documentation of the chain of reasoning, so that values that play a role in quality determinations can be investigated systematically. An accurate presentation of the reasoning will also include the evaluation team's own assumptions and arguments about the quality of the reasoning (E1 Evaluation Documentation). Evaluation users will then be in a better position to apply the evaluation findings in the contexts of their organizations and needs.

A technique that is sometimes very useful to identify the evidentiary and reasoning components for selected types of conclusions is backward mapping. With backward mapping, the evaluation designers start out with the conclusions or types of decisions that need to be made and describe the chain of logic that is needed to support them. Rather than *if-then,* the sequence becomes *therefore-because.* The following application describes the use of backward mapping to design for evidence and logic needed to support expected types of conclusions.

❖ IMPLEMENTING A7 EXPLICIT EVALUATION REASONING

The following are important recommendations for implementing this standard:

1. Begin to make the reasoning explicit as early in the process as possible so that it can be examined, fine-tuned, and adapted to key evaluation questions.

2. In making the reasoning explicit, begin with the most important questions. As time and resources are available, make the needed reasoning explicit for all key evaluation questions, including those related to description, improvement, causal attributions, accountability, and costs related to benefits or effectiveness.

3. Consider using straightforward *if-then* statements to help make the reasoning explicit.

4. After the key lines of the reasoning are made explicit, review and evaluate the statements and the assumptions for completeness.

5. Examine separately the reasoning behind each key evaluation question and the dimensions of quality within the program expected to contribute to the answer. Even if the resulting *if-then* statements overlap, they may all be necessary in order to answer each question effectively and thus optimize accuracy in accomplishing the evaluation purposes.

6. Review the information for pertinence and ability to support reasoning about any newly emphasized dimensions of quality, especially when the important uses and evaluation questions change over the course of the evaluation.

7. Make all assumptions about values explicit, and address the extent to which they must be met for the documentation of quality to be accurate (U4 Explicit Values).

8. Create tables or other summaries (see the following scenario application) that are tailored for the most important questions, interpretations, conclusions, and decisions, and make them available to key users and stakeholders. This will allow the reasoning and the assumption upon which conclusions are based to be explicitly discussed.

❖ HAZARDS

Some possible hazards with regard to A7 are as follows:

1. Overgeneralizing specific reasoning applied to one question to other questions by not making the specific dimensions of quality and attendant reasoning explicit for each key evaluation question

2. Using only one line of reasoning or one source of evidence for drawing firm conclusions when multiple lines and sources would be more accurate

3. Failing to compare and contrast different interpretations and conclusions that could result from important and different dimensions of quality, assumptions, or stipulations
4. Not investigating whether emphasis on desirable conclusions and interpretations has played too large a role in decisions about which information to collect or ways to analyze information to support the reasoning
5. Not addressing the limitations of specific information or analyses with regard to how well they support desirable conclusions and interpretations
6. Leaving out important steps or assumptions in the evaluation reasoning
7. Not addressing key alternative explanations based on whether key assumptions are met
8. Not encouraging all members of the evaluation team, as well as different user and stakeholder groups, to raise questions or concerns about the reasoning from information to conclusions, especially with regard to threats and to lines of reasoning that have been omitted
9. Assuming that having a high-status, gold-standard design, such as a randomized field trial, means that all assumptions involved in the reasoning are accounted for without explicit attention to the situation and the design implementation
10. Assuming a priori that a specific design approach is inherently more logical, without reference to contexts, evaluation purposes, and implementation fidelity
11. Not dealing with threats to valid causal conclusions thoroughly in the context of the specific evaluation design and the expected conclusions and decisions

Application Number Seven for the Accuracy Case Scenario

The scenario that supports this application, including background information about the program, context, and key players, can be read at the end of the Accuracy Overview on page 161.

As part of their internal metaevaluation, near the end of Year 1, the evaluation team reviews the purposes and uses for the evaluation (E2 Internal Metaevaluation). They start first with a review of the Utility, Feasibility, and Propriety Standards. When they turn their attention to accuracy, it is accuracy in the service of intended uses (and preventing misuse) conditioned by feasibility and propriety that they work on, rather than accuracy as an ultimate, stand-alone goal. Even though they know that needs or purposes might change for Year 2, the documented goals for the evaluation included the following:

1. Provide an accurate and complete description of the Summer Institute, so that stakeholders know how it was implemented and experienced from the perspectives of the leaders, staff, and key groups of participants.
2. Provide findings related to how well the Summer Institute met specific identified needs of participating preservice and in-service teachers, teacher educators, and administrators (investigate and identify Summer Institute outcomes).
3. Provide evidence leading to improved decisions about which features or components in the Summer Institute need to be maintained, deleted, or improved based on the dimensions of quality that evaluation users identified.
4. Prepare for randomized field trials in Years 2 and 3 that compare a residential summer institute with a virtual summer institute organized for teachers in their own local education areas.

After reviewing these general evaluation purposes, Huseyin and the team meet to develop some initial lines of reasoning. They view this as a first step leading to further communication and development with Consuela and the steering committee. Huseyin alerts the team that each of the four evaluation goals will address different key evaluation questions, and that the specific reasoning to address each must be specified.

Rather than assigning different members of the team the task of developing the reasoning for each key question, Huseyin decides that they should all work together on the first goal, then in small groups on the other questions. They produce the following initial incomplete table. They backward-map from intended uses to possible findings to the conditions that must be met for the findings to be sound. Some team members have the Accuracy Standards in front of them and others just work from memory. While discussing the first column, the team members invariably brainstorm some other lines of reasoning that will be necessary and keep notes about them to come back to.

Uses, such as decisions or judgments	*Conditions (If-statements)*
Leaders and steering committee members will identify aspects of the Summer Institute in need of improvement.	If • the specified dimensions of quality adequately reflect ongoing priorities of specific intended evaluation users • accurate indicators of the dimensions of quality can be created or selected and implemented accurately • the context description accurately identifies the factors that have a significant effect on the functioning of the program and its components with regard to these dimensions of quality

(Continued)

(Continued)

Uses, such as decisions or judgments	*Conditions (If-statements)*
	• the context, program, and program component descriptions use language that conveys shared meanings to those who supply information, those who analyze and summarize information, and those who use the information • the information sources adequately convey the complexity and scope of the program and its components from the perspectives of key subgroups with different backgrounds • the information, design, and analyses are dependable and of high quality • the information is well-managed, so that it is adequately free of inconsistencies, distortions, and misconceptions • the case study design is appropriate for the purposes and the specified dimensions of quality and is well-implemented

Huseyin and the team discuss whether the table makes their reasoning adequately explicit. For example, in describing the Summer Institute via flowcharts, presentations, and narrative, they had organized evidence in the following categories.

1. the key contextual factors which interact with the Summer Institute
2. intended process, output, and outcome goals
3. intended and actual participants
4. intended and actual resources (costs)
5. intended and actual program theories guiding the Summer Institute
6. activities as actually experienced by staff and participants
7. actual outputs, including documented participation and products
8. actual changes, results, and outcomes for participants and other beneficiaries as observed, assessed, and documented

The evaluation team knows it must review the accuracy of evidence and conclusions with regard to each of the subcomponents above, in accordance with the purposes of the evaluation and intended users' needs. Depending on the selected dimensions of quality in the Summer Institute, different specific subcomponents may need greater or lesser attention. For example, they are not at all sure they have the conditions in place to draw conclusions about the 14 consultants' individual program theories. Team members turn their attention to what they must do to ensure that each condition needed for sound reasoning is discussed and any limitations are made explicit.

They know that formal, systematic evaluation practice helps create commitment to the underlying accuracy that high-quality use demands. However, some of the processes required for accuracy fade into the background once it is achieved. For example, the evaluation team will include these specific tables in their technical reports and use them for recommendations, executive summaries, PowerPoint slides, theoretical and empirical evaluation papers, and other reporting to stakeholders. Nevertheless, some evaluation users will only be interested in the evaluation findings, not the quality of the specific processes that lead to them.

Huseyin and the team members then briefly discuss the most pressing evaluation questions and how to make the reasoning explicit to justify conclusions at the end of the process. Huseyin views conclusions related to descriptions and program descriptions as particularly important in this situation because the program and program components will be changing over time in response to the needs of participants. Participants and their needs will likely change, and these changes should be described. He is very pleased to see that the team understands that drawing conclusions about what the program and its components actually are is both highly important and demands explicit reasoning.

Team members volunteer to work out the initial reasoning lines for each of the other three evaluation goals and the specific questions they engender over the next month. Huseyin decides to spend his time on Evaluation Goal Four, the comparison between the residential and the virtual summer institutes resulting in conclusions about costs and benefits. Costs seem to be rather straightforward. He will certainly look at facilities needed, especially rooms and equipment, personnel, time, and money. Defining *benefits* is conceptually more challenging. The evaluation team will have to identify key evaluation information users and find out from them the quality dimensions defining benefits that they have in mind and how to weigh them. For example, if a summer institute produces renewed and greater enthusiasm leading to lowered likelihood of burnout, is that a valued outcome? How should burnout prevention be weighed compared to knowledge or skill improvements in teachers, or compared to affective or academic student outcomes? Huseyin knows that they should make charts for explicit reasoning using this comparative design for a few specific outcomes, present them to Consuela and the steering committee, and then be ready for new subquestions and or changes in dimensions of quality as they come.

❖ SUPPORTING DOCUMENTATION

Davidson, E. J. (2005). *Evaluation methodology basics: The nuts and bolts of sound evaluation.* Thousand Oaks, CA: Sage.

Fournier, D. M. (1995). Establishing evaluative conclusions: A distinction between general and working logic. In D. M. Fournier (Ed.), *Reasoning in evaluation: Inferential links and leaps: New Directions for Evaluation, 68,* 15–32.

House, E. R. (1980). *Evaluating with validity.* Beverly Hills, CA: Sage.

House, E. R. (1995). Putting things together coherently: Logic and justice. In D. M. Fournier (Ed.), *Reasoning in evaluation: Inferential links and leaps: New Directions for Evaluation, 68,* 33–48.

Mark, M. M., Henry, G. T., & Julnes, G. (2000). *Evaluation: An integrated framework for understanding, guiding, and improving policies and programs.* San Francisco: Jossey-Bass.

Rog, D. J. (1995). Reasoning in evaluation: Challenges for the practitioner. In D. M. Fournier (Ed.), *Reasoning in evaluation: Inferential links and leaps: New Directions for Evaluation, 68,* 93–100.

Scriven, M. (1991). *Evaluation thesaurus* (4th ed.). Newbury Park, CA: Sage.

Scriven, M. (1995). The logic of evaluation and evaluation practice. In D. M. Fournier (Ed.), *Reasoning in evaluation: Inferential links and leaps: New Directions for Evaluation, 68,* 49–70.

A8 Communication and Reporting

Evaluation communications should have adequate scope and guard against misconceptions, biases, distortions, and errors.

❖ RATIONALE AND CLARIFICATION

Accurate evaluations are built on accurate communication. Some of the most important communication processes and products where accuracy is an issue include

- conversations among evaluators, clients, sponsors, and other stakeholders about the program, the evaluation, and related topics
- formal in-person information collection, such as interviews with stakeholders or focus groups with participants
- any kinds of written communications such as surveys, background documents, and formal and informal reports
- formal and informal presentations
- formal contracts and agreements (P2 Formal Agreements)
- communication via multimedia, dramatizations, photography, other visual arts, or other kinds of descriptions and representations of programs, program components, and their contexts

Accurate communication is needed throughout all phases of the evaluation, for example, to understand and operationalize evaluation purposes (U3 Negotiated Purposes); to investigate and represent the program, its components, and its context (A4 Explicit Program and Context Descriptions); and to select and build shared representations that are validated for the evaluation purposes (A2 Valid Information). Accurate communication is especially important in those phases of the evaluation where the methods and designs are discussed, selected, and implemented (A3 Reliable Information, A5 Information Management, and A6 Sound Designs and Analyses). In the absence of accurate instructions and explanations during data collection, for example, respondents may not understand what the data collection tasks are asking of them. Accurate communication is required to support evaluation reasoning leading to sound findings and for interpretations and conclusions serving the evaluation purposes (A7 Explicit Evaluation Reasoning, A1 Justified Conclusions and Decisions, and U8 Concern for Consequences and Influence).

Some discussions of accuracy in evaluation communication focus on trust and authenticity, especially with regard to the evaluators. Other discussions of accurate communication emphasize evaluation documents, such as formal reports and contracts (see also P2 Formal Agreements). Traditional treatments of report accuracy have emphasized impartiality, objectivity (in the sense of formal consistency or dependability), and freedom from bias. These three subdimensions of accuracy are certainly important for communication in general and for reports specifically.

However, overemphasis on paper reports can easily lead to undervaluing the other key roles that accurate communication plays in facilitating the accurate collection and sharing of information throughout the evaluation. Accurate evaluations require an inclusive model of human communication based on cooperation and negotiation. Accurate communication results when all those involved in the evaluation share their understandings with one another cooperatively and reciprocally with shared understanding as a goal. This is an active and ongoing process that serves to detect and repair misconceptions. It allows individuals to express and check their understandings against those of others. In addition, accuracy is furthered when professional evaluators as well as stakeholders are candid about their disciplinary and other background characteristics so that they can be attentive to any biases or unique perspectives that might affect the accuracy of their communications.

Accurate communication supports shared sense-making and is not based on unwarranted assumptions and unexamined, unexplained terms that might mean very different things to different stakeholders (U6 Meaningful Processes and Products). Accuracy for all stakeholders will improve through commitment to openness and transparency, flexibility in listening to others' ideas and concepts, and willingness to give and take until some common ground of understanding is created. Achieving this accuracy requires that all communicators avoid intentional and unintentional distortion and be flexible and open about others' understandings of reality as they experience and communicate them.

❖ IMPLEMENTING A8 COMMUNICATION AND REPORTING

The following are important recommendations for implementing this standard:

1. Develop a communication plan to support evaluation accuracy. (It should also support utility, feasibility, propriety, and evaluation accountability.) Plans should be responsive to needs and changes in needs in the evaluation setting and discussed thoroughly among the key partners.
2. Schedule formal and informal reporting at points during the evaluation determined by information users' needs. Multiple reporting mechanisms that deliver updates regularly may contribute to accuracy if the quality of the information is continuously upgraded and improved (U7 Timely and Appropriate Communicating and Reporting).
3. Build in checks to determine if key identified information users understand the reports in ways that are congruent with and aligned with report writers' intentions and understandings of the information. Follow up as needed to increase accuracy of shared understandings.
4. Consider information collection events as occasions for formal and informal reporting. A focus group interview could begin or end with a brief report on preliminary findings about or descriptions of program components.
5. Prior to formal reporting, conduct pilot work on how best to present reports given the specific audiences and their needs. For example, descriptions of the program, evaluation methodology, design, and logic, or preliminary reports informing interpretations and conclusions can be tested and validated in a number of communication settings, including town meetings, focus groups, and formal presentations.
6. Provide information about evaluators' and others' background characteristics that may affect accuracy in formal and informal reporting situations.
7. Attend carefully to translation and explanation when multiple languages are involved or the potential for misunderstanding is great because of other background differences. Some concepts are very

difficult, if not impossible, to translate or explain in a different language with one equivalent word or phrase.

8. Select or create guidelines to ensure that formal reports are accurate in detail and scope.
9. Where appropriate and where they will increase accuracy, use approaches such as film, dramatizations, and photography to convey the experiences of stakeholders, program outcomes, or other important evaluation processes or products (U6 Meaningful Processes and Products).

❖ HAZARDS

Some possible hazards with regard to A8 are as follows:

1. Viewing formal reports as the only communication products of the evaluation that need to be checked for accuracy
2. Not communicating clearly enough to prevent misunderstandings and misconceptions about information sources, data collection methods, and alternative approaches
3. Assuming that everyone wants to communicate accurately and that the accuracy of all communications does not need to be evaluated
4. Not communicating in ways that help to build shared understandings of important concepts
5. Failing to allow interviewees and other information providers opportunities to review the information they provided. Such reviews and member checks can help correct mistakes and misconceptions and improve accuracy
6. Not attending to stakeholders' and users' communication needs in support of full and complete understanding given the evaluation purposes
7. Failing to review and revise communications plans and procedures as needed in order to avoid inconsistency, corruptions, and misconceptions
8. Assuming without evidence that communication is accurate when diverse languages, cultures, and other background factors may influence communication in unpredictable ways
9. Assuming without evidence that previously successful communication strategies have achieved acceptable levels of accuracy in the current setting

10. Letting the communications needs of one stakeholder group disproportionately affect communication priorities or allocating resources to some aspects of communication only, resulting in oversights, mistakes, or distortions

11. Focusing on the accuracy of reports and presentations from the perspective of the report writers and presenters rather than checking to see that the users' understandings and meanings are accurate

Application Number Eight for the Accuracy Case Scenario

The scenario that supports this application, including background information about the program, context, and key players, can be read at the end of the Accuracy Overview on page 161.

When it comes to communication, Huseyin draws on many skills that are not immediately apparent to everyone. For example, not everyone knows that Huseyin was a prodigy on the *saz* (or *bağlama,* a stringed Middle Eastern instrument related to the lute). He is a highly respected musician both in Turkey and in certain circles in the United States. His expertise is rooted in a deep understanding of composition, conducting, and improvisation. One of his favorite pastimes is communicating with other musicians and with his audiences through the act of creating musical performances.

When Huseyin conceptualizes communication in evaluation settings, he is informed by analogies to musical performance. Like musical skill, all evaluation work is informed by training and practice. Evaluation requires many people playing many roles to implement high-quality methods and designs. Much of this is guided by preexisting technical skills, knowledge, and methods, but evaluations always require innovation and improvisation in order to reach the highest quality. As a composer, conductor, and player in the evaluation, he knows that he must attend sequentially and then simultaneously in balanced fashion to all aspects of evaluation quality (utility, propriety, feasibility, accuracy, and accountability). He knows that communication affects all aspects of quality and is what brings an evaluation to life. It requires extensive planning, technical skill, and the best execution possible.

Huseyin is a veteran of numerous evaluations, and he knows that the development of a communication plan for the evaluation is essential. Not only does sound communication serve accuracy, communications themselves must be accurate. From his perspective, striving for accurate communication is at the core of the accuracy standards.

Huseyin and his team began planning for communication at the very beginning of the evaluation. They drafted their plan with attention to utility, feasibility, and propriety. As they review their plan with regard to accuracy, two interrelated questions come to mind.

- Which communication processes and products are required for evaluation accuracy?
- Which communication processes and products need to be evaluated with regard to their own accuracy?

They begin to list the key evaluation processes and products from the overall communication plan that should contribute to evaluation accuracy. In a second column, they comment on concerns and efforts needed to achieve adequate accuracy.

Communication Plan Processes and Products: Focus on Accuracy

Event	*Comments*
Initial and ongoing conversations with clients and other stakeholders	The conversations with Consuela, steering committee members, and participating teachers and administrators are an excellent time to attend to key concepts and representations that affect the accuracy of the information, such as ELL and academic outcomes. It's important for us to begin to understand the program and context-specific language (jargon) that different staff and stakeholders use.
Needs assessments	We have engaged in formal and informal assessments of two different sets of needs: (1) teachers' professional development needs to be met by specific program components, for example, the ELL Summer Institute and (2) needs to be met by the evaluation. The concern for accurate communication addresses how the respondents define key concepts related to their needs and how well those concepts capture the needs that can potentially be addressed by program components. Respondents have to understand our questions and survey items, and we have to understand what our communication partners actually mean. We have employed multiple approaches to increase accuracy, such as surveys, focus group interviews, and informal telephone conversations. The latter two in particular have helped us notice and clarify misunderstandings.
Evaluation team meetings	We have tried to be meticulous as an evaluation team in being sure that we understand one another and report to one another all pertinent concerns about miscommunications.
On-demand reports	We are committed to rapid response reporting in order to meet the needs of the staff and leaders. For example, when information from a focus group interview or survey needs to be reported very quickly, we do what we can to assure adequate accuracy. However because of resource constraints, we cannot provide rapid responses that are sufficiently accurate with regard to all matters but rather only for those that have urgency and immediate consequences for quality and improvement. Then we build accurate, broader scope reports later.
Formal outcomes surveys	We were originally concerned that Summer Institute participants might not be sufficiently thorough and reflective to provide accurate information. In previous evaluations, it's been a constant struggle to find time for participants to fill out surveys. Sometimes, workshop leaders reschedule the survey as the last event of the day, moving their final closing remarks ahead of it, and then leave before the surveys are distributed. Some participants leave at the same time and others hurry through their responses. This, of course, diminishes the accuracy of the surveys as measures of workshop outcomes. In general we are committed to helping staff members "own" the evaluation and support the value of the survey for reaching evaluation goals. Staff members' ideas about how to word key ideas and how to clarify concepts have contributed greatly to the survey as it was being developed, modified, and finalized.

Event	*Comments*
Materials and documents	We are working on ways to investigate and communicate the accuracy of all materials and documents. For example, when we requested the curriculum for one of the miniworkshops for the Summer Institute, we were instructed by the trainer to download the handouts and lecture notes from the website. We did so and planned the outcomes assessment for this miniworkshop accordingly. However, based on our observations in the miniworkshop and handouts we received in the actual sessions, we found those materials to be significantly modified and shortened from the reference materials on the Web.
Semiannual and annual reports	The most difficult dilemma we have faced with regard to reporting is the trade-off between our commitment to nuance and detail and the brevity and succinctness desired by many users. What good is a long, accurate report if no one has time to integrate it into their understanding of the program? What good is a brief summary if it does not adequately explain complexity and leads to overgeneralizations, misconceptions, and poor decisions? We will work hard on building executive and other short summaries that acknowledge their own limitations and include references to more thorough treatments and documentation. We will embrace paradoxes, conflicts, and dilemmas as they appear rather than provide oversimplistic generalizations.

As they work on accurate communication in the service of evaluation accuracy, Huseyin and the team decide on an adaptive reporting plan. They agree on detailed technical reports that adequately document the program, its components, and its outcomes as well as all evaluation procedures and products. These technical reports make the reasoning leading to conclusions explicit and summarize information quality, conceptual underpinnings, methods, designs, analyses, participant involvement, staffing, management decisions, and key context features (affecting either the program or its evaluation). These technical reports provide the reference material for other concise evaluation reports. They also provide a foundation for accountability (E1 Evaluation Documentation). Huseyin and his team believe that conducting this specific evaluation without creating technical reports would undermine the overall communication quality.

At the same time, Huseyin knows that their communication plan needs to emphasize shorter reports and oral presentations that focus exclusively yet accurately on specific needs. Some stakeholders, especially legislators, are less concerned with a detailed summary of the actual program that was implemented. They just want a two-page summary of the major outcomes and a weighted summary of quality indicators. Others are interested in a more detailed discussion of the arguments for and against the impact of the program on ELLs' academic learning. Still others want a guidebook for starting a similar Summer Institute elsewhere. Huseyin wonders which of these they can provide with adequate quality given their restricted evaluation resources. He knows that careful planning can increase their efficiency and that they will rely repeatedly on the technical reports for the quality information they need.

The reporting plan is beginning to take shape as Huseyin and other evaluation team members identify audiences and decide how to provide accurate information packaged into various levels of detail. In order to emphasize accuracy while working to achieve utility, feasibility, and propriety, they will incorporate references to the longer documents and note the limitations of the short reports, encouraging users to refer to the longer materials for more scope and perspective as needed.

❖ SUPPORTING DOCUMENTATION

Alkin, M. C., Christie, C. A., & Rose, M. (2006). Communicating evaluation. In I. F. Shaw, J. C. Greene, & M. M. Mark (Eds.), *The Sage handbook of evaluation* (pp. 384–403). London: Sage.

Fitzpatrick, J. L., Sanders, J. R., & Worthen, B. R. (Eds.). (2004). *Program evaluation* (3rd ed.). Boston: Pearson.

Greene, J. C. (2004). The educative evaluator: An interpretation of Lee J. Cronbach's vision of evaluation. In M. C. Alkin (Ed.), *Evaluation roots* (pp. 169–180). Thousand Oaks, CA: Sage.

Rallis, S. F., & Rossman, G. B. (2001). Communicating quality and qualities: The role of the evaluator as critical friend. In R. E. Stake (Series Ed.), A. Benson, D. M. Hinn, & C. Lloyd (Vol. Eds.), *Advances in program evaluation: Vol. 7. Visions of quality: How evaluators define, understand, and represent program quality* (pp. 107–120). Oxford, UK: Elsevier Science.

Scriven, M. (2005). *Key evaluation checklist.* Retrieved April 14, 2010, from http://www.afdc.org.cn/shipdet/cn/UploadFile/200853037848345.doc

Snow, D. (2001). Communicating quality. In R. E. Stake (Series Ed.), A. Benson, D. M. Hinn, & C. Lloyd (Vol. Eds.), *Advances in program evaluation: Vol. 7. Visions of quality: How evaluators define, understand, and represent program quality* (pp. 29–42). Oxford, UK: Elsevier Science.

Wholey, J. S. (2001). Defining, improving, and communicating program quality. In R. E. Stake (Series Ed.), A. Benson, D. M. Hinn, & C. Lloyd (Vol. Eds.), *Advances in program evaluation: Vol. 7. Visions of quality: How evaluators define, understand, and represent program quality* (pp. 201–216). Oxford, UK: Elsevier Science.

Willis, G. B. (2005). *Cognitive interviewing: A tool for improving questionnaire design.* Thousand Oaks, CA: Sage.

Part V

Evaluation Accountability Standards

STANDARD STATEMENTS

E1 Evaluation Documentation	*Evaluations should fully document their negotiated purposes and implemented designs, procedures, data, and outcomes.*
E2 Internal Metaevaluation	*Evaluators should use these and other applicable standards to examine the accountability of the evaluation design, procedures employed, information collected, and outcomes.*
E3 External Metaevaluation	*Program evaluation sponsors, clients, evaluators, and other stakeholders should encourage the conduct of external metaevaluations using these and other applicable standards.*

❖ EVALUATION ACCOUNTABILITY OVERVIEW

Accountability refers to the responsible use of resources to produce value. Program evaluations support program accountability by investigating

- how programs are implemented;
- how programs could be improved;
- how worthwhile, significant, or important the programs are to stakeholders; and
- how program costs, including opportunity costs, compare to benefits.

Similarly, assessments of evaluation accountability investigate

- how evaluations are implemented;
- how evaluations could be improved;
- how worthwhile, significant, or important evaluations are to their stakeholders; and
- how evaluation costs, including opportunity costs, compare to benefits.

In short, documenting and improving evaluation accountability requires similar efforts to those required for program accountability. It requires an evaluation of the evaluation, called a *metaevaluation*. How to conduct internal and external metaevaluations is the major emphasis in this chapter.

The three evaluation accountability standards guide this process. The first, E1 Evaluation Documentation, supports evaluation accountability through documenting evaluation contexts, resources, processes, products, and results. The second, E2 Internal Metaevaluation, describes how those in the organizations housing the program or the evaluation can systematically apply these and other standards to their own evaluations. The third, E3 External Metaevaluation, parallels E2 but focuses on engaging outside evaluators to investigate and report on evaluation quality. Taken together, these three standards support the development of evaluation capacity, continuous evaluation improvement (formative purposes), and judgments about evaluation quality once the evaluation is completed (summative purposes).

The Importance of Evaluation Accountability

Attending to evaluation accountability is important for three reasons. First, attention to accountability guides improvements during all phases of evaluation design and implementation. Second, attention to evaluation accountability can lead to improved decisions about programs. Making evaluation strengths and limitations explicit helps stakeholders better understand the warranted uses of the evaluation as they make decisions. Third, reflecting on evaluation accountability helps practitioners and other stakeholders become more skillful in their future practice. It can also support organizational development and help build capacity for evaluation. In the long run, better evaluation practice and capacity can lead to widespread improvements in evaluation and greater positive impact of programs and projects.

At its core, attention to evaluation accountability encourages reflection and a metaevaluative perspective in evaluators and evaluation users. A metaevaluative perspective seeks the key features of evaluation quality in each specific situation and identifies what is needed to judge and improve evaluation quality. It also creates a meaningful learning set for evaluators and evaluation users, so that their experiences can lead to better evaluations and uses of evaluations in the future.

What Is Metaevaluation and How Does it Serve Evaluation Accountability?

The term *metaevaluation* denotes systematic evaluation of evaluations and their subcomponents. Anyone who applies the utility, feasibility, propriety, accuracy, and evaluation accountability standards to judge the quality of evaluations and their components is engaging in metaevaluation. Just like other evaluations, metaevaluations require evidence, analysis, communication, and follow-through with stakeholders.

Individual metaevaluations differ on a number of dimensions, for example, scope, complexity, duration, resource allocation, settings, and uses. However, all metaevaluations apply evidence pertaining to selected standards to reach conclusions about the quality of evaluations or their subcomponents. They can be guided and supported by checklists, forms, tables, and narratives, so that end users can follow the evidence, standards, criteria, logic, and conclusions to reach their own conclusions and decisions (A1 Justified Conclusions and Decisions).

One very basic approach to metaevaluation, sometimes described as a *desk audit,* relies entirely on existing documentation. Like other approaches, it can support both formative and summative purposes and can be repeated by evaluators and other stakeholders at different times for different purposes. Its quality is highly dependent on the suitability and quality of the available documentation for the metaevaluative purposes.

When the stakes are high and the program evaluation quality should be unimpeachable, more complex and better-resourced metaevaluations are warranted. This is the case when issues of evaluation quality are important for decision making on a large scale. For example, some metaevaluations might require additional monitoring and data collection to address evaluation quality and use over longer periods of time. With additional data collection, metaevaluations can also address the long-term impact and utility of specific program evaluations or evaluation approaches.

Some metaevaluations investigate a single evaluation or a specific evaluation component. Typically these metaevaluations go through a four-step process:

- Identify the purposes and needs to be served.
- Select and align dimensions of quality for judging the evaluation.
- Secure documentation about the evaluation or its subcomponents that is adequate to reach trustworthy conclusions.
- Prepare and communicate findings, judgments, and conclusions in preparation for decision making.

At other times, metaevaluations compare two or more program evaluations or subcomponents in order to make decisions about their comparative quality in a specific context or contexts. For example, when two or more evaluations reach quite different conclusions about the quality of similar or replicated programs, comparative external metaevaluation can address the soundness of the evaluations (E3 External Metaevaluation). In other situations, comparative metaevaluation can be part of evaluation planning. After securing funding to design and implement a program, staff may issue a request for evaluation proposals. They will then metaevaluate the proposed evaluation designs against specific standards or other dimensions of quality before awarding the evaluation contract. They might follow the same four-step process mentioned above to compare the multiple designs. Similarly, two evaluation subcomponents can be compared in the context of one evaluation to determine which works better in light of these standards or other dimensions of evaluation quality. In general, when the situation is appropriate and justifies the expense, replicated evaluations, with or without planned variation, can provide a basis for metaevaluation.

Who Is Responsible for Evaluation Accountability?

As knowledgeable professionals, program evaluators have a primary responsibility for formative and summative evaluation accountability (E2 Internal Metaevaluation). In addition, program evaluators should also inform clients, sponsors, and other users of their specific responsibilities for maintaining evaluation accountability and for accurately communicating the strengths and limitations of the evaluation (A8 Communicating and Reporting).

Evaluators, clients, and sponsors all share responsibility for specifying the documentation required for the most pressing accountability questions and for ensuring sufficient resources for the required evidence. In addition, evaluators, clients, and sponsors must decide which resources to allocate for internal and external metaevaluation and formative and summative purposes (E2 Internal Metaevaluation and E3 External Metaevaluation). All stakeholders (not just evaluators, clients, and sponsors) are responsible for understanding whether the quality of the evaluation is sufficient for their intended and actual uses. When evaluation quality is substandard, users can modify their conclusions and actions to limit misuse (U8 Concern for Consequences and Influence).

The accountability standards call for attention to both internal and external metaevaluations. In contrast to internal metaevaluators, external metaevaluators are not members of the organizations that house the program or the evaluation and have no other roles in the program or the evaluation. Once they are hired, the duties of external metaevaluators may replicate and complement those of internal evaluators. For example, just like internal evaluation, external metaevaluation can serve both formative and summative purposes. However, when both internal and external metaevaluations are planned, sometimes the external metaevaluator takes on a greater responsibility for summative metaevaluation.

An external metaevaluator has no other roles in the program, the evaluation, or the organizations that staff them. However, nuances of involvement often make this distinction between internal and external less clear-cut. In addition, role confusions and opportunities for conflicts of interests and the appearance of conflicts of interests are constant concerns (P6 Conflicts of Interests). For example, can two evaluators from different organizations metaevaluate each other's evaluations without a conflict of interest? Can a former employee metaevaluate for a previous employer and still be viewed as an external metaevaluator? In general, the common belief that external evaluators and metaevaluators automatically provide more objectivity should be viewed with caution. The three evaluation accountability standards discuss these issues in more detail.

Evaluating Metaevaluations

Metaevaluations can also be evaluated. However, no special term is needed, such as *meta-metaevaluation*. In addition, diminishing returns from external metaevaluations of metaevaluations (limited or no increased benefits along with increased costs) make them infrequent. In practice, metaevaluations should be held accountable for their quality but do not usually require formal external metaevaluation. It is often sufficient to rely on applicable standards to help control and assure metaevaluation quality. Moreover, the clients for metaevaluations are often quite skilled in evaluation and may be able to judge the quality of the metaevaluation and contribute to its improvement and the documentation of its strengths and limitations.

Evaluation Accountability Case Scenario

The case applications for these Evaluation Accountability Standards build on the earlier scenario and applications from the Utility Standards (page 9). In this scenario, Jamaal, a beginning evaluator with the firm Centerville Research and Evaluation Specialists (CRES), is hired by the board of directors of the Centerville Health for Eco-educated Residents (CHEERS) program to serve as an external evaluator and to help prepare annual reports. CHEERS is eligible to receive multiple years of annual funding from a philanthropic organization on the condition that the evaluation findings from each year demonstrate that the program continues to support the values of the organization and meets annual goals. Should the program qualify for a third year of funding, the philanthropic organization will also fund a summative, external metaevaluation in order to judge the accuracy of the evaluation and whether the program is deserving of continued long-term support. Readers can review the full background and prior development of the CHEERS evaluation in the Utility scenario (p. 9) and in the applications following each Utility Standard.

E1 Evaluation Documentation

Evaluations should fully document their negotiated purposes and implemented designs, procedures, data, and outcomes.

❖ RATIONALE AND CLARIFICATION

The rationale for this standard parallels the rationale for A4 Explicit Program and Context Descriptions. Just like programs, evaluations and their contexts should be documented with adequate detail and scope. When pertinent details about evaluations and their contexts are not sufficiently documented, judgments about evaluation quality may be seriously limited. In collecting, analyzing, and communicating information about evaluations, all the pertinent accuracy standards apply (for example, A2 Valid Information, A3 Reliable Information, A5 Information Management, and A6 Sound Designs and Analyses).

Evaluation documentation serves accountability by providing the basis for judging evaluation quality (E2 Internal Metaevaluation and E3 External Metaevaluation). Documentation should be accurate, sufficient, and pertinent, given the metaevaluation purposes. In practice, evaluators who are responsible for documenting evaluations usually begin to anticipate and collect the needed evidence in advance of its systematic use for metaevaluation. Planning for evaluation documentation should take place as the evaluation is planned.

The quality of the documentation will often depend on available resources and their efficient use. When the evaluation staff and stakeholders adopt a metaevaluative perspective and anticipate metaevaluation-related information needs, it is often possible to collect low-cost evidence across the span of the evaluation that will serve formative and summative purposes as implemented in both internal and external metaevaluations. The best-resourced external metaevaluations can then augment that documentation with additional information collection as needed.

Documenting an evaluation accurately can also serve other instrumental and conceptual uses in addition to evaluation accountability and improvement. For example, those who are designing similar but new programs or program evaluations may begin their design work by reviewing previous, related evaluations. Similarly, program designers interested in how to embed evaluations in their programs may benefit from specific evaluation documentation. Evaluation documentation also provides many theoretical and operational definitions that benefit others engaged in similar work (A2 Valid Information). Documentation will also contribute to knowledge about how these and other standards are used.

❖ IMPLEMENTING E1 EVALUATION DOCUMENTATION

The following are important recommendations for implementing this standard:

1. Determine who will need the evaluation documentation for which purposes and specify the dimensions of quality, needs, and questions to be addressed by the documentation.
2. After the accountability-related needs and questions have been specified, plan a case data set (A6 Sound Designs and Analyses) describing the documentation and information to address these needs and questions.
3. Once the selected dimensions of quality have been aligned with the accountability-related questions and needs, catalogue the existing documentation.
4. Build a table of needed information and review the available documentation with regard to its completeness, quality, and value on a regular basis. It must have sufficient scope, detail, and alignment to be useful.
5. Based on the table of needed and available documentation above, decide whether and how to secure additional documentation.
6. The metaevaluative orientation and perspective can also extend to documenting evaluation consequences and influences after the evaluation is completed. While collecting all needed information is

unlikely during the evaluation, evaluators and metaevaluators can facilitate later information collection by anticipating how and from whom it might be collected.

❖ HAZARDS

Some possible hazards with regard to E1 are as follows:

1. Not fully anticipating the documentation that will be needed for the ensuing metaevaluations and accountability judgments
2. Over- or under-resourcing the collection of evaluation documentation through lack of ongoing review of evaluation documentation needs
3. Not considering the return on investment for evaluation documentation when making decisions about how to provide resources for it
4. Continuing with an internal or external metaevaluation in the absence of adequate information
5. In designing and collecting documentation, not attending to changing priorities, values, needs, purposes, and contexts
6. Failing to consider risks, costs, and benefits of specific evaluation documentation approaches

---

Application One for Evaluation Accountability, Based on the Utility Case Scenario

The scenario that supports this application, including background information about the program, context, and key players, can be read at the end of the Utility Overview on page 9.

Jamaal returns to his office to prepare for a meeting with Janet Chipperfield, PhD, a CRES senior associate and his immediate supervisor and mentor. She has suggested to Jamaal that they review the first year of the evaluation. She has assured him that the meeting is intended to support his growth as an evaluator. The CHEERS evaluation is his first CRES project as the lead evaluator, and the meeting is intended to be an informal discussion. Jamaal considers how to prepare for the meeting. He remembers that he and Camilla, the CHEERS administrative assistant, have collected documentation of the evaluation processes and products. As he reviews the CHEERS files on his computer, he notices that they can tell quite a story. He opens a new table and begins to chart the file names and the different forms of documentation connected to each one. After a while, he stops to review what he has produced.

Evaluation Activity	*Documentation Within File*	*Purposes*
Start-Up	• Letter of introduction • Program staff pictures: "What is evaluation?" • Process to obtain consent to record evaluation working meetings	• Introduce evaluator and set the tone for evaluation • Examine staff expectations for evaluation • Establish working protocols
Contract	• Evaluation design, budget, and deliverables	• Establish initial reference points for decision making
Program Description	• Stakeholder maps for each of five CHEERS projects and the CHEERS program as a whole • Logic models for each project and the program	• Document the program's reach and possible influence • Create a baseline for reviewing accuracy and feasibility of program expectations
Communications	• List of formal deliverables and required reports • Negotiations to establish participatory approaches for evaluation • Formal agreement with Suparna that she track project leaders' experiences of participatory activities • E-mails to program staff • Agreement with Suparna that program communications stored with Camilla be available to the evaluation	• Make explicit the quantity and quality of required communications with program staff • Record renegotiated evaluation purposes and processes • Share communication responsibilities with program director • Track regular program communications • Demonstrate connections with the program administrator
Data Collection	• Summaries of meetings to clarify stakeholders' information needs and the purposes for evaluation findings and how findings could be used • Summaries of meetings to brainstorm and select evaluation questions • Surveys and instrumentation developed and pilot tested • Interview protocols drafted	• Investigate key evaluation questions
Data Analysis	• Pilot data analyzed leading to revised survey	• Improve subsequent data collection

Reporting	• Submissions by Suparna and Jamaal to the board of directors • Weekly updates posted on the office administrative bulletin boards • Formal reports to program funders and program staff	• Document the linkage between the board and program director's accounts of evaluation progress. • Evidence of emergent reporting process. • Demonstrate how reports are adapted to meet audience need
Evaluator E-Log	• Reflections based on meetings with program staff and other stakeholders	• Monitor my own learning and concerns about the progress of the evaluation

Jamaal realizes that he still needs to add the various documents he has created for the formative, developmental, and outcome evaluation activities associated with the different projects. His data collection and data analysis notes are quite extensive and help him describe the purposes of most of the documents associated with these processes.

As Jamaal prepares the documentation for the meeting, he begins to feel more confident about his use of standards to guide decision-making processes throughout the first-year evaluation. He also notes evidence that the bulk of his attention has been focused on supporting the participatory processes that guided the design. In retrospect, this seems to have been the right choice for various reasons, especially since none of the program staff had previous experience with evaluations. As he reviews the documentation, he thinks about their experiences together this last year. He hopes that everyone from CHEERS will be back for Year 2.

During the last year, Jamaal has reflected, often with probing from Janet, about the quality of his evaluation work. All things considered, he is satisfied that the evaluation was well conducted and that his attention to the utility, feasibility, propriety, accuracy, and accountability standards was appropriate. However, he realizes that he could have made more notes about applications of the individual standards than he did. He also wishes that he had paid more attention to the metaevaluation standards and to developing a metaevaluative perspective from the very beginning. He resolves to sit down with *The Program Evaluation Standards* and once again review the documentation that he has collected. His goal will be to identify the standards that were central to his decision making and the documentation that demonstrates how the standards guided his work. In doing this he realizes that it will also become obvious which standards he did not explicitly use and that he should be able to discuss his choices and rationales.

In addition, he knows that some of the standards, for example, the Accuracy Standards, will play a much bigger role in next year's evaluation. He also realizes he should apply the Accuracy Standards to the quality of the evaluation documentation he is preparing. Moreover, by reviewing all the standards at this time, he can anticipate standards that are likely to come to the forefront next year and consider in advance what he should be collecting as documentation. Jamaal is not sure he can complete the review of documentation before he meets with Janet next week. However, he can at least present his evaluation accountability approach.

Jamaal also realizes that Janet will be part of the internal metaevaluation, too. As he reflects and prepares, he understands that a metaevaluative perspective has guided much of her probing and mentoring over the course of this first year, but that it has been nuanced and subtle. As a last thought, Jamaal considers the merits of adding a new column to the chart with the heading *Feedback*. In this column, he will record any suggestions he receives from Janet that apply to the quality of this or next year's evaluation work.

❖ SUPPORTING DOCUMENTATION

Frink, D. D., & Ferris, G. R. (1998). Accountability, impression management, and goal setting in the performance evaluation process. *Human Relations, 51,* 1259–1283.

Gregory, A., & Watson, T. (2008). Defining the gap between research and practice in public relations programme evaluation—towards a new research agenda. *Journal of Marketing Communications, 14,* 337–350.

King, J. (2008). Bringing evaluation learning to life. *American Journal of Evaluation, 29,* 151–155.

Mabry, L. (2001). Representing the truth about program quality or the truth about representing program quality. In A. Benson, D. M. Hinn, & C. Lloyd (Eds.), *Visions of quality: How evaluators define, understand, and represent program quality* (pp. 19–27). New York: JAI/ Elsevier Science.

O'Connor, M. K., & Netting, F. E. (2008). Faith-based evaluation: Accountable to whom, for what? *Evaluation and Program Planning, 31,* 347–355.

Schwarts, R., & Mayne, J. (2005). Assuring the quality of evaluative information: Theory and practice. *Evaluation and Program Planning, 28,* 1–14.

United States Government Accounting Office. (2003). *Government auditing standards.* Accessed January 21, 2010, at http://www.gao.gov/govaud/yb/2003/html/TOC.html

E2 Internal Metaevaluation

Evaluators should use these and other applicable standards to examine the accountability of the evaluation design, procedures employed, information collected, and outcomes.

❖ RATIONALE AND CLARIFICATION

Standards E2 Internal Metaevaluation and E3 External Metaevaluation complement one another to present a full picture of systematic metaevaluation. The two standards are both important in their own right but are best reviewed and applied together. Both have to be considered in planning and budgeting processes to ensure that evaluation resources are well managed (F4 Resource Use). In many situations, including both internal and external metaevaluation in a complementary and collaborative effort can produce the best results.

The internal-external distinction exists for both evaluators and metaevaluators. In general, an internal evaluator is defined as one employed by the organization that hosts the program. In contrast, external evaluators are employed elsewhere and have no other duties in the programs they evaluate. External evaluators can work collaboratively with internal evaluators and program staff without damage to their status or independence. Collaborations of internal and external evaluators on the same evaluation produce blended evaluations with both an internal and external perspective.

Neither internal nor external metaevaluation is necessarily more valuable than the other. They are often complementary and their relative values are often situation-specific. In addition, internal metaevaluations are not necessarily less objective, although they are often viewed as less so. Among employees of the same organization, the degree to which an internal evaluator is independent from or enmeshed in the program can vary widely. For example, when the internal evaluator reports to a supervisor with strong, preconceived opinions, the stresses on the evaluator may not allow for a feasible, useful evaluation (F3 Contextual Viability). On the other hand, when internal evaluators report to independent units, work autonomously, have few if any conflicts of interests affecting the evaluation processes and outcomes, and are not subject to job-related consequences regardless of what they report, they may approach or even exceed the autonomy of external evaluators. When the entire organization has developed a commitment to evaluation capacity building and desires the most useful and accurate evaluation possible, the expected gap in independence between internal and external evaluators may disappear. Regardless of whether an evaluation is internal or external, its quality depends on how well it addresses these program evaluation standards and any other dimensions of quality required in the specific situation.

The distinctions between internal and external metaevaluations are similar, but with important nuances. For example, often the same evaluators design and implement both the program evaluation and its internal metaevaluation. Thus both internal and external program evaluators can be internal metaevaluators. As a consequence, internal metaevaluators can be employees of organizations that house either the program, the evaluation, or both. These and other complexities are described more fully in Standard E3 External Metaevaluation.

As with internal and external evaluation, internal and external metaevaluations share important similarities. Both types of metaevaluations systematically identify factors that must be addressed to improve the evaluation and support decisions about the final quality of the evaluation as proposed and implemented. Typical metaevaluation users are the program staff, clients, and sponsors; the members of the program evaluation team; and other stakeholders with an interest in the evaluation information. Both types of metaevaluation can take place at any point when the quality of the evaluation needs addressing for summative or formative purposes. Both can help evaluation stakeholders know how much they can trust the evaluation.

Internal metaevaluations also provide some special benefits. Because they directly increase communication between evaluators and evaluation users, they help resolve differences in perspectives, backgrounds, and prior knowledge about the program and the evaluation processes. This improved communication can also contribute to metaevaluation process use. It has the potential for indirect, positive effects on evaluation utility, feasibility, propriety, accuracy, and accountability independent of specific findings directed toward evaluation improvement. For example, communication related to internal metaevaluation may positively affect U1 Evaluator Credibility and support U4 Explicit Values. It may help clarify F3 Contextual Viability and P6 Conflicts of Interests. Accuracy may also be enhanced through processes to clarify construct validity, identify backgrounds and assumptions, and illuminate cultural differences (A2 Valid Information). Internal metaevaluations communicate that the evaluators take their own accountability seriously and devote resources to it. This awareness may positively affect stakeholders' views about holding the program accountable and the evaluation's value in doing that.

Internal metaevaluation often provides a necessary basis for external metaevaluation. The work of the external metaevaluators will be greatly facilitated by complete and accurate evaluation documentation and well-designed and executed internal metaevaluation.

❖ IMPLEMENTING E2 INTERNAL METAEVALUATION

The following are important recommendations for implementing this standard:

1. Remember that internal metaevaluation creates value for identified users through reflective practice informed by high-quality documentation (E1 Evaluation Documentation).
2. Adopt a metaevaluative perspective and plan the internal metaevaluation addressing utility, feasibility, propriety, and accuracy from the beginning of the evaluation.
3. Ensure that resources are adequate for the internal metaevaluation.
4. Select at least one person with adequate expertise to manage the internal metaevaluation processes throughout the evaluation.
5. Regularly review the intended uses of the internal metaevaluation and its potential contributions to quality and value.
6. Collect complementary information and documentation about how the program evaluation was implemented and experienced by other involved stakeholders.

❖ HAZARDS

Some possible hazards with regard to E2 are as follows:

1. Relying on beliefs about what happened that are not well investigated and corroborated (their accuracy is not determined)
2. Metaevaluating the evaluation only as conceptualized and intended rather than as actually implemented, experienced, and used by others

3. Relying on insider knowledge only. Internal metaevaluators, by virtue of their roles in the evaluation (and sometimes in the program) may accept without adequate skepticism all manner of insider knowledge, some accurate and some inaccurate, about the program and the program evaluation
4. Undermining the original evaluation by transferring needed resources from it to the internal metaevaluation
5. Paying too little attention to the internal metaevaluation, thus detracting from its potential to document evaluation quality and lead to evaluation improvement

Application Two for Evaluation Accountability, Based on the Utility Case Scenario

The scenario that supports this application, including background information about the program, context, and key players, can be read at the end of the Utility Overview on page 9.

On his way to the CHEERS office to meet Suparna, the program director, and Jase, the assistant program director, Jamaal takes delight in knowing that everyone is feeling very upbeat about the first year's evaluation report. The board of directors is impressed with the quality of information and style of report that he and the program staff created for the five individual projects and the program as a whole. Just this morning, Suparna sent Jamaal a copy of the e-mail she received from the sponsor commending CHEERS on their first year evaluation report and confirming funding for a second year. This news confirms that Jamaal and the program staff would all be working together again on the Year 2 evaluation.

Gradually, however, Jamaal finds himself wrestling with some ambivalence. When he first met the CHEERS personnel he was an outsider. After 11 months of developmental and collaborative work, he is becoming more like their colleague. On the one hand, he realizes that he is an external evaluator. On the other hand, he recognizes that over the year he has grown quite supportive of the CHEERS program. He appreciates their efforts and admires their dedication to using evaluation to learn about their individual projects. In addition, the evaluation findings have demonstrated fiscal responsibility combined with high levels of satisfaction from program users and volunteers. Jamaal realizes that in some ways he is now a quasimember of the program staff even though he directly reports to and is paid by CRES.

In spite of the ambivalence about his role, Jamaal is pleased that the Year 1 evaluation findings have identified ways that the program as a whole and each of the five projects can be improved. The program staff will have the opportunity to demonstrate over the next year their ability to implement evidence-informed decision making as a program improvement strategy. By demonstrating a commitment to improvement, CHEERS can strengthen its case for sustainable funding.

Jamaal enters the CHEERS office hoping that today he and the senior staff will discuss the value of the Year 1 evaluation. They can reflect on how the Year 2 evaluation can contribute to their goal of demonstrating value to the sponsor. They begin by revisiting their first report. Jamaal asks, "So were you satisfied with the way the evaluation went?" Suparna and Jase looked surprised. Jase reacted first. "Well of course. We got renewed funding, didn't we!" Jamaal reminds Jase that while this was critical, all the staff began the evaluation wondering whether it could be conducted without interfering with the program (U1 Evaluator Credibility and F2 Practical Procedures). He also reminds Suparna that she expressed some real doubt about whether collaborative and participatory approaches would add value to the program and its evaluation (U4 Explicit Values). Both consider these concerns to be no longer important, but Jamaal pushes them to consider these issues seriously. "We get to work together for another year." Jamaal emphasizes, "We should be certain that next year's evaluation meets your needs and those of the sponsors and stakeholders."

Jamaal introduces a more formal inquiry process to help all of them with decision making about this and next year's evaluation. It involves revisiting questions they had about the evaluation and identifying the first year evidence that addressed these questions. Suparna and Jase are a little skeptical about the need for this, but they have grown to have confidence in Jamaal. Jamaal is also a bit nervous about this, since he has never conducted this form of internal metaevaluation. In about 30 minutes they have constructed four questions that capture the concerns that Suparna, Jase, and the CHEERS staff had expressed at the beginning of the evaluation. Jamaal notes that *The Program Evaluation Standards* influenced these questions.

- Were the evaluation activities practical and responsive to the way the program operates?
- Was the evaluation responsive to stakeholders and the project communities?
- Were the evaluation activities, descriptions, findings, and judgments meaningful to stakeholders?
- Did the evaluation encourage use of processes and findings?

After the meeting is over, Jamaal returns to his office with the questions to identify evidence that can address them. Reflecting on *The Program Evaluation Standards,* he also sees a relationship between these questions and the five dimensions of quality used to describe evaluation quality (evaluation utility, feasibility, propriety, accuracy, and accountability). He uses these dimensions to build a framework. As he works, he can see how the framework will help shape the Year 2 design and document reallocation of resources.

Jamaal schedules an hour-long meeting with Suparna and Jase to begin work on the internal metaevaluation. In advance, he asks Suparna to put together a folder of all of the e-mails she received from project directors about their experiences in implementing evaluation activities. Because of her skepticism toward participatory evaluation, Suparna had purposely canvassed her project directors about their experiences during the first 4 months of the evaluation. Jamaal arrives for the meeting with a file of materials that he and Camilla have put together. He connects his computer to their LCD projector and opens his working document for Suparna and Jase to review.

Q: Were the evaluation activities practical and responsive to the way the program operates?	Dimension of Quality: Feasibility	
Available Documentation	*Analysis*	*Decisions for Year 2*
1. Project leaders' reports on their evaluation activities as found in monthly staff meeting minutes filed by Camilla 2. The program director's regular correspondence with project directors regarding the evaluation's influence on project implementation plans		

Almost immediately, Jase asks Jamaal why he has not included any of the documents they accumulated when working with the local reporter who created the blog about CHEERS (U7 Timely and Appropriate Communicating and Reporting Application). Jamaal confesses that he overlooked this information because it was not part of the original design but was produced in response to the unexpected opportunity to be featured both inside and outside their community. They add the files to the list and Camilla is able to retrieve them almost immediately.

They plan to review these documents for evidence addressing the primary questions. While Jamaal knows that he might complete this task fairly quickly by himself, he wants Suparna and Jase to participate in answering the questions as a way of setting the direction for next year's evaluation. It takes them more than an hour to consider this first question. After they complete their review and analysis of information, they compose a brief answer to the question. They then turn their attention to the implications for the second year evaluation, given what they have learned.

Q: Were the evaluation activities practical and responsive to the way the program operates?	A: This improved over time.	Dimension of Quality: Feasibility
Available Documentation	*Analyses and Findings*	*Decisions for Year 2*
1. Project leaders' reports on their evaluation activities as found in monthly staff meeting minutes filed by Camilla 2. The program director's regular correspondence with project directors regarding the evaluation's influence on project implementation plans	• Over the first 5 months, project leaders became increasingly adept at reporting on how they were integrating evaluation meetings and activities into project routines. Most concerns arose when Jamaal pushed them on the accuracy of their evaluation work.	• Project leaders will not require the same level of hands-on support in Year 2. Consider making the new evaluation emphasis for project leaders a more in-depth understanding of evaluation accuracy and its importance for decision making. • Jamaal will facilitate a meeting of all program staff where they revisit and formalize problem-solving strategies that have contributed to good decision making.

3. The file from Camilla documenting the processes that led to a publicity on the program by the local blogger	• Jamaal's visits to project sites were initially seen as interruptions to regular routines. Over time, reports from project directors focused on Jamaal's contribution to program discussions and his help with program problem-solving. • Both the senior staff and Jamaal relied heavily on Camilla to prepare for the visit from the press. • Jamaal had a formal report on preliminary findings available within 2 days. • Senior staff were able to comfortably discuss with the blogger the evaluation processes, and early findings; project directors were less able to do so. • Jamaal's availability to support the program during this unexpected event was only one example of his efforts to represent the program accurately to those outside the program.	• A new agenda item for the monthly staff meeting will be *Taking Stock.* Project leaders will ask project directors for a report on the problems that required considerable time, personnel, or financial resources to resolve. Jamaal will track these over time and assess whether the problems are common across projects. If so, they might be better addressed at program level by senior staff. • Do a better job of highlighting Camilla's program roles by conducting a formal assessment of her contributions and using this information to create a job description for the position. • Promote evaluation sustainability by having project directors take more responsibility for reporting on evaluation activities at the project sites during the monthly staff meetings. • Revisit the amount of reporting of evaluation findings, both preliminary and final, including communication both within and outside the program with important audiences. Use reporting as a way to enhance the program's overall profile.

Suparna, Jase, and Jamaal repeat this process using the question: "Was the evaluation responsive to stakeholders and the project communities?" Jamaal explains how this question is primarily about whether the evaluation was conducted in a proper, fair, and acceptable way. Analysis of the documents investigating the needs of stakeholders suggests that the answer is "Not as well as we might have." Three adjustments are made to the Year 2 evaluation plan. One of these allows program users to complete either a paper and pencil survey or a telephone survey. A small but significant segment of project users struggle with literacy and their opinions were absent in the Year 1 data set.

The team realizes in working through their first question that it is the board of directors who will ultimately be responsible for negotiating the program's future with the sponsor. In doing so the board will need to feel assured that the information and analyses take into account the needs, expectations, and cultural contexts of clients and other stakeholders. A challenge for the second-year evaluation will be to help board members become more fluent in discussing the program, the evaluation, and its findings, including any deficits or weakness that emerged during the year.

Finally, the documentation also suggests that by selecting and training a small group of volunteers to help with the data collection, the evaluation has increased stress within the volunteer community by creating an in-group. Suparna, Jase, and Jamaal resolve that anyone interested in being part of the Year 2 data collection team will be included in the training and have the opportunity to help according to their abilities and interests. They also plan to develop incentives in order to create a bigger pool of volunteers for evaluation work as part of their evaluation capacity building.

At subsequent meetings and through electronic file sharing, Jamaal, Jase, and Suparna work through the remaining two questions. When they are satisfied with their analyses, they draft and post a report of the internal metaevaluation processes and findings on the office administrative bulletin board. Camilla and the project leaders are charged with reviewing the summaries and bringing their comments and suggestions to the next staff meeting.

It is now time for Jamaal to finalize the documentation, including his metaevaluative work with Suparna and Jase, and provide a copy to Janet. Over the next few weeks, she will perform a desk audit and then set up a time to discuss her metaevaluation and any questions she has. Jamaal is eager, if a bit nervous, to hear what she will have to say.

❖ SUPPORTING DOCUMENTATION

Bickman, L. (1997). Evaluating evaluation: Where do we go from here? *Evaluation Practice, 18*(1), 1–16.

Cooksy, L. J., & Caracelli, V. J. (2005). Quality, context, and use: Issues in achieving the goals of metaevaluation. *American Journal of Evaluation, 26,* 31–42.

Cooksy, L. J., & Caracelli, V. J. (2009). Metaevaluation in practice: Selection and application of criteria. *Journal of MultiDisciplinary Evaluation, 6*(11), 1–15.

Conley-Tyler, M. (2005). A fundamental choice: Internal or external evaluation? *Evaluation Journal of Australasia, 4* (1 & 2), 3–11.

Hanssen, C. E., Lawrenz, F., & Dunet, D. O. (2008). Concurrent metaevaluation: A critique. *American Journal of Evaluation, 29,* 572–582.

Mathison, S. (1999). Rights, responsibilities, and duties: A comparison of ethics for internal and external evaluators. In J. Telfair, L. C. Leviton, & J. S. Merchant (Eds.), *Evaluating health and human service programs in community settings: New Directions for Evaluation, 82,* 25–34.

Schwarts, R., & Mayne, J. (2005). Assuring the quality of evaluative information: Theory and practice. *Evaluation and Program Planning, 28,* 1–14.

Scriven, M. (2009). Meta-evaluation revisited. *Journal of MultiDisciplinary Evaluation, 6*(11), iii-viiii.

E3 External Metaevaluation

Program evaluation sponsors, clients, evaluators, and other stakeholders should encourage the conduct of external metaevaluations using these and other applicable standards.

In general, the rationale for and the benefits of internal and external metaevaluation are similar to each other. Both internal and external metaevaluations can focus on formative and summative purposes. Both can support continuous or one-time improvements or document the strengths and limitations of evaluations after they are completed. Both can serve a few or a wide variety of evaluation audiences, including program staff, evaluators, and other stakeholders. Internal and external metaevaluators can also form one team providing for a combined approach.

External and internal metaevaluations also differ from one another in important ways. As indicated previously, external metaevaluators are not members of organizations that house the program or the evaluation and do not have a direct role in the program or its evaluation. They have a structural distance from the program and its evaluation that is intended to reduce conflicts of interests and result in fewer biases (or at least different biases).

In contrast to the complete lack of connection required in external evaluators, internal metaevaluators can be internal in various ways. For example, they may have one or more roles in the program, the evaluation, or the organizations that house the evaluation or the program. The following table summarizes the various ways that metaevaluators can have internal connections to the program or its evaluation.

Table E3.1 Types of Internal Metaevaluators

	INTERNAL, T1	INTERNAL, T2	INTERNAL, T3	EXTERNAL
PROGRAM	YES The metaevaluator directs, is a staff member in, or is a participant in the program or the organization that houses the program.	NO The metaevaluator is *not* a contributor to or a participant in the program and not a member of the organization that houses the program.	YES The metaevaluator contributes to or participates in the program or is a member of the organization that houses the program.	NO The metaevaluator is *not* a contributor to or a participant in the program or a member of the organization that houses the program.
EVALUATION	YES The metaevaluator directs, is a staff member, or has a responsible role in the evaluation or the organization that houses it.	YES The metaevaluator directs, is a staff member, or has a responsible role in the evaluation or the organization that houses it.	NO The metaevaluator does *not* direct, implement, or have a responsible role in the evaluation or the organization that houses it.	NO The metaevaluator does *not* direct, implement, or have a responsible role in the evaluation or the organization that houses it.

The labels T1, T2, and T3 denote the different types of internal metaevaluators. Type 1 internal metaevaluators are by definition also internal program evaluators. In contrast, Type 2 internal evaluators are external program evaluators. Type 3 internal metaevaluators have roles in the organizations that house the program but have no program evaluator role.

External metaevaluations are often viewed as more objective. Ideally, they will provide an independent perspective on the quality of the evaluation from the vantage point of an expert third party. However, structural independence does not guarantee quality. External metaevaluators' dispositions, cultural perspectives, beliefs, and values; personal, financial, and other interests; and prior experiences can have significant effects on processes and findings. Just as in any evaluation, metaevaluators' conflicts of interests (P6 Conflicts of Interests) and credibility (U1 Evaluator Credibility) need explicit attention.

Being structurally independent from the program and its evaluation does not mean that external metaevaluators need to insulate themselves from the program and its evaluation. On the contrary, involvement in the program, the evaluation, and the contexts can take many forms. For example, external metaevaluators may contact key stakeholders to better understand their needs related to metaevaluation. They can communicate with key stakeholders to gain knowledge about evaluation processes, products, and outcomes. When working contemporaneously during program and evaluation implementation, external metaevaluators may have considerable contact with the program participants and staff and may be responsible for formative contributions and suggesting ways to improve the evaluation. They may engage in regular contact with the evaluators.

On the other hand, external metaevaluations may sometimes be distant from the evaluation and its processes. It is entirely possible for some summative external metaevaluations to take place long after the program and its evaluation are completed and to rely completely on reports and existing documentation.

Having no direct access to insiders' knowledge can be a sizable challenge in some external metaevaluations. Internal knowledge may be needed to fully understand program and evaluation quality and value. In these situations, external metaevaluators will be even more dependent on the accuracy (scope, pertinence, dependability, and validity) of the evaluation documentation and less able to rely on their own and key informants' knowledge and understanding of the situation. External metaevaluators may be operating without sufficient knowledge about what actually took place or with documents that present an inaccurate picture of what took place. External (and internal) metaevaluators should be diligent in documenting the adequacies and inadequacies of the information on which they rely (E1 Evaluation Documentation). For more thorough and better-resourced external metaevaluations, additional information may be collected even after the program and its evaluation are completed.

Many possibilities exist for tailoring external metaevaluations. For example, sponsors may commission well-resourced, formal external metaevaluations to improve or document the quality of high-stakes evaluations. At the other extreme, interested external individuals or groups working without funding might metaevaluate using existing information for specific limited purposes aligned with their preferred values and standards. Some metaevaluators might undertake targeted metaevaluations of similar or contrasting evaluations as a way to contribute to knowledge about which kinds of evaluation approaches are most efficient and effective in specific situations. In all of these examples, one or more external metaevaluations may take place at the same time, with the metaevaluators operating from different concerns and with different specific purposes, needs, and audiences in mind.

Because evaluations require judgment, reflective practice, and problem solving, the major advantage of external metaevaluations may be that they provide a fresh perspective on the evaluation. By not having participated in the original evaluation and not having obligations to the organization that housed it, external metaevaluators can bring a new way of thinking about the evaluation and its value. The entire system can be viewed from a new vantage point. Sometimes this new way of thinking is critical for increasing evaluation accountability and for creative approaches to evaluation improvement.

❖ IMPLEMENTING E3 EXTERNAL METAEVALUATION

The following are important recommendations for implementing this standard: Those who are responsible include sponsors, evaluators, and metaevaluators.

1. Clarify expectations about the needs and purposes that the external metaevaluation will serve (U2 Attention to Stakeholders and U5 Relevant Information).
2. Identify the relative advantages and disadvantages of internal, external, and blended metaevaluations and decide whether, how, and when to launch the selected types.
3. List the resources required for the needed external metaevaluation, including the adequacy of any preexisting evaluation documentation (E1 Evaluation Documentation and F4 Resource Use).
4. Review resources, documentation, and additional data collection needs (F3 Contextual Viability).
5. When sponsoring a funded external metaevaluation, identify one or more credible metaevaluation experts and make the necessary recruitment, selection, and contractual arrangements (U1 Evaluator Credibility and P2 Formal Agreements).
6. In collaboration with selected stakeholders, review and refine the purposes and needs that the metaevaluation will serve (U3 Negotiated Purposes).
7. Identify the values, standards, and other dimensions of quality needed for metaevaluative judgments (A7 Explicit Evaluation Reasoning).
8. Review and align the available information and documentation with values, standards, and other dimensions of quality needed for the metaevaluative judgments (A1 Justified Conclusions and Decisions).

9. Communicate with intended users about purposes, needs, evidence, findings, and judgments, so that the best uses of the metaevaluation can be facilitated and that misuse or nonuse is minimized (A8 Communication and Reporting, U7 Timely and Appropriate Communicating and Reporting, and U8 Concern for Consequences and Influence).
10. Because metaevaluations are a specific type of evaluation, monitor metaevaluation processes and products for quality assurance and control using these program evaluation standards and other dimensions of quality.

❖ HAZARDS

Some possible hazards with regard to E3 are as follows:

1. Not addressing and clarifying the purposes the external metaevaluation will serve
2. Commissioning external metaevaluations when the needs and potential return on investment do not warrant it
3. Not securing adequate resources for the external metaevaluation and thus undermining its ability to achieve its purposes
4. Assuming that external metaevaluations are unbiased and without conflicts of interests on the basis of their structural independence only
5. Not addressing and communicating the alignment of selected values, standards, purposes, and needs with the evidence
6. Not adequately preparing for the external metaevaluation early in the evaluation process, thus making it more difficult or impossible to secure adequate resources and evidence
7. Investing resources in metaevaluation focuses that will not be used or will produce insufficient benefits to justify their costs

Application Three for Evaluation Accountability, Based on the Utility Case Scenario

The scenario that supports this application, including background information about the program, context, and key players, can be read at the end of the Utility Overview on page 9.

After the Year 1 metaevaluation is completed, Jamaal meets with the senior staff of the CHEERS program. Together they propose a new set of primary evaluation purposes to the board of directors, specifically that the evaluation

- provide evidence about program adaptation and effectiveness,
- investigate expanding program significance in the community,
- support evidence-informed program improvement,
- guide the program staff in presenting the strongest possible case for continued and sustainable funding based on 2 years of evaluation processes and findings.

Jamaal is particularly focused on this last purpose. Evidence of program effectiveness in Year 2 will put CHEERS in a strong position to qualify for continued funding. The Year 2 evaluation will need to provide an accurate investigation of summative program quality. It should investigate program outcomes and gather additional evidence of the value of CHEERS as a new core program in the sponsor's portfolio.

After the meeting, Suparna shares some news with Jamaal. The sponsor has notified her that at the end of Year 2, they will conduct an external metaevaluation of the CRES evaluation to determine its accuracy and utility in supporting their decisions about continued funding. If the CRES evaluation work is satisfactory, the sponsors will rely on CRES to conduct much of the data collection for the Year 3 summative report, leading to the decision about continued funding for CHEERS.

Jamaal arranges a meeting with Janet to discuss how best to prepare for the external metaevaluation at the end of Year 2. Janet is confident based on the Year 1 internal metaevaluation that they can easily be ready for the external metaevaluation. She asks Jamaal to take a little time to think about what the sponsors will want to see in the Year 2 report. Then they will continue their planning.

Jamaal understands that in leading a participatory evaluation and by becoming so involved with program staff, participants, and the board, he could easily create the impression that he is more invested in program improvement and success than in conducting the impartial assessment of merit, worth, and significance that will be required for funding decisions. At this point in the evaluation planning process, he is also concerned with how to create a summative evaluation that will be useful to the sponsors as they judge the quality of the program and its evaluation.

In the Year 1 internal metaevaluations, Jamaal focused more on utility, feasibility, and propriety, leaving few resources to address accuracy. This restricted focus was justified because the program was developing and these specific needs were more pressing. Now Jamaal needs to create an evaluation and an internal metaevaluation that will focus on program and evaluation quality sufficient for improvement and accountability judgments.

Jamaal takes an afternoon to draft some questions for the Year 2 internal metaevaluation based on the Accuracy Standards. For two of the questions (A3 reliable Information and A6 Sound Designs and Analyses) he also lists some documentation that could be used as evidence that the standards have been met.

Dimension of Quality: Accuracy	
Questions Based on Evaluation Standards	Evidence of Meeting the Standard
A1 Justified Conclusions and Decisions: Were evaluation conclusions and decisions explicitly justified in the cultures and contexts where they have consequences?	
A2 Valid Information: Did the evaluation information serve the intended purposes and support valid interpretations?	2.1. Copies of data collection instruments and protocols 2.2. An analysis of the logic lines connecting these tools to the questions they were intended to answer 2.3. Drafts of data gathering instruments that demonstrate revisions based on concerns for reliability and validity
A3 Reliable Information: Did the evaluation procedures yield sufficiently dependable and consistent information for the intended uses?	
A4 Explicit Program and Context Descriptions: Were the program and its contexts documented with appropriate detail and scope for the evaluation purposes?	
A5 Information Management: Is there evidence of systematic information collection, review, verification, and storage?	
A6 Sound Designs and Analyses: Was the design technically adequate and were the analyses appropriate for the evaluation purposes?	6.1. A paper trail of how evaluation purposes were negotiated and evaluation questions determined 6.2. Samples of the data analysis procedures demonstrating efforts to minimize bias or unfairness
A7 Explicit Evaluation Reasoning: Was evaluation reasoning leading from information and analyses to findings, interpretations, conclusions, and judgments clearly and completely documented?	
A8 Communicating and Reporting: Did evaluation communications have adequate scope and guard against misconceptions, biases, distortions, and errors?	

When he shares the questions with Janet, she is pleased with his efforts. She reminds him that they can be well prepared for the external metaevaluation by continuing to prepare their evaluation documentation and maintaining their ongoing internal metaevaluation.

❖ SUPPORTING DOCUMENTATION

Grasso, P. G. (1999). Meta-evaluation of an evaluation of reader focused writing for the Veterans Benefits Administration. *American Journal of Evaluation, 20,* 355–370.

Greene, J. C. (1992). A case study of evaluation auditing as metaevaluation. *Evaluation and Program Planning, 15*(1), 71–74.

Patel, M. (2002). A meta-evaluation, or quality assessment, of the evaluations in this issue, based on the African Evaluation Guidelines: 2002. *Evaluation and Program Planning, 25,* 329–332.

Sanders, J. R. (1999). Metaevaluation of "The effectiveness of comprehensive, case management interventions: Evidence from the national evaluation of the Comprehensive Child Development Program." *American Journal of Evaluation, 20,* 577–582.

Stufflebeam, D. L. (2001). The metaevaluation imperative. *American Journal of Evaluation, 22,* 183–209.

Stufflebeam, D. L., & Shinkfield, A. J. (2007). Evaluation theories, models, and applications. San Francisco: Jossey-Bass

Appendix A

THE 1981 PROGRAM EVALUATION STANDARDS

Utility Standards

❖ SUMMARY OF THE STANDARDS

A Utility Standards

The Utility Standards are intended to ensure that an evaluation will serve the practical information needs of given audiences. These standards are:

A1 Audience Identification

Audiences involved in or affected by the evaluation should be identified, so that their needs can be addressed.

A2 Evaluator Credibility

The persons conducting the evaluation should be both trustworthy and competent to perform the evaluation, so that their findings achieve maximum credibility and acceptance.

A3 Information Scope and Selection

Information collected should be of such scope and selected in such ways as to address pertinent questions about the object of the evaluation and be responsive to the needs and interests of specified audiences.

A4 Valuational Interpretation

The perspectives, procedures, and rationale used to interpret the findings should be carefully described, so that the bases for value judgments are clear.

A5 Report Clarity

The evaluation report should describe the object being evaluated and its context, and the purposes, procedures, and findings of the evaluation, so that the audiences will readily understand what was done, why it was done, what information was obtained, what conclusions were drawn, and what recommendations were made.

A6 Report Dissemination

Evaluation findings should be disseminated to clients and other right-to-know audiences, so that they can assess and use the findings.

A7 Report Timeliness

Release of reports should be timely, so that audiences can best use the reported information.

A8 Evaluation Impact

Evaluations should be planned and conducted in ways that encourage follow-through by members of the audiences.

Feasibility Standards

❖ SUMMARY OF THE STANDARDS

B Feasibility Standards

The Feasibility Standards are intended to ensure that an evaluation will be realistic, prudent, diplomatic, and frugal; they are:

B1 Practical Procedures

The evaluation procedures should be practical, so that disruption is kept to a minimum, and that needed information can be obtained.

B2 Political Viability

The evaluation should be planned and conducted with anticipation of the different positions of various interest groups, so that their cooperation may be obtained, and so that possible attempts by any of these groups to curtail evaluation operations or to bias or misapply the results can be averted or counteracted.

B3 Cost Effectiveness

The evaluation should produce information of sufficient value to justify the resources expended.

Propriety Standards

❖ SUMMARY OF THE STANDARDS

C Propriety Standards

The Propriety Standards are intended to ensure that an evaluation will be conducted legally, ethically, and with due regard for the welfare of those involved in the evaluation, as well as those affected by its results. These standards are:

C1 Formal Obligation

Obligations of the formal parties to an evaluation (what is to be done, how, by whom, when) should be agreed to in writing, so that these parties are obligated to adhere to all conditions of the agreement or formally to renegotiate it.

C2 Conflict of Interest

Conflict of interest, frequently unavoidable, should be dealt with openly and honestly, so that it does not compromise the evaluation processes and results.

C3 Full and Frank Disclosure

Oral and written evaluation reports should be open, direct, and honest in their disclosure of pertinent findings, including the limitations of the evaluation.

C4 Public's Right to Know

The formal parties to an evaluation should respect and assure the public's right to know, within the limits of other related principles and statutes, such as those dealing with public safety and the right to privacy.

C5 Rights of Human Subjects

Evaluations should be designed and conducted, so that the rights and welfare of the human subjects are respected and protected.

C6 Human Interactions

Evaluators should respect human dignity and worth in their interactions with other persons associated with an evaluation.

C7 Balanced Reporting

The evaluation should be complete and fair in its presentation of strengths and weaknesses of the object under investigation, so that strengths can be built upon and problem areas addressed.

C8 Fiscal Responsibility

The evaluator's allocation and expenditure of resources should reflect sound accountability procedures and otherwise be prudent and ethically responsible.

Accuracy Standards

❖ SUMMARY OF THE STANDARDS

D Accuracy Standards

The Accuracy Standards are intended to ensure that an evaluation will reveal and convey technically adequate information about the features of the object being studied that determine its worth or merit. These standards are:

D1 Object Identification

The object of the evaluation (program, project, material) should be sufficiently examined, so that the form(s) of the object being considered in the evaluation can be clearly identified.

D2 Context Analysis

The context in which the program, project, or material exists should be examined in enough detail, so that its likely influences on the object can be identified.

D3 Described Purposes and Procedures

The purposes and procedures of the evaluation should be monitored and described in enough detail, so that they can be identified and assessed.

D4 Defensible Information Sources

The sources of information should be described in enough detail, so that the adequacy of the information can be assessed.

D5 Valid Measurement

The information-gathering instruments and procedures should be chosen or developed and then implemented in ways that will assure that the interpretation arrived at is valid for the given use.

D6 Reliable Measurement

The information-gathering instruments and procedures should be chosen or developed and then implemented in ways that will assure that the information obtained is sufficiently reliable for the intended use.

D7 Systematic Data Control

The data collected, processed, and reported in an evaluation should be reviewed and corrected, so that the results of the evaluation will not be flawed.

D8 Analysis of Quantitative Information

Quantitative information in an evaluation should be appropriately and systematically analyzed to ensure supportable interpretations.

D9 Analysis of Qualitative Information

Qualitative information in an evaluation should be appropriately and systematically analyzed to ensure supportable interpretations.

D10 Justified Conclusions

The conclusions reached in an evaluation should be explicitly justified, so that the audiences can assess them.

D11 Objective Reporting

The evaluation procedures should provide safeguards to protect the evaluation findings and reports against distortion by the personal feelings and biases of any party to the evaluation.

Appendix B

THE 1994 PROGRAM EVALUATION STANDARDS

Utility Standards

❖ SUMMARY OF THE STANDARDS

U **Utility Standards** The Utility Standards are intended to ensure that an evaluation will serve the information needs of intended users. These standards are as follows:

U1 ***Stakeholder Identification*** Persons involved in or affected by the evaluation should be identified, so that their needs can be addressed.

U2 ***Evaluator Credibility*** The persons conducting the evaluation should be both trustworthy and competent to perform the evaluation, so that the evaluation findings achieve maximum credibility and acceptance.

U3 ***Information Scope and Selection*** Information collected should be broadly selected to address pertinent questions about the program and be responsive to the needs and interests of clients and other specified stakeholders.

U4 ***Values Identification*** The perspectives, procedures, and rationale used to interpret the findings should be carefully described, so that the bases for value judgments are clear.

U5 ***Report Clarity*** Evaluation reports should clearly describe the program being evaluated, including its context, and the purposes, procedures, and findings of the evaluation, so that essential information is provided and easily understood.

U6 ***Report Timeliness and Dissemination*** Significant interim findings and evaluation reports should be disseminated to intended users, so that they can be used in a timely fashion.

U7 ***Evaluation Impact*** Evaluations should be planned, conducted, and reported in ways that encourage follow-through by stakeholders, so that the likelihood that the evaluation will be used is increased.

Feasibility Standards

❖ SUMMARY OF THE STANDARDS

F Feasibility Standards The Feasibility Standards are intended to ensure that an evaluation will be realistic, prudent, diplomatic, and frugal. The standards are as follows:

F1 Practical Procedures The evaluation procedures should be practical, to keep disruption to a minimum while needed information is obtained.

F2 Political Viability The evaluation should be planned and conducted with anticipation of the different positions of various interest groups, so that their cooperation may be obtained, and so that possible attempts by any of these groups to curtail evaluation operations or to bias or misapply the results can be averted or counteracted.

F3 Cost Effectiveness The evaluation should be efficient and produce information of sufficient value, so that the resources expended can be justified.

Propriety Standards

❖ SUMMARY OF THE STANDARDS

P Propriety Standards The Propriety Standards are intended to ensure that an evaluation will be conducted legally, ethically, and with due regard for the welfare of those involved in the evaluation, as well as those affected by its results. These standards are as follows:

P1 Service Orientation Evaluations should be designed to assist organizations to address and effectively serve the needs of the full range of targeted participants.

P2 Formal Agreements Obligations of the formal parties to an evaluation (what is to be done, how, by whom, when) should be agreed to in writing, so that these parties are obligated to adhere to all conditions of the agreement or formally to renegotiate it.

P3 Rights of Human Subjects Evaluations should be designed and conducted to respect and protect the rights and welfare of human subjects.

P4 Human Interactions Evaluators should respect human dignity and worth in their interactions with other persons associated with an evaluation, so that participants are not threatened or harmed.

P5 Complete and Fair Assessment The evaluation should be complete and fair in its examination and recording of strengths and weaknesses of the program being evaluated, so that strengths can be built upon and problem areas addressed.

P6 ***Disclosure of Findings*** The formal parties to an evaluation should ensure that the full set of evaluation findings along with pertinent limitations are made accessible to the persons affected by the evaluation, and any others with expressed legal rights to receive the results.

P7 ***Conflict of Interest*** Conflict of interest should be dealt with openly and honestly, so that it does not compromise the evaluation processes and results.

P8 ***Fiscal Responsibility*** The evaluator's allocation and expenditure of resources should reflect sound accountability procedures and otherwise be prudent and ethically responsible, so that expenditures are accounted for and appropriate.

Accuracy Standards

❖ SUMMARY OF THE STANDARDS

A **Accuracy Standards** The Accuracy Standards are intended to ensure that an evaluation will reveal and convey technically adequate information about the features that determine worth or merit of the program being evaluated. The standards are as follows:

A1 ***Program Documentation*** The program being evaluated should be described and documented clearly and accurately, so that the program is clearly identified.

A2 ***Context Analysis*** The context in which the program exists should be examined in enough detail, so that its likely influences on the program can be identified.

A3 ***Described Purposes and Procedures*** The purposes and procedures of the evaluation should be monitored and described in enough detail, so that they can be identified and assessed.

A4 ***Defensible Information Sources*** The sources of information used in a program evaluation should be described in enough detail, so that the adequacy of the information can be assessed.

A5 ***Valid Information*** The information gathering procedures should be chosen or developed and then implemented so that they will assure that the interpretation arrived at is valid for the intended use.

A6 ***Reliable Information*** The information gathering procedures should be chosen or developed and then implemented so that they will assure that the information obtained is sufficiently reliable for the intended use.

A7 ***Systematic Information*** The information collected, processed, and reported in an evaluation should be systematically reviewed and any errors found should be corrected.

A8 ***Analysis of Quantitative Information*** Quantitative information in an evaluation should be appropriately and systematically analyzed so that evaluation questions are effectively answered.

A9 ***Analysis of Qualitative Information*** Qualitative information in an evaluation should be appropriately and systematically analyzed so that evaluation questions are effectively answered.

A10 ***Justified Conclusions*** The conclusions reached in an evaluation should be explicitly justified, so that stakeholders can assess them.

A11 ***Impartial Reporting*** Reporting procedures should guard against distortion caused by personal feelings and biases of any party to the evaluation, so that evaluation reports fairly reflect the evaluation findings.

A12 ***Metaevaluation*** The evaluation itself should be formatively and summatively evaluated against these and other pertinent standards, so that its conduct is appropriately guided and, on completion, stakeholders can closely examine its strengths and weaknesses.

Appendix C

Resources and Support

The Joint Committee on Standards for Educational Evaluation (JCSEE) is a 501(c)(3) nonprofit corporation dedicated to the development and dissemination of practice standards for program, student, and educational personnel evaluations. Initially created in 1975 as a joint committee of three organizations (the American Educational Research Association, the National Council on Measurement in Education, and the American Psychological Association), the JCSEE originally grew out of efforts to create standards for educational and psychological testing. However, with its central focus on the development of program evaluation standards, the founders quickly recognized the need to include a much larger group of researchers, practitioners, and stakeholders. Today 17 organizations sponsor the work of the JCSEE.

The JCSEE follows an inclusive set of procedures to develop standards. The procedures involve members of the sponsoring organizations and scholars, educators, and practitioners around the globe. Its standards development process includes an initial needs assessment, a review of pertinent practice literature and scholarship, drafting of standards, review of the draft standards by national and international panels of reviewers, revision of the drafts based on the panel reviews, field trials of the draft standards, and national hearings to both inform individuals and organizations about the standards and gain feedback to improve the draft materials. The standards are then "published" on the Web for final review and feedback. At this time an independent validation panel undertakes a review of the development process and the resulting standards. The validation panel prepares a written report (available at www.jcsee.org) and presents its findings at a meeting of the JCSEE. The JCSEE membership can choose to approve the standards based on the work to that point or can require additional steps to be taken. In the case of these program evaluation standards, the JCSEE accepted the validation panel report at its 2008 annual meeting and then approved the final document at the 2009 annual meeting after a 45-day American National Standards Institute comment period. Following that approval the standards were submitted to the American National Standards Institute for certification as an American National Standard (currently pending).

❖ THE SPONSORING ORGANIZATIONS

American Association of School Administrators

American Counseling Association

American Educational Research Association

American Evaluation Association

American Indian Higher Education Consortium

American Psychological Association

Canadian Evaluation Society

Canadian Society for the Study of Education

Consortium for Research on Educational Accountability and Teacher Evaluation

Council of Chief State School Officers

National Association of Elementary School Principals

National Association of School Psychologists

National Association of Secondary School Principals

National Council on Measurement in Education

National Education Association

National Legislative Program Evaluation Society

National Rural Education Association

❖ VALIDATION PANEL

Chair

Marvin C. Alkin, University of California at Los Angeles

Members

Jeffrey Braden, North Carolina State University

Joy Frechtling, WESTAT

Floraline I. Stevens, Floraline Stevens and Associates

Sandy Taut, Pontificia Catholic University of Chile

Kevin Welner, University of Colorado at Boulder

Ann T. Vo, Research Assistant to the Panel, University of California at Los Angeles

❖ NATIONAL AND INTERNATIONAL REVIEWERS

Max Arinder, Mississippi Joint Legislative Committee on Performance Evaluation and Expenditure Review

Dennis Affholter, Affholter and Associates

Jeanne Alnot, University of Iowa

James Altschuld, Ohio State University

Oumoul Khayri Ba Tall, oktconsult and International Organization for Cooperation in Evaluation

Dede Bailer, Fairfax County Public Schools

Donna Baird, University of Maryland University College

John Balong, University of Northern Iowa

Eric Barela, Los Angeles Unified School District

Thomas Barrett, World Health Organization

Philip Bashook, University of Illinois–Chicago

A. Alexander Beaujean, Baylor University

Lisa Bischoff, Rockhurst University

Dina Blanc, University of Iowa

Suzanne Blanc

Rolf Blank, Council on Chief State School Officers

Katrina Bledsoe, The College of New Jersey

Kathleen Bolland, University of Alabama

Jeff Braden, North Carolina State University

Valerie Caracelli, U.S. Government Accountability Office

Vickie Cartwright, Orange County Public Schools, Florida

Kara Collins-Gomez, OPPAGA, Florida Legislature

Leslie Cooksy, University of Delaware

Lois-Ellin Datta, Datta Analysis

Kathleen Del Monte, OPPAGA, Florida Legislature

André Luiz Freitas Dias, Universidade Federal de Minas Gerais, Brazil

Kim Dielmann, University of Central Arkansas

Joy Frechtling, WESTAT

Marie-Luise Friedemann, Florida International University

Michi Fu

Rebecca Gajda, University of Massachusetts–Amherst

Amy Germuth, EvalWorks

Jennifer Greene, University of Illinois at Urbana-Champaign

Kelly Hannum, Center for Creative Leadership

Abigail Harris, Fordham University

Steve Henry, REASolutions LLC

Ida Hernandez

Stafford Hood, Arizona State University

Gerunda Hughes, Howard University

Scott Imig, University of North Carolina–Wilmington

Michelle Jay, University of South Carolina

Rahel Kahlert, University of Texas–Austin

Jean King, University of Minnesota

Emily Lai, University of Iowa

Richard Lambert, University of North Carolina–Charlotte

Frances Lawrenz, University of Minnesota

Laura Leviton, The Robert Wood Johnson Foundation

Arnold Love, Independent Evaluation Consultant, Toronto, Canada

Bridgitte Maicher, Net Results & Associates

Sumbal Malik, University of Ottawa

Keith A. Markus, John Jay College of Criminal Justice, CUNY

Mary K. Marlock, Webster University

Patricia McDivitt, Data Recognition Corporation

Kathy McGuire, OPPAGA, Florida Legislature

Patrick McKnight, George Mason University

Donna Mertens, Gallaudet University

Michael Morris, University of New Haven

Susan Munley, OPPAGA, Florida Legislature

Marco Muñoz, CREATE and Jefferson County Public Schools

Georgetta Myhlhousen-Leak, University of Iowa

Catherine Packer, University of South Carolina

Sherry Palamara

Alison Picucci, Resources for Learning

Iris PrettyPaint, University of Montana

Carol Price, Data Recognition Corporation

Barbara Rogers, State of Wyoming

Patricia Rogers

Todd Rogers, University of Alberta

Normand Rondeau

Scott Rosas, Concept Systems, Inc.

Darlene Russ, Oregon State University

John R. Sanders, JRS Consulting

Marilyn Scheffler, University of Nebraska-Lincoln

Linda Schrader, Florida State University

Iris Smith, Emory University

Sandra Speer, Independent Evaluator, Wiesbaden, Germany

Arlene Stanton, SAMHSA, US Department of Health And Human Services

Yvette Tazeau, Independent Practice, Los Gatos, CA

David Turner, New Zealand Ministry of Justice

Jon Twing, Pearson

Gary Vanlandingham, OPPAGA, Florida Legislature

Tamara Walser, University of North Carolina–Wilmington

Iris Weiss, Horizon Research Inc.

Ryan Wells, University of Iowa

Karen Wetherill, University of North Carolina–Wilmington

Thomas Widmer, Institut für Politikwissenschaft, Universität Zürich

Marilyn Willis, Fanshawe College

Stacia Wissink, University of Iowa

Mary Yakimowski, University of Connecticut

Ismail Yuksel, Anadolu University, Turkey

Courtney Zmach, American Institutes for Research

❖ NATIONAL HEARING PARTICIPANTS

Meltem Alemdar, Georgia State University

Marie France Allen, l'Institut de réadaptation en déficience physique de Québec

Frank Amankwah, Health Canada

John Anderson, University of Victoria

Kathryn Anderson Alvestad, University of Maryland

Michelle Anderson-Draper, Alberta Children and Youth Services

Gala Arh, Ontario Tobacco Research Unit

Mariane Arsenault, Universalia Management Group

Nancy Baenen, Wake County Public Schools

Philip Bahsook, University of Illinois–Chicago

Gail Barrington, Barrington Research Group, Inc.

Oumoul Khayri Ba Tall, oktconsult and International Organization for Cooperation in Evaluation

Jonathan Beard, University of Iowa

Erica Bell-Lowther, Interior Health Authority, British Columbia

Myriam Boivin-Villeneuve, Gouvernement du Québec

Ghislain Blais, Ministère de l'Agriculture, des Pêcheries et de l'Alimentation

Shelley Borys, Environment Canada

Brigitte Bouchard-Morris, Prairie Research Associates Inc.

Carolyn Boyce, U.S. Government Accountability Office

Noruand Brault, Gouvernement du Québec

Glenda Breaux, Michigan State University

Pierre Brochu, Council of Ministers of Education, Canada

Tanya Brown, Cambridge Health Alliance/Duquesne University

Elizabeth Buckingham, Hallux Consulting Inc.

Michael Burke, RTI International

Joanne Butler, Office of the Auditor General of Canada

Monique Campbell, Atlantic Canada Opportunities Agency

Vickie Cartwright, Orange County Public Schools, Orlando

Jennifer Carey, J. Carey Consulting and Evaluations Plus Ltd.

Guy Cauquil, French Evaluation Society

Melissa Chapman, University of Iowa

Lucie Charbonneau, Centre Jeunesse de la Monteregie

Kaireen Chaytor, Chaytor Consulting and Dalhousie University

Shu-Huei Cheng, University of Minnesota

Soon Chew Chia, Ministry of Education, Singapore

Ruth Childs, University of Toronto

David Cohen, DPRA Canada

Susan Cole, Public Works

Nanci Comtois, Human Resources and Social Development Canada

Ross Conner, University of California–Irvine

Leslie Cooksy, University of Delaware

Elizabeth Costa, Department of Education and Early Childhood Development, Prince Edward Island

Julie Cote-Stordy, Canadian Food Inspection Agency

Nancy Cote, Canada Revenue Agency

Bea Courtney, Goss Gilroy Inc.

Stephen Court, Wichita Public Schools

Jim Cullen, Thomas More Institute

Cindy Crusto, Yale University School of Medicine

Richard Cummings, Murdoch University, Perth, Western Australia

Katie Dahlke, University of South Carolina

Evangeline Danseco, Provincial Centre of Excellence for Child and Youth Mental Health at CHEO

Brian Dates, Southwest Counseling Solutions

Yantio Debasov, Ministry of Agriculture and Rural Development

Pauline de Jong, Northwest Territories Business Development and Investment Corporation

Sylvie Demer, Société d'habitation du Québec

Sylvie Desmarais, Canadian Space Agency

Sandra DeVries, Transport Canada

David Dibbon, Memorial University

Emily Dickinson, Human Resources Research Organization

Eugenia Didenko, Canadian Institutes of Health Research

Francois Dumaine, Prairie Research Associates Inc.

Alex Duran, Sunnyside Unified School District, Arizona

Andrew Dzuba, Royal Canadian Mounted Police

Reed Early, Auditor General of British Columbia

Lori Ebbesen, Public Health Agency of Canada

Pauline Egelson, College of Charleston

John Ehlert, University of Minnesota–Twin Cities

Susan Elgie

Jessica Eliot, New Hanover County Schools, Wilmington, NC

Nicole Ethier, Porcupine Health Unit, Ontario

Helen Evans, Michael Smith Foundation for Health Research

Judith Evans, Capital Health, Edmonton

Andrée Fafard, Agence de la santé et des services sociaux Chaudière-Appalaches

Mary Kay Falconer, Ounce of Prevention Fund of Florida

Kevin Favor, Lincoln University

Ray Fenton, Fenton Research

Bret Feranchak, Cincinnati Public Schools

Elizabeth Foster, University of North Carolina–Wilmington

Kathy Fox, University of North Carolina–Wilmington

Suzanne Franco, Wright State University

Linda H. Frazer, Wilmington College

Dominic Fung, Ministry of Attorney General, Province of British Columbia

Angela Gallant, Canada Revenue Agency

Dorinda Gallant, Ohio State University

Chloé Gaumont, Centre jeunesse de la Montérégie

Kathy Gerber, Consulting and Audit Canada

Brad Gerhart, Ministry of Environment, Province of British Columbia

Marie Gervais, Laval University

Leonard Giambra, United States Coast Guard Academy

Warrant Gooden, Cheyney University of Pennsylvania

Leslie Goodyear, Education Development Center

Leslie Grant, College of William and Mary

Anne-Marie Grenier, Développement économique Canada

James Griffith, Claremont Graduate University

Rolen Guilland, Heart and Stroke Foundation of Ontario

Colleen Hamilton, Goss Gilroy Inc.

R. Dwight Hare, Mississippi State University

Tracy Hargrove, University of North Carolina–Wilmington

Colonel Hawkins, Coppin State University

Anne Heberger, National Academies Keck Futures Initiative

Laurie Hellsten, University of Saskatchewan

Ramona Helm, Fisheries and Oceans Canada

Steve Henry, REASolutions, LLC

Michael Herrick, Herrick Research

Clare Hildebrandt, Calgary Alberta Health Services

Zelda Holcomb

Stafford Hood, Arizona State University

Lesli Hutchins, Mississippi State University

Kent Hutchinson, OPPAGA, Florida Legislature

Marthe Hurteau, Université du Québec à Montréal

Patricio Ibarra, Province of British Columbia

Donna Innes, Marian College of Fond du Lac

Johann Jacob, Centre de recherche et d'expertise en évaluation

Andy Jackl, Wake County Public Schools

Andrea Johnston, Johnston Research

Jeff Jorgensen, Industry Canada

Rahel Kahlert, University of Texas–Austin

Sue Keller-Olaman, Public Health Services, City of Hamilton, Ontario

Nicole Kennedy, Indian and Northern Affairs Canada

Yangboon Kim, Korean Educational Development Institute

Natalie Kishchuk

Don A. Klinger, Queen's University

Rick Kowalewski, U.S. Department of Transportation

Jane Knox, Provincial Auditor Saskatchewan

Keiko Kuji-Shikatani, Ministry of Education, Ontario

Richard Kunkel, Florida State University

David Kurfust, Citizenship and Immigration Canada

Linda Ladouceur, Department of Canadian Heritage

Clay Lafleur, Claymar International and The Learning Partnership

Robert Lalanpe, Department of Canadian Heritage

Deborah Langille, Nova Scotia Health Research Foundation

Francis Lacasse, Department of Canadian Heritage

Luey Larrison, Bryan Independent School District, Texas

Birgitta Larsson, BIM Larrson and Associates

Michel Laurendeau, École nationale d'administration publique, Gatineau

Paule Lavoie, Centre de réadaptation en déficience intellectuelle de Québec l'École nationale d'administration publique, Gatineau

Louise Leclerc, Raymond Chabot Grant Thornton

Ser Ming Lee, Ministry of Education, Singapore

John C. Long, University of Manitoba

Felix Meisels, Ministère de la Culture, des Communications et de la Condition féminine du Québec

Dieudonne Mouafo, Department of Canadian Heritage

Marco Muñoz, CREATE and Jefferson County Public Schools

Augusto Legaspi, Bow Alley College

Anna Lenk, University of Ottawa

Danielle Levesque, L'Institut de réadaptation en déficience physique de Québec

Jeremy Lingle, Georgia State University

Charles Losthaus, Universalia Management Group

Brian Lotven, Mississippi Energy Resources Conservation Board

Laura Macdonald, University of Manitoba

Sharon Margison, Canada Mortgage and Housing Corporation

Danielle Markel, Public Health Agency of Canada

John Mayne, Independent Consultant, Ontario, Canada

Nelly McEwen, Alberta Educational

Brian McGowan, Brian R. McGowan Consulting

D'Arcy McGuire, Health Canada

Martha McGuire, Cathexis Consulting

Marlene Merrill, Kansas City, Kansas Public Schools

Mechthild Meyer, University of Ottawa and Genhum Consulting

Stephane Mercure, Science Metrix

Nicole Michaud, Social Sciences and Humanities Research Council of Canada

Tess Miller, Queen's University

Daphne Minner, Education Development Center

Joy Mordica, WESTAT

Vernita Morgan, University of Iowa

Marie Moisan, Ministère de la Famille et des Aînés, Québec

Michael P. Mueller, Hospital for Sick Children, Toronto

Cindy Nantais, Service Canada

Brian Noonan, University of Manitoba

Marie-Eve Normandeau, École nationale d'administration publique

Carolynn Oliver, Industry Canada

Kathleen O'Neill, Southport Elementary School

Seema Opal, Ontario Ministry of Training, Colleges and Universities

Colleen Paeplow, Wake County Public School System

Jason Pelletier, Health Canada

Martine Perrault, Environment Canada

Tracy Perry, Canada School of Public Service

Elena Petrus, Service Canada

Barthelemy Pierrelus, Natural Resources Canada

Mario Pimpare, Commission de la santé et de la sécurité du travail du Québec

Sylvie Poirier, Ministère de l'Agriculture, des Pêcheries et de l'Alimentation

Nancy Porteous, Public Health Agency of Canada

Stacey Prieur, Government Consulting Services (PWGSC)

Lisa Punit, Department of Fisheries and Oceans, Canada

Jean Serge Quesnel, United Nations Systems Staff College and Carleton University

Francis Remedios, Alberta Justice

Stephanie Roberge, Human Resources and Social Development Canada

Todd Rogers, University of Alberta

Sandra Ryan, Mary Immaculate College, University of Limerick, Ireland

Miguel Ramos, University of Houston

Gunter Rochow, CAPRA International Inc.

Betty Rogers, Consulting and Audit Canada

Valery Roy-Gosselin, Ministère des Ressources naturelles et de la Faune, Québec

Valerie Ruhe, University of Minnesota

Pat Sadowy, University of Manitoba

Christine Samson, Ministère de l'Emploi et de la Solidarité sociale, Québec

Sue Sarber, Arlington Public Schools, Virginia

Patricia Saunders, Dalhousie University

Evelyn Shapka, Ontario College of Teachers

Robert Schwantz, Ontario Tobacco Research Unit

Susan Scott, SPS Research Evaluation Inc. and Lakehead University, Orilla Campus

Sherrilyn Sklar, Peel Children's Centre, Ontario

Helen Slaughter, University of Hawaii

John Stapleton, University of Manitoba

Hugh Stoddard, University of Nebraska

Mary P. Stutzman, Florida State University

Lisa Styles, Royal Canadian Mounted Police

Penelope Swenson, California State University–Bakersfield

Emily Tsoa, Region of Peel, Ontario

Maurice Turcot, Developpement Economique Canada

Ronit Tutsja, Agriculture and Agri-food Canada

Shirley Von Sychowski, Heart and Stroke Foundation of Ontario

Ausage Faasalele Tanuvasa, University of Otago, New Zealand

Robin Taylor, Auburn University

George Teather, National Research Council of Canada

Megh Thapa, Baltimore City Public School System

Damon Thompson, American Evaluation Association

Sheila Thompson, Precision Research & Evaluation, LLC

Tracy Fiander Trask, Department of Economic Development, Nova Scotia

Charles Ungerleider, Canadian Council on Learning

Ari Uotila, World Vision Canada

Diane Vaneasse, Ministère de l'Emploi et de la Solidarité sociale

Jamos VanHaneghan, University of South Alabama

Sara Veilleux, Ministère de la Santé et des Services sociaux

Trinidad Villegas, University of Illinois–Urbana-Champaign

Jacob Walker, Mississippi State University

Hillel Weinberg, United States Office of the Special Inspector General for Iraq Reconstruction

Menno Wiebe, Konterra Group, LLC

Brenda Williams, College of William and Mary

Ed Williams, Little Rock School District

Jennifer E. Williams, University of Cincinnati Hospital and JE Williams and Associates

Derek Wilson, Fraser Health Authority

Jim Wohleeb, Little Rock School District

Raynie Wood, SAIT Polytechnic

Linda Wurzback, Resources for Learning, LLC

Juanita Yancey, North Carolina Smart Start Early Childhood Initiative

Brian Yates, American University

Jenna Zacamy, Empirical Education Inc.

Rochelle Zorzi, Cathexis Consulting

❖ FIELD-TEST PARTICIPANTS

Jessica Adams, Duquesne University

Lenell Allen, National Science Foundation

Bernice G. Alston, NASA

Todd Bailey, University of Wisconsin

Teri Balser, University of Wisconsin

Janet Branchaw, University of Wisconsin

Nancy Brooks, University of Wisconsin

Matthew Calvert, University of Wisconsin

Molly Carnes, University of Wisconsin

Melissa Chapman, University of Iowa

Sharad Chandarana, University of Wisconsin

Will Clifton, University of Wisconsin

Kara Collins-Gomez, OPPAGA, Florida Legislature

Mark Connolly, University of Wisconsin

Jennifer Cook, University of Iowa

Disa Cornish, University of Northern Iowa

Ashleigh Crabtree, University of Iowa

Mary Crave, University of Wisconsin

Francine Delvicchio, Queen's University

Christine Doe, Queen's University

Scott Gillam, Queen's University

Don Gillian-Daniel, University of Wisconsin

Douglas Grane, University of Iowa

Ann Groves Lloyd, University of Wisconsin

Doug Henderson, University of Wisconsin

Karen Holden, University of Wisconsin

Mary Hoddy, University of Wisconsin

Bharati (Maya) Holtzman, University of Wisconsin

Caesar Jackson, National Science Foundation

Kris Juffer, Action Research Inc.

Steve Kosciuk, University of Wisconsin

Moira Lafayette, University of Wisconsin

Wilhelmena Lee-Ougo, MayaTech Corporation

Sally Leong, University of Wisconsin

Wei Cheng Liu, University of Iowa

King Luu, Queen's University

Setina MacLean, Queen's University

Christine Maidl Pribbenow, University of Wisconsin

Deepa Mansharamani, Queen's University

Chris Mattatall, Queen's University

Yvette McCulley, Iowa Department of Education

David McCullough, University of Wisconsin

Cheryl Michie, University of Wisconsin

Cathy Middlecamp, University of Wisconsin

Vernita Morgan, University of Iowa

Margaret Mwenda, University of Iowa

Susan Nossal, University of Wisconsin

Ruby Paredes, University of Wisconsin

Gary Phye, Iowa State University

Ellen Taylor Powell, University of Wisconsin

Suzanne Randolph, MayaTech Corporation

Jerry Roberts, University of Wisconsin

Sharon Ross, Duquesne University

Hanna Santbury, Queen's University

Tara Shochet, University of Iowa

Kusum Singh, National Science Foundation

Abby Smith, Queen's University

Kelly Smith, Queen's University

Jay Stampen, University of Wisconsin

Alison Struchelli, Queen's University

Hazel Symonette, University of Wisconsin

Veronica G. Thomas, Howard University

Elizabeth VanderPutten, National Science Foundation

Michelle Villeneuve, Queen's University

Nola Walker, University of Wisconsin

Harry Webne-Behrman, University of Wisconsin

❖ Glossary ❖

Terms are defined in this glossary as they are used in this volume, in the context of program evaluation. In other contexts, a number of the terms may have broader or different definitions. For links and references to other evaluation glossaries and for ongoing updates and comments on this glossary, go to http://www.jcsee.com

Accountability Demonstrated responsibility for the use of resources, activities, or decisions made in the course of a program and/or its evaluation.

Accuracy The extent to which an evaluation is truthful or valid in the scope and detail of what it communicates about a context, program, project, or any of their components.

Adversarial/advocacy group A group of people who enter into cross-examination of counter plans, strategies, or outcomes.

Advocacy teams Groups of people who are brought together to develop competing strategies for achieving a given set of objectives.

Affective dimension The psychological concept that refers to a person's feelings, emotions, or degree of acceptance or rejection of something or someone.

Anonymity (provision for) Evaluator action to ensure that the identity of subjects cannot be ascertained during the course of a study, in study reports, or in any other way.

Archival search An examination of existing records, reports, and documents pertaining to the object of the evaluation.

Assessment The determination of relative or absolute position on some variable of interest based on qualitative and/or quantitative evidence.

Attrition Loss of subjects from the defined sample during the course of a study.

Audiences Those persons who will experience and learn from evaluation information and findings.

Audit (of an evaluation) An independent examination and verification of the quality of an evaluation plan, the adequacy with which it was implemented, the accuracy of results, and the validity of conclusions.

Benefit The instrumental or conceptual worth to stakeholders of a program, service, procedure, or evaluation or any component of them.

Bias A consistent alignment with one point of view to the detriment of other equally important points of view.

Bounded activity Defines the time period, beginning and ending, in project management for a specific project.

Budget A description of the resources (people, money, materials, infrastructure, and time) and how they will be allocated to support programs or evaluations.

Case study An intensive, detailed description and analysis of one or more projects, programs, or any of their specific components or participants in the context of their environments.

Clients Those with whom the evaluator(s) negotiates evaluation purposes and intended uses, often the individuals, groups, or organizations who hire the evaluator. Clients are also stakeholders.

Code (information) To translate a given set of data or items into a set of quantitative or qualitative symbols.

Coefficient A value expressing the degree to which some characteristic or relation is to be found in specified instances; e.g., the coefficient of correlation is a value expressing the degree to which two variables vary concomitantly.

Cognitive ability The psychological concept that refers to such processes as perceiving, knowing, recognizing, feeling, conceptualizing, judging, and reasoning.

Comparison group (in quasiexperimentation) A group that provides a basis for contrast with a treatment group (i.e., the group of people participating in the program, project, or other intervention being evaluated). The comparison group is not subjected to the intervention (independent variable) or is subjected to another type of treatment thus creating a means for comparison with the group that does receive the intervention of interest.

Competent evaluator An evaluator who possesses the necessary knowledge, skills, and dispositions to conduct a high-quality evaluation.

Complexity A characteristic of programs, contexts, and evaluations entailing intricate linkages, multi-level interactions, emergent events, adaptation, unpredictable outcomes, and that can be more in substance that the sum of its parts.

Conceptual use The effects of evaluation processes and findings on stakeholders' representations of reality, especially their cognitive and affective schema, perceptions, understandings, and responses.

Conclusions (of an evaluation) Final judgments and recommendations.

Content analysis The process of identifying and listing—in accordance with a parsimonious classification system—categories of expression contained in a variety of information sources.

Context (of an evaluation) The combination of the factors accompanying the evaluation that may have influenced its processes or findings. These factors include the geographic location; its timing; the political, social, cultural, and economic influences in the region at that time; the other relevant professional activities that were in progress; and/or any other pertinent factors.

Contract A written or oral agreement between the evaluator and the client that is enforceable by law. It is a mutual understanding of expectations and responsibilities for both parties.

Control group A group that by virtue of random selection or assignment is as closely as possible equivalent to an experimental group (one that is exposed to a program, project, or instructional material), and exposed to all the conditions of the investigation except the program, project, or other intervention being studied.

Correlation A statistical measure of the degree of relationship between or among variables. It is expressed in the form of an index that may vary from -1.00 to +1.00, with 0 representing the absence of covariation, and +1 and -1 represent per covariation, albeit in different directions.

Cost The monetary and nonmonetary resources required for an evaluation, program, or other identifiable entity.

Cost effectiveness The extent to which a program, project, or one of their components produces equal or better results than competitors that cost about the same amount of time, effort, and resources; or the extent to which an object produces the same results as competitors but is less costly.

Covariate A variate occurring concomitantly with the variate of primary interest and measured for the purpose of making informed adjustments on the variate of primary interest (e.g., measuring pretest performance of two groups in order to adjust their posttest scores so that they take account of differences between groups that existed prior to the treatment of one of the groups).

Cultural Context All group related identity factors and features that may have an influence on or are pertinent to the processes and products of the evaluation. The cultural context is bounded by the total of all cultural backgrounds of all stakeholders, stakeholder groups, organizations and other human units in the context.

Cultural competency Individuals, including evaluators, have varying degrees of competence in the specific cultures in which they live. Cultural competency with regard to evaluators refers more specifically to the special skill set needed to recognize and respond to the diverse cultural backgrounds in the evaluation context so that the needs, values and contributions from different perspectives are recognized and responded to in ways that result in the most useful, feasible, proper, accurate, and accountable evaluations possible in this context.

Culturally responsive evaluation This way of evaluating recognizes the need for attention to diversity in the populations served by programs and evaluations. Culturally responsive evaluations attend to all aspects of the evaluation approach, planning, design, methods, implementation, use, and follow-through from the perspective of the full-spectrum of stakeholder variability. The goal of culturally responsive evaluations is to recognize diversity as a source of values and resources that can result in broadened, enriched, and maximally useful processes, findings, and influences.

Criterion A standard by which something can be judged.

Criterion-referenced tests Tests whose scores are interpreted by reference to well-defined domains of content or behaviors, rather than by reference to the performance of some comparable group of people.

Data Material gathered during the course of an evaluation which serves as the basis for information, discussion, and inference.

Data access The extent to which the evaluator will be permitted to obtain data during the course of an evaluation.

Decision rule A rule for choosing between optional interpretations or courses of action given certain evidence (e.g., a rule by which teachers pass or fail students in a course based on their test scores and other performances in the course; a rule by which a government agency ranks project proposals for funding based on their contents and the ratings assigned to them by judges; or a rule by which an evaluator decides that the difference between the test scores of students exposed to different programs is statistically significant).

Dependent variable A measure (e.g., a student's performance on a test) that is assumed to vary as a result of some influence (often taken to be the independent variable).

Design (evaluation) A plan for conducting an evaluation; e.g., data collection schedule, report schedules, questions to be addressed, analysis plan, management plan, etc. Designs may be either preordinate or emergent.

Dissemination The communication of evaluation processes and products, especially results and conclusions, by written, oral, and/or other means to foster knowledge and use by all stakeholders with a right-to-know.

Editorial authority The extent of the evaluator's authority to edit evaluation reports prior to dissemination.

Education The development of cognitive, psychomotor, and affective skills and knowledge over the lifespan through formal and informal means.

Emergent design An implementation plan in which the specification of every step depends upon the results of previous steps, sometimes also known as a cascading or rolling design.

Escrow agent A third party who, by agreement, controls certain information, such as the names on tests, submitted by a first party, so that this information is not obtained by the second party.

Evaluability Describes the degree to which it is possible to meaningfully evaluate a specific program at a specific time and place. (See Feasibility Overview)

Evaluability assessment The steps taken by an evaluator to determine if a program or project has the necessary resources, level of development, potential for evaluation utility, and context features to warrant an evaluation.

Evaluation-Systematic investigation of the value, importance, or significance of something or someone along defined dimensions (e.g., a program, project, or specific program or project component).

Evaluation checklist A list prepared by the evaluator or from another source that serves as a reminder of the processes, procedures, and tasks that need to be addressed in an evaluation. An evaluation checklist does not serve as the management plan for the evaluation.

Evaluation report A presentation of information resulting from evaluative activity.

Evaluation users Those with a vested interest in the quality and substance of the evaluation's processes or products; particularly those who are likely to act (make decisions) based on the evaluation processes, descriptions, and findings. Evaluation users are stakeholders.

Executive report An abbreviated report that has been tailored specifically to address the concerns and questions of one or more specific people whose function is to administer a program or project.

Executive summary A nontechnical summary statement designed to provide a quick overview of the full-length report on which it is based.

Experimental design The plan of an experiment, including selection of subjects, order of administration of the experimental treatment, the kind of treatment, the procedures by which it is administered, and the recording of the data (with special reference to the particular statistical and other analyses to be performed).

Experimental group A group of subjects randomly selected or assigned to receive an intervention (independent variable), the effects of which are measured (dependent variable). Often comparisons are made between these effects and those observed for a comparison or randomly selected or assigned control (nontreatment) group.

Experimental research Scientific investigation in which an investigator manipulates and controls one or more independent variables to determine their effects on the outcome (dependent) variable.

External evaluator An evaluator from outside the organization which houses the program, project, or component being evaluated.

Extrapolate To infer an unknown from something that is known. (Statistical definition—to estimate the value of a variable outside its observed range.)

Feasibility The extent to which resources and other factors allow an evaluation to be conducted in a satisfactory manner.

Field test The study of a program, project, or instructional material in a setting similar to that in which it is to be used. Field tests may range from preliminary primitive investigations to full-scale summative studies.

Focus group A group selected for its relevance to an evaluation that is engaged by a trained facilitator in a series of discussions designed for sharing insights, ideas, and observations on a topic of concern.

Formative evaluation Evaluation designed and used to improve an object, especially when it is still being developed.

Generalizability The extent to which information about a program, project, or instructional material collected in one setting can be used to reach a valid judgment about how it will perform in other settings.

Goal An end that one strives to achieve.

Guideline A procedural suggestion intended to help evaluators and their audiences to meet the requirements of the evaluation standards; strategy to avoid mistakes in applying the standards.

Hazard A difficulty or mistake that can result from applying standards inappropriately or without adequate reflection and caution or from not applying the standard at all.

Information Numerical and nonnumerical findings, representations, or presentations—including narratives, graphs, pictures, maps, displays, statistics, and oral reports—that help illuminate issues, answer questions, and increase knowledge and understanding of a program or other object.

Information needs Information requirements of the evaluator, clients, and other pertinent audiences to be met by the evaluation.

Information sources The persons, groups, and documents from which data are obtained.

Informed consent Agreement by the participants based on adequate information provided to them concerning their participation in a study, especially about the uses of their names and/or information supplied by them in specified ways, for stated purposes, and in light of possible consequences prior to the collection and/or release of this information.

Instrument An assessment device adopted, adapted, or constructed for the purpose of the evaluation.

Instrumental use The effects of evaluation findings and processes on the evaluated program or project, on any of their specific components, or on any evaluative decisions, such as decisions leading to resource allocations, improvements or to continue funding or not.

Internal evaluator A staff member or unit functioning in an evaluative capacity and coming from the organization which houses the program, project or component.

Key Stakeholders Persons who have the most to gain or lose as a result of the evaluation and persons who have the most knowledge about the program.

Learning The acquiring of cognitive, psychomotor, and affective knowledge and skill, which in combination with other developmental factors results in growth over time.

Logic model A mapping approach that connects in schematic overviews with or without narrative explanations the program, project or subproject goals with needed resources, intended activities, expected outputs, and desired outcomes.

Matching An experimental procedure in which the subjects are so divided, by means other than lottery, that the groups are regarded for the purposes at hand to be of equal merit or ability. (Often matched groups are created by ensuring that they are the same or nearly so on such variables as sex, age, grade point averages, and past test scores.)

Materials evaluation Evaluations that assess the merit or worth of content-related physical items, including books, curricular guides, films, tapes, and other tangible instructional products.

Mean (arithmetic) A measure of central tendency calculated by dividing the sum of all the values by the number of the values.

Merit The excellence of an object as assessed by its intrinsic qualities or performance.

Metaevaluation Evaluation of an evaluation.

Modus operandi analysis Deducing the cause of effects based upon analysis of events, process, or properties associated with the effects; analogous to procedures used in detective work.

Monetary and Non-Monetary costs Evaluation expenses for which money is expended such as personnel salaries, evaluation team travel, and survey printing compared to other costs, such as the of time for a teacher or parent to participate in a focus group. (see **Opportunity cost)**

Nonreactive measures Assessments done without the awareness of those being assessed.

Norm A single value, or a distribution of values, constituting the typical performance of a given group.

"No significant difference" A decision that an observed difference between two statistics occurred by chance.

Null hypothesis The hypothesis of no difference or no differential effects.

Objective Something aimed at or striven for, more specific than a goal.

Objectives-referenced test A test whose scores are referenced to the attainment of the objectives the test was designed to measure, rather than to the performance on the test by somc comparison group of people.

Object of the evaluation The program, project, or component being evaluated. In these standards, the term *program* is sometimes used to subsume all components that are evaluated.

Opportunity cost The value lost from precluded and foregone resource uses in order to engage in another use or activity, for example, not being able to spend money of one type of data collection because it has been used on other things is an opportunity cost.

Operational definition A definition of a concept, often an outcome or other key construct, achieved by stating the operations or procedures employed to specify, concretize, and implement it.

Overview A conceptual/introductory statement that gives essential definitions; provides a general rationale; and presents summarized procedures, common problems, and special difficulties that are applicable.

Parallel forms Multiple forms of a test constructed to be as comparable and interchangeable as possible in their content, length, and procedures of administration, and in the scores and test properties (e.g., means, variances, and reliability indices).

Pilot test A brief and simplified preliminary study designed to try out methods to learn whether a proposed project or program seems likely to yield valuable results.

Political Context The sum total of group and individual interests related to power, resources, and the values that guide their operations and allocations in the environment in which a program and/or its evaluation occurs.

Population All the persons in a particular identified group.

Posttest A test to determine performance after the administration of a program, project, subproject, or specific component.

Pretest A test to determine performance prior to the administration of a program, project, subproject, or specific component.

Primary evaluation users A subset of evaluation users who have the authority to make decisions about the applications of evaluation descriptions and findings.

Programs Orchestrated initiatives that dedicate resources and inputs to a series of activities intended to achieve specific process, product, services, output, and outcome goals. Programs can include one or more projects, subprojects, and specific components.

Projects Specific initiatives that dedicate resources to a series of activities intended to achieve specific product and/or service goals. Programs are often organized into specific projects that can include one or more sub-projects.

Propriety The extent to which the evaluation has been conducted in a manner that evidences uncompromising adherence to the highest principles and ideals (including professional ethics, civil law, moral code, and contractual agreements).

Purpose Something one intends to do; intention; aim.

Purposes (of an evaluation study) The objectives of an evaluation (e.g., to judge the relative merits of competing textbooks, or to monitor and report on how well a project plan is implemented) and the intended use of its reports (e.g., to help teachers choose a textbook or to help a school district carry out a special project).

Qualitative information Representations of experiences, performances, characteristics, or other descriptions presented in narrative or other symbolic but not numerical form.

Quantitative information Representations of experiences, performances, characteristics, or other descriptions modeled by or summarized by ordered numerical systems.

Random Determined by chance.

Random sampling Drawing a number of items of any sort from a larger group or population so that every individual item has a specified probability to be chosen.

Randomized field trials Experiments in natural settings that rely on random sampling or random assignment to programs, projects, or other interventions and to control groups in order to study the net outcomes of the programs, projects or other interventions.

Regression effect The tendency of examinee scoring above or below the mean of a distribution on a pretest to score closer to the mean on the posttest.

Reliability Consistency and precision, freedom from random error. (Also, see **Generalizability**.)

Replicate To repeat an evaluation or a component of an evaluation with all essentials unchanged.

Report A presentation of information resulting from evaluative activity.

Sample A part of a population, usually selected following specified, replicable procedures.

School profile A description (graphic, numeric, or variable) of the status of a school with respect to a set of concepts or variables.

Secondary data analysis A reanalysis of data using the same or other appropriate procedures to verify the accuracy of the results of the initial analysis or for answering different questions.

Self-report instrument A device in which persons make and report judgments about the functioning of their project, program, or instructional material.

Significant difference (statistically) A decision that an observed difference between two statistics probably did not occur by chance.

Sponsor The individuals, groups, or organizations that provide the financial or other resources required for the evaluation.

Stakeholder Individuals or groups served by, affected by, or with a legitimate interest in the program or the evaluation.

Stakeholder map A representation in narrative or schematic form of key stakeholders from the perspective of selected individuals in an evaluation or program, depicting the proximity or other relationships among all identified stakeholders.

Standard A principle commonly agreed to by experts in the conduct and use of evaluation, that when implemented will lead to greater evaluation quality.

Standardized test A sample of items or situations with specific directions for administration and scoring, often accompanied by reliability, validity, and normative or other interpretive information.

Statistic A summary number that is typically used to describe a characteristic of a sample.

Stratified random sample A grouping achieved by dividing the population to be surveyed into a number of nonoverlapping classes or categories which together include all cases, followed by taking cases at random from within the categories.

Subprojects The subordinate, specific initiatives that are part of overarching projects and/or programs that dedicate resources to a series of activities intended to achieve specific product and/or service goals.

Summative evaluation An evaluation designed to present conclusions about the merit or worth of an object and recommendations about whether it should be retained, altered, or eliminated.

Table of specifications A two-way grid, sometimes called a test blueprint, that lists major areas of content to be covered by the test as row headings and major kinds of abilities to be developed and tested as column headings.

Tacit knowledge Cognitive, psychomotor, and affective perceptual and performance capabilities which are largely unarticulated and unexpressed but which may be essential components of individual expertise and competence. Sharing of tacit knowledge is difficult because it may be difficult or impossible to express via language alone. Discovery and sharing of tacit knowledge generally requires extensive reflection, effort, time, and trust.

Test retest reliability The extent to which two administrations of the same test to the same group of subjects yield consistent results.

Time series study A study in which periodic measurements are obtained prior to, during, and following the introduction of an intervention or treatment in order to reach conclusions about effects of the intervention.

Triangulation The use of multiple sources and methods to gather similar information about an object of inquiry, such as a program component or specific outcome.

Unit of analysis The level at which assessment information and measures are taken and analyzed.

Utility The extent to which evaluations are aligned with stakeholders' needs such that process uses, findings uses, and other appropriate influences are possible.

Validity The truthfulness of information and the soundness of the inferences made from representations of it.

Value Refers to the real or perceived worth or importance of a program and/or evaluation to stakeholders, such as policymakers, recipients and potential recipients of services, community members, policymakers, and evaluators. (See Feasibility Overview).

Values clarification techniques Procedures used to help groups recognize the different values held in the groups, to discern conflicts among these values, and to consider how these conflicts might be resolved.

Variable A characteristic that can take on different values.

Variate The quantitative measure of a variable.

Worth The value of an object in relationship to needs or identified purposes.

❖ Documentation Reference Lists ❖

❖ UTILITY REFERENCES

Abma, T. A. (2006). The practice and politics of responsive evaluation. *American Journal of Evaluation, 27*(1), 31–43.

Abma, T. A. (2007). Situated learning in communities of practice. *Evaluation, 13*(1), 32–47.

Adler, M. D., & Posner, E. A. (2006). *New foundations of cost-benefit analysis.* Cambridge, MA: Harvard University Press.

Alexander, H. (2003). Health-service evaluations: Should we expect the results to change practice? *Evaluation 9*(4), 405–414.

Alkin, M. C. (2004). Utilization of evaluation. In S. Mathison (Ed.), *Encyclopedia of evaluation* (pp. 434–436). Thousand Oaks, CA: Sage.

Alkin, M. C., Christie, C. A., & Rose, M. (2006). Communicating evaluation. In I. F. Shaw, J. C. Greene, & M. M. Mark (Eds.), *The Sage handbook of evaluation.* London: Sage.

Alkin, M. C., & Taut, S. (2003). Unbundling evaluation use. *Studies in Educational Evaluation, 29*(1), 1–12.

Altschuld, J. (1999). The certification of evaluators: Highlights from a report submitted to the board of directors of the American Evaluation Association. *American Journal of Evaluation, 20*(3), 481–493.

Amos, C., & Cousins, J. B. (2009). Reconnecting knowledge utilization and evaluation utilization domains of inquiry. *Canadian Journal of Program Evaluation, 23*(1), 81–85.

Atkinson, D. D., Wilson, M., & Avula, D. (2005). A participatory approach to building capacity of treatment programs to engage in evaluation. *Evaluation and Program Planning, 28*(3), 329–334.

Avalos, B., & Assael, J. (2006). Moving from resistance to agreement: The case of the Chilean teacher performance evaluation. *International Journal of Educational Research, 45*(4–5), 254–266.

Azaam, T., (2010). Evaluator responsiveness to stakeholders. *American Journal of Evaluation, 31,* 45–65.

Balthasar, A. (2006). The effects of institutional design on the utilization of evaluation: Evidenced using qualitative comparative analysis (QCA). *Evaluation, 12,* 353–371.

Balthasar, A. (2009). A contribution to a theory of evaluation influence based on Swiss experience. *Evaluation Review, 33*(3), 226–256.

Barbier, J.-C. (1999). Inter-governmental evaluation: Balancing stakeholders' expectations with enlightenment objectives? *Evaluation 5,* 373–386.

Berlo, D. K., Lemert, J. B., & Mertz, R. J. (Winter, 1969–1970). Dimensions for evaluating the acceptability of message sources. *Public Opinion Quarterly 33*(4), 563–576.

Beywl, W., Potter, P. (1998). RENOMO—a design tool for evaluations: Designing evaluations responsive to stakeholders' interests by working with nominal groups using the moderation method. *Evaluation, 4,* 53–71.

Bezzi, C. (2006). Evaluation pragmatics. *Evaluation, 12*(1), 56–76.

Birkeland, S., Murphy-Graham, E., & Weiss, C. (2005). Good reasons for ignoring good evaluation: The case of the drug abuse resistance education (D.A.R.E.) program. *Evaluation and Program Planning, 28*(3), 247–256.

Birman, D. (2007). Sins of omission and commission. *American Journal of Evaluation, 28*(1), 79–85.

Botcheva, L., Shih, J., & Huffman, L. (2009). Emphasizing cultural competence in evaluation. *American Journal of Evaluation, 30,* 176–188.

Bozeman, B. (2004). The Internet's impact on policy evaluation: Information compression and credibility. *Evaluation Review, 28*(2), 156–174.

Brandon, P. R., & Singh, J. M. (2009). The strengths of the methodological warrants for the findings on research on program evaluation use. *American Journal of Evaluation, 30*(2), 123–157.

Brousselle, A., Contandriopoulos, D., & Lemire, M. (2009). Using logic analysis to evaluate knowledge transfer initiatives: The case of the research collective on the organization of primary care services. *Evaluation, 15,* 165–183.

Brown, J. (2006). Interviewer as instrument: Accounting for human factors in evaluation research. *Evaluation Review, 30*(2), 188–208.

Burton, P. (2009). Conceptual, theoretical, and practical issues in measuring the benefits of public participation. *Evaluation, 15,* 263–284.

Burton, P., Goodlad, R., & Croft, J. (2006). How would we know what works?: Context and complexity in the evaluation of community involvement. *Evaluation, 12,* 294–312.

Caracelli, V. J. (2001). Evaluation use at the threshold of the twenty-first century. In V. J. Caracelli & H. Preskill (Eds.), *The expanding scope of evaluation use: New Directions for Evaluation, 88,* 99–111.

Caracelli, V. J., & Preskill, H. (Eds.). (2001). *The expanding scope of evaluation use: New Directions for Evaluation, 88.*

Cartland, J., Ruch-Ross, H., Mason, M., & Donohue, W. (2008). Role sharing between evaluators and stakeholders in practice. *American Journal of Evaluation, 29,* 460–477.

Chelimsky, E. (1998). The role of experience in formulating theories of evaluation practice. *American Journal of Evaluation, 19,* 35–55.

Chelimsky, E. (2006). The purposes of evaluation in a democratic society. In I. F. Shaw, J. C. Greene, & M. M. Mark (Eds.), *The Sage handbook of evaluation* (pp. 27–48). London: Sage.

Chen, H.-T. (2005). *Practical evaluation program.* Thousand Oaks, CA: Sage.

Christie, C. A. (2007). Reported influence of evaluation data on decision makers' actions. *American Journal of Evaluation, 28,* 8–25.

Cohen, D. J., Leviton, L. C., Isaacson, N., Tallia, A. F., & Crabtree, B. F. (2006). Online diaries for qualitative evaluation. *American Journal of Evaluation, 27,* 163–184.

Cook, P. F., Friedman, R., Lord, A., & Bradley-Springer, L. A. (2009). Outcomes of multimodal training for healthcare professionals at an AIDS education and training center. *Evaluation & the Health Professions, 32*(1), 3–22.

Cooksy, L. J., Gill, P., & Kelly, P. A. (2001). The program logic model as an integrative framework for a multimethod evaluation. *Evaluation and Program Planning, 42*(2), 119–128.

Cousins, J. B. (2004). Commentary: Minimizing evaluation misuse as principled practice. *American Journal of Evaluation, 25,* 391–397.

Cousins, J. B. (Ed.). (2008). *Process use in theory, research, and practice: New Directions for Evaluation, 116.*

Cousins, J. B., Cullen, J., Malik, S., & Maicher, B. (2009). Debating professional designations for evaluators: Reflections on the Canadian process. *Journal of MultiDisciplinary Evaluation, 6*(11), 71–82.

Cousins, J. B., & Shulha, L. M. (2006). A comparative analysis of evaluation utilization and its cognate fields. In I. F. Shaw, M. M. Mark, & J. C. Greene (Eds.), *The Sage handbook of evaluation* (pp. 266–291). London: Sage.

Crunkilton, D. D. (2009). Staff and client perspectives on the journey mapping online evaluation tool in a drug court program. *Evaluation and Program Planning, 32*(2), 119–128.

Curran, J. A., Murphy, A. L., Abidi, S. S. R., Sinclair, D., & McGrath, P. J. (2009). Bridging the gap: Knowledge seeking and sharing in a virtual community of emergency practice. *Evaluation & the Health Professions, 32*(3), 314–327.

Daigneault, P., & Jacob, S. (2009). Toward accurate measurement of participation: Rethinking the conceptualization and operationalization of participatory evaluation. *American Journal of Evaluation, 30,* 330–348.

Datta, L. (2000). Seriously seeking fairness: Strategies for crafting non-partisan evaluations in a partisan world. *American Journal of Evaluation, 21,* 1–15.

De Vito, C., Carmelo Nobile, G., Furnari, G., Pavia, M., De Giusti, M., Angelillo, I. F., et al. (2009). The role of education in improving physicians' professional use of economic evaluations of health interventions: Some evidence from a cross-sectional survey in Italy. *Evaluation & the Health Professions, 32,* 249–263.

Denzin, N. K., & Lincoln, Y. S. (2007). *Strategies of Qualitative Inquiry.* Thousand Oaks, CA: Sage.

Donaldson, S. I., Gooler, L. E., & Scriven, M. (2002). Strategies for managing evaluation anxiety: Toward a psychology of program evaluation. *American Journal of Evaluation, 23,* 261–273.

Donaldson, S. I., & Lipsey, M. W. (2006). Roles for theory in evaluation practice: Developing practical knowledge. In I. F. Shaw, J. C. Greene, & M. M. Mark (Eds.), *The Sage handbook of evaluation* (pp. 27–48). London: Sage.

Donaldson, S. I., & Scriven, M. (Eds.). (2003). *Evaluating social programs and problems: Visions for the new millennium.* Thousand Oaks, CA: Sage.

Duignan, P. (2003). Mainstreaming evaluation or building evaluation capability? Three key elements. In J. J. Barnette & J. R. Saunders (Eds.), *The mainstreaming of evaluation: New Directions for Evaluation, 99,* 7–21.

Escoffery, C., Glanz, K., Hall, D., & Elliott, T. (2009). A multi-method process evaluation for a skin cancer prevention diffusion trial. *Evaluation & the Health Professions, 32,* 184–203.

Fernie, S., Green, S. D., Weller, S. J., & Newcombe, R. (2003). Knowledge sharing: Context, confusion, and controversy. *International Journal of Project Management, 21,* 177–187.

Fetterman, D. M. (2001). *Foundations of empowerment evaluation.* Thousand Oaks, CA: Sage.

Fetterman, D. M. (2002). Empowerment evaluation: Building communities of practice and a culture of learning. *American Journal of Community Psychology, 30*(1), 89–102.

Fitzpatrick, J. L., Sanders, J. R., & Worthen, B. R. (2004). *Program evaluation: Alternative approaches and practical guidelines* (3rd ed.). Upper Saddle River, NJ: Pearson.

Fjellstrom, M. (2008). A learner-focused evaluation strategy: Developing medical education through a deliberative dialogue with stakeholders. *Evaluation, 14*(1), 91–106.

Fleischer, D. N., & Christie, C. A. (2009). Evaluation use: Results from a survey of U.S. American Evaluation Association members. *American Journal of Evaluation, 30,* 158–175.

Fredericks, K., Deegan, M., & Carman, J. (2008). Using system dynamics as an evaluation tool. *American Journal of Evaluation, 29,* 251–267.

Friedman, S. R., Reynolds, J., Quan, M. A., Call, S., Crusto, C. A., & Kaufman, J. S. (2007). Measuring changes in interagency collaboration: An examination of the Bridgeport Safe Start Initiative. *Evaluation and Program Planning, 30,* 294–306.

Friedman, V. J., Rothman, J., & Withers, B. (2006). The power of why. *American Journal of Evaluation, 27,* 201–218.

Gajda, R., & Koliba, C. (2007). Evaluating the imperative of intraorganizational collaboration. *American Journal of Evaluation, 28,* 26–44.

Gastic, B., Irby, D. J., & Zdanis, M. (2008). When stakeholders rebel: Lessons from a safe schools program. *Studies in Educational Evaluation, 34*(4), 208–211.

Gilliam, A., Davis, D., Barrington, T., Lacson, R., Uhl, G., & Phoenix, U. (2002). The value of engaging stakeholders in planning and implementing evaluations. *AIDS Education and Prevention, 14,* 5–17.

Grasso, G. F. (2003). What makes an evaluation useful? Reflections from experience in large organizations. *American Journal of Evaluation, 24,* 507–514.

Greene, J. C. (2001). Evaluation extrapolations. *American Journal of Evaluation, 22,* 397–402.

Greene, J. C. (2002). Mixed-method evaluation: a way of democratically engaging with Difference. *Evaluation Journal of Australasia, 2*(2), 22–29.

Greene, J. C. (2005). Stakeholder involvement. *Encyclopedia of Evaluation* (p. 397). Thousand Oaks, CA: Sage.

Grobb, G. F. (2003). A truly useful bat is one found in the hands of a slugger. *American Journal of Evaluation, 24,* 499–505.

Hahn Severance, J. (2009). Community health program evaluation using accreditation as a framework. *Evaluation & the Health Professions, 32*(1), 59–68.

Hansen, H. F. (2005). Choosing evaluation models: A discussion on evaluation design. *Evaluation, 11*(4), 447–462.

Hansoon, A. (2006). Organizational use of evaluations: Governance and control in research evaluation. *Evaluation, 12*(2), 159–178.

Harnar, M. A., & Preskill, H. (2007). Evaluators' descriptions of process use: An exploratory study. In J. Bradley Cousins (Ed.), *Process Use in Theory, Research, and Practice: New Directions for Evaluation, 116,* 27–44.

Hart, D., Diercks-O'Brien, G., & Powell, A. (2009). Exploring stakeholder engagement in impact evaluation planning in educational development work. *Evaluation, 15*(3), 285–306.

Hellstrom, T., (2003). Knowledge without goals? Evaluation of knowledge management programs. *Evaluation, 9,* 55–72.

Henry, G. T. (2003). Influential evaluation. *American Journal of Evaluation, 24,* 515–524.

Henry, G. T., & Mark, M. M. (2003). Beyond use: Understanding evaluation's influence on attitudes and actions. *American Journal of Evaluation, 24,* 293–314.

Hodges, S. P., & Hernandez, M. (1999). How organizational culture influences outcome information utilization. *Evaluation and Program Planning 22,* 183–197.

Hofstetter, C., & Alkin, M. C. (2003). Evaluation use revisited. In T. Kellaghan, D. L. Stufflebeam, & L. A. Wingate (Ed.), *International handbook of educational evaluation* (p. 196). Dordrecht, Netherlands: Kluwer.

Hogard, E. (2007). Using consultative methods to investigate professional–client interaction as an aspect of process evaluation. *American Journal of Evaluation, 28,* 304–317.

Hogard, E. (2008). Purpose and method for the evaluation of interpersonal process in health and social care. *Evaluation and Program Planning, 31*(1), 34–40.

Holte-McKenzie, M., Forde, S., & Theobald, S. (2006). Development of a participatory monitoring and evaluation strategy. *Evaluation and Program Planning, 29*(4), 365–376.

Horelli, L. (2009). Network evaluation from the everyday life perspective: A tool for capacity-building and voice. *Evaluation, 15*(2), 205–223.

House, E. (2001). Responsive evaluation (and its influence on deliberative democratic evaluation. In J. C. Greene & T. A. Abma (Eds.), *Responsive evaluation: New Directions for Evaluation, 92,* 23–30.

House, E. R. (2008). Blowback: Consequences of evaluation for evaluation. *American Journal of Evaluation, 29,* 416–426.

House, E. R., & Howe, K. R. (1998). The issue of advocacy in evaluations. *American Journal of Evaluation, 19,* 233–236.

House, E. R., & Howe, K. R. (1999). *Values in evaluation and social research.* Thousand Oaks, CA: Sage.

Hurley, C., Renger, R., & Brunk, B. (2005). Learning from a challenging fieldwork evaluation experience: Perspectives of a student and an instructor. *American Journal of Evaluation, 26,* 562–578.

Hurteau, M., Houle, S., & Mongiat, S. (2007). How legitimate and justified are judgments in program evaluation? *Evaluation, 13*(3), 307–319.

Iriti, J. E., Bickel, W. E., & Nelson, C. A. (2009). Using recommendations in evaluation. *American Journal of Evaluation, 26,* 464–479.

Jajosky, R. A., & Groseclose, S. (2004). Evaluation of reporting timeliness of public health surveillance systems for infectious diseases. *BMC Public Health 4*(29), 1–9.

Johnson, B., & Christensen, L. B. (2007). *Educational Research: Quantitative, qualitative, and mixed approaches* (3rd ed.). Thousand Oaks, CA: Sage.

Johnson, K., Greenseid, L. O., Toal, S. A., King, J. A., & Lawrenz, F. (2009). Research on evaluation use: A review of empirical literature from 1986 to 2005. *American Journal of Evaluation, 30,* 377–410.

Jonas, R. K., (Ed.). (1999). *Legislative program evaluation: Utilization-driven research for decision makers: New Directions for Evaluation, 81,* 1–107.

Kahn, L. S., Tumiel-Berhalter, L., Cadzow, R., Watkins, R., Leonard, K. M., & Taylor, J. S. (2007). The impacts of subsidized health insurance on employees' use of preventive health services. *Evaluation & the Health Professions, 30*(1), 22–34.

Karlsson, P., Beijer, E., Eriksson, B., & Leissner, T. (2008). Evaluation workshops for capacity building in welfare work: Some Swedish examples. *Evaluation, 14*(4), 483–498.

King, G., Servais, M., Kertoy, M., Specht, J., Currie, M., Rosenbaum, P., et al. (2009). A measure of community members' perceptions of the impacts of research partnerships in health and social services. *Evaluation and Program Planning, 32*(3), 289–299.

King, J. A. (1999). Involving practitioners in evaluation studies. How viable is collaboration in schools? In J. B. Cousins & L. M. Earl (Eds.), *Participatory evaluation in education: Studies of Evaluation Use and Organizational Learning.* London: Falmer Press. (115–139).

King, J. A., Cousins, J. B., & Whitmore, E. (2007). Making sense of participatory evaluation: Framing participatory evaluation. In S. Mathison (Ed.), *Enduring issues in evaluation: The 20th anniversary of the collaboration between NDE and AEA: New Directions for Evaluation, 114,* 83–105.

King, J. A., & Ehlert, J. C. (2008). What we learned from three evaluations that involved stakeholders. *Studies in Educational Evaluation, 34*(4), 194–200.

King, J. A., Stevahn, L., Ghere, G., & Minnema, J. (2001). Toward a taxonomy of essential evaluator competencies. *American Journal of Evaluation, 22,* 229–247.

Kirkhart, K. E. (2000). Reconceptualizing evaluation use: An integrated theory of influence. In V. J. Caracelli & H. Preskill (Eds.), *The expanding scope of evaluation use: New Directions for Evaluation, 88,* 5–23.

Launso, L., Rieper, J., & Rieper, O. (2007). Evaluative feedback as a contribution to learning between groups of professionals. *Evaluation, 13*(3), 306–322.

Lawrenz, F., Gullickson, A., & Toal, S. (2007). Dissemination. *American Journal of Evaluation, 28,* 275–289.

Lee, Y., Altschuld, J. W., & White, J. L. (2007). Effects of multiple stakeholders in identifying and interpreting perceived needs. *Evaluation and Program Planning, 30*(1), 1–9.

Lehn, B. (2008). Evaluator's role in accountability relationships: Measurement technician, capacity builder, or risk manager? *Evaluation, 14*(3), 323–343.

Lehoux, P., Hivon, M., Denis, J., & Tailliez, S. (2008). Health technology assessment in the Canadian health policy arena: Examining relationships between evaluators and stakeholders. *Canadian Journal of Program Evaluation, 14*(3), 295–321.

Leviton, L. C. (2001). Presidential address: Building evaluation's collective capacity. *American Journal of Evaluation, 22,* 1–12.

Leviton, L. C. (2003). Evaluation use: Advances, challenges, and applications. *American Journal of Evaluation, 24,* 525–535.

Lonsdale, J. (2008). Balancing independence and responsiveness: A practitioner perspective on the relationships shaping performance audit and evaluation. *Evaluation, 14*(2), 227–248.

Louis, K. S. (1996). Do we need a new theory of dissemination and knowledge utilization? In B. B. Gundem & K. Z. Ozerk (Eds.), *Dissemination and utilization of research knowledge.* Olso, Norway: University of Oslo, Institute for Educational Research.

Lusk, C., Delclos, G. L., Burau, K., Drawhorn, D. D., & Aday, L. A. (2007). Mail versus internet surveys: Determinants of method of response preferences among health professionals. *Evaluation & the Health Professions, 30*(2), 186–201.

MacLellan, M. F., Patten, S., dela Cruz, A., & Flaherty, A. (2007). A participatory approach to the development of an evaluation framework: Process, pitfalls, and payoffs. *Canadian Journal of Program Evaluation, 22*(1), 99–124.

Mark, M. M. (2006). Introduction: The evaluation of policies, programs, and practices. In I. F. Shaw, J. C. Greene, & M. M. Mark (Eds.), *The Sage handbook of evaluation* (pp. 1–26). London: Sage.

Mark, M. M., Henry, G. T., & Julnes, G. (2000). *Evaluation: An integrative framework for understanding, guiding, and improving policies and programs.* San Francisco: Jossey-Bass.

Mathie, A., & Greene, J. C. (1997). Stakeholder participation in evaluation: How important is diversity? *Evaluation and Program Planning, 20*(3), 279–285.

McDonald, D. (2008). Revisiting a theory of negotiation: The utility of Markiewicz (2005) proposed six principles. *Evaluation and Program Planning, 31*(3), 259–265.

Mcdougal, J. A., Brooks, C. M., & Albanese, M. (2005). Achieving consensus on leadership competencies and outcome measures: The pediatric pulmonary centers' experience. *Evaluation & the Health Professions, 28*(4), 428–446.

McNall, M., & Foster-Fishman, P. G. (2007). Methods of rapid evaluation, assessment, and appraisal. *American Journal of Evaluation, 28,* 151–168.

McNamee, S. (2003). Appreciative evaluation within a conflicted educational context. In H. Preskill & A. T. Coghlan (Eds.), *Using appreciative inquiry in evaluation: New Directions for Evaluation, 100,* 23–40.

Mertens, D. M. (2005). *Research and evaluation in education and psychology: Integrating diversity with quantitative, qualitative, and mixed methods.* Thousand Oaks, CA: Sage.

Mertens, D. M. (2007). Transformative considerations. *American Journal of Evaluation, 28,* 86–90.

Miller, R. L., & Campbell, R. (2006). Taking stock of empowerment evaluation: An empirical review. *American Journal of Evaluation, 27,* 296–319.

Morell, J. A. (2005). Why are there unintended consequences of program action, and what are the implications for doing evaluation? *American Journal of Evaluation, 26,* 444–463.

Naccarella, L., Pirkis, J., Kohn, F., Morley, B., Burgess, P., & Blashki, G. (2007). Building evaluation capacity: Definitional and practical implications from an Australian case study. *Evaluation and Program Planning, 30,* 231–236.

O'Sullivan, R. G. (2004). *Practicing evaluation: A collaborative approach.* Thousand Oaks, CA: Sage.

O'Sullivan, R. G., & D'Agitino, A. (2002). Promoting evaluation through collaboration: Findings from community-based programs for young children and their families. *Evaluation, 8*(3), 372–387.

Parkinson, S. (2009). Power and perceptions in participatory monitoring and evaluation. *Evaluation and Program Planning, 32*(3), 229–237.

Patton, M. Q. (2001). Evaluation, knowledge management, best practices, and high quality lessons learned. *American Journal of Evaluation, 22*(3), 329–336.

Patton, M. Q. (2006). Evaluation for the way we work. *Nonprofit Quarterly, 12*(1), 28–33.

Patton, M. Q. (2008). *Utilization-focused evaluation* (4th ed.). Thousand Oaks, CA: Sage.

Plottu, B., & Plottu, E. (2009). Approaches to participation in evaluation. *Evaluation, g15*(3), 343–359.

Poth, C., & Shulha, L. (2008). Encouraging stakeholder engagement: A case study of evaluator behavior. *Studies in Educational Evaluation, 34*(4), 218–223.

Preskill, H. (2006). *Reframing evaluation through appreciative inquiry.* Newbury Park, CA: Sage.

Preskill, H., & Boyle, S. (2008). A multidisciplinary model of evaluation capacity building. *American Journal of Evaluation, 29,* 443–459.

Rebolloso, E., Fernandez-Ramirez, B., & Canton, P. (2005). The influence of evaluation on changing management systems in educational institutions. *Evaluation, 11*(4), 463–479.

Rolfsen, M., & Torvatn, H. (2005). How to 'get through': Communication challenges in formative evaluation. *Evaluation, 11*(3), 297–309.

Ross, J., & Ben Jaafar, S. (2006). Participatory needs assessment. *Canadian Journal of Program Evaluation, 21*(1), 131–154.

Rossi, P. H., Lipsey, M. W., & Freeman, H. E. (2004). *Evaluation: A systematic approach.* Thousand Oaks, CA: Sage.

Ryan, K. E., Chandler, M., & Samuels, M. (2007). What should school-based evaluation look like? *Studies in Educational Evaluation, 33*(3–4), 197–212.

Ryan, K. E., & Johnson, T. D. (2000). *Democratizing evaluation: Meanings and methods from practice: New Directions for Evaluation, 85.*

Scarinci, I. C., Johnson, R. E., Hardy, C., Marron, J., & Partridge, E. E. (2009). Planning and implementation of a participatory evaluation strategy: A viable approach in the evaluation of community-based participatory programs addressing cancer disparities. *Evaluation and Program Planning, 32*(3), 221–228.

Schwandt, T. A., & Burgon, H. (2006). Evaluation and the study of lived experience. In I. F. Shaw, J. C. Greene, & M. M. Mark (Eds.). *The Sage handbook of evaluation* (pp. 85–101). London: Sage.

Schwarz, C., & Struhkamp, G. (2007). Does evaluation build or destroy trust? Insights from case studies on evaluation in higher education reform. *Evaluation, 13*(3), 323–339.

Schweigert, F. J. (2006). The meaning of effectiveness in assessing community initiatives. *American Journal of Evaluation, 27*(4), 416–436.

Scriven, M. (1996). Types of evaluation and types of evaluator. *Evaluation Practice, 17*(2), 151–161.

Scriven, M. (1997). Truth and objectivity in evaluation. In E. Chelimsky & W. R. Shadish (Eds.), *Evaluation for the 21st century: A handbook* (pp. 477–500). Thousand Oaks, CA: Sage.

Sevdalis, N., Norris, B., Ranger, C., & Bothwell, S. (2009). Closing the safety loop: Evaluation of the national patient safety agency's guidance regarding wristband identification of hospital inpatients. *Journal of Evaluation in Clinical Practice, 15*(2), 311–315.

Shaw, I. F., Greene, J. C., & Mark, M. M. (2006). *The Sage handbook of evaluation.* London: Sage.

Shulha, L. M. (2000). Evaluative inquiry in university/school professional learning partnerships. In V. J. Caracelli & H. Preskill (Eds.), *The expanding scope of evaluation use: New Directions for Evaluation, 88,* 39–54.

Shulha, L. M., & Wilson, R. J. (2003). Collaborative mixed-methods research. In A. Tashakkori & C. Teddlie (Eds.), *Handbook of mixed methodology.* Thousand Oaks, CA: Sage.

Skolits, G. J., Morrow, J. A., & Mehalic Burr, E. (2009). Reconceptualizing evaluator roles. *American Journal of Evaluation, 30,* 275–295.

Smits, P., & Champagne, F. (2008). An assessment of the theoretical underpinnings of practical participatory evaluation. *American Journal of Evaluation, 29,* 427–442.

Sobeck, J., & Agius, E. (2007). Organizational capacity building: Addressing a research and practice gap. *Evaluation and Program Planning, 30*(3), 237–246.

Sridharan, S. (2003). Introduction to Special Section on "What is a Useful Evaluation?" *American Journal of Evaluation, 24,* 483–487.

Sridharan, S., Campbell, B., & Zinzow, H. (2006). Developing a stakeholder-driven anticipated timeline of impact for evaluation of social programs. *American Journal of Evaluation, 27*(2), 148–162.

Stacey, R. D. (2001). *Complex responsive processes in organizations: Learning and knowledge creation.* London: Routledge.

Stake, R. E. (2009). The incredible lightness of evidence: Problems of synthesis in educational evaluation. *Studies in Educational Evaluation, 35*(1), 3–6.

Stufflebeam, D. L. (2000). Lessons in contracting for evaluations. *American Journal of Evaluation, 21,* 293–314.

Suarez-Herrera, J. C., Springett, J., & Kagan, C. (2009). Critical connections between participatory evaluation, organizational learning, and intentional change in pluralistic organizations. *Evaluation, 15,* 321–342.

Sutherland, S., & Katz, S. (2005). Concept mapping methodology: A catalyst for organizational learning. *Evaluation and Program Planning, 28*(3), 257–269.

Taut, S. (2007). Methodological and conceptual challenges in studying evaluation process use. *Canadian Journal of Program Evaluation, 22*(2), 1–19.

Taylor, J. R., & Van Every, E. J. (2000). *The emergent organization: Communication as its site and surface.* Mahwah, NJ: Erlbaum.

Thayer, C., & Fine, A. (2001). Evaluation and outcome measurement in the non-profit sector: Stakeholder participation. *Evaluation and Program Planning, 24,* 103–108.

Toal, S. A., King, J. A., Johnson, K., & Lawrenz, F. (2009). The unique character of involvement in multi-site evaluation settings. *Evaluation and Program Planning, 32*(2), 91–98.

Torres, R. T., Preskill, H. S., & Piontek, M. E. (2004). *Evaluation strategies for communicating and reporting: Enhancing learning in organizations* (2nd ed.). Thousand Oaks, CA: Sage.

Trevisan, M. S. (2004). Practical training in evaluation: A review of the literature. *American Journal of Evaluation, 25,* 255–272.

Trevisan, M. S. (2007). Evaluability assessment from 1986 to 2006. *American Journal of Evaluation, 28*(3), 290–303.

Vaessen, J. (2006). Programme theory evaluation, multicriteria decision aid and stakeholder values: A methodological framework. *Evaluation, 12*(4), 397–417.

Wallace, T. L. (2008). Process of evaluation: Focus on stakeholders. *Studies in Educational Evaluation, 34*(4), 192–193.

Weiss, C. H., Murphy-Graham, E., & Birkeland, S. (2005). An alternate route to policy influence: How evaluations affect D.A.R.E. *American Journal of Evaluation, 26,* 12–30.

Westley, F., Zimmerman, B., & Patton, M. Q. (2006). *Getting to maybe: How the world is changed.* Toronto, ON: Random House Canada.

Zuckerman, B., & Preskill, H. (2001). Throwing a curveball in the game of evaluation: Deception and the misuse of findings. *Advances in Developing Human Resources, 3*(1), 55–68.

❖ FEASIBILITY REFERENCES

Abma, T. (2006). The practice and politics of responsive evaluation. *American Journal of Evaluation, 27,* 31–43.

Abma, T. (2006). The social relations in evaluation. In I. F. Shaw, J. C. Greene, & M. M. Mark (Eds.), *The Sage handbook of evaluation* (pp.184–199). London: Sage.

Alkon, A., Tschann, J., Ruane, S., Wolff, M., & Hittner, A. (2001). A violence-prevention and evaluation project with ethnically diverse populations. *American Journal of Preventive Medicine, 20,* 48–55.

Barrington, G. (1999). Commentary: When management changes: Advice for a young evaluator. *American Journal of Evaluation, 20,* 377–380.

Bell, J. B. (2004). Managing evaluation projects. In J. S. Wholey, H. P. Hatry, & K. Newcomer (Eds.), *Handbook of practical program evaluation* (2nd ed., pp. 571–603). San Francisco, CA: Jossey-Bass.

Brandon, P. R. (1998). Stakeholder participation for the purpose of helping ensure evaluation validity: Bridging the gap between collaborative and non-collaborative evaluations. *American Journal of Evaluation, 19,* 325–337.

Chelimsky, E. (1995). The political environment of evaluation and what it means for the development of the field. *Evaluation Practice, 16,* 215–225.

Chelimsky, E. (1998). The role of experience in formulating theories of evaluation practice. *American Journal of Evaluation, 19,* 35–55.

Chelimsky, E. (2008). A clash of cultures: Improving the "fit" between evaluative independence and the political requirements of a democratic society. *American Journal of Evaluation, 29,* 400–415.

Clayson, Z. C., Castañeda, X., Sanchez, E., & Brindis, C. (2002). Unequal power—changing landscapes: Negotiations between evaluation stakeholders in Latino communities. *American Journal of Evaluation, 23,* 33–44.

Compton, D. W., & Baizerman, M. (Eds.). (2009). *Managing program evaluation: Towards explicating a professional practice: New Direction for Evaluation, 121.*

Datta, L.-E. (2000). Seriously seeking fairness: Strategies for crafting non-partisan evaluations in a partisan world. *American Journal of Evaluation, 21,* 1–14.

Davidson, E. J. (2005). *Evaluation methodology basics: The nuts and bolts of sound evaluation.* Thousand Oaks, CA: Sage.

Fitzpatrick, J., Sanders, J., & Worthen, B. (2004). *Program evaluation: Alternative approaches and practical guidelines* (3rd ed.). Boston: Allyn & Bacon.

Henry, G., & Mark, M. M. (2003). Beyond use: Understanding evaluation's influence on attitudes and actions. *American Journal of Evaluation, 24,* 293–314.

Hood, S. (2001). Nobody knows my name: In praise of african american evaluators who were responsive. In J. C. Greene and T. A. Abma (Eds.), *Responsive evaluation: New Directions for Evaluation, 92,* 31–43.

Hood, S. (2005). Culturally responsive evaluation. In S. Mathison (Ed.), *Encyclopedia of evaluation (*pp. 96–100). Thousand Oaks, CA: Sage.

Hopson, R. K., Lucas, K. J., & Peterson, J. A. (2000). HIV/AIDS talk: Implications for prevention intervention and evaluation. In R. K. Hopson (Ed.), *How and why language matters in evaluation: New Directions for Evaluation, 86,* 29–42.

House, E. R., & Howe, K. R. (1998). The issues of advocacy in evaluations. *American Journal of Evaluation, 19,* 233–236.

House, E. R., & Howe, K. R. (1999). *Values in evaluation and social research.* Thousand Oaks, CA: Sage.

Johnson, E. (2005). The use of contextually relevant evaluation practices with program designed to increase participation of minorities in science, technology, engineering, and mathematics (STEM) education. In S. Hood, R. K. Hopson, & H. Frierson (Eds.), *The role of culture and cultural context: A mandate for inclusion, the discovery of truth, and understanding in evaluative theory and practice* (pp.217–235). Greenwich, CT: Information Age.

Johnson, E., Kirkhart, K., Madison, A. M., Noley, G., & Solano-Flores, G. (2008). The impact of narrow views of scientific rigor on evaluation practices for under-represented groups. In N. Smith & P. Brandon (Eds.), *Fundamental issues in evaluation* (pp. 197–218). New York: Guilford Press.

Joint Committee on Standards for Educational Evaluation. (1994). *The program evaluation standards* (2nd ed.). Thousand Oaks, CA: Corwin.

Kirkhart, K. (1995). Seeking multicultural validity: A postcard from the road. *Evaluation Practice, 12,* 1–12.

Kirkhart, K. (2000). Reconceptualizing evaluation use: An integrated theory of influence. In V. Caracelli & H. Preskill (Eds.), *The expanding scope of evaluation use: New Directions for Evaluation, 88,* 5–23.

Kirkhart, K. (2005). Through a cultural lens: Reflections on validity and theory in evaluation. In S. Hood, R. K. Hopson, & H. Frierson (Eds.), *The role of culture and cultural context: A mandate for inclusion, the discovery of truth, and understanding in evaluative theory and practice.* (pp. 21–39). Greenwich, CT: Information Age.

Letiecq, B. L., & Bailey, S. J. (2004). Evaluating from the outside: Conducting cross-cultural evaluation research on an American Indian reservation. *Evaluation Review, 28,* 342–357.

Levin, H., & McEwan, P. (2001). *Cost-effectiveness analysis* (2nd ed.). Thousand Oaks, CA: Sage.

Lewis, J. P. (2002). *Fundamentals of project management: Developing core competencies to help outperform the competition* (2nd ed.). New York: American Management Association.

Madison, A.-M. (1992). Primary inclusion of culturally diverse minority program participants in the evaluation process. In A.-M. Madison (Ed.), *Minority issues in program evaluation: New Directions for Program Evaluation 53,* 35–43.

Nelson-Barber, S., LaFrance, J., Trumbull, E., & Aburto, S. (2005). Promoting culturally reliable and valid evaluation practice. In S. Hood, R. K. Hopson, & H. Frierson (Eds.), *The role of culture and cultural context: A mandate for inclusion, the discovery of truth, and understanding in evaluative theory and practice* (pp. 61–85). Greenwich, CT: Information Age.

Patton, M. Q. (1997). *Utilization-focused evaluation: The new century text* (3rd ed.). Thousand Oaks, CA: Sage.

Preskill, H., & Torres, R. (1999). *Evaluative inquiry for learning in organizations.* Thousand Oaks, CA: Sage.

Project Management Institute. *A guide to the project management body of knowledge (PMBOK® guide)* (3rd ed.). (2004). Newtown Square, PA: Author.

Rossi, P., Lipsey, M., & Freeman, H. (2004). *Evaluation: A systematic approach* (7th ed.). Thousand Oaks, CA: Sage.

Scriven, M. (1991). *Evaluation thesaurus* (4th ed.). Newbury Park, CA: Sage.

SenGupta, S., Hopson, R., & Thompson-Robinson, M. (2004). Cultural competence in evaluation: An overview. In M. Thompson-Robinson, R. Hopson, & S. SenGupta (Eds.), *In search of cultural competence in evaluation: Toward principles and practices: New Directions for Evaluation, 102,* 5–19.

Shulha, L. (2000). Evaluative inquiry in university-school professional learning partnerships conceptualizing evaluation use. In V. Caracelli & H. Preskill (Eds.), *The expanding scope of evaluation use: New Directions for Evaluation, 88,* 39–53.

Stevenson, W. (2005). *Operations management* (8th ed.). New York, NY: McGraw-Hill/Irwin.

Stufflebeam, D. L. (2000). *Guidelines for developing evaluation checklists: The checklists development checklist (CDC).* Retrieved December 14, 2009, from www.wmich.edu/evalctr/checklists

Stufflebeam, D. L. (2001). Evaluation checklists: Practical tools for guiding and judging evaluations. *American Journal of Evaluation, 22,* 71–79.

Stufflebeam, D. L. (2004). *Evaluation design checklist.* Retrieved December 14, 2009, from www.wmich.edu/evalctr/checklists

Taut, S. M., & Alkin, M. C. (2003). Program staff perceptions of barriers to evaluation implementation. *American Journal of Evaluation, 24,* 213–226.

Taylor, J. (1998). *A survival guide for project managers.* New York: American Management Association.

Thomas, V. G. (2004). Building a contextually responsive evaluation framework: Lessons from working with urban school interventions. In V. G. Thomas & F. I. Stevens (Eds.), *Co-constructing a contextually responsive evaluation framework: The talent development model of school reform: New Directions for Evaluation, 101,* 3–23.

Thomsett, M. (1990). *The little black book of project management.* New York: American Management Association.

Walker, R., & Wiseman, M. (2006). Managing evaluations. In I. F. Shaw, J. C. Greene, & M. M. Marks (Eds.), *The Sage handbook of evaluation* (pp. 360–383). London: Sage.

Weiss, C. (1998). *Evaluation* (2nd ed.). Upper Saddle River, NJ: Prentice Hall.

Weiss, C. (1998). Have we learned anything new about the use of evaluation? *American Journal of Evaluation, 19,* 21–33.

Weiss, C. (2000). The experimenting society in a political world. In L. Bickman (Ed.), *Validity and social experimentation* (pp. 283–301). Thousand Oaks, CA: Sage.

Weiss, C., Murphy-Graham, E., & Birkeland, S. (2005). An alternate route to policy influence. *American Journal of Evaluation, 26,* 12–30.

Wholey, J. (1987). Evaluability assessment: Developing program theory. In *Using program theory in evaluation: New Directions in Program Evaluation, 33,* 77–92.

Wholey, J. (2004). Evaluability assessment. In J. S. Wholey, H. P. Hatry, & K. E. Newcomer (Eds.), *Handbook of practical program evaluation.* (2nd ed., pp. 33–66). San Francisco, CA: Jossey-Bass.

Wysocki, R., Beck, R., Jr., & Crane, D. (1995). *Effective project management.* New York: John Wiley.

❖ PROPRIETY REFERENCES

Abma, T. (2006). The social relations of evaluation. In I. F. Shaw, J. C. Greene, & M. M. Mark, (Eds.), *The Sage handbook of evaluation.* London: Sage.

Alkin, M. C., Christie, C. A., & Rose, M. (2006). Communicating evaluation. In I. F. Shaw, J. C. Greene, & M. M. Mark (Eds.), *The Sage handbook of evaluation* (pp. 337–354). London: Sage.

American Association of University Professors. (2001). Report: Protecting human beings: Institutional review boards and social science research. *Academe, 87*(3), 55–67.

American Evaluation Association. (2007). *Guiding principles for evaluators.* Retrieved June 26, 2007, from http://www.eval.org/Publications/GuidingPrinciples.asp

Australasian Evaluation Society. (2006). *Guidelines for the ethical conduct of evaluations.* Retrieved May 1, 2007, from http://www.aes.asn.au

Australian Institute of Aboriginal and Torres Strait Islander Studies. (2000). *Guidelines for ethical research in indigenous studies.* Canberra, Australian Capital Territory: Author.

British Educational Research Association. (2004). *Revised ethical guidelines for educational research.* Notts, UK: Author.

Bustelo, M. (2006). The potential role of standards and guidelines in the development of an evaluation culture in Spain. *Evaluation, 12*(4), 437–453.

Centre for Social Research and Evaluation. (2004). *Guidelines for research and evaluation with Maori.* Ministry of Social Development, New Zealand.

Chelimsky, E. (1999). The political environment of evaluation and what it means for the development of the field. *Evaluation Practice, 16*(3), 215–225.

Chen, H.-T. (2002). Designing and conducting participatory outcome evaluation of community-based organizations' HIV prevention programs. In Evaluating HIV Prevention Programs [Supplement], *AIDS Education and Prevention, 14,* 18–26.

Cooksy, L. (2007). Ethical challenges: Should we call the whole thing off? *American Journal of Evaluation, 28,* 76–78.

Cram, C., McCreanor, T., Smith, L., Nairn, R., & Johnstone, W. (2006). Kaupapa Mäori research and Päkehä social science: Epistemological tensions in a study of Mäori health. *Hülili, 3,* 41–68.

Cronbach, L. J., Ambron, S. R., Dornbusch, S. M., Hess, R. D., Hornik, R. C., Phillips, D. C., et al. (1980). *Toward reform of program evaluation.* San Francisco: Jossey-Bass.

Davidson, E. J. (2005). *Evaluation methodology basics: The nuts and bolts of sound evaluation.* Thousand Oaks, CA: Sage.

Davis, J. E. (1992). Reconsidering the use of race as an explanatory variable in program evaluation. In A.-M. Madison (Ed.), *Minority issues in evaluation: New Directions for Program Evaluation, 53,* 55–65.

Dial, M. (1994). The misuse of evaluation in educational programs. In C. J. Stevens & M. Dial (Eds.), *Preventing the misuse of evaluation: New Directions for Program Evaluation, 64,* 61–67.

Drummond, M. F., O'Brien, B., Stoddart, G. L., & Torrance, G. (2004). *Methods for the economic evaluation of health care programmes,* (2nd ed.). Oxford, UK: Oxford University Press.

Fitzpatrick, J. L., & Morris, M. (Eds.). (1999). *Current and emerging ethical challenges in evaluation: New Directions for Evaluation, 82.*

Fitzpatrick, J. L., Sanders, J. R., & Worthen, B. R. (2004). *Program evaluation: Alternative approaches and practical guidelines* (3rd ed.). White Plains, NY: Longman.

Fraser, D. (2004). National evaluation standards for Australia and New Zealand: Many questions but few answers. In C. Russon & G. Russon (Eds.), *International perspectives on evaluation standards: New Directions for Evaluation, 104,* 67–78.

Frierson, H., Hood, S., & Hughes, G. B. (2002). Strategies that address culturally responsive evaluations. In J. Frechtling (Ed.), *The 2002 user-friendly handbook for project evaluation* (NSF 02–057). Arlington, VA: National Science Foundation, Directorate for Education and Human Resources.

Gondolf, E. W. (2000). Human subject issues in batterer program evaluation. *Journal of Aggression, Maltreatment, & Trauma, 4,* 279–297.

Greene, J. C. (2005). Evaluators as stewards of the public good. In S. Hood, R. K. Hopson, & H. Frierson (Eds.), *The role of culture and cultural context in evaluation: A mandate for inclusion, the discovery of truth, and understanding in evaluative theory and practice* (pp. 7–20). Greenwich, CT: Information Age.

Greene, J. C. (2006). Evaluation, democracy, and social change. In I. F. Shaw, J. C. Greene, & M. M. Mark (Eds.), *The Sage handbook of evaluation,* (pp. 102–122). London: Sage.

Greene, J. C., & Abma, T. A. (Eds.). (2001). *Responsive evaluation: New Directions for Evaluation, 92.*

Grinyer, A. (2002). The anonymity of research participants: Assumptions, ethics, and practicalities. *Social Research Update,* 36.

Guba, E., & Lincoln, Y. (1981). *Effective evaluation.* San Francisco: Jossey-Bass.

Henry, G. T., Julnes, G., & Mark, M. M. (Eds.). (1998). *Realist evaluation: An emerging theory in support of practice: New Directions for Evaluation, 78.*

Holt, L. (2004). The 'voices' of children: De-centering empowering research relations. *Children's Geographies, 2*(1), 13–27.

Hood, S. (1998). Responsive evaluation Amistad style: Perspectives of one African-American evaluator. In R. Davis (Ed.), *Proceedings of the stake symposium on educational evaluation.* University of Illinois at Urbana-Champaign.

Hood, S. (2001). Nobody knows my name: In praise of african american evaluators who were responsive. In J. C. Greene & T. A. Abma (Eds.), *Responsive valuation: New Directions for Evaluation, 92,* 31–43.

Hostetler, K. (2005). What is "good" education research? *Educational Researcher, 34*(6), 16–21.

House, E. R. (1991). Evaluation and social justice: Where are we? In M. W. McLaughlin & D. C. Phillips (Eds.), *Evaluation and education: At quarter century.* Ninetieth Yearbook of the National Study for the Study of Education. Chicago: The University of Chicago Press.

House, E. R., & Howe, K. R. (1998). The issue of advocacy in evaluation. *American Journal of Evaluation, 19*(2), 233–236.

House, E. R., & Howe, K. R. (1999). *Values in evaluation and social research.* Thousand Oaks, CA: Sage.

Kushner, S. (2000). *Personalizing evaluation.* London: Sage.

Levin, H. (2004). Cost effectiveness. *Encyclopedia of evaluation* (p. 90). Thousand Oaks, CA: Sage.

Levin, H. M., & McEwan, P. J. (2001). *Cost-effectiveness analysis: Methods and applications.* Thousand Oaks, CA: Sage.

Lincoln, Y. S. (1991). The arts and sciences of program evaluation. *Evaluation Practice, 12,* 1–7.

Lincoln, Y. S., & Tierney, W. G. (2004). Qualitative research and institutional review boards. *Qualitative Inquiry, 10,* 219–234.

Mabry, L. (1999). Circumstantial ethics. *American Journal of Evaluation, 20,* 199–213.

Mabry, L. (2003). In living color: Qualitative methods in educational evaluation. In T. Kellaghan, D. L. Stufflebeam, & L. Wingate (Eds.), *International handbook of educational evaluation* (pp. 167–188). Dordrecht, Netherlands: Kluwer.

Madison, A. M. (2000). Language in defining social problems and in evaluating social programs. In R. K. Hopson (Ed.), *How and why language matters in evaluation: New Directions for Evaluation, 86,* 17–28.

Mark, M. M., Greene, J. C., & Shaw, I. F. (2006). The evaluation of policies, programs, and practices. In I. F. Shaw, J. C. Greene, & M. M. Mark (Eds.), *The Sage handbook of evaluation* (pp. 1–26). London: Sage.

Mark, M. M., Henry, G. T, & Julnes, G. (2000). *Evaluation: An integrated framework for understanding, guiding, and improving policies and programs.* San Francisco: Jossey-Bass.

Martin, J. I., & Meezan, W. (2003). Applying ethical standards to research and evaluations involving lesbian, gay, bisexual, and transgendered populations. *Journal of Gay and Lesbian Social Services, 15,* 181–201.

Mertens, D. M. (1999). Inclusive evaluation: Implications of transformative theory for evaluation. *American Journal of Evaluation, 20,* 1–14.

Mertens, D. M. (2005). *Research and evaluation in education and psychology: Integrating diversity with quantitative, qualitative, and mixed methods* (2nd ed.). Thousand Oaks, CA: Sage.

Morris, M. (2003). Ethical considerations in evaluation. In T. Kellaghan & D. L. Stufflebeam (Eds.), *International handbook of educational evaluation* (pp. 303–328). Dordrecht, Netherlands: Kluwer.

Morris, M. (Ed.). (2008). *Evaluation ethics for best practice: Cases and commentaries.* New York: Guilford Press.

Morris, M., & Cohn, R. (1993). Program evaluators and ethical challenges. *Evaluation Review, 17*(6), 621–642.

Moskowitz, J. M. (1993). Why reports of outcome evaluations are often biased or uninterpretable. *Evaluation and Program Planning, 16,* 1–9.

National Commission for the Protection of Human Subjects in Biomedical and Behavioral Research. (1979). *The Belmont report: Ethical principles and guidelines for the protection of human subjects of research.* Washington, DC: U.S. Department of Health, Education, and Welfare.

Newman, D. L., & Brown, R. D. (1996). *Applied ethics for program evaluation.* Thousand Oaks, CA: Sage.

Oakes, J. M. (2002). Risks and wrongs in social science research: An evaluator's guide to the IRB. *Evaluation Review, 26*(5), 443–478.

Pandiani, J. A., & Banks, S. M. (1998). Personal privacy versus public accountability: A technological solution to an ethical dilemma. *Journal of Behavioral Health Services & Research, 25,* 456–464.

Patton, M. Q. (1997). *Utilization-focused evaluation.* Thousand Oaks, CA: Sage.

Patton, M. Q. (2002). A vision of evaluation that strengthens democracy. *Evaluation, 8*(1), 125–139.

Picciotto, R. (2005). The value of evaluation standards: A comparative assessment. *Journal of MultiDisciplinary Evaluation, 3,* 30–59.

Posavac, E. J., & Carey, R. J. (2003). *Program evaluation: Methods and case studies.* (6th ed.). Upper Saddle River, NJ: Prentice Hall.

Pring, R. (2000). *Philosophy of educational research.* London: Continuum.

Ramcharan, P., & Cutcliffe, J. R. (2001). Judging the ethics of qualitative research: Considering the "ethics as process" model. *Health and Social Care in the Community, 9*(6), 358–366.

Rosenthal, R. (1994). Science and ethics in conducting, analyzing, and reporting psychological research. *Psychological Science, 5*(3), 127–134.

Sanders, J. R. (1983). Cost implications of the standards. In M. C. Alkin & L. C. Solmon (Eds.), *The costs of evaluation* (pp. 101–117). Beverly Hills, CA: Sage.

Schwandt, T. A. (2001). Ethics of qualitative inquiry. In *Dictionary of qualitative inquiry* (2nd ed., pp. 73–77). Thousand Oaks, CA: Sage.

Schwandt, T. A. (2002). Traversing the terrain of role, identity, and self. In K. Ryan & T. A. Schwandt (Eds.), *Exploring evaluator roles and identity.* Greenwich, CT: Information Age.

Scriven, M. (1983). Evaluation costs: Concept and theory. In M. C. Alkin & L. C. Solmon (Eds.), *The costs of evaluation* (pp. 27–44). Beverly Hills, CA: Sage.

Scriven, M. (2003). Evaluation theory and metatheory. In T. Kellaghan & D. L. Stufflebeam (Eds.), *International handbook of educational evaluation* (pp. 15–20). Dordrecht, Netherlands: Kluwer.

Shaw, I. F. (2003). Ethics in qualitative research and evaluation. *Journal of Social Work, 3*(1), 9–29.

Simons, H. (2006). Ethics in evaluation. In I. F. Shaw, J.C. Greene, & M. M. Mark (Eds.), *The Sage handbook of evaluation.* London: Sage.

Stake, R. E. (1973). Program evaluation, particularly responsive evaluation. Keynote address at the conference "New Trends in Evaluation," Institute of Education, University of Göteborg, Sweden, October.

Stake, R. E. (1986). Quieting reform: Social science and social action in an urban youth program. Urbana, IL: University of Illinois Press.

Stevens, C. J., & Dial, M. (Eds.). (1994). *Preventing the misuse of evaluation: New Directions for Program Evaluation, 64.*

Stufflebeam, D. L. (2000). Lessons in contracting for evaluation. *American Journal of Evaluation, 21,* 293–314.

Thomas, V. G., & McKie, B. K. (2006). Collecting and utilizing evaluation research for public good and on behalf of African American children. *Journal of Negro Education, 75*(3), 341–352.

Thurston, P. W., Ory, J. C., Mayberry, P. W., & Braskamp, L. A. (1984). Legal and professional standards in program evaluation. *Educational Evaluation and Policy Analysis, 6*(1), 15–26.

United Nations. (2005). The Universal Declaration of Human Rights. Retrieved on June 26, 2006, from http://www.un.org/Overview/rights.html

Vroom, P. I., Colombo, M., & Nahan, N. (1994). Confronting ideology and self-interest: Avoiding misuse of evaluation. In C. J. Stevens & M. Dial (Eds.), *Preventing the misuse of evaluation: New Directions for Program Evaluation, 64,* 49–59.

Worthen, B. (1987). *Evaluating educational and social programs: Guidelines for proposal review, onsite evaluation, evaluation contracts, and technical assistance.* Boston: Kluwer-Nijhoff.

❖ ACCURACY REFERENCES

Abma, T. A. (2006). The social relations of evaluations. In I. F. Shaw, J. C. Greene, & M. M. Mark (Eds.), *The Sage handbook of evaluation* (pp. 184–199). London: Sage.

Alkin, M. C. (2004). Context-adapted utilization: A personal journey. In M. C. Alkin (Ed.), *Evaluation roots: Tracing theorists' views and influences* (pp. 293–303). Thousand Oaks, CA: Sage.

Alkin M. C., Christie, C. A., & Rose, M. (2006). Communicating evaluation. In I. F. Shaw, J. C. Greene, & M. M. Mark (Eds.), *The Sage handbook of evaluation* (pp. 384–403). London: Sage.

American Educational Research Association, American Psychological Association, & National Council on Measurement in Education (1999, in revision). *Standards for educational and psychological testing.* Washington, DC: American Educational Research Association.

Angrosino, M. V., & Mays de Perez, K. A. (2000). Rethinking observation: From method to context. In N. K. Denzin & Y. S. Lincoln (Eds.), *Handbook of qualitative research* (2nd ed., pp. 673–702). Thousand Oaks, CA: Sage.

Banse, R. (2003). Beyond verbal self-report: Priming methods in relationship research. In J. Musch & K. C. Klauer (Eds.), *The psychology of evaluation* (pp. 245–274). Hillsdale, NJ: Lawrence Erlbaum.

Belgrave, L. L., & Smith, K. J. (2002). Negotiated validity in collaborative ethnography. In N. K. Denzin & Y. S. Lincoln (Eds.), *The qualitative inquiry reader* (pp. 233–255). Thousand Oaks, CA: Sage.

Berk, R. A. (Ed.). (1981). *Educational evaluation methodology: The state of the art.* Baltimore: The Johns Hopkins University Press.

Bhola, H. S. (2003a). Introduction. In T. Kellaghan, D. L. Stufflebeam, & L. A. Wingate (Eds.), *International handbook of educational evaluation, part one: Perspective* (pp. 389–415). Dordrecht, Netherlands: Kluwer Academic.

Bhola, H. S. (2003b). Social and cultural contexts of evaluation: A global perspective. In T. Kellaghan, D. L. Stufflebeam, & L. A. Wingate (Eds.), *International handbook of educational evaluation, part one: Perspective* (pp. 397–415). Dordrecht, Netherlands: Kluwer Academic.

Bickman, L. (2000). Summing up program theory. In P. J. Rogers, T. A. Hacsi, A. Petrosino, & T. A. Huebner (Eds.), *Program theory in evaluation: Challenges and opportunities: New Directions for Evaluation, 87,* 103–112.

Bledsoe, K. L. (2005). Using theory-driven evaluation with underserved communities. In S. Hood, R. K. Hopson, & H. Frierson (Eds.), *The role of culture and cultural context: A mandate for inclusion, the discovery of truth, and understanding in evaluative theory and practice* (pp. 179–199). Greenwich, CT: Information Age.

Boruch, R. F. (2004). A trialist's notes on evaluation theory and roots. In M. C. Alkin (Ed.), *Evaluation roots: Tracing theorists' views and influences* (pp. 88–113). Thousand Oaks, CA: Sage.

Brandon, P. R. (1998). Stakeholder participation for the purpose of helping ensure evaluation validity: Bridging the gap between collaborative and non-collaborative evaluations. *American Journal of Evaluation, 19,* 325–337.

Brandt, R. M. (1981). *Studying behavior in naturalistic settings.* New York: University Press of America.

Brennan, R. L. (2001). *Generalizability theory.* New York: Springer-Verlag.

Bronfenbrenner, U. (1979). *The ecology of human development.* Cambridge, MA: Harvard University Press.

Brown, A. L, & Campione, J. C. (1990). Communities of learning and thinking or a context by any other name. In D. Kuhn (Ed.), *Developmental perspectives on teaching, learning, and thinking skills* (pp. 108–126). Basel, Switzerland: Karger.

Brown, J. D. (1990). Short-cut estimators of criterion-referenced test consistency. *Language Testing, 7,* 77–97.

Browne, C., & Mills, C. (2001). Theoretical frameworks: Ecological model, strengths perspective, and empowerment theory. In R. Fong & S. Furuto (Eds.), *Culturally competent practice: Skills, interventions, and evaluations* (pp. 10–32). Boston: Allyn & Bacon.

Candoli, C., & Stufflebeam, D. L. (2003). The context of educational program evaluation in the United States. In T. Kellaghan, D. L. Stufflebeam, & L. A. Wingate (Eds.), *International handbook of educational evaluation, part one: Perspective* (pp. 417–427). Dordrecht, Netherlands: Kluwer Academic.

Caracelli, V. J., & Greene, J. C. (1997). Crafting mixed-method evaluation designs. In J. C. Greene & V. J. Caracelli (Eds.), *Advances in mixed-method evaluation: The challenges and benefits of integrating diverse paradigms: New Directions for Evaluation, 74,* 19–32.

Charmaz, K. (2000). Grounded theory: Objectivist and constructivist methods. In N. K. Denzin & Y. S. Lincoln (Eds.), *Handbook of qualitative research* (2nd ed., pp. 509–535). Thousand Oaks, CA: Sage.

Chen, H.-T. (1990). *Theory-driven evaluation.* Newbury Park, CA: Sage.

Chen, H.-T. (1997). Applying mixed methods under the framework of theory-driven evaluations. In J. C. Greene & V. J. Caracelli (Eds.), *Advances in mixed-method evaluation: The challenges and benefits of integrating diverse paradigms: New Directions for Evaluation, 74,* 61–72.

Chen, H.-T. (2004). The roots of theory-driven evaluation: Current views and origins. In M. C. Alkin (Ed.), *Evaluation roots: Tracing theorists' views and influences* (pp. 132–152). Thousand Oaks, CA: Sage.

Chen, H.-T. (2005). *Practical program evaluation.* Thousand Oaks, CA: Sage.

Cherin, D., & Meezan, W. (1998). Evaluation as a means of organizational learning. *Administration in Social Work, 22*(2), 1–21.

Chiseri-Strater, E., & Sunstein, B. S. (1997). *Field working.* Upper Saddle River, NJ: Prentice-Hall.

Clarke, A. (2006). Evidence-based evaluation in different professional domains: Similarities, differences, and challenges. In I. F. Shaw, J. C. Greene, & M. M. Mark (Eds.), *The Sage handbook of evaluation* (pp. 559–581). London: Sage.

Cochran-Smith, M., & Donnell, K. (2006). Practitioner inquiry: Blurring the boundaries of research and practice. In J. L. Green, G. Camilli, & P. B. Elmore (Eds.), *Handbook of complementary methods in education research* (pp. 503–518). Mahwah, NJ: Lawrence Erlbaum.

Conner, R. F. (2004). Developing and implementing culturally competent evaluation: A discussion of multicultural validity in two HIV prevention programs for

Latinos. In M. Thompson-Robinson, R. K. Hopson, & S. SenGupta (Eds.), *In search of cultural competence in evaluation: Toward principles and practices: New Directions for Evaluation, 102,* 51–65.

Cook, T. D. (1997). Lessons learned in evaluation over the past 25 years. In E. Chelimsky & W. R. Shadish (Eds.), *Evaluation for the 21st century* (pp. 30–52). Thousand Oaks, CA: Sage.

Cook, T. D. (2000). Toward a practical theory of external validity. In L. Bickman (Ed.), *Validity and social experimentation: Donald Campbell's legacy* (pp. 3–43). Thousand Oaks, CA: Sage.

Cook, T. D. (2004). Causal generalization: How Campbell and Cronbach influenced the theoretical thinking on this topic in Shadish, Cook, and Campbell. In M. C. Alkin (Ed.), *Evaluation roots: Tracing theorists' views and influences* (pp. 88–113). Thousand Oaks, CA: Sage.

Cook, T. D., & Sinha, V. (2006). Randomized experiments in educational research. In J. L. Green, G. Camilli, & P. B. Elmore (Eds.), *Handbook of complementary methods in education research* (pp. 551–565). Mahwah, NJ: Lawrence Erlbaum.

Cooksy, L. J., Gill, P., & Kelly, P. A. (2001). The program logic model as an integrative framework for a multimethod evaluation. *Evaluation and Program Planning, 24,* 119–128.

Creswell, J. W. (2003). *Research design: Qualitative, quantitative, and mixed methods approaches* (2nd ed.). Thousand Oaks, CA: Sage.

Cronbach, L. J. (1982). *Designing evaluations of educational and social programs.* San Francisco: Jossey-Bass.

Datta L.-E. (1997a). Multimethod evaluations: Using case studies together with other methods. In E. Chelimsky & W. R. Shadish (Eds.), *Evaluation for the 21st century* (pp. 344–359). Thousand Oaks, CA: Sage.

Datta, L.-E. (1997b). A pragmatic basis for mixed-method designs. In J. C. Greene & V. J. Caracelli (Eds.), *Advances in mixed-method evaluation: The challenges and benefits of integrating diverse paradigms: New Directions for Evaluation, 74,* 33–46.

Datta, L.-E. (2006). The practice of evaluation: Challenges and new directions. In I. F. Shaw, J. C. Greene, & M. M. Mark (Eds.), *The Sage handbook of evaluation* (pp. 419–438). London: Sage.

Davidson, E. J. (2000). Ascertaining causality in theory-based evaluation. In P. J. Rogers, T. A. Hacsi, A. Petrosino, & T. A. Huebner (Eds.), *Program theory in evaluation: Challenges and opportunities: New Directions for Evaluation, 87,* 17–26.

Davidson, E. J. (2005). *Evaluation methodology basics: The nuts and bolts of sound evaluation.* Thousand Oaks, CA: Sage.

Davies, B. (2000). Grice's cooperative principle: Getting the meaning across. In D. Nelson & P. Foulkes (Eds.), *Leeds Working Papers in Linguistics and Phonetics* (No. 8), 1–26.

Davies, P., Newcomer, K., & Soydan, H. (2006). Government as structural context for evaluation. In I. F. Shaw, J. C. Greene, & M. M. Mark (Eds.), *The Sage handbook of evaluation* (pp. 163–183). London: Sage.

Delgado, M. (1996). Puerto Rican elders and gerontological research: Avenues for empowerment and participation. *Activities, Adaptation, & Aging, 21*(2), 77–89.

Denzin, N. K., & Lincoln, Y. S. (Eds.). (2002). *The qualitative inquiry reader.* Thousand Oaks, CA: Sage.

Denzin, N. K., & Lincoln, Y. S. (2000). Introduction: The discipline and practice of qualitative research. In N. K. Denzin & Y. S. Lincoln (Eds.), *Handbook of qualitative research* (2nd ed., pp. 1–28). Thousand Oaks, CA: Sage.

Donaldson, S. I. (2003). Theory-driven program evaluation in the new millennium. In S. I. Donaldson & M. Scriven (Eds.), *Evaluating social programs and problems: Visions for the new millennium* (pp. 109–141). Thousand Oaks, CA: Sage.

Donaldson, S. I., & Lispey, M. W. (2006). Roles of theory in contemporary evaluation practice: Developing practical knowledge. In I. F. Shaw, J. C. Greene, & M. M. Mark (Eds.), *The Sage handbook of evaluation* (pp. 56–75). London: Sage.

Drummond, M. F., O'Brien, B., Stoddart, G. L., & Torrance, G. W. (1997). *Methods for the economic evaluation of health care programmes* (2nd ed.). New York: Oxford University Press.

Dwyer, J., Stanton, P., & Thiessen, V. (2004). *Project management in health and community services.* London: Routledge.

Eisenhart, M. (2006). Representing qualitative data. In J. L. Green, G. Camilli, & P. B. Elmore (Eds.), *Handbook of complementary methods in education research* (pp. 567–581). Mahwah, NJ: Lawrence Erlbaum.

Eisenhart, M., & DeHaan, R. L. (2005). Doctoral preparation of scientifically based education researchers. *Educational Researcher, 34*(4), 3–13.

Eisenhart, M., & Towne, L. (2003). Contestation and change in national policy on "scientifically based" educational research. *Educational Researcher, 32*(7), 31–38.

Ercikan, K., & Roth, W. M. (2003). What good is polarizing research into qualitative and quantitative? *Educational Researcher, 35*(5), 14–23.

Ferguson, M., & Bargh, J. (2003). The constructive nature of automatic evaluation. In J. Musch & K. C. Klauer (Eds.), *The psychology of evaluation* (pp. 169–188). New Jersey: Lawrence Erlbaum.

Fetterman, D. M. (1992). Theory in evaluation: We think, therefore we theorize (an ethnographer's perspective). In H.-T. Chen & P. H. Rossi (Eds.), *Using theory to improve program and policy evaluations* (pp. 115–126). Westport, CT: Greenwood Press.

Fine, M., Weis, L., Weseen, S., & Wong, L. (2000). For whom? Qualitative research, representations, and social responsibilities. In N. K. Denzin & Y. S. Lincoln (Eds.), *Handbook of qualitative research* (2nd ed., pp. 107–131). Thousand Oaks, CA: Sage.

Finney, J. W., & Moos, R. H. (1992). Four types of theory that can guide treatment evaluations. In H.-T. Chen & P. H. Rossi (Eds.), *Using theory to improve program and policy evaluations* (pp. 15–27). Westport, CT: Greenwood Press.

Fitzpatrick, J. L., Sanders, J. R., & Worthen, B. R. (Eds.). (2004). *Program evaluation* (3rd ed.). Boston: Pearson.

Fong, R., & Furuto, S. B. C. L. (Eds.). (2001). *Culturally competent practice: Skills, interventions, and evaluations.* Boston: Allyn & Bacon.

Fontana, A., & Frey, J. H. (2000). The interview: From structured questions to negotiated text. In N. K. Denzin & Y. S. Lincoln (Eds.), *Handbook of qualitative research* (2nd ed., pp. 645–672). Thousand Oaks, CA: Sage.

Fournier, D. M. (1995). Establishing evaluative conclusions: A distinction between general and working logic. In D. M. Fournier (Ed.), *Reasoning in evaluation: Inferential links and leaps: New Directions for Evaluation, 68,* 15–32.

Freeman, M., deMarrais, K., Preissle, J., Roulston, K., & St. Pierre, E. A. (2007). Standards of evidence in qualitative research: An incitement to discourse. *Educational Researcher, 36*(1), 25–32.

Frechtling, J. (Ed.), *The 2002 user-friendly handbook for project evaluation.* (NSF 02–057). Arlington, VA: National Science Foundation, Directorate for Education and Human Resources.

Frow, J., & Morris, M. (2000). Cultural studies. In N. K. Denzin & Y. S. Lincoln (Eds.), *Handbook of qualitative research* (2nd ed., pp. 315–346). Thousand Oaks, CA: Sage.

Gilbert, D. J., & Franklin, C. (2001). Developing culturally sensitive practice evaluation skills with Native American individuals and families. In R. Fong & S. Furuto (Eds.), *Culturally competent practice: Skills, interventions, and evaluations* (pp. 396–411). Boston: Allyn & Bacon.

Gliner, J. A., & Sample, P. (1996). A multimethod approach to evaluate transition into community life. *Evaluation and Program Planning, 19*(3), 225–233.

Grant, D. (2001). Evaluation skills with African American organizations and communities. In R. Fong & S. Furuto (Eds.), *Culturally competent practice: Skills, interventions, and evaluations* (pp. 355–369). Boston: Allyn & Bacon.

Green, B. L., Mulvey, L., Fisher, H. A., & Woratschek, F. (1996). Integrating program and evaluation values: A family support approach to program evaluation. *Evaluation Practice, 17*(3), 261–272.

Greene, J. C. (2000). Understanding social programs through evaluation. In N. K. Denzin & Y. S. Lincoln (Eds.), *Handbook of qualitative research* (2nd ed., pp. 981–999). Thousand Oaks, CA: Sage.

Greene, J. C. (2001). The relational and dialogic dimensions of program quality. In R. E. Stake (Series Ed.), A. Benson, D. M. Hinn, & C. Lloyd (Vol. Eds.), *Advances in program evaluation: Vol. 7. Visions of quality: How evaluators define, understand, and represent program quality* (pp. 57–71). Oxford, UK: Elsevier Science.

Greene, J. C. (2004). The educative evaluator: An interpretation of Lee J. Cronbach's vision of evaluation. In M. C. Alkin (Ed.), *Evaluation roots: Tracing theorists' views and influences* (pp. 169–180). Thousand Oaks, CA: Sage.

Greene, J. C. (2006). Evaluation, democracy, and social change. In I. F. Shaw, J. C. Greene, & M. M. Mark (Eds.), *The Sage handbook of evaluation* (pp. 118–140). London: Sage.

Greene, J. C., & Caracelli, V. J. (1997). Defining and describing the paradigm issue in mixed-method evaluation. In J. C. Greene & V. J. Caracelli (Eds.), *Advances in mixed-method evaluation: The challenges and benefits of integrating diverse paradigms: New Directions for Evaluation, 74,* 5–17.

Guba, E. G., & Lincoln, Y. S. (1981). *Effective evaluation: Improving the usefulness of evaluation results through responsive and naturalistic approaches.* San Francisco: Jossey-Bass.

Guba, E. G., & Lincoln, Y. S. (1989). *Fourth generation evaluation.* Newbury Park: Sage.

Guba, E. G. (Ed.). (1990). *The paradigm dialog.* Newbury Park, CA: Sage.

Guzman, B. L. (2003). Examining the role of cultural competency in program evaluation: Visions for new millennium evaluators. In S. I. Donaldson & M. Scriven (Eds.), *Evaluating social programs and problems: Visions for the new millennium* (pp. 167–182). Thousand Oaks, CA: Sage.

Hacsi, T. A. (2000). Using program theory to replicate successful programs. In P. J. Rogers, T. A. Hacsi, A. Petrosino, & T. A. Huebner (Eds.), *Program theory in evaluation: Challenges and opportunities: New Directions for Evaluation, 87,* 71–78.

Haertel, E. H. (2006). Reliability. In R. L. Brennan (Ed.), *Educational measurement* (4th ed., pp. 65–110). Westport, CT: Praeger.

Hodder, I. (2000). The interpretation of documents and material culture. In N. K. Denzin & Y. S. Lincoln (Eds.), *Handbook of qualitative research* (2nd ed., pp. 703–715). Thousand Oaks, CA: Sage.

House, E. R. (1980). *Evaluating with validity.* Beverly Hills, CA: Sage.

House, E. R. (1995). Putting things together coherently: Logic and justice. In D. M. Fournier (Ed.), *Reasoning in evaluation: Inferential links and leaps: New Directions for Evaluation, 68,* 33–48.

Hubbs-Tait, L., Nation, J. R., Krebs, N. F., & Bellinger, D. C. (2005). Neurotoxicants, micronutrients, and social environments. *Psychological Science in the Public Interest, 6*(3), 57–121.

Huebner, T. A. (2000). Theory-based evaluation: Gaining a shared understanding between school staff and evaluators. In P. J. Rogers, T. A. Hacsi, A. Petrosino, & T. A. Huebner (Eds.), *Program theory in evaluation: Challenges and opportunities: New Directions for Evaluation, 87,* 79–89.

Johnson, E. (2005). The use of contextually relevant evaluation practices with programs designed to increase participation of minorities in science, technology, engineering, and mathematics (STEM) education. In S. Hood, R. K. Hopson, & H. Frierson (Eds.), *The role of culture and cultural context: A mandate for inclusion, the discovery of truth, and understanding in evaluative theory and practice* (pp. 217–235). Greenwich, CT: Information Age.

Kane, M. T. (2006). Validation. In R. L. Brennan (Ed.), *Educational measurement* (4th ed., pp. 17–64). Westport, CT: Praeger.

Kincheloe, J. L., & McLaren, P. (2000). Rethinking critical theory and qualitative research. In N. K. Denzin & Y. S. Lincoln (Eds.), *Handbook of qualitative research* (2nd ed., pp. 279–313). Thousand Oaks, CA: Sage.

King, J. A., Nielsen, J. E., & Colby, J. (2004). Lessons for culturally competent evaluation from the study of a multicultural initiative. In M. Thompson-Robinson, R. K. Hopson, S. SenGupta (Eds.), *In search of cultural competence in evaluation: Toward principles and practices: New Directions for Evaluation, 102,* 67–80.

Kirkhart, K. E. (1995). Seeking multicultural validity: A postcard from the road. *Evaluation Practice, 16*(1), 1–12.

Kirkhart, K. E. (2005). Through a cultural lens: Reflections on validity and theory in evaluation. In S. Hood, R. K. Hopson, & H. Frierson (Eds.), *The role of culture and cultural context: A mandate for inclusion, the discovery of truth, and understanding in evaluative theory and practice* (pp. 21–39). Greenwich, CT: Information Age.

Koehler, D. J. (1991). Explanation, imagination, and confidence in judgment. *Psychological Bulletin, 110*(3), 499–519.

Kushner, S. (2001). Culture, standards, and program qualities. In R. E. Stake (Series Ed.), A. Benson, D. M. Hinn, & C. Lloyd (Vol. Eds.), *Advances in program evaluation: Vol. 7. Visions of quality: How evaluators define, understand, and represent program quality* (pp. 121–134). Oxford, UK: Elsevier Science.

Kvale, S. (2002). The social construction of validity. In N. K. Denzin & Y. S. Lincoln (Eds.), *The qualitative inquiry reader* (pp. 299–325). Thousand Oaks, CA: Sage.

Lakoff, G., & Johnson, M. (1980). *Metaphors we live by.* Chicago: The University of Chicago Press.

Landauer, T. K., & Dumais, S. T. (1997). A solution to Plato's problem: The latent semantic analysis theory of acquisition, induction, and representation of knowledge. *Psychological Review, 104*(2), 211–240.

Lather, P. (1986). Issues of validity in openly ideological research: Between a rock and a soft place. *Interchange, 17*(4), 63–84.

Lather, P. (1993). Fertile obsession: Validity after poststructuralism. *The Sociological Quarterly, 34*(4), 673–693.

LeCompte, M. D. (1993). *Ethnography and qualitative design in educational research* (2nd ed.). San Diego: Academic Press.

Levin, J. R. (2006). Probability and hypothesis testing. In J. L. Green, G. Camilli, & P. B. Elmore (Eds.), *Handbook of complementary methods in education research* (pp. 519–537). Mahwah, NJ: Lawrence Erlbaum.

Lincoln, Y. S. (2002). Emerging criteria for quality in qualitative and interpretive research. In N. K. Denzin & Y. S. Lincoln (Eds.), *The qualitative inquiry reader,* (pp. 327–345). Thousand Oaks, CA: Sage.

Lincoln, Y. S., & Guba, E. G. (1985). *Naturalistic inquiry.* Beverly Hills, CA: Sage.

Lincoln, Y. S., & Guba, E. G. (2000). Paradigmatic controversies, contradictions, and emerging confluences. In N. K. Denzin & Y. S. Lincoln (Eds.), *Handbook of qualitative research* (2nd ed., pp. 163–188). Thousand Oaks, CA: Sage.

Lincoln, Y. S., & Guba, E. G. (2004). The roots of fourth generation evaluation: Theoretical and methodological origins. In M. C. Alkin (Ed.), *Evaluation roots: Tracing theorists' views and influences* (pp. 225–241). Thousand Oaks, CA: Sage.

Linn, R. L., Baker, E. L., & Dunbar, S. B. (1991). Complex, performance-based assessment: Expectations and validation criteria. *Educational Researcher, 20*(8), 15–21.

Lloyd, C. (2001). Understanding program quality: A dialectic process. In R. E. Stake (Series Ed.), A. Benson, D. M. Hinn, & C. Lloyd (Vol. Eds.), *Advances in program evaluation: Vol. 7. Visions of quality: How evaluators define, understand, and represent program quality* (pp. 43–54). Oxford, UK: Elsevier Science.

Mabry, L. (2001). Representing the truth about program quality or the truth about representing program quality. In R. E. Stake (Series Ed.), A. Benson, D. M. Hinn, & C. Lloyd (Vol. Eds.), *Advances in program evaluation: Vol. 7. Visions of quality: How evaluators define, understand, and represent program quality* (pp. 19–27). Oxford, UK: Elsevier Science.

Mackie, J. L. (1980). *The cement of the universe: A study of causation.* New York: Oxford University Press.

Madison, A. M. (2000). Language in defining social problems and in evaluating social programs. In R. K. Hopson (Ed.), *How and why language matters in evaluation: New Directions for Evaluation, 86,* 17–28.

Mark, M. M., Feller, I., & Button, S. B. (1997). Integrating qualitative methods in a predominantly quantitative evaluation: A case study and some reflections. In J. C. Greene & V. J. Caracelli (Eds.), *Advances in mixed-method evaluation: The challenges and benefits of integrating diverse paradigms: New Directions for Evaluation, 74,* 47–59.

Mark, M. M., Greene, J. C., & Shaw, I. F. (2006). The evaluation of policies, programs, and practices. In I. F. Shaw, J. C. Greene, & M. M. Mark (Eds.), *The Sage handbook of evaluation* (pp. 1–30). London: Sage.

Mark, M. M., Henry, G. T., & Julnes, G. (2000). *Evaluation: An integrated framework for understanding, guiding, and improving policies and programs.* San Francisco: Jossey-Bass.

Maxwell, J. A. (2004). Causal explanation, qualitative research, and scientific inquiry in education. *Educational Researcher, 33*(2), 3–11.

Mertens, D. M. (2005). *Research and evaluation in education and psychology: Integrating diversity with quantitative, qualitative, and mixed methods* (2nd ed.). Thousand Oaks, CA: Sage.

Messick, S. (1995). Validity of psychological assessment. *American Psychologist, 50*(9), 741–749.

Messick, S. (1998). Test validity: A matter of consequence. *Social Indicators Research, 45,* 35–44.

Miller, M. D., Linn, R. L., & Gronlund, N. E. (2009). *Measurement and assessment in teaching* (10th ed.). Upper Saddle River, NJ: Pearson.

Mishler, E. G. (1990). Validation in inquiry-guided research: The role of exemplars in narrative studies. *Harvard Educational Review, 60*(4), 415–442.

Nelson-Barber, S., LaFrance, J., Trumbull, E., & Aburto, S. (2005). Promoting culturally reliable and valid evaluation practice. In S. Hood, R. K. Hopson, & H. Frierson (Eds.), *The role of culture and cultural context: A mandate for inclusion, the discovery of truth, and understanding in evaluative theory and practice* (pp. 61–85). Greenwich, Connecticut: Information age.

Northcutt, N., & McCoy, D. (2004). *Interactive qualitative analysis.* Thousand Oaks, CA: Sage.

Norwood, P. M., Atkinson, S. E., Tellez, K., & Saldana, D. C. (1997). Contextualizing parent education programs in urban schools: The impact on minority parents and students. *Urban Education, 32*(3), 411–432.

Padgett, D. K. (Ed.). (2004). *The qualitative research experience.* Belmont, CA: Wadsworth.

Patton, M. Q. (1997). *Utilization-focused evaluation* (3rd ed.). Thousand Oaks, CA: Sage.

Patton, M. Q. (2002). *Qualitative research and evaluation methods* (3rd ed.). Thousand Oaks, CA: Sage.

Pawson, R., & Tilley, N. (1997). An introduction to scientific realist evaluation. In E. Chelimsky & W. R. Shadish (Eds.), *Evaluation for the 21st century* (pp. 405–418). Thousand Oaks, CA: Sage.

Preissle, J. (1984). *Ethnography and qualitative design in educational research.* Orlando: Academic Press.

Preskill, H. (2003). The evaluation profession as a sustainable learning community. In T. Kellaghan, D. L. Stufflebeam, & L. A. Wingate (Eds.), *International handbook of educational evaluation, part one: Perspective* (pp. 361–372). Dordrecht, Netherlands: Kluwer Academic.

Rallis, S. F., & Rossman, G. B. (2001). Communicating quality and qualities: The role of the evaluator as critical friend. In R. E. Stake (Series Ed.), A. Benson, D. M. Hinn, & C. Lloyd (Vol. Eds.), *Advances in program evaluation: Vol. 7. Visions of quality: How evaluators define, understand, and represent program quality* (pp. 107–120). Oxford, UK: Elsevier Science.

Reimers, F. (2003). The social context of educational evaluation in Latin America. In T. Kellaghan, D. L. Stufflebeam, & L. A. Wingate (Eds.), *International handbook of educational evaluation, part one: Perspective* (pp. 441–463). Dordrecht, Netherlands: Kluwer Academic.

Reynolds, A. J. (1998). Confirmatory program evaluation: A method for strengthening causal inference. *American Journal of Evaluation, 19,* 203–221.

Richardson, L. (2000). Writing: A method of inquiry. In N. K. Denzin & Y. S. Lincoln (Eds.), *Handbook of qualitative research* (2nd ed., pp. 923–948). Thousand Oaks, CA: Sage.

Riggin, L. J. C. (1997). Advances in mixed-method evaluation: A synthesis and comment. In J. C. Greene & V. J. Caracelli (Eds.), *Advances in mixed-method evaluation: The challenges and benefits of integrating diverse paradigms: New Directions for Evaluation, 74,* 87–94.

Rog, D. J. (1995). Reasoning in evaluation: Challenges for the practitioner. In D. M. Fournier (Ed.), *Reasoning in evaluation: Inferential links and leaps: New Directions for Evaluation, 68,* 93–100.

Rog, D. J. (2006). Using evaluation as a tool for treatment improvement. *American Journal of Evaluation, 27*(1), 28–30.

Rogers, P. J., Petrosino, A., Huebner, T. A., & Hacsi, T. A. (2000). Program theory evaluation: Practice, promise, and problems. In P. J. Rogers, T. A. Hacsi, A. Petrosino, & T. A. Huebner (Eds.), *Program theory in evaluation: Challenges and opportunities: New Directions for Evaluation, 87,* 5–13.

Rogers, P. J., & Williams, B. (2006). Evaluation for practice improvement and organizational learning. In I. F. Shaw, J. C. Greene, & M. M. Mark (Eds.), *The Sage handbook of evaluation* (pp. 76–97). London: Sage.

Rossi, P. H., Lipsey, M. W., & Freeman, H. E. (2004). *Evaluation: A systematic approach* (7th ed.). Thousand Oaks, CA: Sage.

Ryan, G. W., & Bernard, H. R. (2000). Data management and analysis methods. In N. K. Denzin & Y. S. Lincoln (Eds.), *Handbook of qualitative research* (2nd ed., pp. 769–802). Thousand Oaks, CA: Sage.

Schwandt, T. A. (2000). Introduction: Three epistemological stances for qualitative inquiry: Interpretivism, hermeneutics, and social constructionism. In N. K. Denzin & Y. S. Lincoln (Eds.), *Handbook of qualitative research* (2nd ed., pp. 189–213). Thousand Oaks, CA: Sage.

Schwarts, R., & Mayne, J. (2005). Assuring the quality of evaluative information: Theory and practice. *Evaluation and Program Planning, 28,* 1–14.

Scriven, M. (1991). *Evaluation thesaurus* (4th ed.). Newbury Park, CA: Sage.

Scriven, M. (1995). The logic of evaluation and evaluation practice. In D. M. Fournier (Ed.), *Reasoning in evaluation: Inferential links and leaps: New Directions for Evaluation, 68,* 49–70.

Scriven, M. (1997). Truth and objectivity in evaluation. In E. Chelimsky & W. R. Shadish (Eds.), *Evaluation for the 21st century* (pp. 477–500). Thousand Oaks, CA: Sage.

Scriven, M. (2005). *Key Evaluation Checklist.* Retrieved from http://www.wmich.edu/evalctr/checklists/kec.htm

Shadish, W. R., Cook, T. D., & Campbell, D. T. (2002). *Experimental and quasi-experimental design.* Boston: Houghton Mifflin.

Shadish, W. R., Cook, T. D., & Leviton, L. C. (1991). *Foundations of program evaluation: Theories of practice.* Newbury Park, CA: Sage.

Shepard, L. (2006). Classroom assessment. In R. L. Brennan (Ed.), *Educational measurement* (4th ed., pp. 623–646). Westport, CT: Praeger.

Silverman, D. (2000). Analyzing talk and text. In N. K. Denzin & Y. S. Lincoln (Eds.), *Handbook of qualitative research* (2nd ed., pp. 821–834). Thousand Oaks, CA: Sage.

Smith, G. T. (2005). On the complexity of quantifying construct validity: Reply. *Psychological Assessment, 17*(4), 413–414.

Smith, M. L. (1997). Mixing and matching: Methods and models. In J. C. Greene & V. J. Caracelli (Eds.), *Advances in mixed-method evaluation: The challenges and benefits of integrating diverse paradigms: New Directions for Evaluation, 74,* 73–85.

Smith, N. L. (2002). International students' reflections on the cultural embeddedness of evaluation theory. *American Journal of Evaluation, 23*(4), 481–492.

Snow, D. (2001). Communicating quality. In R. E. Stake (Series Ed.), A. Benson, D. M. Hinn, & C. Lloyd (Vol. Eds.), *Advances in program evaluation: Vol. 7. Visions of quality: How evaluators define, understand, and represent program quality* (pp. 29–42). Oxford, UK: Elsevier Science.

Stake, R. E. (1995). *The art of case study research.* Thousand Oaks, CA: Sage.

Stake, R. E. (2000). Case studies. In N. K. Denzin & Y. S. Lincoln (Eds.), *Handbook of qualitative research* (2nd ed., pp. 435–454). Thousand Oaks, CA: Sage.

Stake, R. E. (2001). Representing quality in evaluation. In R. E. Stake (Series Ed.), A. Benson, D. M. Hinn, & C. Lloyd (Vol. Eds.), *Advances in program evaluation: Vol. 7. Visions of quality: How evaluators define, understand, and represent program quality* (pp. 3–11). Oxford, UK: Elsevier Science.

Stake, R. E. (2004). *Standards-based and responsive evaluation.* Thousand Oaks, CA: Sage.

Stevenson, J., & Thomas, D. (2006). Intellectual contexts. In I. F. Shaw, J. C. Greene, & M. M. Mark (Eds.), *The Sage handbook of evaluation* (pp. 200–224). London: Sage.

Stufflebeam, D. L. (2004). The 21st-century CIPP model: Origins, development, and use. In M. C. Alkin (Ed.), *Evaluation roots: Tracing theorists' views and influences* (pp. 245–266). Thousand Oaks, CA: Sage.

Tedlock, B. (2000). Ethnography and ethnographic representation. In N. K. Denzin & Y. S. Lincoln (Eds.), *Handbook of qualitative research* (2nd ed., pp. 455–486). Thousand Oaks, CA: Sage.

Vestman, O. K., & Conner, R. F. (2006). The relationship between evaluation and politics. In I. F. Shaw, J. C. Greene, & M. M. Mark (Eds.), *The Sage handbook of evaluation* (pp. 225–242). London: Sage.

W. K. Kellogg Foundation (2001). *Logic model development guide.* Battle Creek, MI: Author.

Weaver, H. N. (2001). Organization and community assessment with First Nations people. In R. Fong & S. Furuto (Eds.), *Culturally competent practice: Skills, interventions, and evaluations* (pp. 178–195). Boston: Allyn & Bacon.

Weiss, C. H. (1998). *Evaluation* (2nd ed.). New Jersey: Prentice Hall.

Wholey, J. S. (1997). Trends in performance measurement: Challenges for evaluators. In E. Chelimsky & W. R. Shadish (Eds.), *Evaluation for the 21st century* (pp. 124–133). Thousand Oaks, CA: Sage.

Wholey, J. S. (2001). Defining, improving, and communicating program quality. In R. E. Stake (Series Ed.), A. Benson, D. M. Hinn, & C. Lloyd (Vol. Eds.), *Advances in program evaluation: Vol. 7. Visions of quality: How evaluators define, understand, and represent program quality* (pp. 201–216). Oxford, UK: Elsevier Science.

Wholey, J. S. (2004). Using evaluation to improve performance and support policy design making. In M. C. Alkin (Ed.), *Evaluation roots: Tracing theorists' views and influences* (pp. 267–275). Thousand Oaks, CA: Sage.

Willis, G. B. (2005). *Cognitive interviewing: A tool for improving questionnaire design.* Thousand Oaks, CA: Sage.

Winberg, A. (1991). Maximizing the contribution of internal evaluation units. *Evaluation and Program Planning, 14,* 167–172.

Wyer, R. S., Jr., & Radvansky, G. A. (1999). The comprehension and validation of social information. *Psychological Review, 106*(1), 89–118.

Yen, W. M., & Fitzpatrick, A. R. (2006). Item response theory. In R. L. Brennan (Ed.), *Educational measurement* (4th ed., pp. 111–154). Westport, CT: Praeger.

Yin, R. K. (1992). The role of theory in doing case study research and evaluations. In H.-T. Chen & P. H. Rossi (Eds.), *Using theory to improve program and policy evaluations* (pp. 97–114). Westport, CT: Greenwood Press.

Yin, R. K. (2009). *Case study research* (4th ed.). Thousand Oaks, CA: Sage.

Zulli, R. A., & Frierson, H. T. (2004). A focus on cultural variables in evaluating an upward bound program. In M. Thompson-Robinson, R. K. Hopson, & S. SenGupta (Eds.), *In search of cultural competence in evaluation: Toward principles and practices: New Directions for Evaluation, 102,* 81–93.

❖ EVALUATION ACCOUNTABILITY

Bickman, L. (1997). Evaluating evaluation: Where do we go from here? *Evaluation Practice, 18*(1), 1–16.

Christie, C. A., Ross, R. M., & Klein, B. M. (2004). Moving toward collaboration by creating a participatory internal-external evaluation team: A case study. *Studies in Educational Evaluation, 30,* 125–134.

Conley-Tyler, M. (2005). A fundamental choice: Internal or external evaluation? *Evaluation Journal of Australasia, 4* (1 & 2), 3–11.

Cooksy, L. J. (1999). The meta-evaluand: The evaluation of project TEAMS. *American Journal of Evaluation, 20,* 123–136.

Cooksy, L. J., & Caracelli, V. J. (2005). Quality, context, and use: Issues in achieving the goals of metaevaluation. *American Journal of Evaluation, 26,* 31–42.

Cooksy, L. J., & Caracelli, V. J. (2009). Metaevaluation in practice: Selection and application of criteria. *Journal of MultiDisciplinary Evaluation, 6*(11), 1–15.

Datta, L. (1999). CIRCE's demonstration of a close-to-ideal evaluation in a less-than-ideal world. *American Journal of Evaluation, 20*(2), 354–354.

Frink, D. D., & Ferris, G. R. (1998). Accountability, impression management, and goal setting in the performance evaluation process. *Human Relations, 51*(10), 1259–1283.

Gale, P. S. (2004). A summative metaevaluation synthesis. *UMI Dissertation Services.* (University Microfilms No. 3134839)

Grasso, P. G. (1999). Meta-Evaluation of an evaluation of reader focused writing for the Veterans Benefits Administration. *American Journal of Evaluation, 20*(2), 355–370.

Greene, J. C. (1992). A case study of evaluation auditing as metaevaluation. *Evaluation and Program Planning, 15*(1), 71–74.

Gregory, A., & Watson, T. (2008). Defining the gap between research and practice in public relations programme evaluation—towards a new research agenda. *Journal of Marketing Communications, 14*(5), 337–350.

Hanssen, C. E., Lawrenz, F., & Dunet, D. O. (2008). Concurrent metaevaluation: A critique. *American Journal of Evaluation, 29,* 572–582.

King, J. (2008). Bringing evaluation learning to life. *American Journal of Evaluation, 29,* 151–155.

Lynch, D. C., Greer, A. G., Larson, L. C., Cummings, D. M., Harriett, B. S., Dreyfuss, K. S., et al. (2003). Descriptive metaevaluation: Case study of an interdisciplinary curriculum. *Evaluation and the Health Professions, 26*(4), 447–461.

Mabry, L. (2001). Representing the truth about program quality or the truth about representing program quality. In A. Benson, D. M. Hinn, & C. Lloyd (Eds.), *Visions of quality: How evaluators define, understand, and represent program quality* (pp. 19–27). New York: JAI/ Elsevier Science.

Mathison, S. (1999). Rights, responsibilities, and duties: A comparison of ethics for internal and external evaluators. *New Directions for Evaluation, 82,* 25–34.

O'Connor, M. K., & Netting, F. E. (2008). Faith-based evaluation: Accountable to whom, for what? *Evaluation and Program Planning, 31*(4), 347–355.

Patel, M. (2002). A meta-evaluation, or quality assessment, of the evaluations in this issue, based on the African Evaluation Guidelines: 2002. *Evaluation and Program Planning, 25,* 329–332.

Posavac, E. J. (1994). Misusing program evaluation by asking the wrong question. In C. J. Stevens & M. Dial (Eds.), *Preventing the misuse of evaluation: New Directions for Program Evaluation, 64,* 69–78.

Sanders, J. R. (1999). Metaevaluation of "The Effectiveness of Comprehensive, Case Management Interventions: Evidence for the National Evaluation of the Comprehensive Child Development Program." *American Journal of Evaluation, 20,* 577–582.

Schwarts, R., & Mayne, J. (2005). Assuring the quality of evaluative information: Theory and practice. *Evaluation and Program Planning, 28,* 1–14.

Scriven, M. (1969). Introduction to metaevaluation. *Educational Product Report, 2,* 36–38.

Scriven, M. (1991). *Evaluation thesaurus* (4th ed.). Newbury Park, CA: Sage.

Scriven, M. (2009). Meta-evaluation revisited. *Journal of MultiDisciplinary Evaluation, 6*(11), iii-viiii.

Stake, R. E. (2004). *Standards-based and responsive evaluation.* Thousand Oaks, CA: Sage.

Stufflebeam, D. L. (1981). Metaevaluation: Concepts, standards, and uses. In R. A. Berk (Ed.), *Educational evaluation methodology: The state of the art.* Baltimore: The Johns Hopkins University Press.

Stufflebeam, D. L. (2001). The metaevaluation imperative. *American Journal of Evaluation, 22,* 183–209.

Stufflebeam, D. L., & Shinkfield, A. J. (2007). *Evaluation theories, models, and applications.* San Francisco: Jossey-Bass.

United States Government Accounting Office (2003). Government auditing standards. Last accessed January 21, 2010, at http://www.gao.gov/govaud/yb/2003/html/TOC.html

Index